The Sisters' Arts

The Sisters' Arts

THE WRITING AND PAINTING OF VIRGINIA WOOLF AND VANESSA BELL

Diane Filby Gillespie

SYRACUSE UNIVERSITY PRESS

Syracuse, New York 13244-5160

First published 1988

First Edition
95 94 93 92 91 90 89 88 5 4 3 2 1

The paper used in this publication meets the minimum requirements of American National Standard for Information Sciences—Permanence of Paper for Printed Library Materials, ANSI Z39.48-1984. ∞™

Library of Congress Cataloging-in-Publication Data

Gillespie, Diane F.
The sisters' arts : the writing and painting of Virginia Woolf and Vanessa Bell / Diane Filby Gillespie. — 1st ed.
p. cm.
Bibliography: p.
Includes index.
ISBN 0-8156-2430-1 (alk. paper)
1. Woolf, Virginia, 1882–1941—Criticism and interpretation.
2. Bell, Vanessa, 1879–1961—Criticism and interpretation.
3. Painting, English. 4. Painting, Modern—20th century—England.
5. Art and literature—England—History—20th century. 6. Sisters—England. I. Title.
PR6045.072Z644 1988
820'.9'00912—dc 19 88-2086
CIP

MANUFACTURED IN THE UNITED STATES OF AMERICA

To my sister,
CAROLE FILBY KOLBE

DIANE FILBY GILLESPIE, Associate Professor of English at Washington State University, is the co-editor (with Elizabeth Steele) of *Julia Duckworth Stephen: Stories for Children, Essays for Adults* (Syracuse University Press, 1987). She has published articles and presented papers on Virginia Woolf as well as Dorothy Richardson and May Sinclair. Currently she is editing a collection of essays entitled *Virginia Woolf and the Other Arts*. Having also published articles on modern drama, she is writing a book on British women dramatists, 1900–1940.

Contents

Acknowledgments

Excerpts from the works of Virginia Woolf are reprinted by permission of Harcourt Brace Jovanovich, Inc., and by permission of the estate of Virginia Woolf and the Hogarth Press. Several Hogarth Press covers plus selected illustrations by Vanessa Bell are reproduced by permission of the estate of Vanessa Bell and the Hogarth Press. I am especially indebted to Angelica Garnett for permission to reproduce the Vanessa Bell paintings and decorative works in this book as well as for permission to reproduce some by Duncan Grant; to Mrs. Garnett and Professor Quentin Bell for kindly allowing me to quote from Vanessa Bell's unpublished letters and memoirs; and to Professor Bell for permission to quote from Clive Bell's unpublished letters, to reproduce Virginia Stephen's early drawings and bookplate designs, and to include a photograph from Stella Duckworth's album.

I am also indebted to the following galleries, libraries, and individuals for providing photographs, permissions, or both: the Anthony d'Offay Gallery, London; Christie's, London; the City of Manchester Art Galleries; the Courtauld Institute Galleries, London; John Murray, London; the National Gallery, London; the National Galleries of Scotland, Edinburgh; the National Portrait Gallery, London; the National Trust; the Royal Academy of Arts, London; the Tate Gallery, London; the Watts Gallery, Compton; the Henry W. and Albert A. Berg Collection, the Astor Lenox and Tilden Foundation at the New York Public Library; the Huntington Library, San Marino, California; the Leonard and Virginia Woolf Library and Bloomsbury Collection at Washington State University Libraries; Lady Clark; Mrs. Patricia Kapp; and Mrs. Trekkie Parsons. To those who waived or reduced their fees I am doubly grateful. My thanks, too, to *Studies in the Humanities*, which published a version of chapter 4 of this study.

Many other individuals have been helpful: Caroline Cuthbert, formerly of the Anthony d'Offay Gallery and, more recently, Robin Vousden and Linda Wright; Richard Jefferies of the Watts Gallery; Graham Sutherland of Christie's; Peter Miall of the National Trust; John Guido and especially Leila Luedeking of Manuscripts, Archives and Special Collections, Washington State University Libraries; Michael Halls of the King's College Library, Cambridge; Elizabeth Inglis of the University of Sussex Library; the staff at the New York Public Library; and Cathy Henderson and staff, Harry Ransom Humanities Research Center at the University of Texas at Austin. I would also like to thank Fred Lucas, formerly of the Bow Windows Book Shop, Lewes, Sussex; Richard Shone; Isabelle Anscombe; Sandra Lummis; Professors S. P. Rosenbaum, Susan Dick, Frances Spalding, and J. J. Wilson; Richard Outram; Jean Peters; and Hugh Lee of the Charleston Trust. All of these people provided important information and assistance at crucial times.

I owe a special thanks to those people willing to read part or all of versions of this study: Leila Luedeking, Dr. Roberta Armstrong, Professors Jane Lilienfeld, Joan Burbick, Frances Spalding, Virginia Hyde, and especially S. P. Rosenbaum. Valuable suggestions also came from unnamed outside reviewers of the typescript. Professor Thomas Faulkner provided good procedural advice.

I am grateful to the American Association of University Women for granting me a postdoctoral fellowship in 1980–81 to work on the first draft of this book; to the E. O. Holland Fund and the Dean of Humanities and Social Sciences Project Completion Funds at Washington State University for travel and other money; to the Washington State University administration for occasional reduced teaching loads and for professional leaves in 1980–81 and 1986–87; and to the Ella and Basil Jerard Fund of the Department of English at Washington State University for help with photographic and permission costs.

My parents, Waino and Saima Filby, deserve credit for instilling in me the desire and the discipline to learn. A more direct influence on this book was my husband, Richard Domey, who did all my research photography, accompanied me on research trips, helped me to solve many of the practical problems that arose, and encouraged me when the frustrations began to outweigh the excitement of scholarly research and writing. To him, above all, my thanks.

Abbreviations

All references in the text to the works of Virginia Woolf are to the following editions:

AROO	*A Room of One's Own* (1929). New York: Harcourt Brace Jovanovich, 1957.
BA	*Between the Acts* (1941). New York: Harcourt Brace Jovanovich, 1969.
BP	*Books and Portraits: Some Further Selections from the Literary and Biographical Writings of Virginia Woolf*. Ed. Mary Lyon. New York: Harcourt Brace Jovanovich, 1977.
CE I, II, III, IV	*Collected Essays*. New York: Harcourt, Brace and World, 1967.
CSF	*Complete Shorter Fiction of Virginia Woolf*. Ed. Susan Dick. London: Hogarth, 1985.
CW	*Contemporary Writers*. New York: Harcourt, Brace and World, 1965.
D I, II, III, IV, V	*Diary of Virginia Woolf*. Ed. Anne Olivier Bell. New York: Harcourt Brace Jovanovich, *1915–1919* (1974); *1920–1924* (1978); *1925–1930* (1980); *1931–1935* (1982); *1936–1941* (1984).
F	*Flush: A Biography*. New York: Harcourt Brace Jovanovich, 1976.
FW	*Freshwater*. Ed. Lucio Ruotolo. New York: Harcourt Brace Jovanovich, 1976.
HH	*A Haunted House and Other Stories* (1944). New York: Harcourt Brace Jovanovich, 1972.
JR	*Jacob's Room* (1922). New York: Harcourt Brace Jovanovich, 1978.

L I, II, III, IV, V, VI	*Letters of Virginia Woolf*. Ed. Nigel Nicolson and Joanne Trautmann. New York: Harcourt Brace Jovanovich, *1888–1912* (1975); *1912–1922* (1976); *1923–1928* (1977); *1929–1931* (1978); *1932–1935* (1979); *1936–1941* (1980).
MB	*Moments of Being: Unpublished Autobiographical Writings*. Ed. Jeanne Schulkind. New York: Harcourt Brace Jovanovich, 1976.
MD	*Mrs. Dalloway* (1925). New York: Harcourt Brace Jovanovich, 1953.
MDP	*Mrs. Dalloway's Party: A Short Story Sequence*. Ed. Stella McNichol. New York: Harcourt Brace Jovanovich, 1973.
MT	*Monday or Tuesday* (1921). New York: Harcourt Brace, 1921.
ND	*Night and Day* (1919). New York: Harcourt Brace Jovanovich, 1948.
O	*Orlando: A Biography* (1940). New York: Harcourt Brace Jovanovich, 1956.
P	*The Pargiters: The Novel-Essay Portion of "The Years."* Ed. Mitchell A. Leaska. New York: Harcourt Brace Jovanovich, 1978.
RF	*Roger Fry: A Biography* (1940). New York: Harcourt Brace Jovanovich, 1976.
TG	*Three Guineas* (1938). New York: Harcourt Brace Jovanovich, 1966.
TTL	*To the Lighthouse* (1927). New York: Harcourt Brace Jovanovich, 1955.
VO	*The Voyage Out* (1915). New York: Harcourt Brace Jovanovich, 1948.
W	*The Waves* (1931). New York: Harcourt Brace Jovanovich, 1978.
Y	*The Years* (1937). New York: Harcourt, Brace and World, 1965.

Holders of unpublished materials are abbreviated in the notes as follows:

AG	Angelica Garnett.

HRHRC	Harry Ransom Humanities Research Center, University of Texas at Austin.
KCL	Charleston Papers, King's College Library, Cambridge, England. These are photocopies of originals sold in July 1980 at Sotheby's, London.
NYPL	Henry W. and Albert A. Berg Collection, New York Public Library.
QB	Quentin Bell.
USL	Monks House Papers, University of Sussex Library, Falmer, England.
WSUL	Leonard and Virginia Woolf Library and Bloomsbury Collection; Manuscripts, Archives, and Special Collections; Washington State University Libraries, Pullman, Washington.

Illustrations

The Sisters' Arts

Introduction

RAIDING AND WRITING

In *Walter Sickert: A Conversation*, Virginia Woolf defines two kinds of artists: "Some . . . bore deeper and deeper into the stuff of their own art; others are always making raids into the lands of others" (CE II 243; cf RF 239–40). Sickert is a raider. He satisfies fellow painters interested in pure color and form, but he also pleases viewers with a more literary bent. Woolf is also a raider. So is the novel as she redefines it. That "cannibal . . . which has devoured so many forms of art," she says, threatens to devour "even more." It will incorporate drama, poetry, and, ultimately, "the power of music, the stimulus of sight" (CE II 224–25, 229). Woolf's own voracious fiction pleases fellow novelists concerned with human relationships as well as readers more interested in visual responses to the world around them and in the overall design of the work.

Statements like "for though they must part in the end, painting and writing have much to tell each other," "the novelist after all wants to make us see," and "all great writers are great colourists" (CE II 241) are well known. Writers on Woolf and Bloomsbury recognize her interest in the visual arts,[1] but they do not accurately define her motives, strategies, or goals. Woolf's image of the raider with its visual associations of gallops on horseback into and out of alien territory relates in a curious way to an equestrian image she varies constantly in her diaries when she tries to describe both her life and her creative process. The image was a familiar one: her sister, Vanessa Bell, also used it to describe creative activity. In 1908 she said that she hesitated to write to "such a gifted beast as Billy [Virginia] with all his wits & graces & who has probably been spending his morning caracolling about on his genius."[2] In 1922 Walter Sickert wrote that Vanessa Bell's "medium bends beneath her like a horse that knows its rider."[3] A year later, Woolf recorded that work is "the root & source

& origin of all health & happiness, provided of course that one rides work as a man rides a great horse, in a spirited & independent way; not a drudge, but a man with spurs in his heels" (D II 259). Equating her art with a traditionally masculine sense of freedom and power, Woolf sees her books as fences she must take at a gallop or as the galloping horses themselves. Sometimes her pen is the horse she gallops in her fiction and canters in her diary. Whatever the gait, she says, "having got astride my saddle the whole world falls into shape; it is this writing that gives me my proportions" (D III 343). Writing, like riding, is mastering and governing a powerful force.

Riding, however, includes raiding, if one connects the image from the Sickert essay with the one from the diary. The connection is worth making; it helps define the nature of the relationship between Woolf's writing and the visual arts. As writer, rider, and raider, Woolf is in control. At the same time, her motivation is necessity; the sense of mastery and proportion that writing gives her is essential to her health and happiness, but the dimension that raiding provides is also necessary to her writing. If Woolf is a raider, she is no Homeric sacker of cities. She invades the realm of the visual arts to learn and to commune with an outlook she finds not only alien but also compatible.

The purposes of this study are three: to shift the emphasis in the ongoing discussion of Virginia Woolf and the visual arts from Roger Fry to Vanessa Bell; to shift the emphasis in the discussions of the sisters from the psychological to the professional and aesthetic; and, in these contexts, to define and reveal more fully the pervasive role of the visual arts in Woolf's writing. According to most writers on Virginia Woolf, Roger Fry is the ruler of the territory she raids. The attention given Fry's theories in her creative life is justified. "You have . . . kept me on the right path, so far as writing goes, more than anyone," she wrote to him in 1927 (L III 385). In the Preface to *Orlando* in the following year she wrote, "to the unrivalled sympathy and imagination of Mr. Roger Fry I owe whatever understanding of the art of painting I may possess." Yet Nigel Nicolson concludes from his work on Woolf's letters that she "learned to understand painting through . . . [Vanessa Bell's] eyes" (L II xxi).[4] Since the two sisters were intimates long before either met Fry, why do many writers on her work, and Woolf herself, credit him so exclusively? Woolf's remarks can be explained by the competition between the sisters, combined with Virginia's perception of Fry as more willing to discuss art because he was more verbal and theoretical than Vanessa. Fry's reputation in the history of art in England, his abundant and accessible comments on the visual arts, the published selection of his letters, and Woolf's biography of him all help to solidify the connection between the two artists in the critical commentary. In contrast, Vanessa Bell's place in the history of English art is only now being established.[5] Many of the paintings Woolf saw and commented upon no longer exist. Others, in private collections, are unknown or inaccessible to scholars. Bell's comments on the visual arts are also fewer that Fry's, and only fragments are in print. For these reasons the artistic relationship between the sisters is more difficult to document. At the same time, a common tendency may be operating here: when they must account for the formal characteristics of women's works, critics often invoke the principle of *cherchez l'homme*: you'll find a man at the bottom of it.[6] In Woolf's case, the man is Fry or, less frequently, Clive Bell. In Vanessa Bell's case, again the man is Fry, or he is Duncan Grant.

One cannot ignore Fry or the other men in the lives of Woolf or Bell; neither must one limit the discussion to them. Like her sister, Vanessa Bell acknowledged Fry's influence. She accepted enthusiastically some of his theories but, both before and after she met him, she was willing to draw her own conclusions about art. Similarly, although she sometimes feared that her work was inferior to Duncan Grant's, she was certain it was different. She wrote to Fry in 1922 that she dreaded suffering, like so many women, the submergence of her work in a man's.[7] In spite of her worries, most recent art historians have accorded Bell's work the integrity it merits.[8] But if literary critics mention Vanessa when they discuss her sister's novels, they rarely consider her as a painter. With some partial exceptions, the few who do note relationships between the sisters' writing and painting do not define clearly, develop thoroughly, or illustrate their insights.[9]

Woolf observes in *A Room of One's Own* that women painters and composers have had even fewer chances than women writers of being taken seriously as artists. If writers on Woolf do not respect Vanessa Bell as a professional painter, then they are less likely to credit her with any significant artistic impact on her sister. Even Virginia often sees Vanessa as more procreative than creative, as more the artist in life than the artist per se. Trying to come to terms with Vanessa's engagement to Clive Bell, for example, Virginia pronounced her sister "no genius" although she had "all the human gifts" (L I 276). It is tempting, as the increasing number of biographical studies indicate, to dwell on the psychological tugs of war and intimacies between the sisters at the expense of their relationship as professional artists.[10] The two cannot be separated, but the emphasis can be shifted. The title of this study embodies that shift.

The phrase "the sisters' arts" modifies "the sister arts," which invokes the classical tradition of *ut pictura poesis*. According to that tradition, the visual and verbal arts are related much as sisters are: in spite of individual differences, a family resemblance remains. The long history of this metaphorical sisterhood, as Jean Hagstrum's *The Sister Arts* indicates, is one of collaboration and competition.[11] The visual and verbal arts, however, are not just siblings; they are female siblings, perhaps because of the Muses.[12] These goddesses personified areas of creative endeavor; they also inspired the creators who, traditionally, have been male. While we have no brother arts, we do have brotherhoods of artists.

To change the traditional metaphorical label, "the sister arts," into "the sisters' arts" has political, metaphysical, and aesthetic implications. "Sisters' arts" operates on a literal level. Woolf and Bell formed an artistic sisterhood and practiced in art media conceived of, metaphorically, as sisters. "Sisters'" in my title is also plural and possessive. Virginia Woolf and Vanessa Bell are two among many often unrecognized women who, over the centuries, were active in one art medium or the other. If "sister arts" suggests the family resemblance between two different art media, "sisters' arts" suggests, in addition, that women artists often have something in common, as Woolf recognized: a set of experiences, related values, and a desire to embody their perceptions in appropriate artistic forms.

"But it is obvious," Woolf writes in *A Room of One's Own*, "that the values of women differ very often from the values which have been made by the other sex. . . . Yet it is the masculine values that prevail" (AROO 76–77). Similarly in *Three Guineas* she notes that while men and women "see the same world," they "see it through different eyes" (TG 18). Elaine Showalter, advocating feminist criticism "based on a model of women's culture," cautions that "there can be no writing or criticism totally outside of the dominant structure; . . . women's writing is a 'double-voiced discourse' that always embodies the social, literary, and cultural heritages of both the muted [female] and the dominant [male]."[13] Putting it another way, she says that "If a man's text, as Bloom and Edward Said have maintained, is fathered, then a woman's text is not only mothered but parented; it confronts both paternal and maternal precursors and must deal with the problems and advantages of both lines of inheritance."[14] So Woolf inevitably thinks back not only through her literary mothers (AROO 79) but also through her fathers.

In the context of this study, it is equally appropriate to talk of sisters and brothers. The latter represent the educational and political privileges of the dominant culture, however thoroughly some men may question its values. As the critical and biographical writings establish, Virginia Woolf and Vanessa Bell were artistically "brothered" by a number of their male contemporaries, and many of the ideas the sisters shared and reinforced in each other were also those of male writers, painters, and critics. The art of Woolf and Bell, however, was also "sistered" by a few female contemporaries and especially by each other. They were artists with a common family background, with educations and experiences limited in some ways because they were women, and with an abiding awareness of these facts and of each other's activities.[15]

In spite of all they shared, a dualistic structure inevitably dominates discussions of Virginia Woolf and Vanessa Bell, in part because each woman caricatured the other as her opposite. At the same time, each occasionally recognized that her view of her sister was inadequate. Bell confessed to Fry in 1913 that perhaps she had been too ready to laugh at Virginia, to ignore her brave and sound perspective on life.[16] Woolf, in turn, confessed to Duncan Grant four years later, "I have invented such a myth about her [Vanessa] that I scarcely know one from tother" (L II 146). Not surprisingly, Lily Briscoe concludes in *To the Lighthouse* that "half one's notions of other people were . . . grotesque. They served private purposes of one's own" (TTL 293). It serves the purposes of Virginia Woolf or Vanessa Bell, or their later biographers or critics, to think of the virginal, barren woman versus the sensual, maternal one; the domestically inept versus the practical and competent; the dependent versus the independent; the conversationalist versus the silent listener; the mentally unstable versus the sane.[17] My emphasis is not on sexuality, domesticity, sociability, or pathology; it is on artistic productivity. Nevertheless, a recognition of the family relationships between these two women as artists and between their art forms calls into question some of the other dualities as well. A few people have acknowledged Woolf's practicality and domesticity; her sensuality, diffuse as it may have been; and her healthy ability to analyze herself and her creative processes. Likewise a few have acknowledged Vanessa Bell's reservations about maternity; her depressions and, as Woolf herself put it, the "volcanoes underneath her sedate manner" (L I 31); and her emotional and practical dependencies on other people. The direction of Woolf's art and thought, as many have recognized, is to dissolve the false and transcend even the true dichotomies between men and women, solitude and society, the human and the natural worlds, permanence and change, reason and emotion, life and art.

To separate Virginia Woolf and Vanessa Bell as writer and painter from the prevailing dualistic model is to recognize that both on occasion defined what they did as opposed when they were actually working along similar lines. Sibling rivalry accounts in part for Virginia's early development to be in the verbal and Vanessa's to be in the visual arts, or at least such development, as Vanessa says, reduced the jealousy between them.[18] Still, in addition to her experiments with drawing, Virginia imitated Vanessa at her easel by writing at a stand-up desk (D I 247, n. 17). Each sister's apologetic attitude about her comments on the other's medium relates to the rivalry, the fear of infringing on the other's territory combined with the desire to do so. The two women created caricatures of writers and painters, each generalizing partially from her experience of the other. Because of Virginia's admiration for her sister and the unconventional life that painting seemed both to necessitate and to foster, Virginia felt that she, as a writer, was on the defensive. Vanessa admitted that when the Post-Impressionist paintings from France were creating so much controversy and excitement during the years 1909–14, "the writers were pricking up their ears and raising their voices lest too much attention . . . be given to painting."[19] Vanessa, on the other hand, grew up in a family of writers and in a country dominated by the literary not the visual arts. As a result, she and the other Bloomsbury painters felt not only rebellious but also defensive, capable of getting the artistic stimulation and appreciation they needed only in France. There was also the tendency in the art criticism of Roger Fry as well as Clive Bell, even though they emphasized a basic unity among the arts, to reject certain kinds of links between painting and literature. In the published and unpublished writings of the Bloomsbury critics and artists, including Vanessa Bell, "literary," in the sense of depending upon outside associations or suggestions of character and story rather than on formal elements within the picture itself, is a pejorative term.

For these reasons, the sisters never fully developed their potentials for dual creativity. To Virginia Woolf, although she does wish to exclude from fiction material more appropriate to the essay, the novel in general is a more inclusive art form; it can do some of what painting does and more. Vanessa Bell is the other kind of painter mentioned in Woolf's essay on Sickert. To her, painting is a pure, inviolable medium, divorced from the confusions and muddles of human relationships and the psychological self-analysis upon which literature depends. A painting, unlike a novel, is not a cannibal, at least not in theory; it does not devour other genres and media. It fasts, lives off itself; at the most, it devours the shapes and colors of people and trees, fruits and flowers. My focus, however, is not on the extent to which each sister failed to develop her creative potential but on the extent to which she did. If each respected, or at least claimed to respect fundamental territorial boundaries, at the same time the amount of potential each did fulfill was due in large part to the professional example of the other.

Because my methods are primarily those of literary criticism, I do not offer definitive analyses or evaluations of Vanessa Bell's paintings. Those tasks are underway among art historians and critics. Instead, this book uses her work as well as the professional relationship between the sisters to illuminate, from a different angle, certain characteristics of Virginia Woolf's writing. In the process, aspects of Vanessa Bell's creativity inevitably emerge. The book is divided, therefore, into two parts. Both incorporate biographical material about the quantity and quality of the sisters' contact as artists; both include analyses of related aspects of Woolf's writing. The first three chapters, however, deal primarily with Virginia and Vanessa as sisters intensely aware of each other's artistic activities and, while territorial about their own, willing to exchange ideas on both media and even to collaborate professionally.

Each sister, as we shall see, experimented not only with her own but also with the other's medium. Virginia wrote essays, but she also practiced drawing and copied the works of artists who had abilities in both media. Vanessa drew and painted, but she also tried her hand at the critical essay. Watching and commenting on the early stages of each other's artistic careers, involving themselves in groups that discussed ideas and art, looking at paintings together in London and abroad, and discussing painted and written renditions of the world around them, the sisters both forged separate professional identities and identified with each other as artistic rebels and experimenters.

Their early discussions of art may not have been highly theoretical, but Virginia and Vanessa did recognize differences between a medium that is essentially static and one that can embody the actual creative process that results in the finished work of art. As an early diary entry reveals, Virginia realized this distinction as early as 1904 when she and Vanessa looked at some paintings by Perugino. She also recognized that both painter and writer aim at beauty although perhaps of a different kind. The sisters observed too that the writer is more interested in the consciousness of color and other visual stimuli than in colors or forms themselves; the writer subordinates the purely visual to human concerns. In later years, the sisters elaborated on their artistic differences. Vanessa Bell's lecture at Leighton Park School in the twenties defines her art in contrast to that of writers, her sister being her primary example. Virginia Woolf's *Walter Sickert: A Conversation* in the thirties is a counterpart. Instigated by Vanessa, who also designed the cover, and written with an understanding of Vanessa's approach to painting, Virginia still asserts a literary bias. Much of Woolf's self-conscious exploration of her medium arises from her continual awareness of what her sister and other modern painters are doing. Virginia interrupts and interprets Vanessa's silence with words; yet paradoxically, by writing about what transcends language and by choosing and arranging her words with care, Virginia aspires to a parallel silence.

Walter Sickert is, in many respects, Woolf's culminating piece of formal art criticism, written as it was after two introductions to her sister's exhibitions as well as various other essays on the visual arts. In all of them Woolf follows the workings of a common viewer's mind, although one with a distinct verbal orientation. Like some of the characters in her fiction, Woolf is both repelled by and attracted to the silence and impersonality of painting. She likes to exercise her imagination on traditional narrative or didactic works; she also rejects them. Like verbal clichés, such pictures, which the mind is all too ready to call up on its own if no sentimental painting is present, lend a false significance to human activities.[20] Visual images, like words, can be hackneyed. At their best, paintings make Woolf conscious of the inadequacy of words to embody deep emotion, the essence of a human personality, or perceptions that go beyond the individual, time-bound ego. When words fail, she and her characters frequently turn to visual images to express themselves. Paradoxically, Woolf also goes to paintings for verbal stimulation. Their silence stops words, creates a hiatus in the phrases that bubble up so constantly, but, by doing so, allows the unconscious mind to generate fresher words and phrases.

Although they acknowledged differences between their media, each sister saw the world in part through the other's professional eyes. Each could imagine what the other would do with certain material or what she would do herself if she worked in the other medium. If she were a painter, Virginia Woolf noted repeatedly in her diaries and letters, she would render a particular scene in certain colors. If Virginia had seen this view or heard that conversation, Vanessa Bell wrote in letters to her sister, she would have been able to capture it in words. Each deprecated her ability to create works of art in the other's medium and to criticize it, yet each showed some facility in the forbidden territory. Virginia's drawings and comments on the visual arts are sensitive; Vanessa's ability to use words is far greater than she gave herself credit for, and her responses to literature, although often stern, are provocative.

Each sister valued the other's reactions to her own work and felt that the criticism of another creative person, even one working in a different medium, was important. Virginia especially depended upon Vanessa's approval, a situation which sometimes made commenting difficult for her. Although Virginia, when she wrote about painting, usually tried to acknowledge formal criteria and insisted that she was not responding exclusively to suggestions of character and emotion, Vanessa, when she wrote about literature, emphasized form. Knowing this, Virginia even wondered if she had not made *The Waves* too abstract in her attempts to please. Responding to Virginia's novels, however, Vanessa often had trouble with objectivity. She knew the material her sister drew upon and the workings of her sister's mind and tongue so well that she had trouble applying what was, for both of them, the highest aesthetic criteria: the ability of a work of art to transport them into a world quite separate from the one they knew. Increasingly, however, Vanessa was able to see the formal aspects of her sister's work and even to attribute her own strong personal responses to Virginia's ability to create a cohesive and separate aesthetic realm. Virginia had no difficulty seeing a separate world in Vanessa's work; her critical process was more likely to involve detecting and then defining a more personal, emotional dimension to her initial aloof response.

Because the sisters shared values and a view of reality, they often found themselves stimulated by each other's work or capable of creating parallel works. Just as Woolf was tempted to produce verbal versions of some of her sister's paintings and did use Vanessa Bell's words—her story of the giant moths at Cassis—as the impetus for *The Waves*, so Vanessa found pictures forming when she read Virginia's stories. With her illustrations to some of her sister's works, Vanessa gave visible form to a few of these pictures. Insisting that they were not equivalents of passages in the text, she still revealed a sensitivity to Woolf's experiments with point of view as well as to the motifs and fundamental oppositions and harmonies that recur in her writing. The 1919 and 1927 editions of *Kew Gardens* provide the best examples of Bell's visual embroidery of Woolf's text. Not dependent on the illustrations, the text nevertheless is vitalized by the wordless commentary and, in some instances, challenged by some visual self-assertion.

Virginia Woolf made many condescending remarks about the visual arts as part of her competition with her sister. She also liked to equate her professional and financial successes with Vanessa Bell's domestic ones. When Vanessa succeeded as a painter, however, Virginia had two reactions. On the one hand, she did not think it fair that Vanessa should have professional achievements in addition to children; on the other, identifying with her sister as closely as she did, Virginia felt more certain of her own artistic gifts. Throughout their lives the sisters measured themselves against each other. Who was more successful, who more unconventional? They assessed their pasts and projected their futures. Experimenters and rebels as well as late bloomers, Virginia decided, each ultimately conquered her medium and faced similar problems with overall structure. In writing as in painting, the evanescent had to be given solid form. Virginia was one of several to encourage Vanessa to paint larger canvases, just as Vanessa, who liked Virginia's letters and shorter pieces better than her first novel, may have counseled her to keep her books succinct. Virginia paid more attention to the formal dimension of her work because of her sister's critical eye. Although Vanessa's influence on Virginia probably exceeded Virginia's on Vanessa, the latter's own delight in her everyday environment may have been affirmed by Virginia's. For whatever reason and in spite of her theories, Vanessa rarely excluded representational elements from her art.

Both sisters were aware, to varying degrees and at different times in their lives, of the problems inherent in being artists who were also women. Virginia Woolf especially saw that she and Vanessa were subject to restrictions, conflicts, and feelings of inferiority that were less likely to plague male artists. The woman writer had the Angel in the House (defined by Coventry Patmore for the male establishment) to impose the traditional feminine role upon her. The woman painter had the sometimes greater obstacles of getting proper training as well as equipment, a studio, and models. Both had work interrupted by family, visitors, servants, domestic duties, and illness. Even with men in their lives who accepted them as artists, the sisters sometimes found time and privacy difficult to obtain. Vanessa, as a young student, was aware of negative attitudes towards women painters, experienced inferiority feelings then and later when she and others compared her work with Duncan Grant's, and found it especially hard at times to subordinate domestic and human concerns to her art. An apparent ignorance of female predecessors, unlike Virginia Woolf's view backwards at prominent woman writers, may have been an added difficulty. Still both sisters, like Lily Briscoe in *To the Lighthouse*, struggled to assert their own views and needs in the face of traditional domestic pressures and artistic theories and did so with sufficient vigor to be productive professionals.

The sisters shared many assumptions. Most important was their conviction that art is valuable, that the activity of those who are sincere in communicating their perceptions is worthwhile in itself and necessary to generate the few geniuses each age produces. Both struggled to communicate what they perceived, not what traditions dictated; each explored her medium, and Virginia raided Vanessa's, in search of appropriate ways to embody her perceptions. At the same time that they made their works coherent, both tried to retain the childlike freshness and spontaneity with which they viewed the everyday world. In the background of both their orientations towards art is an awareness, first, of the extent to which one can transcend the individual ego and the complexities of human relationships and, second, of the thin and variable lines between individual and communal and between humankind and both humanmade and natural external worlds.

My last three chapters shift the focus to three kinds of paintings Vanessa Bell produced and her involvement with each, but the emphasis is on the many uses in Virginia Woolf's thinking and writing of portrait, still life, and landscape painting. Her direct and indirect allusions to painters and paintings in all three genres, to mention only one issue, have received little critical attention when, in fact, they provide her throughout her career with a valuable technique comparable to her literary allusions.[21] Most interesting, however, are the ways portraiture, still-life, and landscape overlap in both sisters' work. People appear indoors among solid objects that embody their interests and statuses or outside in landscape settings that suggest states of mind or that transcend individual egos. In both sisters' art works, moreover, interior and exterior worlds interpenetrate. Still lifes or people appear in front of or through windows. Virginia Woolf's fictional people look out of windows to escape from the difficulties of human relationships, to assuage curiosity or boredom, or to escape from the personal realm altogether. Woolf slips between the interior worlds of her characters' minds and the exterior worlds of rooms or nature. Even still lifes perceived by Woolf's characters sometimes become landscapes. All is ultimately subordinated to the individual consciousness; it, in turn, is subsumed in larger spaces and patterns. As Mrs. Ramsay realizes in *To the Lighthouse*, the unity of individuals around the dinner table partakes "of eternity." She concludes that "there is a coherence in things, a stability; something . . . is immune from change, and shines out . . . in the face of the flowing, the fleeting, the spectral, like a ruby." She rests in "the still space that lies about the heart of things . . . " (TTL 158).

In their depictions of people neither sister sought verisimilitude in the traditional sense, although both claimed to be able to judge portraits in the other's medium only in those terms. Both had to recognize the similar demands for a likeness placed on the commissioned portrait painter and the authorized biographer. In other work, however, likeness was less a matter of the subject's external appearance than of some inner essence, or even an ultimate elusiveness expressed by presenting the subject from more than one point of view or by subordinating the figure to a larger pattern. When each sister portrayed the other, for example, she often merged her subject with the overall design. The sometimes featureless faces of Vanessa Bell's paintings become in Woolf's work individual identities lost in the communal. Such experiences can be negative or positive, but most frequently they are the latter. In Woolf's fiction portraits also become presences and appear in various guises to aid in characterization. She associates characterization with portraiture, as she does biography and various diary exercises in which she tries to capture people's appearances or conversation. People's words, in fact, seem more suitable than their appearances for a verbal portrait. Yet words constantly fail to express what people do not or cannot say; repeatedly Woolf and her characters use visual images to solve that problem.

Still-life paintings and descriptions reveal the pleasure of both sisters in their immediate surroundings. Woolf usually employs such descriptions, not for their own sakes, but to characterize individuals. As with the featureless faces, solid objects suggest a reality beyond the individual ego. Objects outlast people who, like fruits and flowers, perish although the species continues. Often such a realization calms one of Woolf's characters. Flowers are still-life subjects especially attractive to both sisters. In her writing Woolf uses them in a variety of ways. Frequently associating them with women, she defines or challenges the traditional feminine role. That flowers are equally prominent in Vanessa Bell's dust-jacket designs for her sister's books is appropriate. Because she continually counterpoints them to human concerns, however, Woolf's use of solid and perishable objects is more complex than Vanessa Bell's. The same is true of Woolf's landscape descriptions. Even when, as in the introductory passages to sections of *The Waves*, a relatively impersonal narrative voice describes, we still do not get visual description unalloyed. Combined with images of sound and smell as well as motion, visual images become parts of larger conceptions.

The number of Woolf's characters who feel the need to escape into a more impersonal realm than that of human relationships, and the number who are calmed or charmed by scenes framed by windows or by arrangements of fruits or flowers, suggest Woolf's own visual tendencies as well as her ability to see the world through her sister's eyes. The visual arts, especially as represented by Vanessa, remind Virginia of an austere realm, free of individual egos, tangled personal relationships, and social problems. This realm, although it repels, also attracts her. She not only incorporates it in her characters' experiences but also reflects it in her own interest in the formal dimension in her writing.

This overview of the book raises the issue of how to discuss the relationships between the visual and verbal arts in the modern period.

I could emphasize the unity of the two art media or their independent identities and still be accurate. Which emphasis critics choose depends to some extent upon which prevails; when the similarities between the two art media are stressed too often, the obvious differences, which no one would deny, are reasserted.[22] In this study I try to do justice to both. While acknowledging differences, I also recognize attempts by Virginia Woolf and Vanessa Bell to simulate the effects of the other medium or to use it to stimulate creativity in their own. To simulate or stimulate, however, is not to equate; nor is it always to imitate. Often painters and writers modify traditions in their own media in parallel directions according to similar assumptions about reality and about the limitations of words or paint. Fiction, for example, can include vivid descriptive passages which intentionally or unintentionally suggest paintings.[23] Beyond that difficulty, however, others exist. Assuming that one can identify and define relationships between the visual and verbal arts, one has to recognize that these relationships are neither universal nor constant. Similarities between the two art media can always be found, but different comparisons dominate in different time periods.[24] Parallels in subject matter have been most characteristic; beginning with the movement loosely termed "Romanticism," however, likenesses in motivation, states of mind, or creative processes, as well as parallel artistic strategies, patterns, or structures have prevailed.[25]

The relationship between modern visual and verbal art forms derives from these tendencies. Although many late nineteenth- and early twentieth-century painters consciously separated themselves from literature and tried in varying degrees to present the image pure, free of verbal and especially "literary" associations, they merely shifted their alliance from traditional literary forms to those more evocative than anecdotal, moral, or even descriptive.[26] Howard Nemerov describes this new alliance by noting that both poets and painters use images; that both have languages, the painter's, in fact, having preceded and generated the writer's; and that both use their languages to try to communicate "the silence behind the language, the silence within the language."[27] By silence, Nemerov means the eternal, essential, transcendent. Other commentators define this parallel as the tendency to express, often unconsciously, basic forms and themes common to all times and places.[28]

Although many modern painters avoid the literary in the traditional narrative sense, they ally themselves with verbal expression in yet another way: they depend heavily "on an elaborate verbal apologetics, the ersatz metaphysics of 'art theory'"[29] which, in turn, "had its effect on what painters were encouraged to do." In fact, deciding whether the explanations or the characteristics they illuminate came first became impossible.[30] As Dennis Farr points out, modern painters broke with literature when they insisted that art was important for its own sake and not for its subject-matter, but they also followed literature, which was experiencing its own rebellion against tradition. Thus Whistler was in conflict with Ruskin but in agreement with Gautier, Baudelaire, and Mallarmé.[31] Most people who currently write about the relationships between the visual and verbal arts, therefore, attempt neither to posit universals in motivation or in terminology nor to establish clear cause-and-effect patterns. Recent critics limit themselves, instead, to specific relationships within "a given style or period" and work empirically and flexibly with the data at hand.[32]

Marianna Torgovnick, who recently has tried to sort out the various comparative approaches to the sister arts, offers a continuum to assist critics who want to define a writer's use of the visual arts. A "decorative" use may include characters who happen to be artists, isolated painterly descriptions, or occasional metaphors and allusions indicating a knowledge of the other medium. One can also look at the "biographical" facts that link a writer's work with the visual arts. An "ideological" focus may reveal how an author's aesthetic theory derives from a pictorial one or how a writer communicates major themes through a variety of pictorially based methods. At the "interpretive" end of the continuum, characters within a novel as well as readers of the novel respond to "art objects or pictorial objects" in ways that are central to the author's meaning. Torgovnick admits "considerable overlapping" among these categories.[33] Indeed, as readers of my study will see, the overlapping is continual, because Woolf runs the gamut, even within a single novel, from superficial to metaphysical uses of the visual arts.

Although by itself the fact does not define their professional relationship, Virginia Woolf and Vanessa Bell are part of the tendency in the arts known as "Modernism." Attempts to define this term usually raise as many questions as they answer. Does Modernism reject the past or revise our view of it? Is it order-seeking and authoritarian, or is it anarchic, apocalyptic, or nihilistic? Is it spiritual in some noninstitutional sense or defiantly secular? Is it personal or impersonal? Does it reflect hope or despair? Most writers on Modernism agree that behind it is a sense of historical transition and crisis; human beings are arrested in ways that result in altered views of reality, artistic self-examination, multiple styles, and individual solutions to aesthetic problems but, overall, a greater emphasis on form and an increasingly elitist art.[34] Malcolm Bradbury and James McFarland, who synthesize many other efforts to define Modernism, conclude that some early twentieth-century artists experienced an exhilarating freedom from traditional restraints; "art could now fulfil *itself*," and it did, often in sophisticated, technically difficult ways.[35] The other side of this freedom, however, was "bleakness, darkness, alienation, disintegration."[36] Throughout most of her career, Woolf manifests the more positive, liberating aspect of Modernism, as Bradbury says in another essay,[37] and a similar exhilaration and freedom is apparent in Vanessa Bell's work and in the proclamations about the visual arts in the criticism of Clive Bell and Roger Fry. "Cézanne," Clive Bell says, "is the Christopher Columbus of a new continent of form."[38] His admirers are its eager explorers and devoted cartographers.

"In or about December, 1910," Woolf said in 1924, "human character changed" (CE I 320). Her remark is much quoted and its meaning variously interpreted. The link between her date, however, and the first Post-Impressionist Exhibition at the Grafton Galleries (November 8, 1910 to January 15, 1911) is undisputed. Here, all together, were about twenty paintings each by Cézanne and Van Gogh and well over thirty by Gauguin. Manet, Matisse, and several others were also represented. "It is impossible . . . that any other single exhibition can ever have had so much effect as did that on the rising generation," Vanessa Bell wrote later. "That autumn of 1910," she said, "is to me a time when everything seemed springing to new life."[39] In 1913 Clive Bell proclaimed painting to be "the one manifest triumph of the young age." Unlike the novel, poetry, drama, or even music, painting had attained a purity that he equated with religious inspiration.[40] Later writers on this period echo the emphasis on purity in art. José Ortega y Gasset, for instance, comments, "Even though pure art may be impossible there doubtless can prevail a tendency toward a purification of art. Such a tendency," he adds, "would affect a progressive elimination of the human, all too human, elements predominant in romantic and naturalistic production."[41] The painter can distort or omit details, but how can the novelist, who like Woolf sees characterization as the center of fiction, begin to eliminate human elements? Taking cues from modern painting, she can render the self elusive through multiple and partial points of view; she can place her individuals in larger social, historical, and natural contexts, have the characters themselves realize their places in larger patterns, and subordinate them to the overall form of her own work of art. Working spatially with the consciousnesses of her characters and aiming for "synchronicity" rather than a linear, sequential view of history or of human life, she can also approximate painting.[42] She can even present characters engaged in similar abstracting processes, whether as painters, writers, viewers, or readers of works of art.

Woolf does not actually mention painting when she dates the change in character as "in or about December, 1910." As one might expect, she mentions literature, specifically Butler and Shaw (CE I 320). It was a year, she writes, in which "all human relations . . . shifted—those between masters and servants, husbands and wives, parents and children." All aspects of life and art reflected these changes (CE I 321). One cause of the shift in human relations was the women's movement. Nineteen ten was also the year when Virginia Woolf did volunteer work for women's suffrage. She soon decided to spend her time creating books that gave value as well as appropriate artistic form to individual women's inner lives; she chose to challenge authoritarian points of view, conventional narrative sequences, and certain kinds of emphases on external facts, to engage in political aesthetics rather than in politics.[43] Still, the coincidence is worth noting; the suffrage movement and the avant-garde artists, both of whom challenged the status quo and increasingly aroused public indignation, felt some sympathy with each other. The violent acts of the more militant suffragists, which included the hacking of paintings, coincided with more frequent displays of avant-garde art. The Vorticist writers and painters asked, condescendingly, that the women discriminate in their acts of violence so that they did not "destroy a / Good Picture by Accident," but they commended the militants for their bravery and vitality.[44]

Feminine vitality was constructive as well as destructive. As Judith Gardiner notes, "Feminist literary historians are now defining the contribution[s] of women to modernism" like, for instance, differences between the male model of the integrated individual who is part of a clearly defined sexual hierarchy and the female model who is more comfortably multiple and democratic.[45] Woolf suggests an additional contribution: "Aren't things spoilt by saying them?" asks Lily Briscoe in the manuscript version of *To the Lighthouse*. She speculates that women are "more expressive silently gliding high together, side by side, in . . . curious dumbness, . . . with the kingdoms of the world displayed down beneath. . . ."[46] In 1932 another novelist, Dorothy Richardson, contrasted men to women, whom she called "humanity's silent half, without much faith in speech as a medium of communication"; she also contrasted the sound to the silent film. The latter, with "its power to evoke, suggest, reflect, express from within its moving parts and in their totality of movement, something of the changeless being at the heart of all becoming," Richardson called "essentially feminine." In the silent film's "insistence on contemplation it provided a pathway to reality."[47] Woolf did not explicitly use "feminine" and "masculine" to oppose her sister's silent art works to talky conventional narrative paintings or works of literature. Yet something of that opposition is there, more easily perceived perhaps by readers of later decades than by those of Woolf's time, and complicated by the fact that silence, like sound, can be carried to destructive extremes. Women not only look for words and sentences suited to their experiences, but they also, like painters, recognize and value the many varieties of communication without words. My treatment of Virginia Woolf and Vanessa Bell, therefore, is part of a new history of Modernism which, until recently, has slighted not only women artists' perspectives but also their relationships as professionals.

Woolf rightly feared any critical attitude toward literature that "pinches the mind," that puts it "in whalebones, . . . or pinches the foot like too tight shoes." For the critic she advocates, instead, "that state of mind in which it seems possible . . . to write the book, not to read it." Such a mental state is filled with many disorganized, opposing sensory impressions, but out of them "one or two gradually become significant."[48] In Woolf's case, as she realized herself, visual impressions dominated (D III 297). Sometimes she thought of her whole mind as an "insatiable" eye (D III 29, 130). "The look of things has a great power over me," she noted on another occasion. "But what a little I can get down with my pen of what is so vivid to my eyes . . ." (D III 191). In 1933 she even defined the imagination as "the picture making power" (D IV 176).[49] An examination of

Woolf's work in the context of the visual arts, therefore, requires a plunge into the fertile and highly visual creative state of mind from which her writing emerged.

To stress the visual dimension is not to deny the impact of traditional and contemporary literature or of other art forms upon Woolf's work. Her visual orientation complements these other characteristics of her complex creative process and reveals how her art diverged from and converged with Vanessa Bell's. To stress the artistic link between the sisters, moreover, is not to deny important links with other people, periods of relative estrangement, or times when their lives inevitably took different directions. It is not to deny varying degrees of reciprocal or sometimes one-sided psychological dependencies between them. Nor do I mean to dismiss technical and ideological development in Woolf's work. This study teases out from an intricate fabric a single thread, one that is so pervasive as to override chronology and one that, more frequently than is recognized, holds larger portions of the design intact.

This study draws upon a large number of published and unpublished letters, diaries, and memoirs and, even more important, the sisters' novels, stories, essays, paintings, illustrations, and decorative works to reveal two visually creative minds at work. Weaving together numerous details from various sources and time periods to reveal a whole range of professional activities has both disadvantages and advantages. The danger of losing conclusions in a plethora of subtle variations and even contradictions, however, is more often outweighed by the ability to make accurate statements about the artistic relationship between the sisters and about the pervasiveness of the visual in Woolf's creative process. Out of this wealth of available materials emerge assumptions these two women had about art works and creative activity. Sometimes articulated, sometimes not, these assumptions resulted in works which, more often than Virginia Woolf and Vanessa Bell realized, communicated similar perceptions and values by means of parallel artistic strategies. If Virginia moved away from the traditional "realistic," plotted novel to a form as compact and evocative as poetry, and if Vanessa moved away from traditional representational and narrative paintings in a similar direction, then one might, with certain reservations, call the work of both "poetic." Both women use images and the relationships among them to evoke essences beyond the language of words or the language of form and color. Competitors and raiders of each other's artistic territories, as well as collaborators and inspirers of each other's art works, Virginia Woolf and Vanessa Bell were, above all, productive professional artists whose relationship as such illuminates the tension and encouragement that exists in the families of both society and the arts.

1

Dual Creativity

VIRGINIA'S DRAWING AND VANESSA'S WRITING

Virginia Woolf and Vanessa Bell each had considerable interest and some ability in the other's art medium. In a draft of "Anon," one of the last essays Woolf wrote, she reaffirmed the close relationship among the arts in the early development of the individual artist as well as in the early history of British literature: "For a moment there is a pause on the threshold of the great Elizabethan house, when the artist sees before him three different paths. Shall he sing, or paint, or make poems? And then there rose from the courtyard the crude tones of the mummers. It was the stage that settled it. Had there been no stage, no actors, Shakespeare might have been Michael Angelo, Spenser Raphael, and Marlowe our first great musician."[1]

Had Virginia Woolf's situation been different, might she have become a visual artist? As a young woman she tried her hand at the visual arts for several reasons: drawing was a recreation in the Stephen family, she wanted to compete with her sister, and she had some genuine sensitivity and interest. Ultimately writing displaced drawing, although her early efforts and Vanessa's continuing commitment to the visual arts contributed to the highly visual nature of Virginia's prose. Vanessa may not have written formal essays on painting or welcomed purely theoretical discussions, but she liked to talk about art. From the beginning, Virginia listened, looked, and defined her own medium in comparison to her sister's. Still, feeling excluded from Vanessa's world, Virginia mocked the painters' preoccupations and insisted that writing was both more difficult and more worthwhile. Her rivalry with Vanessa caused her to contrast their accomplishments, but her close identification with her sister's achievements reduced the competitiveness. A further complication was Vanessa's ability to write.

That Virginia Stephen tried her hand at her sister's medium seems natural. In spite of the literary orientation of the family, many of its members drew. Leslie Stephen, for example, who Virginia said "had . . . no feeling for pictures" (MB 68), still entertained his children with droll animal sketches (Figure 1.1).[2] After his death in 1904 and the move to 46 Gordon Square when Virginia was twenty-two, she wrote about her future to Violet Dickinson: "If Haldane is severe," she said, awaiting the reaction of the liberal statesman to one of her articles, "I shall give up literature and take to art, I am already a draughtsman of great promise," she continued. "I draw for 2 hours every evening after dinner, and make copies of all kinds of pictures, which *Nessa says* show a very remarkable feeling for line. Pictures are easier to understand than subtle literature, so I think I shall become an artist to the public, and keep my writing to myself" (L I 170). The copies of pictures Virginia mentioned in her letter to Violet Dickinson probably were the ones she sent to her friend a month later. They were, she explained, "the first I did when the divine inspiration seized me—and I am now improved, according to severe critics, and draw ponies out of my head, and domestic groups." The family, she reported, still drew after dinner. Vanessa apparently sometimes read, while Virginia drew with the rest. Thoby, she said, "draws murderers escaping and criminals being hung—and once, I'm sorry to say, the back view of God Almighty—and Adrian draws foxes, as large as deer, running along with their tongues out, and a beautiful gent. on a horse, who's himself, galloping up in front of the hounds" (L I 172).[3]

Virginia's drawings of ponies and domestic groups have not, to my knowledge, survived. When Violet Dickinson typed copies of her friend's letters and bound them, however, she included the first drawings in one of the two volumes.[4] "I'd altogether forgotten those old drawings," Virginia Woolf wrote in 1936 upon seeing the collection (L VI 91). Perhaps she would have agreed with Quentin Bell's assessment of them as "weak but not insensitive."[5] One sketch says "my very first work" in the upper left-hand corner. "HYPNOS," the name of the classical god of sleep and brother of death, is printed below (Figure 1.2). The faint pencil drawing, probably a copy of the "Head of Hypnos" (fourth century B.C.) in the British Museum, is of a benign face with eyelids lowered and a wing on one side of the

1.1. Leslie Stephen. Pencil drawings of animals from a copy of George Meredith's *The Egoist* (London, 1880). Courtesy of the Library of Leonard and Virginia Woolf at Washington State University Libraries, Pullman, Washington.

1.2. Virginia Stephen. *Hypnos*, 1904. Courtesy of Quentin Bell.

head.[6] Two of the drawings are copies of works by Dante Gabriel Rossetti, probably taken from the first volume of *Memorials of Edward Burne-Jones*.[7] Virginia labeled one "Mrs. Morris from the drawing by D. G. Rossetti" and drew, again in fine, faint pencil, a woman's head (Figure 1.3). The other says "Mrs. D. G. Rossetti drawing by Rossetti" (Figure 1.4).

Two drawings after Blake have darker, more pronounced lines. One, executed on an upside-down piece of stationery which says "46 Gordon Square," is inscribed in Virginia's hand, "Death & life by Blake" (Figure 1.5). It depicts a nude male figure, head in profile, looking towards the upper right. His torso faces front and he sits with one knee up and the other leg, drawn with some difficulty, bent under at the knee. Virginia paid some attention to the muscles in the arms and legs and provided minimal shading to give roundness to the figure, but the overall effect, like Blake's, is two-dimensional. She sketched only the "life" portion of this design for Blair's *The Grave*, omitting the stooped, white-bearded man below who, supported by a

1.3. Virginia Stephen. *Mrs. Morris from the drawing by D. G. Rossetti*, 1904. Courtesy of Quentin Bell.

crutch, enters a door into darkness or death. Her second "Drawing by Blake" also depicts, somewhat stiffly, a nude form. This time it leaps into the picture space, arms and legs extended (Figure 1.6). Blake's original appears at the beginning of chapter one of *Urizen*.

1.4. Virginia Stephen. *Mrs. D. G. Rossetti drawing by Rossetti*, 1904. Courtesy of Quentin Bell.

The works Virginia Stephen copied are by artists known for their dual creativity. If she was not aware of this duality then, she certainly was in later life. In "Notes for Reading at Random," written shortly before her death, she isolates as an issue

> The connection between seeing & writing:
> Michael Angelo. Leonardo. Blake. Rossetti.
> a twin gift. Wh. shall be born. depends on
> Nin Crot & Pulley.[8]

"Nin Crot & Pulley," Woolf's whimsical way of referring to combinations of environmental forces which affect individual artists at each

1.5. Virginia Stephen. *Death and Life by Blake*, 1904. Courtesy of Quentin Bell.

period in their development and in each historical period, influenced her to become a writer instead of a painter. Had she become a painter, her work might have been as false as she considered Benjamin Haydon's. Reviewing this nineteenth-century painter's memoirs

1.6. Virginia Stephen. *Drawing by Blake*, 1904. Courtesy of Quentin Bell.

in 1926, she concluded that "his genius is a writer's." His visual sense prompts vivid prose, but a "malicious accident" of some kind "made him, when he had to choose a medium, pick up a brush when the pen lay handy" (CE IV 11–12). Woolf also hesitated between the two but ultimately used her visual sensitivity to augment her verbal gift.

Virginia also sent Violet Dickinson what she called "two of my masterpieces" done on a "silver point press" her sister had purchased. "One is a Rose," she reported, "which I use as a bookplate in Fitzgeralds books, the other is a copy of Shakespeare's death mask!—rather elongated you will see, but I have not yet mastered my medium, which is a very fascinating one" (L I 174). The bookplates still exist in the volumes where Virginia placed them.[9] The rose design shows one opened bloom with stem and leaves as well as one bud, its stem almost meeting the other atop the intertwined initials

1.7. Virginia Stephen. Rose bookplate, 1904. From vol. 4 of *Letters and Literary Remains of Edward Fitzgerald*, 7 vols. (London: Macmillan, 1903). Courtesy of the Library of Leonard and Virginia Woolf at Washington State University Libraries, Pullman, Washington, and of Quentin Bell.

AVS, for Adeline Virginia Stephen (Figure 1.7). Two stages in the life of a flower doomed to fade is appropriate for what must have been her new volumes of a poet whose work repeatedly invokes the rose as a symbol of mortality.[10]

The bookplate Virginia Stephen made for her new Whitehall Shakespeare volumes was, as she indicated to Violet Dickinson, the death mask of the bard (Figure 1.8). It is a face with a bald head,

1.8. Virginia Stephen. Shakespeare's death mask bookplate, 1904. From a copy of *The Works of William Shakespeare* (The Whitehall Edition), 12 vols. (Westminster, 1893–98). Courtesy of the Library of Leonard and Virginia Woolf at Washington State University Libraries, Pullman, Washington, and of Quentin Bell.

furrowed brow, closed eyes, strangely flattened nose, mustache, and small beard. The abundant life of the figures Virginia copied from Blake juxtaposed with the vivid but ephemeral rose and the death mask indicate from the beginning a preoccupation with intense life and inevitable death which permeates her work. Yet the death mask in the volumes of Shakespeare's plays also recalls the immortality of the bard, if not in body, at least through his artistic creations.[11]

Virginia Stephen gave up her experimentation with the visual arts fairly early, although in 1910 she was still trying her hand. She wrote to Lady Cecil that she had been attempting to draw her the previous day. "When shown to the company," however, her drawing "was pronounced 'head of a male, unknown'" (L I 426). Although less enthusiastic about her own efforts in the visual media, Virginia continued some of them even after her marriage in 1912. In August of 1915, Vanessa Bell indicated her desire to see the copies her sister had made of some unidentified paintings by her and Duncan Grant. That Virginia had copied her work was a compliment, she said; no one else was ever likely to do so.[12] "I try to paint and embroider," Virginia wrote a month later, "but these arts are so vapid after writing" (L II 64). By 1918 she seems to have given up anything but an occasional sketch or various attempts at needlework or other decorative art forms.

Like their creator, a number of Woolf's fictional characters have dual creative inclinations. In *Mrs.Dalloway* Sally Seton, as a girl, plans to paint and write; ultimately she does neither. Septimus Smith, whose interests have been literary, draws naked caricatures of the self-satisfied, hypocritical people in his office. His papers at home contain not only poems, conversations, and "messages from the dead" but also, "Diagrams, designs, little men and women brandishing sticks for arms, with wings—were they?—on their backs; circles traced round shillings and sixpences—the suns and stars; zigzagging precipices with mountaineers ascending roped together, exactly like knives and forks; sea pieces with little faces laughing out of what might perhaps be waves: the map of the world" (MD 223–24).

Like Septimus, Bernard in *The Waves* tries to express the contents of his mind both visually and verbally. Contemplating strangers, he says, "I could make a dozen stories of what he said, of what she said—I can see a dozen pictures" (W 144). Both arts arise from observation. Later he recalls how he "made notes for stories; drew portraits in the margin of my pocket-book. . ." (W 242). Orlando too occasionally uses visual images to express herself, although she is primarily a writer. In the nineteenth century, when she tries to write and her quill makes a blot instead of words on the page, "she tried to decorate the blot with wings and whiskers, till it became a round-headed monster, something between a bat and a wombat" (O 238). And the narrator of *A Room of One's Own*, while doing the research for a lecture on women and fiction, angrily draws a caricature of the Professor Von X who has proclaimed women inferior (AROO 31).

Virginia Woolf's own potential dual creativity takes many forms. She may not illustrate her own works, but she frequently develops arguments by a series of highly visual passages. The argument of *A Room of One's Own*, for instance, turns upon three main pictures in addition to that of the angry professor. The first two, the luncheon at Oxbridge and the dinner at Fernham, suggest others, like "a scene of masons on a high roof some five centuries ago. Kings and nobles brought treasure in huge sacks and poured it under the earth. This scene was forever coming alive in my mind and placing itself by another of lean cows and a muddy market and withered greens and the stringy hearts of old men—these two pictures, disjointed and disconnected and nonsensical as they were, were forever coming together and combating each other and had me entirely at their mercy" (AROO 19). Having defined by means of contrasting pictures the discrepancy between men's and women's circumstances as well as her own initial reaction to the injustice, Woolf provides a third main picture, a man and woman entering a cab, to restore her "unity of . . . mind" (AROO 100–101).

Woolf's procedure in an earlier piece, "The Plumage Bill" (1920), is similar. Her subject is the defeat of a bill that would outlaw the killing of birds for their feathers. "But what do women care?" she asks. To answer her question, she looks from her window and watches a woman with a striking figure and "a stupid face" gaze greedily at some egret plumes attractively displayed in a shop window. "But since we are looking at pictures," Woolf says, "let us look at another which has the advantage of filling in certain blank spaces in our rough sketch of Regent Street in the morning." The second picture is an imaginary "blazing South American landscape" (D II 337). "In the foreground" are blinded, tortured birds used as decoys. Other pictures are of tiny birds in nests, hungry but deprived of their parents; of wounded birds; of hunters blinding birds. The picture of the greedy, vain woman must be balanced by those of brutal male hunters and opportunistic male profiteers. Woolf distributes blame by means of verbal pictures.

Virginia Woolf used her early interest in drawing and her dual creativity in these and, as we shall see, other ways. Such inclinations emerge, to a great extent, from her close relationship with her sister. That Virginia and Vanessa discussed art during the years they were growing up is clear from a letter Vanessa wrote to Clive Bell in 1906. She and her sister, she said, had discussed not only their own intimacy and their views of various actual and potential suitors but also "her art" and "art altogether."[13] The generally accepted notion that Vanessa Bell rarely talked or wrote in a theoretical, analytical way about either painting or writing is one possible reason why she is slighted as an artistic influence on Virginia Woolf. A traditionally male-dominated critical establishment may favor theoretical discussions; expressed, as they often are, in writing, theories are also possible to document. Nevertheless, they are not the only kinds of interchanges that have value. Nor are they the only ways in which one creative person can stimulate another. Virginia observed, in both Vanessa's conversation and behavior, her commitment: the enthusiasm and struggle, the confidence and despair she communicated as she evaluated her own work and as she developed and expressed her own artistic priorities. The paintings that remain are visual documents of her commitment but, ironically, in a study like this one Vanessa's spoken words or silent example to her sister must be verified mainly through written reminiscences, diary entries, and letters.

Angelica Garnett is one who recalls her mother's antitheoretical tendencies and adds that, in the case of painting, Vanessa took ideas from Roger Fry and echoed them unquestioningly throughout her life.[14] David Garnett says that "Her brain was original and logical and she was a quick reasoner, never hesitating to put forward her views."[15] Kenneth Clark describes Vanessa as "not at all dogmatic, but she never relaxed her standards, and in a quiet, hesitant voice would expose false values and mixed motives."[16] While all of these comments may be accurate, they give somewhat different impressions of Vanessa Bell. Reconciling them depends upon understanding the situations and topics that prompted her to express certain kinds of opinions. Then one can determine how derivative her views were as well as how much she influenced her sister's creative life. Vanessa Bell's letters and memoirs leave no doubt that she enjoyed talking about art, that she readily pronounced judgment upon the works of both old masters and contemporaries, and that Virginia thoughtfully received many such conclusions. Although she had setbacks and considerable self-doubt, Vanessa charted a relatively independent course in her effort to communicate honestly her own view of reality.

In her letters Vanessa Bell frequently comments enthusiastically on talk about painting. In 1908, for example, she wrote to tell her friend Marjorie Snowden how much she enjoyed the continual discussion of art among the Parisian painters. In the same year she wrote that Henry Lamb was one of the few in England willing to talk to her with any intelligence about painting. Later she recalled that she had founded the Friday Club in 1905 in order to encourage such conversation in London.[17] Leon Edel sees the Friday Club as a competitive response to the Thursday Evenings instituted by her brother, Thoby, earlier in 1905 when his Cambridge friends visited the four Stephenses at 46 Gordon Square. The tone of such gatherings was one of "lofty academicism" and philosophical inquiry. Edel distinguishes between the "theoretical discussion" that Vanessa Stephen disliked and "the aesthetic ideas of her young peers" as well as "the shoptalk of art" which she enjoyed.[18] Vanessa's discomfort with the Thursday Evening group, made up of people who were, with the exception of Clive Bell, "aesthetically blind,"[19] is understandable.

Vanessa, however, may have been competing with Virginia as much as with Thoby. Frances Spalding suggests that Virginia's increasing activity and success as a reviewer may have caused Vanessa to reevaluate her own professional environment and potential.[20] Still, one should not assume that she enjoyed nothing about the Thursday Evening situation or that Virginia was, in contrast, totally at home in it. Vanessa's memoir on Bloomsbury lists among the topics of conversation not only philosophical subjects like "the 'meaning of good,'" but also "books or painting" or even "one's daily doings and adventures." What she liked about the meetings was the sense that the men and women present "seemed to be a company of the young, all free, all beginning life in new surroundings" without adult supervision. To her, at least in retrospect, the group was part of her new liberation from the gloom and the values of Kensington.[21]

Edel's and Spalding's observations are in part just, but Vanessa's reticence about discussions on philosophical questions and her founding of the Friday Club may have resulted not just from competitiveness but from feelings of ignorance and intellectual inferiority as well. In a memoir, she recalls Virginia's assertion that she had had no education: "If she had none, however, I had less, for she did at least teach herself or get herself taught Greek, and was given books to read by my father which may, for all I know, have had educational value."[22] Similarly, a letter to Virginia in 1906 described Vanessa's feelings of intellectual inadequacy. With Robert and Nelly Cecil she had had a dinner-table conversation "in the best old Thursday Evening style." The topic was whether painting was "spiritual or material." Vanessa said she could contribute to the conversation only because both Cecils were present; with Lord Robert alone, she felt "a hopeless fool." Only a genius like her sister, she added, could separate her "subtleties & beautiful reserves" from "pure idiotcy."[23]

Virginia reported with enthusiasm Thursday evening arguments that continued until three in the morning; at the same time she mocked the long silences and satirized the young men's attempts at poetry.[24] Nor did Vanessa's alternative gatherings escape mockery. In *The Voyage Out* Evelyn Murgatroyd expresses to Rachel Vinrace her dissatisfaction with a group that sounds in some respects like the Thursday Evenings but in others like the Friday Club:

> "I belong to a club in London. It meets every Saturday, so it's called the Saturday Club. We're supposed to talk about art, but I'm sick of talking about art—what's the good of it? With all kinds of real things going on round one? It isn't as if they'd got anything to say about art either. So what I'm going to tell 'em is that we've talked enough about art, and we'd better talk about life for a change. Questions that really matter to people's lives, the White Slave Traffic, Woman Suffrage, the Insurance Bill, and so on. . . . My notion's to think of the human beings first and let the abstract ideas take care of themselves. . . . I'm not intellectual or artistic or anything of that sort, but I'm jolly human" (VO 248–49).

Whether she agreed or not, Virginia obviously was aware of such points of view. Comments in her letters on her sister's Friday Club are less severe. The founding committee, she reported to Violet Dickinson, "sat for two hours on very few eggs" and could not agree: "one half of the committee shriek Whistler and French impressionists, and the other half are stalwart British" (L I 201). Still, she saw its quarrels as "healthy," and Vanessa's managerial ability as admirable. "It all seems to interest her," Virginia added, but "it would bore me to death" (L I 213).

With less risk of boredom, perhaps, Virginia and Adrian reinstituted the Thursday Evenings shortly after Thoby's death and Vanessa's marriage to Clive Bell. Unlike Vanessa, who had cut many of her ties with the past, Virginia invited the Cambridge young men as well as friends from the days when the Stephen family was established at Hyde Park Gate.[25] Vanessa did not think that one such gathering sounded "very lively except to read of afterwards. But then its real success," she wrote to her sister, "may have been sacrificed to its literary success."[26] Either Virginia could bring to life what had not been very exciting in actuality, or else the real value of the meeting had been missed by someone like Virginia whose habit was to transform it into words. Vanessa had some interest in the Thursday Evenings, though, because she and Virginia tried to revive them some twenty years later. Vanessa wrote that they had "started a most extraordinary series of entertainments in the line of the old Thursday evenings" except that now "a most miscellaneous collection" met at Gordon Square on Tuesdays. The meetings were "an experiment" and could be abandoned if they got out of hand. But, Vanessa said, they "may be amusing for a time."[27]

There is one more way to account for Vanessa's founding of the Friday Club: its composition. Richard Shone defines the Club as "a place where artists could talk shop, listen to lectures, discuss their work and even from time to time hold exhibitions."[28] Quentin Bell describes the Club's activities and membership less narrowly. Exhibitions and discussions certainly occurred, but not all of the latter were about art. The founding committee, as well as those who attended the meetings, included several nonpainters like Virginia Stephen as well as painters.[29] Occasionally Duncan Grant, Henry Lamb, and other male painters attended, but women made up a large proportion of the Club's membership.[30] Vanessa recalls that in 1904 she felt extremely intimidated by the most advanced group of artists at that time, the New English Art Club. These men, she felt, "seemed somehow to have the secret of the art universe within their grasp, a secret one was not worthy to learn, especially if one was that terrible low creature, a female painter."[31] Her remark suggests that women could benefit from a group in which each artist could take herself and the others seriously. For a similar reason many women students from the Slade, including Vanessa Bell, were willing to help Roger Fry in the Omega Workshop when he founded it in 1913. They were "only too anxious," Isabelle Anscombe notes, "to find a place in what was still very much a man's world."[32]

In addition to the Friday Club, letters served as a forum for the discussion of art. Vanessa's constant readiness to express opinions is especially evident in her early correspondence with Marjorie Snowden. In 1904 Vanessa described her reactions to the early Italian painters and disagreed with Ruskin's desire to read "deep meanings" into them. Influenced perhaps by Thoby, Tintoretto was her great discovery, "an absolute revelation."[33] Virginia was along on this trip, which occurred shortly after their father's death; apparently she looked at paintings with her sister: "till you have seen Tintoretto," she wrote, agreeing with or merely echoing her brother and sister, "you don't know what paint can do" (L I 138). In Florence, Vanessa's responses to some of the early Italian masters was, as Richard Shone puts it, "not at all conventional."[34]

Throughout her life, to a number of correspondents, including Virginia, Vanessa indicated her desire to talk about art, even sometimes about the theoretical questions that her insecurities about her education perhaps caused her to avoid. As early as 1905 she was aware of an issue that preoccupied her friends throughout their lives: the importance of form as opposed to subject in painting. Marjorie Snowden had wondered if she should paint her model with a kitten. Vanessa replied that the treatment was more important than the subject; even a commonplace one could be rendered in an interesting manner.[35] Then, in 1910 or 1912, Vanessa reported that she and Leonard Woolf "had an argument as to whether colour exists, of the kind I always took to."[36] Sometimes Vanessa identified with her sister's or other people's views on art in opposition to those of people like Roger Fry and Clive Bell who were more directly involved with painting or art criticism. She wrote to Virginia in 1913 that Fry had visited them in the country: ". . . The air is teeming with discussion on Art. . . . Roger's views of course are more mature than ours—He is at one pole & Clive at the other & I come somewhere in between on a rather shaky foothold."[37] She does not mention their topic, but a month earlier Vanessa had described to Leonard Woolf where she agreed and disagreed with people like Clive who insisted that aesthetic emotions derive from form alone. She agreed, she said, that she responded primarily to the patterns the artist creates with form and color; she insisted, however, that she found these patterns in the world around her. Abstract art was not the inevitable result.[38] In 1926, the "awful question" still under discussion was "the content of a work of art" about which, she observed to Roger Fry, her opponent agreed with him rather than with her. Both, presumably, attached a different degree of importance to content than she did. She later described her opponent, Stephen Tomlin, as a man she could take only in small doses. Although a sculptor, he "never seems to pay any attention to the looks of anything or notice them at all. All his conversation is theoretical & argumentative & I should die of despair if I had to live with him."[39]

One of Vanessa Bell's most long-lasting dialogues about art went on with Roger Fry. They met in about 1905, became reacquainted in 1910, were lovers from about 1911–13, and remained friends until his death in 1934. Talk about art with Fry, she reported, was far better than talk about it with most other people, even those like Kenneth Clark who ought to know all about it. Fry was a "creative critic," she said, someone far more difficult to find than a good painter.[40] Many of her comments to Fry are colored by her admiration and, at the same time, her need to assert herself and to remain independent of a powerful personality. Although she said she wanted to discuss theoretical matters as well as technique with him, she frequently postponed doing so or referred to her contributions apologetically.[41] Still, over the years she not only attended some of Fry's lectures but also read the copies of lectures and articles he sent her.

Often punctuated with sketches, the letters between Vanessa Bell and Roger Fry included discussions of the importance of form as opposed to content as well as exchanges on the merits and demerits of specific painters, on working from life versus working from sketches, on working indoors versus outdoors and in England versus in France, and on using watercolors as opposed to oils; they also commented on their own projects and predicted failures and successes. In these letters, Vanessa often denounced the color and design of the paintings and decorative art works she saw as "pretty," "sweet," "melodramatic," or "sentimental." Her other pejorative terms were "dull," "silly," "academic," "bad," "feeble," "second-hand," and variations on "commonplace." She looked for a sure sense of color and, by implication, "freshness" and honesty.[42] Writing to Fry about the old masters whose works she saw on her travels in 1920, she reported mixed reactions to the ceiling of the Sistine Chapel and admired Vermeer, Rembrandt, and especially Delacroix for his color and design. Fry agreed with her about Michelangelo but disagreed about Delacroix.[43] Similarly, in 1929 she wrote from the continent about paintings by Giorgione, Raphael, and Rembrandt which she and Fry had obviously discussed before. Although she presented her conclusions apologetically, in one case she tried to help him decide what was wrong with a Giorgione painting; in another, she disagreed with him about a specific painting's merits.[44]

Vanessa Bell told Fry that she could not trust herself as a critic of his paintings,[45] a reluctance that was convenient when she did not want to say how much she disliked his work. She saved her strictures for letters to Clive Bell, but Roger apparently was not fooled. In 1914 Vanessa described his annoyance at the indifference to his painting in England. He blamed this neglect on her and Clive. Roger saw accurately, she wrote, that she thought his work lifeless and colorless. Sometime after 1928 she wrote, again to Clive, that Fry's painting of an old lady was "beyond anything Ive ever seen of his for pure horror. Its not only feeble but quite as vulgar as any R.A. [Royal Academy] portrait & almost exactly like one."[46] What she meant by "vulgar" might be explained by a teasing comment to Virginia a year earlier: "Roger always tells me how good he is but I cant really bring myself to like him. So there must be some peculiar literary fascination in him."[47]

Vanessa's reservations about her critical ability appear mainly in letters to Roger Fry, and not just in comments about his painting. In 1912, she recorded her frustration when she tried to explain her admiration for Giotto. His painting, she said, "makes me feel how little one *can* analyze one's feelings before really great art. One is simply lifted into a different life & carried off in it."[48] Some years later, expressing an opinion about a work by Giorgione, she wanted Fry's reaction: "I really trust your judgment far more than my own though I suppose my feelings would remain the same."[49] She trusted the genuineness of her emotional responses which she separated from her intellectual ability; the latter she was willing to let Fry influence.

Even though she and Fry discussed "Art. Gothic Art. . . . Art. My Art. Roger's Art. Duncan's Art. Art of the Theatre etc,"[50] Vanessa Bell also kept their interchanges at some remove from her actual painting. In 1916 she even wrote to Fry that he had influenced her on a theoretical level, but not "in detail of practice." She did give him credit for prompting her "to paint much more solidly."[51] Vanessa acknowledged that she learned a great deal from Fry about looking at pictures, but her letters show that she sometimes liked to argue for the sake of argument, that she enjoyed having him understand and articulate some of her responses to works of art, and that she already agreed in many instances with what he said. In the memoir she wrote of Fry in 1934, she recalled that when the Post-Impressionist Exhibition occurred in 1910, suddenly "one might say things one had always felt instead of trying to say things that other people told one to feel."[52]

Vanessa, therefore, may have founded her Friday Club to balance Thoby's more philosophical Thursday Evenings and to compete with Virginia's activities as a writer, but she may have had other reasons: an intellectual inferiority complex resulting from her limited education, and her need as a woman artist for support and validation. Her talk about art, as her letters indicate, included theories about the genesis, the components, the goals, and the effects of art; the merits and demerits of work by old masters and contemporaries; her own attempts and experiments; as well as more practical or technical concerns. Vanessa Bell trusted Fry's judgment, but she also trusted her initial responses to works of art. His real value to her, apart from their love affair, was the understanding and validation he gave her as a serious painter.

Vanessa also discussed art with her sister, especially on trips they took during the first decade of the century. In 1906 Vanessa and Virginia, accompanied by Violet Dickinson, Thoby, and Adrian, visited Greece. In 1908, Virginia went with Vanessa and Clive Bell to Siena and Perugia, and in 1909 she accompanied them to Florence. In the journal accounts of these travels, Virginia implies but does not mention her sister's presence. Using the journals to practice and define her own verbal medium, she also considers Vanessa's. When she describes the statues of Apollo and Hermes at Olympia, the colors of the Greek landscape seen from a hill, the Acropolis and the Parthenon at Athens, the sights of Epidauros and Mycenae, and various people she observes, Virginia sounds a theme that echoes throughout her writing: the inadequacy of words. Frustrated, but persistent, she tries to discover what language can and cannot do. She notes, however, that a painter would be equally incapable of capturing the color of the Parthenon in the setting sun. Other parallels between the visual and the verbal occur. What she sees in Greece recalls the words of the Greek poets. Marble statues appeal to the sense of touch as their words appeal to the ear. All aspects of Greece, in fact, whether landscapes, temples, statues, or poems, have a similar coherence and completeness.[53]

In Italy in 1908 Vanessa admired some of Perugino's paintings.[54] When Virginia accompanied her sister to look at them, there is little doubt that they talked about what they saw. Virginia recorded some conclusions that may have been one of her first attempts to compare the creative processes of painters and writers. Her hastily noted responses, based on an experience shared with Vanessa, introduced ideas she embodied in her most successful novels and developed in some of her later essays: the importance of the intense moment of perception, silence versus speech, and the interdependence of parts in a total design. She also suggested a significant difference between painting and literature; both create beauty, but painting is silent, wordless, static, whereas writing documents "the flight of the mind," the very process by which that beauty is perceived and achieved.

> I look at a fresco by Perugino. I conceive that he saw things grouped, contained in certain and invariable forms; expressed in faces, actions—[? which] did not exist; all beauty was contained in the momentary appearance of human beings. He saw it sealed as it were. . . . His fresco seems to me infinitely silent; as though beauty had swum up to the top and stayed there, above everything else, speech, paths leading on, relation of brain to brain, don't exist.
>
> Each part has a dependence upon the others; they compose one idea in his mind. That idea has nothing to do with anything that can be put into words. A group stands without relation to the figure of God. They have come together then because their lines and colours are related, and express some view of beauty in his brain.
>
> As for writing—I want to express beauty too—but beauty (symmetry?) of life and the world, in action. Conflict?—is that it? If there is action in painting it is only to exhibit lines; but with the end of beauty in view. Isn't there a different kind of beauty? No conflict.
>
> I attain a different kind of beauty, achieve a symmetry by means of infinite discords, showing all the traces of the mind's passage through the world; achieve in the end, some kind of whole made of shivering fragments; to me this seems the natural process; the flight of the mind. Do they really reach the same thing?[55]

Although Virginia contrasts Perugino's fresco to her own writing, her reference to the beauty she achieves as a "whole made of shivering fragments" anticipates experiments to come and suggests, perhaps inadvertently, a kind of painting that attempts to communicate the very act of perception. The sisters must have discussed Impressionism prior to this trip to Italy. Vanessa had read Camille Mauclair's *The French Impressionists* when it was translated into English in 1903. Then, in 1904 or 1905, both Vanessa and Virginia had attended a lecture by a Mr. Rutter on Impressionism (MB 163).[56] So Virginia Stephen, in this journal entry, may very well have begun to contrast traditional to modern art as well as painting to writing. But she did not develop her ideas at that time.

Instead, she thought most about the paintings in front of her. As the sights of Greece made Virginia hear the poets, so the landscapes of the Italian hill towns reminded her of backgrounds in paintings by the early Italian masters. Looking at such paintings, she considered the ways people react to them. The works by the old masters, painted centuries ago, have endured the pleasure and interpretations of generations without being possessed or altered. At the same time, the paintings depend for their value on being seen. The individual viewer is both diminished and elevated in importance.

During these early travels, Virginia not only recorded her reactions to paintings, but she also read books and wrote down her responses. In Greece she read and described at length Mérimée's letters to an unknown woman. In Italy she described, in detail, the strengths and weaknesses of Meredith's *Henry Richmond*. Her consciousness of the quality of writing affects her own journal entries. In the Greek journal, she says she tries not to count statues like the guide books or establish relationships among them like the archaeologists. She is also aware, like a painter, of different subjects for her pen: artifacts, landscapes, people. In the Italian journal, she is equally self-conscious about her attempts to write. She inveighs against her own unsatisfactory use of language, her tendency, for example, to make humorous narratives out of the day's activities. She wants to avoid vapid, "ladylike" writing. She is wary, too, of description that is too emphatic, not sufficiently subtle to capture the quality of the landscape any better than it can the essence of a human being. What the writer puts down, she decides, is her own state of mind. She wants to use that mind, in addition to her eye, so that her verbal picture is complete and so that it reveals the truth beneath appearances.

At home in England Virginia Stephen was also extremely conscious of her sister's activities and interests as a painter. "Nessa went to her ——— drawing," she recorded with the resentment of what Louise DeSalvo calls "a voyeur of her family's . . . meaningful work." Virginia made this entry during a period when a doctor was overseeing her health and restricting her activities.[57] Her reactions to Vanessa's drawing and painting were not always so negative. Virginia Woolf recalled a visit Henry Tonks had made to Gordon Square thirty years earlier, an occasion on which he was "so severe on Nessa's pictures" (D IV 285). The diary from 1905 describes Vanessa "in a state of great misery, awaiting Mr Tonks. So I sat in the studio & tried to comfort her. . . . At one Tonks came, a great raw boned man, with a cold bony face, prominent eyes, & a look of mingled severity & boredom." Virginia stayed by Vanessa's side. "We talked valiantly," she wrote, "but it was not easy work. Then he reviewed the pictures, with a good deal of criticism apparently, but also some praise" (D IV 285, quoted in n. 5). In this passage Virginia makes clear not only her sister's insecurities but also her own empathetic observation and support. An early photograph of the Stephen children (Figure 1.9) shows Vanessa, palette in one hand and brush in the other, before her easel, her glance turned towards the camera. Seated beside her is Virginia. Although the book lying open upon her lap suggests her verbal bias, she looks intently at her sister's canvas. The photo underscores Virginia's role as a sometimes resentful, sometimes empathetic onlooker.

Virginia Woolf continued to watch painters and discuss art with them. Like Vanessa she found Roger Fry stimulating but did not leave his theories about art unchallenged. Like her sister, Woolf attended some of Fry's lectures (D II 21, 229; IV 76) and read his and Clive Bell's articles and books on art when they appeared. When she read Fry's *The Artist and Psychoanalysis* in conjunction with Percy Lubbock's *The Craft of Fiction*, for example, she wrote that she wanted Fry to "tidy up" the relationship between form in literature and form in painting (L III 133). A comment in Woolf's diary about Fry's *Vision and Design* reveals another potential area of disagreement, her notion that literature is more complex than painting. Fry's book, she noted, "reads rudimentary compared with Coleridge. Fancy reforming poetry by dicovering something scientific about the com-

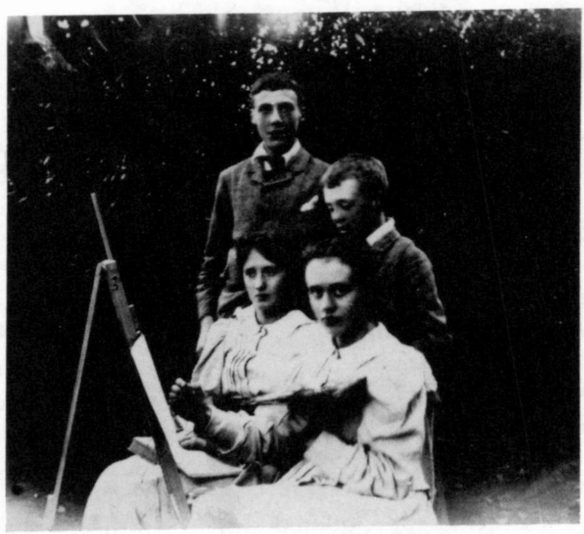

1.9. Virginia, Vanessa, Thoby, and Adrian Stephen. Photograph from Stella Duckworth's album. Courtesy of the Henry W. and Albert A. Berg Collection; the New York Public Library; Astor, Lenox and Tilden Foundations, and of Quentin Bell.

position of light!" (D II 80–81). In her ambivalence about Fry's theories, she wrote to Benedict Nicolson in 1940, "But in fact I am not responsible for anything Roger did or said. My own education and my own point of view were entirely different from his" (L VI 419).

Still, unlike the happily "humming" Vanessa Bell and Duncan Grant, Woolf said, Fry had a "dash of the dragon fly" about him (L III 209) and was someone with whom she could discuss the similarities and differences between art media. That Woolf and Fry were both engaged in solving a similar problem about art, its relationship to life, has been well documented. A "belief that the artist does not describe a given, objective reality," as Allen McLaurin puts it, "lies behind Fry's attack on the 'illusionists'" in painting and "Virginia Woolf's on the 'materialists'" in the novel.[58] As McLaurin and J. K. Johnstone before him point out, however, Woolf did not always agree with Fry, particularly on her own art medium. Like the painter, the writer is concerned with perceiving and communicating relationships; when Fry emphasized unavoidable cause-and-effect patterns as fundamental to fiction, however, Woolf demurred.[59] Both sisters found Fry's ideas about art stimulating, and agreed with him up to a point, but followed their own inclinations when they picked up their brushes or pens.

To Jacques Raverat, a painter who she said was "half chatterbox, as I am wholly chatterbox" (L III 108), Woolf also felt she could argue about some of the differences and similarities between painting and writing. "Is your art as chaotic as ours?" she asked Raverat after the publication of *Jacob's Room* (L II 591). In another letter she said that her wish to have "married a foxhunter. . . . is partly the desire to share in life somehow, which is denied to us writers. Is it to you painters?" (L III 163). When in 1924 she described the "Neo-paganism" (L III 130) of an earlier period of her life, Raverat described the multiple associations the word aroused. But, he concluded, one must embody such an experience visually; the painter and not the writer can achieve the necessary simultaneity. Woolf defended writing as capable of doing what painting could (L III 135–36). *Mrs. Dalloway*, the novel she was working on at the time of this written conversation, is one attempt to transcend some of the linear dictates of traditional literature.[60]

Woolf also read works related to the visual arts by a number of people other than Roger Fry and Clive Bell. In 1917, for example, she read Ezra Pound's *Gaudier-Brzeska: A Memoir* (1916), a discussion of the common ground of the arts (D I 90); in 1928 she read a life of Cézanne (L III 29) and, in 1929, one of Constable (L IV 18) as well as a memoir by Vlaminck (L IV 44); in 1939 she read Delacroix's journals and noted "a sentence of his about the profundity of the painter's meaning; & how a writer always superficializes" (D V 199). Throughout her life Woolf also visited art museums and exhibitions. In 1919 she even proposed, although not seriously, that she and Vanessa and Duncan collaborate on reviews of exhibitions, joining their sublime insights about art with her "perfectly amazing" writing ability (L II 341). Her frequent use of the visual artists' perceptions and vocabulary, therefore, is inevitable. After not writing in her diary for eleven days in 1919, Woolf noted, "Still I think if I were a painter I should only need a brush dipped in dun colour to give the tone of those eleven days. I should draw it evenly across the entire canvas." Nevertheless she voiced reservations. "But painters lack sub[t]lety,"she added; "there were points of light, shades beneath the surface, now, I suppose undiscoverable" (D I 239).

Woolf also had begun to entertain the conclusion that anyone could be a visual artist. She said that Carrington "seems to be an artist—*seems*, I say, for in our circle the current that way is enough to sweep people with no more art in them than Barbara [Bagenal, née Hiles] in that direction. Still I think Carrington cares for it genuinely, partly because of her way of looking at pictures" (D I 184). The attitude parallels one advanced in Leonard Woolf's early novel, *The Wise Virgins* (1914). Harry, who in some ways resembles Leonard himself, is a painter. Although he says very little about painting, one exception is his contemptuous comment, "Anyone can paint—that's the great discovery of modern times."[61] Such a comment may have been a writer's caricature or even misconception of remarks like those Vanessa Bell made later in a lecture at Leighton School. Mechanical skill, she insisted there, is less important than the spontaneous and fresh embodiment of vision and emotion.[62]

Over the years Virginia Woolf made many condescending remarks about the visual arts. She generalized repeatly about the differences between writers and painters, usually to the advantage of writers. Most of her comments were tongue-in-cheek, many were contradictory, but there was often an undercurrent of seriousness about them, especially when she wrote her teasing comments to her sister. Woolf was staggered, for instance, by some clothing Vanessa Bell designed in 1916 for Karin Stephen: It "almost wrenched my eyes from the sockets," she wrote, "—a skirt barred with reds and yellows of the vilest kind, and a pea green blouse on top, with a gaudy handkerchief on her head, supposed to be the very boldest taste. I shall retire," she quipped, "into dove colour and old lavender, with a lace collar, and lawn wristlets" (L II 111). In 1918 she reported to Vanessa Bell her impressions of Jacques Raverat's work and the show at the New English Art Club in which it appeared. "The drowsy stupidity of the painter's point of view appalled me," she said (L II 257). "Why are you artists so repetitious," she asked Vanessa after describing a London Group exhibit. "Does the eye for months together see nothing but roofs?" (L II 300). Returning from a gallery in 1921,

Virginia wrote to her sister about the excessive detail in paintings by the Pre-Raphaelites. "Your art is far more of a joke than mine," she announced (L II 458). Then, in a letter to Vanessa in 1922 she generalized from Wyndham Lewis, who had attacked Clive Bell in print, to all visual artists: "Why do you artists write like that? We dont." But, she added, humorously undercutting her own comment, "Even poor little squint eyed [John Middleton] Murry wouldn't" (L II 520). Such remarks also appear in her fiction during this period, although not always in the mouths of characters whose values Woolf admires. In *Jacob's Room*, for instance, Jacob insists that "the moderns were futile; painting the least respectable of the arts" (JR 122). Painting is "a stupid art," Jacob also tells two painters he meets in Paris (JR 127).

To her nephews, Julian and Quentin Bell, she also mocked painting and elevated writing. Her tone remained teasing. However, as brothers, one of whom was interested in writing and one of whom preferred painting, their situation paralleled hers and Vanessa's. Woolf assumed as well as fomented a similar competitiveness between them and their art forms. When Julian wrote that Quentin considered becoming a painter, their aunt replied, "I dont see why you envy him. Think of being a painter, my God!, when you might be a writer!" (L III 440). Painters, she suggested to Quentin, are "ignorant always" (L III 481). She reproached him ironically for considering such a profession when he wrote as well as he did. "Surely you must see the infinite superiority of the language to the paint? Think how many things are impossible in paint: giving pain to the Keynes', making fun of one's aunts, telling libidinous stories, making mischief—these are only a few of the advantages; against which a painter has nothing to show: for all his merits are also a writers" (L III 492–93). She also wrote to Julian in 1936 that she envied Vanessa and Duncan their detachment from politics: "There they sit, looking at pinks and yellows, and when Europe blazes all they do is to screw up their eyes and complain of a temporary glare in the foreground. Unfortunately politics get between one and fiction."[63] Woolf's tongue-in-cheek assertions that writers can do everything painters can do, and that writers are the more socially responsible artists, have a serious ring. But whether her nephews painted or wrote, Woolf was reluctant to praise them and found herself "irritated" by her sister's "maternal partiality" to whatever they produced (D IV 264, 288–89). She saw them, in part, as rivals for Vanessa's approval.

Letters to other correspondents, as well as Woolf's diaries and essays, contain similar remarks about the differences between painters and writers. Often Vanessa Bell stands in the background as the touchstone against which all painters and their activities are evaluated. She and Duncan and painters in general are, Woolf noted in her diary, "very large in effect . . . ; very little self-conscious; they have smooth broad spaces in their minds where I am all prickles & promontories" (D I 69). Visual artists, Woolf wrote to Roger Fry in 1925, have no need for people. "This is why you painters are, as a rule, such exemplary characters; why calm and well being exhale from you. Certainly this is true of Bell and Grant: I never saw two people humming with heat and happiness like sunflowers on a hot day more than those two" (L III 209). Similarly, Woolf observed to Ethel Sands and Nan Hudson how Vanessa and Duncan and other painters "are so mute and highminded compared with us poor creatures" (L III 400) and how they are better "equipped for life;" painters control life whereas "we writers merely contemplate it" (L III 405–6).

On occasion Woolf felt excluded from the painters' world. Describing a visit to Charleston, she reported in her diary that her reception was unsatisfactory. The painters were preoccupied with a still-life arrangement and "the talk was not entirely congenial" (D II 260). To Edward Sackville-West she confessed that, while she was fond of painters, they made her feel uncomfortable: "'Poor beetle' thats what they say; and at once I have eight legs, all squirming. It is for this reason; their ascendancy is over all objects of daily use: tea pots, chairs, wall paper; so that when they come, their presence is one long criticism, from the heights. We, who deal in ideas, and are moreover, sensitised to draw out, always more and more, other peoples feelings never inflict this chill. How delightful if one could" (L III 294).

Woolf returns frequently to this idea that writers must deal with human aspects of life in ways that painters do not. She describes the novelist as "terribly exposed to life," unlike painters and composers who can "withdraw; they shut themselves up for weeks alone with a dish of apples and a paintbox, or a roll of music paper and a piano." They come out to escape for a while from their work. The novelist, however, cannot escape: "he enjoys presumably all the pleasures of talk and table, but always with a sense that he is being stimulated and played upon by the subject-matter of his art" (CE II 131). The situation, therefore, is dangerous; the novelist must risk deception, distinguish life's "treasure" from its "trash," and ultimately, withdraw and give form to accumulated perceptions (CE II 136). In solitude, the novelist has a more difficult task than the painter who looks at a stationary model or a still-life arrangement. "A writer," in contrast, "has to keep his eye upon a model that moves, that changes, upon an object that is not one object but innumerable objects. Two words alone cover all that a writer looks at—they are, human life" (CE II 162). The writer, moreover, has to learn to embody human life in words, but the education required is "indefinite" and "mixed" (CE II 169).

With this vision of the complexity of the writer's situation, Virginia Woolf sometimes had trouble sharing the painter's excitement over what seemed to her trivialities. By the second Post-Impressionist exhibition, she was saying that "artists are an abominable race. The furious excitement of these people all the winter over their pieces of canvas coloured green and blue, is odious" (L II 15).[64] In 1918, when Maynard Keynes bought a Cézanne painting of seven apples, Woolf described the reaction in her diary in less impatient terms. Her own reaction to the apples in the painting encompassed "their relationship to each other, & their colour, & their solidity." She was, on the whole, impressed. The painters' reaction was different. Roger Fry and Vanessa Bell were concerned with technique: "It was a question of pure paint or mixed; if pure which colour: emerald or veridian; & then the laying on of the paint; & the time he'd spent, & how he'd altered it, & why, & when he'd painted it" (D I 140–41). To Nicholas Bagenal she repeated how taken she was with Cézanne's apples and how "amused" she was by the painters "discussing whether he'd used veridian or emerald green, and Roger knowing the day, practically the hour, they were done by some brush mark in the background." For an audience, though, Woolf exaggerated: "Roger very nearly lost his senses. I've never seen such a sight of intoxication[.] He was like a bee on a sunflower" (L II 230).

Part of Virginia Woolf's irritation with the painters' enthusiasms must have been the product of her rivalry with her sister. Virginia Woolf's biographers note their competitiveness.[65] Her diaries and letters indicate the extent to which she measured her own artistic accomplishments against Vanessa Bell's achievements in both life and art. In 1929 Virginia noted in her diary that "Orlando is recognized for the masterpiece that it is. The Times does not mention Nessa's pictures. Yet, she said last night, I have spent a long time over one of them." The disparity pleased Woolf: "Then I think to myself, So I have something, instead of children, & fall comparing our lives. I note my own withdrawal from those desires; my absorption in what I call, inaccurately, ideas: this vision" (D III 217). During this period, too, Virginia Woolf was exhilarated by the money her writing brought in and exclaimed over what it could buy. Her purchases, she recorded, gave her "pleasure; & set my dander up against Nessa's almost overpowering supremacy. My elder son is coming tomorrow; yes, & he is the most promising young man in King's; & has been speaking at the Apostles dinner. All I can oppose that with is, And I made £2,000 out of Orlando & can bring Leonard here & buy a house if I want. To which she replies (in the same inaudible way) I am a failure as a painter compared with you, & cant do more than pay for my models. And so we go on; over the depths of our childhood" (D III 232–33).

Still, she thought of Vanessa as contented with her accomplishments (D III 298) and, although at times Virginia could say of her success, "Children are nothing to this," she also noted, "whats money, compared with Nessa's children" (D III 298, 241). In 1937, the refrain recurred. The diary noted Vanessa's relief that Virginia's earnings were not so high as reported (D V 117–18). Adding up some figures, she wrote, "This a little shames me in comparison with Nessa's sales: but then I reflect, I put my life blood into writing, & she had children" (D V 120).

Vanessa recognized, from the time her first child was born, her sister's envy. Sometimes she tried to alleviate it. Although Vanessa could not resist some teasing objections, she relayed comments other people had made about Virginia's cleverness and beauty. More important, Vanessa noted the inroads motherhood made on her art: "I suppose you are happy at work again on Mel ["Melymbrosia" or *The Voyage Out*]. I envy you. What wouldn't I give for a steady uninterrupted two months work"; instead she did "vague" sketches through the window or of the baby, or "still vaguer" sketches of animals for him. Similarly, having read one of Virginia's articles, Vanessa noted, "I can't do a stroke of painting as long as I have Julian. Such is maternity. You would turn it to account though," she adds, imagining how a writer would treat the experience.[66]

Vanessa must have complained too much, however, because by the end of 1909 she was writing, "If you *really* knew what I was feeling you would not pity me for having Julian," who "isn't the burden you seem to think." Virginia demurred since Vanessa's next letter says, "Do you really envy me? Well he is very nice when he cuddles into me in bed in the early morning."[67] In later years, when it became clear that Virginia would not herself become a mother, Vanessa's comments to her sister ranged from "One can't let them [children] be unhappy nor can one give up one's own existence to them,"[68] to acknowledgments of Virginia's view of her as "too maternal,"[69] to assertions of her children's and their aunt's mutual affection.

Each sister declared she envied the other. Vanessa's maternity offset Virginia's more flexible schedule and greater earning capacity. From childhood, both sisters were not materialistic, but they were nevertheless money conscious. Vanessa Bell recalls a serial story that she and Virginia evolved night after night in the nursery at Hyde Park Gate: "The plot consisted in the discovery under their nursery floor of immense stores of gold. It then went on to describe the wonderful things they could buy in consequence, especially the food, which was unlimited."[70] These early preoccupations, exacerbated later, perhaps, by Leslie Stephen's exaggerated terror of the poorhouse after his wife's death, resulted in a lifelong concern about money, its benefits and pitfalls. In letters Vanessa frequently noted earnings from the sales of her paintings as well as amounts she could count on after the exhibitor's percentages had been deducted. Even though she wrote to Virginia in 1912, "But I know really that nothing I can do will ever make money,"[71] still she often assessed the failure or success of a show on that basis. Virginia Woolf, too, often recorded in her diary the numbers of copies sold and the purchases her earnings made possible. Income from *To the Lighthouse*, for example, enabled her and Leonard to purchase a car. Again Virginia compared her financial success to her sister's: "Here at the age of 45 are Nessa & I growing little wings again after our lean years. She may rake in another £500; perhaps more" not from her art, but as an inheritance from Clive's father. "Already she has bought a role of linoleum & a cupboard" (D III 152).

Virginia Woolf's independent income and the Hogarth Press enabled her to have a mind of her own; she did not have to write to please editors and reviewers in order to make money. Nevertheless, she was money conscious. From July 1928 to July 1937 she kept, somewhat haphazardly, an account book. This affluent period began after the publication of *Orlando* and ended about the time Virginia turned over to John Lehmann her partnership with Leonard in the Hogarth Press. Just prior to these nine years, the Woolfs altered their financial arrangements; they began to designate individual as opposed to joint funds. Virginia's financial success and independence, then, are documented in her own hand.[72] Vanessa was not so successful. In 1934, Virginia noted that her sister was "very hard up." During a conversation about how to make money, the sisters even considered "some caricatures. issued between us" (D IV 200). They pursued this collaborative project or a similar one prior to the Christmas season in 1937. But "Faces and Voices," which was to have contained twelve lithographs by Vanessa to illustrate incidents written by Virginia, was never completed (D V 57–58, n. 8).

Woolf was critical and curious about her attitude towards money. In 1927 she noted, "I have thought too much, though on purpose, with my eyes open, of making money; & once we have each a nest egg I should like to let that sink into my sub-consciousness, & earn easily what we need" (D III 149). Spending did not give her pleasure, she found, because she fretted over buying foolishly (D III 164–65) and because she had some trouble trusting her ability to earn more (D III 212). Money may provide women with material and intellectual independence, as Woolf notes in *A Room of One's Own*, but they are not used to earning it. The exhilaration that is one response to financial security, even relative abundance, can be muted by self-doubt. So Woolf's financial success, relative to her sister's, had its problematic side.

Woolf measured her achievements not only against Vanessa's maternity and income but also against her sister's domestic arrangements. "Vanessa is living in sin with Duncan Grant," she wrote jokingly to Vita Sackville-West in 1926, and "I have written Mrs Dalloway—which equals living in sin," at least in the eyes of some elderly gentlemen who had come to call (L III 241). Woolf could usually find professional accomplishments to weigh against her sister's personal life; it was more difficult to confront the fact that Vanessa Bell was an artistic success as well. In 1926, Woolf admitted to being "a little alarmed" at the quality of her sister's painting: "(for as you have the children, the fame by rights belongs to me)." She confessed her admiration, however, for her sister's work: "But I was hugely impressed, and kept on saying that your genius as a painter, though rather greater than I like, does still shed a ray on mine. I mean, people will say, What a gifted couple! Well: it would have been nicer had they said: Virginia had all the gifts; dear old Nessa was a domestic character—Alas, alas, they'll never say that now" (L III 271). In 1934 Vanessa Bell's successful show made Woolf feel "so old so cold so dumpish . . . , but not jealous," she insisted (D IV 205). "I will not be jealous," she asserted in 1935 when Clive Bell reported Dunoyer de Segonzac's assessment of Vanessa as "the best painter in England, much better than Duncan . . . , but isnt it odd—thinking of gifts in her? I mean when she has everything else" (D IV 322). As late as 1937, Woolf admitted in a half-mocking, half-serious way that her sister's success made her jealous (L VI 126).

As her comments indicate, Virginia Woolf found Vanessa Bell's success discomfiting because it destroyed the mother-artist duality of which she was fond, but Woolf was also reassured because her sister's reputation enhanced hers and gave her confidence in her own abilities and experiments. "I like you to be praised," she wrote in 1923, "chiefly because it seems to prove that I must be a good writer" (L III 34). Both of them periodically assessed and compared their progress through life. In 1908, Vanessa both supported and refuted her sister's notion that their lives diverged in domestic and artistic directions. She imagined them five years hence when Virginia's reputation would be increasing, then ten years hence when both would be wealthy and Virginia would also be married and have a family. In a subsequent letter she expanded upon her picture. Twenty years from now, she said, both of them would be famous. Both would have families, Virginia's "very odd & small & you with a growing reputation for your works—I with nothing but my capacities as a hostess & my husband's value to live upon." Virginia, she speculated humorously, might be a widow by then, having been careless about boiling her spouse's milk properly, but she would have a "clever & cranky daughter" with whom to argue.[73]

Fifteen years later, in 1923, Virginia Woolf did define them both as "well known women" (D II 246). Then, in 1927, she noted that she and Vanessa Bell were "both mistresses of our medium as never before" (L III 341). She also observed that they were late bloomers as artists. "And our late flowers are rare & splendid. Think of my books, Nessa's pictures—it takes us an age to bring our faculties into play" (D III 141). In 1930 she imagined them both envied by Marjorie Snowden, Vanessa's unmarried, unsuccessful painter friend:

"There are Vanessa & Virginia, they have lives full of novels & husbands & exhibitions. I am fifty & it has all slipped by" (D III 289). Noting her own upcoming fiftieth birthday, Virginia identified with her sister's observation that she felt like "the youngest person" aboard any omnibus (D IV 63). Furthermore, in spite of the artistic reputations they had gained, Virginia concluded in 1933 that they were both "without the publicity sense." She was pleased that Vanessa, who had accompanied her to a dinner during which Virginia was pressured to accept a Doctor of Letters degree from Manchester University, had used her "arguments about the silliness of honours for women" (D IV 148). One advantage of their "notoriety," Virginia noted in 1935, was that neither she nor Vanessa had to risk not being able to paint or write because of a party's aftereffects: "we can see anyone we want," she said, ". . . on our own terms" (D IV 359).

Vanessa Bell could write as well as paint but, aware of Virginia Woolf's claim to the territory, she consistently denied her skill. Even after her sister's death, Vanessa began a memoir on Bloomsbury by saying, "I am no writer and . . . all I can hope to do is to jot down notes for others to use" in constructing a whole picture.[74] She also constantly disclaimed any ability as a letter writer. "Letter writing's not my strong point," she wrote as early as 1904 to Marjorie Snowden. She apologized for writing boring letters, not wanting to list the examples of art and architecture she'd seen and unable to do justice in words to the scenery.[75] To Clive Bell, too, she apologized about her letter writing: "A duller letter than this was never written," she said, "so you neednt hurry to read it." Her letters, she wrote, were not "witty nor clever nor literary." Dolphins, she reminded him, "arent letter writers."[76]

Because each sister feared the other's criticism, however, Vanessa especially denigrated her ability to write in letters to Virginia. "You say so much about the faculty of expression," she wrote in 1904, "that I am quite afraid of putting my feeble sentences before your critical eye."[77] Her letters, she feared, were "imitative" and "stupid" and could not possibly compare with those her sister received from Clive and Lytton: "After them hobbles poor Dolphin fresh from domesticities."[78] She felt especially inadequate, she wrote to Virginia, when she saw "the growing strength of the exquisite critical atmosphere distilled by you & Clive with your wits alert to pounce upon convoluted sentences & want of rhythm."[79] She insisted, however, that although her own letters might be dull they nevertheless expressed her fondness.[80] Vanessa wrote many such comments during or shortly after the period when Clive and Virginia carried on what Quentin Bell calls "a violent and prolonged flirtation," an attempt on Virginia's part "to enter and in entering to break that charmed circle within which Vanessa and Clive were so happy and by which she was so cruelly excluded" and to regain possession of her sister.[81] Virginia's behavior has another dimension. In the ongoing competition between writer and painter, she enlisted Clive on her side. Hurt, and aware of the interest in Virginia's first novel that her husband and her sister shared, Vanessa indicated her feelings of being an outsider by reiterating her ineptitude with the pen.

Vanessa is quick to disclaim any attempts to compete with her sister in writing. Virginia need not worry about a rival, she wrote in 1907 when she was working on a biographical sketch; her writing will be plain, with no consistent style; furthermore, the whole thing will take a long time to complete.[82] Yet each sister looked at the world in part with the other's artistic eye. Virginia saw scenes for Vanessa to paint. In 1935, for example, she wrote from Holland that her sister "ought to paint the tulip fields and the hyacinth fields all laid out flat with about 20 miles of water in and out, 18 sheep, 6 windmills, sun setting, moon rising" (L V 390). More frequently, however, Vanessa heard conversations and saw sights she thought Virginia ought to put into words. Writing from Italy in 1909, for instance, she tried to describe High Mass at Santa Maria Novella: "You would have enjoyed it & perhaps could have described it which unluckily I can't." The ceiling of San Michele, a crisis with her child, even the world of Cleeve house, where Clive's relatives lived and where Vanessa had to spend many boring days, might have been put to good use by Virginia. "If Mrs. Bell's chatter could be heard by you no doubt it would become immortal," she wrote to her sister. Marriage to Clive also brought Vanessa into contact with groups of male sportsmen. From Glencarron Lodge, she wrote to Virginia, "I feel that if only I were writing a novel this would probably be an unequalled opportunity for me to hear what male conversation is really like—for one silent & solitary female I think makes practically no difference to their talk."[83] She was both amused, as she would have been watching an exotic animal, and critical of the men's topics: wine, beer, and cigars. The next day, their subject of conversation was whether venison or grouse made the better gift.[84]

Virginia Woolf addresses the subject of one sex's ignorance of the other, as well as the novelist's need to overcome such a liability, when Terrence Hewet questions Rachel Vinrace in *The Voyage Out* about what women think, say, and do when they are not with men. Vanessa Bell understood the novelist's interest in all types of people. Sometimes she schooled herself to endure boring situations by imagining how Virginia might have found them valuable for her art. On her visits to Cleeve house, too, Vanessa longed for her sister's cleverness to lift her "out of this dead level of commonplaces." She said she "sniff[ed] the air like an old war horse & snort[ed] with delight" when she got something of Virginia's to read.[85] Finally, in 1927 she wrote, "I wish you would write a book about the maternal instinct. . . . In all my wide reading," she added with some self-mockery, "I haven't yet found it properly explored . . . I could tell you a great deal!"[86]

Vanessa Bell used her alleged incapacity as a writer as an excuse sometimes for reticence, sometimes for the quality of her letters, and sometimes for not writing at all. When she tried to express her feelings for Roger Fry, for example, during the period of her greatest love for him, she wished that her view might suddenly become that of a writer so she could find the words. A portrait might be better, she said, if no one examined it too critically.[87] To Virginia she wrote in 1921, "Its unfortunate for you you haven't got a literary sister. Its with the greatest difficulty as you know that I take to the pen."[88] When she did not write sooner and at greater length about her sister's works, she pointed out that when she finally did, her efforts were to be taken as compliments since nothing was harder for her than expressing herself in written form.[89]

There is considerable evidence however, that Vanessa Bell could write reasonably well. Like Virginia's drawing, Vanessa's writing suggests some dual creative ability. To say that she could write is not to claim that her skill equaled or exceeded that of her sister. Perhaps she wrote no better than one would expect of a Stephen. The number of friends and correspondents, including Virginia, who praised her memoir and letter writing, however, indicates that she wrote much better than she thought or claimed. Leonard Woolf, for example, in his account of the Memoir Club, says that Vanessa Bell "developed a remarkable talent in a fantastic narrative of a labyrinthine domestic crisis."[90] Another memoir, *Notes on Virginia's Childhood*, recreates vividly the altercations among the children at Hyde Park Gate. As one might expect from an artist who saw the world as form and color, Vanessa's first memories of her sister are visual. She also remembers her sister's superior verbal skills:

> Why do I see her so clearly, a very rosy chubby baby, with bright green eyes, sitting in a high chair at the nursery table, drumming impatiently for her breakfast? She cannot have been more than two and I therefore only about four and a half. But it is a vivid memory to me. How worried I was too, not much later, because she couldn't speak clearly; I feared she would never do so, which would certainly have been a misfortune. That cannot have lasted long, for we were not very old when speech became the deadliest weapon as used by her. When Thoby and I were angry with each other or with her, we used good straightforward abuse, or perhaps told tales if we felt particularly vindictive. How did she know that to label me "The Saint" was far more effective, quickly reducing me to the misery of sarcasm from the grown-ups as well as the nursery world? One was vaguely aware that it was no good trying to retort in kind. No, our only revenge . . . was to make her, as we said, "purple with rage." I don't remember how we did this, I only remember watching her colour mount till it was the most lively flaming red.[91]

The passage emphasizes Vanessa's concern for her sister as well as their rivalries and developing artistic territories. From an early age, Virginia chose the precise words to caricature Vanessa; with her creative use of language she could control her nursery environment. Vanessa's methods were more direct, and her interest in altering her sister's color is humorously prophetic of some of her later bold experiments with portrait painting.

Vanessa Bell's memoirs also exhibit her sensitivity to the complexities of human relationships. Angelica Garnett describes the difficulty her mother had when Virginia demanded demonstrations of affection: "Vanessa suffered mainly because, much as she loved Virginia and deep though her emotions were, she became almost unbearably self-conscious when called upon to show them. Of her love for Virginia there was no question: she simply wished that it could have been taken for granted."[92] Vanessa Bell's memoir pieces show the same mixture of emotion and reticence, especially when women were involved. As she told Roger Fry in 1911, she was able to get on intimate terms with Sickert much more quickly than she could have with a woman. Men, she concluded, are less complicated.[93] Her description of her early meeting with Helen Fry, Roger's mentally ailing wife, is an example:

> One could not tell how much she understood, but it was clearly impossible to talk to her. She murmured sometimes vaguely to herself & Roger left her out of the conversation so that one could not but do likewise. After lunch we went for a walk rather to my dismay, but Roger of course had noticed no reason why I should not jump over the moon—& I stumbled along in my long loose dress doing my best to keep up for one could not miss the talk. Coming back I found myself alone with Roger & Helen & as we reached the road leading up to Durbins she stopped, murmured something about the children, & wandered off—Rather to my surprise Roger let her go—then said to me "She thinks she hears the children, but its no use theyre away," & Helen gave up her search & followed us to the house. She took me up to her room then, which was the most natural thing she had done & asked me if I were tired. For she I think had seen what no man ever sees, that I was going to have a child. She looked so utterly miserable standing there that I nearly put my arms round her & asked if I couldnt help, but I was too shy, the moment went & we came down. I have never seen her since.[94]

This memoir also includes Vanessa Bell's description of the excitement surrounding the first Post-Impressionist Exhibition in 1910 and the growing intimacy of her relationship with Roger Fry. Vanessa describes vividly the time she and he painted "a dignified Turk" and his wife whom Roger had charmed. Washing her hands in the Turks' well, Vanessa lost "a very pretty old French ring" that Clive had given her. None of the Turk's efforts to retrieve it were successful, his wife cried in distress, and Vanessa, who tried ineffectually to comfort her with an embrace, returned to her hotel feeling "as if something obscure but terrible had happened."[95]

Vanessa Bell's memoir writing includes not only narratives but also brief descriptive sketches which communicate the sensory or emotional impact of interiors: the "snug if stuffy" nursery at Hyde Park Gate, the "cheerful little room, almost entirely made of glass" off the drawing room where she and Virginia spent their afternoons reading and painting, and the contrasting "black paint" and "dull blue walls" of the rest of the gloomy, dark, and silent house.[96] Roger Fry's house, Durbins, prompts a more lengthy description of a different environment, at once brilliantly sunny and austere. Vanessa also describes her sickroom in Broussa, presided over by Roger, as a chaos of "towels, sanitary and otherwise piled high on the floor, spoons, glasses, bottles, all seeming to give birth to others daily, & all put down haphazard on floor or chair, books papers, letters on bed or floor, but also paints canvases, palettes, every kind of object discovered and bought in the bazaars."[97]

Most of the praise for Vanessa Bell's writing, however, was reserved for her letters, which, in spite of the difficulty she claimed to have producing them, were numerous and much in demand. Virginia Woolf praised them: "Your letters rather depress me—my vanity I mean," she wrote in 1928. "They are so expressive—yet you only dip your paw in the ink, and scarcely know one word from another. How is it? We literary gents, Clive and I, never get your effects at all" (L III 456). In the same year she also wrote that she "was enraptured by the account of Seend which is in its way masterly. The accounts in the dining room, the Keys—the lavatory: all my skill never produces that effect." (L III 566) Vanessa attributed such compliments, perhaps rightly, to flattery prompted by her sister's unappeasable desire for letters.[98]

Virginia, however, was not the only recipient who praised Vanessa's letters. In 1938, Clive Bell wrote that her letters were "vivid." Vanessa had described a harrowing journey on the way to Cassis in a way Clive called "striking," even "symbolical."[99] Repeatedly he called his wife's letters "admirable," "amusing," and "fascinating," and emphasized the amount of pleasure they gave him. Janie Bussy, too, wrote from Nice that she had very much enjoyed Vanessa's warm, informative letter. She attributed Vanessa's skill with the pen to Virginia's example and tutelage.[100] Similarly Roger Fry reported in 1927 his delight at receiving a letter from Vanessa; its charm and wit reminded him, he said, of Virginia's. A few years later he reported that Virginia had been reading them one of Vanessa's letters and moving them to both tears and laughter; miseries are of some value, he added, to a person whose words can turn them into art.[101]

In her letters Vanessa reproduces dialogues, includes sketches, and, as in her memoirs, describes and narrates her experiences. A traumatic arrival in Venice in the middle of the night, a "medieval romance" involving an unfortunate woman, a transparent attempt to avoid some undesirable English acquaintances, the notorious Dreadnought Hoax, a visit to two American painters who live together and color-coordinate their clothes and furniture, Virginia's amusing and satisfying wedding, and the doctor's misdiagnosis and mistreatment of Angelica's illness all stimulated Vanessa to generate words.[102] She also could mount a formidable defense on behalf of a principle, as in 1920 when Madge Vaughan planned and then refused to rent Charleston farm from Vanessa because of rumors about her living arrangements.[103]

The tone of her letters ranges from indignation to humor. "Thank goodness there is a funny side to most things," she said. "I dont know what life would be without it & I think its a crime to neglect it."[104] So in 1906 she satirized her brother; her letters from Greece, she wrote, would probably be dull, mostly an "account of the number of bugs found at each hotel—at least that's what seems to excite Adrian most."[105] When her son told her that her ignorance appalled him, she satirized herself: "I had to try & make out that I could teach him a thing or two about darning—but rather feebly."[106] David Garnett reports that Vanessa was "witty and very fond of making bawdy jokes." Her early letters to Maynard Keynes are examples, but the shift to a more serious tone in the twenties suggests that the bawdiness may have been a self-consciously liberated pose, abandoned when Keynes became a better friend and a valuable financial consultant.[107] Vanessa Bell's humor is more often droll than bawdy. "Its rather amusing work," she wrote in 1915 about making artificial flowers, "& they generally seem to me to be much more beautiful than God's attempts! I dont imitate Him of course but take hints sometimes."[108]

Unlike Woolf's, Bell's letters are not remarkable for their figures of speech, although now and then one emerges in striking contrast with her more straightforward prose. To Clive she wrote, long before Woolf's Orlando has a similar experience, "I feel as if I were a fountain pen which wouldnt stop & streams of dull fragmentary remarks issue from me."[109] Being with Fry, she wrote, "is like being on a river & being with most people is like driving a jibbing horse along a bumpy road."[110] A Duncan Grant painting was "eatable," Burne-Jones "deteriorated into a machine," and Queen Victoria was "just the kind of middle class woman I am always wanting to paint, entirely dressed in furniture ornaments."[111]

Just as Virginia sketched with her family, so Vanessa joined family and friends in writing. Competing perhaps with Virginia's early review writing, Vanessa attempted an article on Watts which the *Saturday Review* rejected (L I 178–79). Much later, in 1933, she even wrote a book review that was published, unsigned, in the *New Statesman and Nation*. Her "light but ironic review" of James Strachey Barnes' *Half-a-Life*, Spalding says, "managed to condemn him utterly with his own words."[112] In 1909 Vanessa got involved in a letter-writing game along with Virginia, Lytton Stachey, Walter Lamb, Clive Bell, Saxon Sydney-Turner, and perhaps Adrian Stephen. Each assumed a name and a character, and an epistolary novel was to have been the result. The game failed because, during this period of Clive's and Virginia's flirtation, the disguises tempted the players to reveal what they would otherwise have concealed and, in doing so, to hurt each other.[113] Vanessa also had some interest in poetry. "You know you are almost as sensitive to poetical beauty as you are to artistic," Roger Fry wrote to her in 1923, "and there's something rather piquant about your having exercised it so comparatively little."[114] She had exercised it in 1914, but not in the way Fry meant. From Asheham, she wrote to him, "We have been writing poems—very indecent ones but not I think as successful as sometimes."[115] About the same time she wrote to Clive to see if Mary Hutchinson had liked one of his poetic productions: "I have been suddenly seized with a great desire," she joked, "to write poetry! But dont be afraid I shall."[116]

Other contacts with the written word were even less direct. She helped Clive with his writing, as his 1913 Preface to *Art* indicates: "My wife has been good enough to read both the MS. and proof of this book; she has corrected some errors, and called attention to the more glaring offences against Christian charity."[117] She also must have helped Quentin Bell edit the volume of Julian Bell's writings after his death. "I have been wondering lately," she wrote to Virginia, "how on earth you writers manage—getting Julians letters ready to be printed has nearly done for me." She had difficulty, she confessed, in paying attention to details, which had to be accurate, and even in having the necessary equipment, like scissors and paste, at hand when she had to work on the text.[118]

Virginia Woolf's visual way of thinking and writing, then, was certainly fostered by her early competitive and empathic relationship with her sister. Although Woolf made many condescending remarks about the visual arts, she pondered the relationships between the painter's enthusiasms and capabilities and her own. She and Vanessa continually compared their professional accomplishments. Virginia liked to think of Vanessa's achievements as maternal and domestic and her own as artistic and financial. Bell's success as a painter, therefore, created both resentment in her sister and identification. Woolf realized that both of them had slowly increasing professional reputations and similar professional values. Vanessa's skill with the pen also caused Virginia, who liked to reinforce as well as to foster an image of her sister as nonverbal, to reassess the image she had created. Indeed, both the memoir pieces and the letters exhibit considerably more ability than Vanessa admitted. Although she did not want to intrude upon her sister's territory, she did enough reading and writing to be aware of the kinds of settings and situations that fueled the writer's imagination. Just as Virginia looked at scenes with a painter's eye, so Vanessa noted how skillfully her sister might have handled certain material. Just as often she displayed her own narrative flare, her sensitivity about human relationships, or her argumentative or humorous tendencies. Each sister studied her own art medium; each observed and experimented with the other's but ultimately put her energies into her own. Virginia more than Vanessa, though, incorporated into her own artistic creations what she learned about her sister's art.

2

The Common Viewer

VIRGINIA WOOLF'S PUBLISHED ART CRITICISM

Virginia Woolf's close identification with Vanessa Bell's artistic achievements moderated their rivalry. So did Vanessa's rebellions against certain traditions in the visual arts. Woolf explored the potentials and limitations of her verbal artistic medium by contemplating her sister's work and that of other modern painters and writers who rejected what they perceived as the Victorian emphases on story-telling, didacticism, verisimilitude, sentiment, and solemnity. Because Woolf also sympathized with the problems faced by women writers and especially by women painters in an era that defined the roles of the sexes in restrictive and opposite ways, she admired her sister's commitment to painting. The sisters' explorations of their media took similar directions: the hackneyed visual images or overused phrases which the mind continually records and generates had to be confronted anew, their traditional associations silenced. Virginia and Vanessa continually reassessed and altered the means they used to give artistic form to their intense experiences of the everyday world. The visual arts aided Woolf in her search for new, more appropriate vehicles for her perceptions. Visual images and scenes rescued her and her characters when words proved inadequate to define human relationships or individual lives. Chilly and impersonal as Woolf sometimes found paintings, they made her see more vividly, or they stopped words for her and returned them to her afresh. One way Woolf reveals her assimilation of the visual medium, as we have seen, is by her use of pictures to develop arguments in her essays on a variety of topics. Another is her series of comments, from a writer's point of view, on the visual arts themselves. Many of these remarks originate from her intimate and competitive relationship with her sister.

In January of 1935, "Mrs. Clive Bell and Mrs. Leonard Woolf" were "at home" in Vanessa's studio in Fitzroy Street, London, for a performance of Virginia's *Freshwater: A Comedy*. The play was based on the life of their great-aunt, Julia Margaret Cameron, played by Vanessa. More interesting than the collaboration of the sisters in presenting the play is the satire of tendencies in the visual and verbal art of the Victorian era. Representing painting is George Frederick Watts. With his oft-repeated motto, "The Utmost for the Highest," he paints "Modesty at the feet of Mammon." Woolf satirizes Watts's preoccupation with detail: he has spent six months trying to draw "the great toe of Mammon" perfectly (FW 8). She also mocks his concern with symbolism. The "innumerable stars" of the Milky Way that form the veil enveloping Modesty turn out to represent among the ancients "the fertility of fish" (FW 17–18). In an earlier version of the play, Watts cries, "It shall never be said that George Frederick Watts painted a single hair that did not tend directly—or indirectly—to the spiritual and moral elevation of the British Public" (FW 65).

Watts had done a painting entitled *Mammon* (Figure 2.1) which Woolf probably had in mind, at least in a general way. It does not depict a veiled female figure representing Modesty like the one Watts's young wife, Ellen Terry, poses for in the play. Instead, a nude woman kneels at the feet of a sightless, corpulent male dressed in rich gold brocade and seated, with bags of money on his lap, on a throne upon which two skulls are mounted. The nude's head is on Mammon's knee; his heavy, clawlike hand rests on her neck and hair. At Mammon's feet lies a short-haired and more muscular male nude with the top of his head towards the viewer. One of Mammon's feet, in a shapeless boot or stocking, rests on the man's ribs; the other foot separates the two subjugated figures.[1]

The Stephen sisters knew Watts's work; he was a friend of their mother's family. Woolf's treatment of Watts in *Freshwater* derives not only from the biography written by his wife that she was reading in 1919 (D I 237) but also from Vanessa's memories and remarks. In about 1903, Watts had lectured Vanessa as he worked on a painting of an ivy-covered tree trunk to send to the Royal Academy "as a protest against Impressionism. You see every leaf is clearly painted,"

2.1. G. F. Watts. *Mammon*, 1884–85. Permission of the Tate Gallery, London.

he explained. Rossetti, he told her, is "the greatest genius of all the great men he has known. Further, he said that when he painted a picture, he wanted "to give a message" and was less concerned with the accuracy of his facts or with the value of the work as art.[2] Vanessa considered herself responsible for weaning her sister away from "that family idol, G. F. Watts,"[3] a claim that Virginia Stephen's letters corroborate. In 1905 she wrote to Madge Vaughan that the Watts show she and her sister had attended was "*atrocious:* my last illusion is gone. . . . Some of his work indeed most of it—is quite childlike" (L I 174). Other people, however, still "spoke almost with tears of the greatness and beauty of Watts—and wouldn't admit the possibility of criticism"; the article Vanessa had written on him may have been rejected by the *Saturday Review* for this reason (L I 178–79).

Still, when Vanessa decorated 46 Gordon Square in 1904, she hung Watts's portraits of her parents, and Duncan Grant remembers the Watts portrait of Leslie Stephen hanging at 29 Fitzroy Square when Virginia and Adrian moved there. Vanessa also represented the family heritage by hanging photographs of not only Herschel and Darwin but also Lowell, Meredith, Browning, and Tennyson.[4] In *Freshwater* Tennyson, who recites *Maud* throughout much of the play, represents the literature of the Victorian era. In Woolf's earlier version, he faints at the hideous sound of "twelve *s*'s in ten lines" uttered by Watts (FW 67). "Take care of the sound and the sense will take care of itself," he advises the painter who contemplates changing "Modesty at the feet of Mammon" to "Mammon trampling upon Maternity" (FW 66), a title with a pleasing sound and perhaps a hint of Virginia's ambivalence about her sister's motherhood or about her own childless state. To Tennyson, accomplishment means having written "The moan of doves in immemorial elms, / The murmuring of innumerable bees" as well as "perhaps the loveliest line in the language—The mellow ouzel fluting on the lawn" (FW 16). While Tennyson amusingly insists that his poetry is based on "facts" like the color of the flowers in "For her feet have touch'd the meadows / And left the daisies rosy" (FW 15), he damns facts when any attention due them interrupts his recitation of *Maud*. "Facts are the death of poetry," he proclaims (FW 39). These same facts, in the persons of Watts's young wife and her lover, upset the painter as well.

Tennyson was for Virginia Woolf roughly what Watts was for Vanessa Bell. "Tennysonian sentiment," Woolf says, cast a false golden glow over her mother's first marriage (MB 32). Then Tennyson was among the writers whose works her mother's second husband, Leslie Stephen, read aloud to his family.[5] Appropriately, Mr. Ramsay, the character based on Woolf's father in *To the Lighthouse*, quotes the *Charge of the Light Brigade* as he strides across the lawn. In *Jacob's Room* Jacob, reminiscent of Woolf's dead brother, Thoby, defends "poor old Tennyson" to his more modern, disparaging friends.[6] Virginia reported her annoyance when people asked her about having met Tennyson, whom she remembered less as a great man than as someone who asked her to pass salt or butter at the table (L I 300); but there is also her poignant admission that she sat in a dark corner and read *In Memoriam* at some social event while Vanessa danced (L I 217).

The woman artist in the immediate background, Julia Margaret Cameron, is a somewhat better role model. Vanessa hung several of her great-aunt's photographs of Julia Stephen at 46 Gordon Square. In *Freshwater*, however, Woolf shows the side of Mrs. Cameron that Quentin Bell calls "vague, silly and sentimental."[7] She proposes to be buried with Tennyson's *In Memoriam* beneath her head and *Maud* upon her heart (FW 9). Her photographs, like "Poetry in the person of Alfred Tennyson adoring the Muse," are, like Watts's paintings, allegorical. Like Watts she cannot understand anyone not wanting to pose for her pictures. Echoing both the painter and the poet she declares, "A fact is a fact; art is art" (FW 16).

The irreverent younger generation in this play is embodied in Watts's young wife, Ellen Terry. She finds posing for pictures chilling and tiring; she cannot comprehend how she can be Modesty one minute and a Muse the next; she prefers a swim to the prospect of hanging in the Tate Gallery, life in Bloomsbury to life at the Cameron house on the Isle of Wight, and a young husband to an old man married to his art. However caricatured are its artists and rebels, *Freshwater* still portrays the generation gap that exists in both life and art. When Virginia Woolf was almost sixty years old, she recalled the Edwardian period during which she and Vanessa formed a "conspiracy" against Victorian values and obligations. "By nature," she wrote, "both Vanessa and I were explorers, revolutionists, reformers. But our surroundings were at least fifty years behind the times" (MB 126–27). Those surroundings included their father's and half-brothers' notions about women's role in society and, as *Freshwater* reveals, the painting and literature admired by the family. Although both sisters found ways to escape some of their social obligations each day by learning about their respective art media, they did not find predecessors like Watts and Tennyson adequate models. What these men shared, G. K. Chesterton observes, was a "profound belief in the solemnity, the ceremoniousness, the responsibility and what most men would now . . . call the pomposity of the great arts."[8] The sisters shared, in contrast, a desire to communicate their fresh responses to nature and human nature as directly as possible. Rebellion lessened their rivalry and brought Virginia to Vanessa's defense.

By 1930 Woolf's reputation as a writer was fairly well established. When she unexpectedly volunteered to write the introductory remarks for the catalogue accompanying Vanessa Bell's exhibition at the Cooling Galleries, London, Vanessa confessed some reservations to Clive Bell. Although she was certain that her sister's comments would promote the exhibit effectively, she wondered how other people would react.[9] She may have thought that people would consider Virginia's remarks biased or based on an insufficient knowledge of painting. Fortunately, Vanessa was not worried enough to refuse the offer. The remarks Woolf wrote provide a striking example of what she consistently defined as her layperson's response to the visual arts as well as an assessment of her sister as an artist.

The preface begins with comments on the historical plight of women painters barred from the pursuit of artistic careers by prohibitions against their painting nudes.[10] These remarks were not Woolf's first on the practical difficulties, guilt, and inferiority feelings of women in the visual arts. In 1920, as part of an exchange in the *New Statesman* with Desmond MacCarthy, known in his column as the "Affable Hawk," Woolf had pointed out that painting might now be within women's reach "if . . . there is sufficient money after the sons have been educated to permit of paints and studios for the daughters and no family reason requiring their presence at home. Otherwise they must make a dash for it and disregard a species of torture more exquisitely painful, I believe, than any that man can imagine" (D II 341). She had returned to this theme in *A Room of One's Own* to note that women painters, like women composers, still have a harder time than women novelists when confronted with the notion that women are incapable of significant creative and intellectual activity (AROO

56). While Angelica Garnett does not think anyone said such a thing to the Stephen daughters,[11] Charles Tansley's comment that "Women can't paint, can't write" in *To the Lighthouse* and its psychological impact on Lily Briscoe embody this problem in Woolf's art.

After Vanessa Bell's exhibition, Virginia Woolf returned to the theme. In the essay portion of *The Pargiters*, written in 1932 as a preliminary to *The Years*, Woolf considers the different kinds of problems faced by women writers and women painters and specifically mentions her sister. This time her sympathies are with writers who, she insists, have had a formidable obstacle not confronted by women painters: "the Angel in the House;" that self-abnegating, flattering phantom,

> has a special hatred for writers and with good reason. Her province, you see, is the House. Painters and musicians—it is one of their chief assets—have very little to do with the house. When Vanessa Bell paints a picture it is as often as not a picture of red apples on a plate. Thats all right, says the Angel. It may be a pity to waste your time painting; but if you must paint [*paint apples*] ⟨there is no harm in apples.⟩[12]
>
> . . . But writing is a very different matter—you cannot even review a novel without expressing an opinion upon charac-[ters,] morality, human relations—all matters of vital importance in the conduct of the house, and thus coming directly under the notice of its Angel (P xxxii).

Woolf admits, however, that in some ways women writers have had an easier time than women painters or composers. At least writers can get materials cheaply. "Pianos, models, studios, north lights, masters and mistresses, ⟨Berlin, Paris, Vienna & all the rest of it⟩ are not needed" (P xxviii). Milly Pargiter, who wants to paint, has these practical problems and also has a father who discourages her from going to art school, because "painting at the Slade meant painting from the nude." Submitting to his wishes, Milly sketches outdoors or paints flowers in her room: "Her most successful sketch—of a cottage in Surrey—was hung in the dining room over the mantlepiece under the dagger" (P 29–30).[13] The position of the drawing above the sacred hearth but beneath the dagger echoes both Milly's position in her patriarchal household and the plight of women artists in Victorian society.

The issue reappears briefly in *Three Guineas*. Woolf notes how difficult it was in the mid-nineteenth century for women painters to get proper training. While they had to compete on an equal basis with men in the Royal Academy, they got only half the instruction and no opportunities whatsoever to draw from nude models (TG 136, 183). In spite of her mockery of the painters' enthusiasms, therefore, Virginia Woolf understood some of the practical and psychological difficulties her sister faced. At times, she even tried to alleviate them. One result of her observations in *Three Guineas* was that in 1939 she sent her sister some birthday money and noted that it "is to be spent *simply and solely on Models* Duncan and Angelica are witnesses"; Vanessa was not to use it for household expenses or other necessities (L VI 333). A month later Virginia inquired, "Are you painting from models?" (L VI 338).

Because of her own professional difficulties, Vanessa was also able to sympathize with some of Virginia's. Both sisters, during certain periods of their lives, could not work because of physical or mental illnesses. In Vanessa's case, domestic or maternal activities or an inadequate studio created additional problems. "It's awful being cut off from one's principal occupation isn't it?" Vanessa wrote to her sister on one such occasion. "I'm thankful to be able to paint again. One gets that tetchy without it and is off one's balance."[14] In *A Room of One's Own*, Woolf emphasizes two prerequisites for women's creativity: conquest of material difficulties, like poverty and lack of privacy and time; and conquest of immaterial difficulties, primarily the lack of self-confidence that results from the overt discouragement of people around them. Freedom from the material obstructions, Woolf says, leads to freedom from the psychological ones; a room of one's own leads to a mind of one's own. Vanessa Bell's dust jacket design for her sister's book isolates one of the initial material difficulties to be overcome: the lack of uninterrupted time. Her design is an arch, black inside except for two pink rectangles and a square. These are piled, each slightly embedded in the one below, to form a pyramid in the center. The square at the top has a clock face on it (Figure 2.2). Virginia called Vanessa's design "most attractive—but what a stir you'll cause by the hands of the clock at that precise hour! People will say—" but Virginia said she had no space to elaborate (L IV 81). As the editors of the letters point out, the hands of the clock, set at 11:05, form a "V." The initial, appropriate for both sisters, underscores the significance of the book's commentary for both of

2.2. Vanessa Bell. Dust jacket for *A Room of One's Own* (London: Hogarth, 1929) by Virginia Woolf. Courtesy of the Bloomsbury Collection at Washington State University Libraries, Pullman, Washington; permission of the estate of Vanessa Bell and the Hogarth Press.

their professional lives. In a memoir describing the move to Bloomsbury after Leslie Stephen's death, Vanessa noted that she was especially delighted "to have one's own rooms, be master of one's own time, have all the things in fact which come as a matter of course to many of the young today but so seldom then to young women at least."[15] Older women have even more trouble: "It's so terribly difficult to paint seriously when one is responsible for other things," she wrote, "and hasn't room and space to oneself and we females have to struggle for it all our lives. . . ."[16]

Virginia Woolf admits in her preface to Vanessa Bell's exhibition, however, that a contemplation of the historical difficulties of women in the visual arts is only a way to avoid looking at the pictures and trying to come to conclusions about them. She evades doing so again by commenting briefly upon her sister's reputation in relation to Berthe Morisot's and Marie Laurencin's. Finally, however, after "shillyshallying on the threshold," she turns to the paintings. Her identification with Vanessa Bell's achievements and rebellions and her understanding of the problems of women painters are augmented by a third positive response: a genuine fascination with her sister's artistic process and practice. "What is there to intimidate or perplex?" she asks herself. Vanessa Bell's paintings present a "serene and ordered world." Unlike ninety-nine other painters whose responses to similar scenes Woolf imagines, Bell does not compromise with the public's desire for caricatures and illustrations, for the sentiments and wit that have made England such a literary nation. In her paintings, "No stories are told; no insinuations are made. The hill side is bare; the group of women is silent; the little boy stands in the sea saying nothing. If portraits there are, they are pictures of flesh which happens from its texture or its modelling to be aesthetically on an equality with the China pot or the chrysanthemum."[17]

Unable to proceed further with her line of thought, Woolf approaches the paintings from a more congenial direction: she contrasts her sister's art with literature. When we read a number of novels by the same writer, we can reach conclusions about that person. When we experience a number of Vanessa Bell's paintings, however, we can discover nothing about her interests, her education, or her appearance: ". . . Mrs. Bell says nothing. Mrs. Bell is as silent as the grave. Her pictures do not betray her. Their reticence is inviolable" and that, Woolf admits, is part of their attraction.[18] Their full meaning may be apparent only to painters who understand what she does with the "masses and passages and relations and values of which we know nothing"; nevertheless, they arouse feelings and create perplexities in the lay viewer. How? What the paintings communicate, Woolf decides, cannot be embodied in words; the pictures neither make statements nor prompt actions. The emotions they arouse have nothing to do with associations apart from the pictures themselves; instead, the emotions result from Bell's ability to make her viewers share the "shock of emotion" she has felt in perceiving the world around her. This she does "always by her means, in her language, with her susceptibility, and not ours. That is why," Woolf concludes, "she is so tantalising, so original, and so satisfying as a painter." Vanessa Bell takes her viewers into a "strange painters' world, in which mortality does not enter, and psychology is held at bay, and there are no words." If not mortality, is there morality? That, Woolf concludes, "was the very question I was asking myself as I came in."[19] She does not answer it. Having avoided issues, then confronted them, posed questions and then answered them in a sensitive and articulate way, Woolf circles back to the layperson's uncertainties with which she entered her sister's show. Her amalgamation of decisiveness and indecision leaves the reader as aware of the critic and the critical process as of the painter and her work.

Woolf's approach to art criticism parallels, in some ways, her approach to literary criticism. In her essays about literature, she writes primarily as another creator. Suspicious of criticism in general and eclectic in her tastes and approaches, Woolf does not impose her own literary or metaphysical preconceptions upon individual writers or works. Perhaps because she is relatively nondogmatic and because she is interested in states of mind, her own and other people's, she is commonly labeled an impressionistic or subjective critic.[20]

Woolf is especially wary of the critic's stance when she writes about the visual arts. Unlike Roger Fry or Clive Bell, she does not expound aesthetic theories within the context of art history. Unwilling to limit herself exclusively to the state of mind responsible for many modern paintings yet intrigued by the rejection of narrative and didactic motives, she focuses more often on her own mental processes. More accurately, Woolf in her essays on the visual arts makes of herself a character, one we might dub "the common viewer" or, to use her own Johnsonian coinage, "the common seer" (RF 105). That viewer is also, less commonly, a writer. What a creator who works in a different medium perceives as she confronts not only the paintings but the task of saying something about them determines the structure of her essays. They reflect what she calls "the flight of the mind,"[21] the often associational, imaginative and, in Woolf's case, mocking and self-mocking processes by which she reaches her conclusions.

"Because everyone I most honour is silent—Nessa, Lytton, Leonard, Maynard: all silent; and so I have trained myself to silence; induced to it also by the terror I have of my own unlimited capacity for feeling . . ." (L IV 422). So Virginia Woolf wrote in 1931. While the list of silent people includes only one painter, her sister, still Woolf consistently associated silence and, by implication, emotional control, with the visual arts. Visual artists are "inarticulate," Woolf wrote (L I 60); painting "tends to dumbness" (L II 382); and painters live in a "sublime silent fish-world" (L IV 142). Such reticence both intrigues and repels Woolf. Her response recalls Keats's in "Ode on a Grecian Urn." The "silent form" of the urn "dost tease us out of thought / As doth eternity," but the scene represented is a "Cold Pastoral!"[22] In *To the Lighthouse* Lily Briscoe thinks that the "penalty" of Mrs. Ramsay's beauty is that "It stilled life—froze it" (TTL 264). So the silent world of the visual arts is beautiful and transcendent, but somehow chillingly inhuman.

It suggests death, which also stops words, imposes silence. When Rachel Vinrace in *The Voyage Out* thinks of her restricted life framed by birth and death, she concludes, resentfully, that it is "the only chance she had—the short season between two silences" (VO 82). Her premature death freezes her relationship with Terence Hewet as if it were a work of art. At her deathbed he experiences peace and "perfect happiness. They had now what they had always wanted to have, the union which had been impossible while they lived" (VO 353), but that union is achieved at the cost of Rachel's life. Woolf reverses, however, the advice of the poet to the lover not to grieve since "Forever wilt thou love, and she be fair!" Terence, who leaves the deathbed peacefully, confronts "a world in which he would never see Rachel again" and cries out her name inconsolably (VO 354). We hear no more from him in the novel. In *To the Lighthouse* Mr. Ramsay is similarly bereft, but Lily Briscoe, who in her grief cries out Mrs. Ramsay's name, is also comforted by her recognition that she can understand and use in her painting the dead woman's creative ability to make life stand still. So Bernard, the writer in *The Waves*, holds his own funeral service for Percival in the National Gallery. Among the "cold madonnas" and other paintings that "make no reference; . . . do not point," the dead friend returns, although "differently. I remember his beauty," Bernard says; "I recover what he was to me: my opposite" (W 156). Although the price is high, the silence of death can freeze a relationship between two people as if it were a painting; in reverse, the frozen life of a painting can recall the beauty of a person who is dead.

In 1920, in "Pictures and Portraits," Woolf analyzed her ambivalent reaction to "the silent art." Although she is reviewing *Personalities*, a book of twenty-four drawings by Edmond X. Kapp, she again avoids her subject and follows her own train of thought about the National Gallery, the National Portrait Gallery, and their surroundings. Contrasting the noisy city and the crowds in the galleries with the paintings, she concludes that the latter "are too still, too silent." She suggests that the English generally do not like paintings because they seem aloof and indifferent, devoid of sympathy or solutions for personal or public dilemmas.[23] In *Between the Acts*, too, part of the discussion before the play concerns England's bias for the verbal as opposed to the visual arts. Bart Oliver asks Dodge why "we, as a race, [are] so incurious, irresponsive, and insensitive . . . to that noble art, whereas, Mrs Manressa . . . has her Shakespeare by heart?" The group recites bits of Shakespeare, and Bart considers his point proved. In contrast, he says, nothing emerges when he says "Reynolds! Constable! Crome!" Mrs. Swithin disagrees with him and shows her usual insight. Those names may bring no words to the lips, but "behind the eyes," something happens (BA 54–55).

In *The Waves*, we see behind Bernard's eyes. There is some of the same traditional English bias for words, although his reaction to paintings is more complex. His initial response to a work by Titian in the National Gallery is that painters suffer less than writers: "Painters live lives of methodical absorption, adding stroke to stroke. They are not like poets—scapegoats; they are not chained to the rock." The results are "silence" and "sublimity." But Bernard's next reaction is that Titian suffered too, at least aesthetically: "Yet that crimson must have burnt in Titian's gizzard" and his emotions must have risen and fallen with the lines he drew. Bernard's final response to the painting, however, is frustration: ". . . the silence weighs on me—the perpetual solicitation of the eye." His sensory responses are extremely strong, but "without order." An idea, an interpretation, does not quite take shape, so Bernard stores his visual experience in his mind for future reference (W 157).

Woolf feels the chilly silence of paintings and their tendency to make the individual "fade and dwindle and dissolve." She also feels freed from the "damned egotistical self," which she says elsewhere can destroy the novelist's work (D II 14), and attracted to that silence, as her comments in "Pictures and Portraits" indicate:

> We rise, purged and purified; deprived, it is true, of a tongue, but free from the impertinences and solicitations of that too animated and active member. The silence is hollow and vast as that of a cathedral dome. After the first shock and chill those used to deal in words seek out the pictures with the least of language about them—canvases taciturn and congealed like emerald or aquamarine—landscapes hollowed from transparent stone, green hillsides, skies in which the clouds are eternally at rest. Let us wash the roofs of our eyes in colour; let us dive till the deep seas close above our heads.[24]

Something essential in the human experience transcends words. As Woolf says in "Craftsmanship," they "live in the mind. If you want proof of this, consider how often in moments of emotion when we most need words we find none" (CE II 249). Or we find ourselves as Bernard in *The Waves* does after an eclipse, "unable to speak save in a child's words of one syllable; without shelter from phrases—I who have made so many." Without his phrases, and rendered insignificant by the transformation around him, Bernard's very identity is in doubt: "But how describe the world seen without a self? There are no words. . . . How describe or say anything in articulate words again?" (W 287).

"Pictures and Portraits," which defines the repulsion and attraction Woolf felt for the silent art, also emphasizes her dual reaction to her own medium. In her fiction she constantly explores the nature and boundaries of her verbal art. Some words retain an expressive quality independent of their meanings, just as color and line give pleasure whatever the subject of a painting. In *The Years*, North concludes that "adenoids," taken out of context, is "a good word. . . . wasp-waisted; pinched in the middle; with a hard, shining, metallic abdomen, useful to describe the appearance of an insect" (Y 374). Like a solid object, the word has a shape, a texture, a way of reflecting light. Sometimes the effects are less visual. To the young Orlando words, "even without meaning were as wine" (O 57). So the names "Orlando" and "Shelmerdine" have enormous power over the lovers (O 260). When Terence Hewet reads Milton in *The Voyage Out* and when Mrs. Ramsay reads poetry in *To the Lighthouse*, words also affect them like textures, shapes, or colors.

Woolf's visual imagination affects her response to words and that of her characters. Communication fails sometimes because they have not adequately defined themselves, sometimes because they fear self-exposure, but often because they cannot find a medium to embody what they feel. "But words have been used too often; touched and turned, and left exposed to the dust of the street," concludes the narrator in *Jacob's Room*. "The words we seek hang close to the tree. We come at dawn and find them sweet beneath the leaf" (JR 93). Words are exhausted by overuse; their relationship to the feelings they are supposed to represent is lost. Peggy in *The Years* tries to associate certain emotions with the word "pleasure" just as Eleanor, in a similar way, tries to define "love" (Y 362, 370). Already in *The Voyage Out*, Terence Hewet despairs of "talking, talking, merely talking" as a way of learning what Rachel is really like (VO 219). Rachel, trying to analyze her feelings, thinks back on the experiences of heroines in novels and gets no help. "It seemed to her that her sensations had no name" (VO 223). People in church, she realizes, fall back on stock phrases which misrepresent ideas (VO 228) but, answering letters, she finds herself relying on the standard expressions she so dislikes. Struggling to express their feelings for each other, Terence and Rachel discover that words like "love" are "either too trivial or too large" (VO 280).

The jungle makes communication especially difficult for them. The strange, wordless sounds emphasize the fundamental, nonverbal nature of their experience. A comment on Mrs. Flushing, the painter, suggests that this inarticulate world is related to the realm of painting: Her brush "strokes . . . seemed to serve her as speech serves others" (VO 234). As the narrator in *Jacob's Room* cautions, "if you persist that a command of the English language is part of our inheritance, one can only reply that beauty is almost always dumb" (JR 96). So, when words fail, Rachel relies on a visual image: "When she thought of their relationship she saw rather than reasoned, representing her view of what Terence felt by a picture of him drawn across the room to stand by her side" (VO 224).

Katharine and Ralph in *Night and Day* have as much difficulty as Rachel and Terence in *The Voyage Out* when they try to find words to express their feelings for each other. When Katharine thinks about "romance" in her life, for example, she cannot define what she means: ". . . she could drape it in color, see it in form, hear it in music, but not in words; no, never in words" (ND 287). She tries on one occasion to describe one of her mental pictures, "But she could not reduce her vision to words, since it was no single shape colored upon the dark, but rather a general excitement, an atmosphere, which when she tried to visualize it, took form as a wind scouring the flanks of northern hills and flashing light upon cornfields and pools" (ND 422). "Love" seems to be the only word Katharine and Ralph can find, but they aren't sure what each loves, the other person or some illusory image (ND 423–24). Katharine rejects Ralph's attempts to express what he feels in poetry, but when he tries prose, he again confronts "the inadequacy of the words, and the need of writing under them and over them others which, after all, did no better" (ND 487). Just as Mary Datchet draws involuntarily when she ponders the complexities of her relationship with Ralph, so Ralph draws when he thinks of his with Katharine: ". . . because he could do nothing further with words, he began to draw little figures in the blank spaces, heads meant to resemble her head, blots fringed with flames meant to represent—perhaps the entire universe" (ND 487). To these visual images, especially the dot surrounded by flames, Katharine can respond although Ralph is embarrassed that she has seen it. To him it is a private symbol representing Katharine but, in addition, "that encircling glow which for him surrounded, inexplicably, so many of the objects of life." (ND 493). The image is similar to the "luminous halo," the "semi-transparent envelope" Woolf uses in "Modern Fiction" to suggest the truth fiction tries to capture (CE II 106). Amazingly, Katharine admits to Ralph that she sees the world as he does (ND 493). With him, she can hold "in her hands for one brief moment the globe which we spend our lives in trying to shape, round, whole, and entire from the confusion of chaos" (ND 503); she can create, in other words, the equivalent of a work of art. The circles so common in Vanessa Bell's decorative work are similar embodiments of wholeness.[25]

Like Ralph, Katharine draws, but more abstractly. Seeing

mathematics as "directly opposed to literature" which she dislikes (ND 46), she draws "square boxes halved and quartered by straight lines, and then circles which underwent the same process of dissection" (ND 306) while she helps her mother write about their famous literary ancestor. The exactness of such figures is an antidote to the confusion of the personal relationships her mother's project forces her to consider. Katharine's mental state, however, is not so unlike the writer's as she thinks. In *To the Lighthouse* Lily Briscoe equates the "love which mathematicians bear their symbols" and the love poets have for "their phrases" (TTL 74). Although in this comparison the artist is a poet, Lily herself is something of a geometer in her creative process as a painter. To her Mrs. Ramsay, the subject of her painting, is "an august shape; the shape of a dome" (TTL 80).[26] Reading to James, she becomes a "triangular purple shape" (TTL 81). Lily has tapped some essential characteristic of her subject: Mrs. Ramsay thinks of herself, apart from her relationships to others, as "a wedge-shaped core of darkness" (TTL 95). Both writers and painters try "To clear the truth of the unessential" (D IV 172), in order to achieve form.

Other characters in Woolf's fiction devise abstract visual correlatives for their relationships and their lives. While her characters' images are also part of a literary tradition, they are closely related to Woolf's highly visual orientation and creative process. The characters in *The Waves* see their relationship as a chain and a circle. When they leave the restaurant where they have dined together, "the chain breaks," "the circle is destroyed" (W 142–43). "Meeting and parting," Louis thinks as though looking through a kaleidoscope, "we assemble different forms, make different patterns" (W 170). When Bernard joins his friends at Hampton Court, he perceives that "another arrangement will form, another pattern" (W 210).

Similarly, each character has a visual image for his or her life. Louis sees his destiny as numerous threads that he "must plait into one cable" (W 202). Neville, to himself, is "a net whose fibres pass imperceptibly beneath the world" (W 214). Susan sees "life in blocks, substantial, huge" (W 215). Bernard thinks, "I am wedged into my place in the puzzle" (W 216). His life also appears to him as a "circle of great stones" like Stonehenge (W 241) or as a tree; "The mind grows rings," he thinks late in the book (W 257). Eleanor in *The Years* also thinks of life as a circle. Considering "a long strip" of life behind her, she wonders how all the fragments of memories achieved unity.

"Perhaps there's 'I' at the middle of it . . . a knot; a centre; and again she saw herself sitting at her table drawing on the blotting paper, digging little holes from which spokes radiated" (Y 367).

Woolf and her characters, then, frequently abandon words for silence. For a writer a reverse process also occurs. Silence conceals words. Terence Hewet in *The Voyage Out* wants to get at "the things people don't say" for his "novel about Silence" (VO 216), ironically, by encouraging Rachel to talk on topics that women have not discussed with men before. When the silence is not of a person, however, but of a painting, a different kind of verbal activity occurs. In "Pictures and Portraits" Woolf notes ironically that "after a prolonged dumb gaze" at a painting, silence, colors, shapes, even "the very paint on the canvas begins to distil itself into words" again. These are not, however, "writers' words;" rather they are "sluggish, slow-dropping words that would, if they could, stain the page with colour." Woolf refuses to define such words any further in "Pictures and Portraits." What she is supposed to do, she says, is prove her "unfitness to review the caricatures of Mr. Kapp." She proceeds, therefore, to consider the National Portrait Gallery which has been in her mind from the beginning. Having narrowed her discussion from pictures in general to portraits, she considers the desire to have faces to accompany what she knows about famous people. At this point, reproaching herself for procrastination, Woolf finally turns to Kapp's drawings.

Since all of the personalities Kapp has drawn are well-known, she is not interested in what they look like but, instead, in what the artist "can add . . . to our estimate of their souls." Looking first at the drawings of people she has met, she concludes that Kapp's renditions do not correspond to her own memories. The warmth of Lord Morley's handshake is lost in a portrait in which "The lean, smoke-dried pedant's face looks as if scored upon paper by a pen clogged and corroded . . . with old ink" (Figure 2.3). Shaw appears "diabolic" in Kapp's rendition rather than "shrewd" and a bit quixotic: "Moustache and eyebrows are twisted into points. The fingers are contorted into stamping hooves. There is no hint of blue in the eye" (Figure 2.4). Yet Woolf realizes that the artist must work within his black-and-white medium. Trying to create a work of art, he is concerned primarily with "design, texture, handwriting, the relation of this with that." Woolf finds that when she has no preconceptions about the men portrayed, she can perceive the essence the artist has captured.

2.3. Edmond X. Kapp (1890–1978). *Lord Morley* from *Personalities: Twenty-four Drawings*. New York: Robert M. McBride; London: Secker, 1920. Courtesy of the Barber Institute of Fine Arts, the University of Birmingham, and of Mrs. Patricia Kapp.

The creator of "the Saint" in the nursery at 22 Hyde Park Gate appreciates Kapp's symbolical portraits of *The Politician* and *The Bishop*. She also admires Kapp's ability to suggest and to satirize. She cannot put into words, however, what he has captured and can only conclude the essay with exclamations: "But words, words! How inadequate you are! How weary one gets of you! How you will always be saying too much or too little! Oh to be silent! Oh to be a painter!"[27]

2.4. Edmond X. Kapp. *George Bernard Shaw* from *Personalities: Twenty-four Drawings*. New York: Robert M. McBride; London: Secker, 1920. Courtesy of Mrs. Patricia Kapp.

Both the idea that words other than traditional "writer's words" exist and the idea that painters have some advantages over writers in communicating human experiences continue to intrigue Woolf. Bernard in *The Waves* wishes for "some little language such as lovers use, broken words, inarticulate words, like the shuffling of feet on the pavement" (W 238). Woolf's conclusion to "Craftsmanship" is related. Words, she says, "like ourselves, in order to live at their ease, need privacy. Undoubtedly they like us to think, and they like us to feel, before we use them; but they also like us to pause; to become unconscious. Our unconsciousness is their privacy; our darkness is their light . . . That pause was made, that veil of darkness was dropped, to tempt words to come together in one of those swift marriages which are perfect images and create ever-lasting beauty" (CE II 251). Woolf does not draw the conclusion herself, but the juxtaposition of her comments on visual and verbal expression suggests the proper response to paintings. Devoid of conventional thoughts and feelings, the viewer experiences the hiatus in verbal communication that can stimulate new and subtler words and combinations of words in the unconscious mind.

In 1934 Virginia Woolf wrote another foreword to an exhibition of her sister's paintings, this one at the Lefevre Gallery.[28] In this introduction, as in the earlier one, she alludes to specific paintings, but her comments are brief and her tone is more impersonal; she does not mention her sister by name. The experts, she says, may discuss the artist's development and the formal characteristics of individual paintings. Her focus is the "excitement" of the common viewer whose vision is reeducated to see "familiar things" afresh. Although the paintings are silent, they suggest "conversations" and "intimate relationships" among the people in them. Ultimately, art media merge: "Character is colour. . . . Greens, blues, reds and purples are here seen making love and war and joining in unexpected combinations of exquisite married bliss." What the writer does with human relationships, Woolf suggests, her sister does with colors. More important, "life has been rid of its accidents, shown in its essence." But words cannot capture the truths on these canvases. The best Woolf can do is to declare the painter's world one "of glowing serenity and sober truth."[29]

Woolf wrote this preface during the same period when she was completing *Walter Sickert: A Conversation*. In this long essay, the topic again is the variety of responses to works of visual art. Because *Walter Sickert* is the culmination of Woolf's comments on that subject and of her professional relationship with Vanessa Bell, three brief earlier pieces deserve mention. All three also explain certain characteristics of Woolf's writing. In 1919 she published a short description of a visit to the Royal Academy. The essay is an indulgence in "iconic prose" in the tradition of Philostratus who, as Jean Hagstrum says,

2.5. Alfred Priest (1874–1929). *Cocaine. Royal Academy Illustrated*, 1919. Courtesy of the Royal Academy.

"reads paintings as though they were dramas."[30] In Woolf's case, certain pictures suggest multiple dramatic possibilities. One is entitled *Cocaine* which, although she does not mention the painter's name, is by Alfred Priest (Figure 2.5).[31] Virginia wrote to Vanessa that this painting was "one of the best" she saw on this occasion and encouraged her sister to read her article (L II 378). In it she describes the painting at length:

> A young man in evening dress lies, drugged, with his head upon the pink satin of a woman's knee. The ornamental clock assures us that it is exactly eleven minutes to five. The burning lamp

> proves that it is dawn. He, then, has come home to find her waiting? She has interrupted his debauch? For my part, I prefer to imagine what in painters' language (a tongue well worth separate study) would be called 'a dreary vigil'. There she has sat since eight-thirty, alone, in pink satin. Once she rose and pressed the photograph in the silver frame to her lips. She might have married that man (unless it is her father, of which one cannot be sure). She was a thoughtless girl, and he left her to meet his death on the field of battle. Through her tears she gazes at the next photograph—presumably that of a baby (again the painter has been content with a suggestion). As she looks a hand fumbles at the door. 'Thank God!' she cries as her husband staggers in and falls helpless across her knees, 'thank God our Teddy died!' So there she sits, staring disillusionment in the eyes, and whether she gives way to temptation, or breathes a vow to the photographs, or gets him to bed before the maid comes down, or sits there for ever, must be left to the imagination of the onlooker.
>
> But the queer thing is that one wants to be her. For a moment one pretends that one sits alone, disillusioned, in pink satin (CE IV 209).

Woolf seems equally impatient with the excessive detail that indicates the exact time and with the lack of information about the subjects of the photographs. Her primary response, however, is to the characters and their imagined situations. To these she reacts with a mixture of mockery and sympathy, but she refuses to draw a moral. She would not go so far as Ruskin, whose "eloquence" in *Modern Painters* sometimes overwhelms her but whose insistence on morality in art, she says, disturbs the critics of her day and even a lay art critic like herself (CE I 207). This conclusion echoes Vanessa Bell, who wrote in 1904 that Ruskin, however amusing, was unsatisfactory as a critic of paintings: "He never cares for anything unless it is a symbol or has several deep meanings which doesn't seem to me to be what one wants."[32] The paintings Woolf views at the Royal Academy seem "to radiate the strange power to make the beholder more heroic and more romantic," but they also exaggerate. Their painters had indulged in emotion to such an extent that the viewer becomes glutted with "Honour, patriotism, chastity, wealth, success, importance, position, patronage, power" (CE IV 210–11). Woolf is both intrigued by and suspicious of such nonaesthetic appeals and the conventional values they represent.

2.6. Berthe Morisot (1841–95). *Summer's Day*. 1879. Courtesy of the Trustees, The National Gallery, London.

In 1918 Virginia Woolf wrote to her sister about a visit to the National Gallery. Dismissing a list of traditional artists and subjects, Woolf admitted to having been "at once amused and very much pleased" by the French. Perhaps she knew that her preference would please her sister; nevertheless, Woolf did discriminate among individual artists and paintings, complimenting Berthe Morisot for "her picture of 2 women in a boat" (Figure 2.6). "It gives me great pleasure," she wrote, "and I seem able to understand it." She singled out another painting of women caught in an undramatic moment, Renoir's *The Umbrellas* (Figure 2.7). Vuillard's "still life on a mantelpiece" (probably *The Chimneypiece*, 1905), and a Boudin beach scene also pleased her (L II 260). The diary entry about this same trip to the National Gallery says little about individual painters; instead it explains and defends Woolf's attraction to certain works: "But I see why I like pictures; its as things that stir me to describe them; but then only certain pictures do this; & I insist (for the sake of my

2.7. Pierre-Auguste Renoir (1841–1919). *The Umbrellas*, c. 1885–86. Courtesy of the Trustees, The National Gallery, London.

aesthetic soul) that I don't want to read stories or emotions or anything of the kind into them; only pictures that appeal to my plastic sense of words make me want to have them for still life in my novel" (D I 168). A visit to the Victoria and Albert Museum to see a Rodin exhibition prompted a similar reaction. "But I see I shall have to write a novel entirely about carpets, old silver, cut glass and furniture," she wrote to Vanessa Bell. "The desire to describe becomes almost a torment" (L II 284). To Roger Fry she defined this desire as similar to "the lusts of the flesh" (L II 285).

A letter to Duncan Grant in 1920 helps to clarify what she meant by paintings and other objects that appeal to her "plastic sense of words." Although her tone is teasing, the letter also reveals how tempted Woolf sometimes was to pursue another goal of the iconic prose writers—to rival painting with equally sensuous words:[33] "But as I say I won't tell you what I think of your pictures. This is the more vexatious, as I should immensely like to describe them—its the sort of thing I do rather well—I should begin with the naked Venus and go all the way round, keeping my crescendo for the right place, descending thence in curves and spirals like an alighting swan—but I won't do it—dont be nervous—my masterpiece shall give way to yours . . ." (L II 421). Woolf's description, in other words, would have a shape that paralleled the formal elements of Grant's painting. Words and, presumably, the ideas they convey, can be chosen, juxtaposed, and arranged in as pleasing a fashion as colors and shapes. They can be worked with, as though they had tangible qualities and textures. Because of their protean meanings, Woolf says in "Craftsmanship," words cannot be used for practical purposes, as a craftsman handles "solid matter" to create "useful objects" (CE II 245). But the writer can combine words, if their variability be recognized and respected, to create enduring although "many-sided" truths and "everlasting beauty" (CE II 247, 251). In 1935 Woolf wrote about manipulating, like a painter, not words but components of character: "I have . . . reached a further stage in my writers advance. I see that there are 4? dimensions; all to be produced; in human life; & that leads to a far richer grouping and proportion: I mean: I: & the not I: & the outer & the inner. . . . New combinations in psychology & body—rather like painting." This realization would affect the biography of Fry, she noted, as well as the novel after *The Years* (D IV 353).[34]

In the twenties, however, Woolf was still trying to put into words some of her less complex reactions to painting. "Pictures," which appeared in the *Nation* in April of 1925, contains a response to paintings like *Cocaine* that is considerably more severe than the one in the earlier essay on the Royal Academy visit. Now modifying Samuel Johnson on women preachers, she says that "A story-telling picture is as pathetic and ludicrous as a trick played by a dog, and we applaud it only because we know that it is as hard for a painter to tell a story with his brush as it is for a sheep-dog to balance a biscuit on its nose." A painter telling a story is like a writer embodying visual beauty in words: often it is not done well because of the limitations of each medium, but the attempt is fascinating.[35] Woolf concludes, as she had in her diary, that when paintings influence writers, it is not because they suggest stories. The influence of painting on writing is a relatively new and different phenomenon evident in Hardy and Conrad, Flaubert, and especially Proust. These writers go to landscapes, still lifes, and portraits because paintings ultimately stimulate them verbally:

> That picture of a wet marsh on a blowing day shows us much more clearly than we could see for ourselves the greens and silvers, the sliding streams, the gusty willows shivering in the wind, and sets us trying to find phrases for them, suggests even a figure lying there among the bulrushes, or coming out of the farmyard gate in top-boots and mackintosh. That still-life, they proceed, pointing to a jar of red-hot pokers, is to us what a beefsteak is to an invalid—an orgy of blood and nourishment, so starved we are on our diet of thin black print. We nestle into its colour, feed and fill ourselves with yellow and red and gold till we drop off, nourished and content. Our sense of colour seems miraculously sharpened. We carry those roses and red-hot pokers about with us for days, working them over again in words. From a portrait, too, we get almost always something worth having—somebody's room, nose, or hands, some little effect of character or circumstance, some knick-knack to put in our pockets and take away.[36]

The references to red-hot pokers recall still-life paintings done in the early twenties by both Vanessa Bell (Figure 2.8) and Duncan Grant[37] and anticipate a reference a year later in a letter to Vanessa. Before her sister's renditions of "hot pokers," Woolf says, her "mind shivers with joy" (L III 271). Writers do not respond to the art of such paintings per se; they come to vitalize their visual senses and to pilfer visual images, like these brilliant flowers, which they try to turn into words. Woolf tries in the early draft of *To the Lighthouse*. There the pokers, planted by Mrs. Ramsay, "burst their clear red coal against the blue" of the bay.[38] In "Pictures," Woolf also speaks

2.8. Vanessa Bell. *Red-Hot Pokers*, 1921. Courtesy of the Manchester City Art Galleries.

of writers in galleries as if they were naughty children pulling works of art to pieces, stuffing their pockets, and getting away before anyone detects their pranks. The passage quoted above associates them, less amusingly, with starved people gulping food and with feeding parasites. The paintings they feed upon have nothing to do with words, although some painters come closer to speech than others. Matisse, Derain, and Grant approach speech more often, Woolf says, than do Picasso, Sickert, and her sister, Vanessa Bell. These last three are "all mute as mackerel."[39] The desire to describe visual experiences in words is a barrier, however thin, between writer and painter; they are not entirely fit companions, Woolf concludes, in art galleries.

One more relevant essay precedes *Walter Sickert*. "Three Pictures" (1929) examines, not writers' reactions to paintings in galleries, but mental pictures. Woolf's lack of intimacy with people she only glimpses enables her to exaggerate with relative impunity. She provides an example. A quick visual image becomes in her mind a fully detailed picture entitled, like a traditional narrative painting, "The Sailor's Homecoming." It pleases her and makes "most things appear much brighter, warmer, and simpler than usual." Such pictures resolve questions of right and wrong as well as imbue life with meaning (CE IV 151). Woolf uses the idyllic mental picture of the sailor to ward off another dark and terrifying one of "an obscure human form, almost without shape, raising a gigantic arm in vain against some overwhelming iniquity" (CE IV 152). The happy, idealized picture of the sailor masks unpleasant realities, but not for long. A third mental picture reveals his death from some "foreign fever" and the grief of his young wife (CE IV 154). The pictures of human life which we create in our minds, like the idyllic traditional paintings hanging in our galleries, are both tempting and false.[40]

Like words, then, visual images do not always serve. The theme recurs in Woolf's fiction. Lily Briscoe thinks of "Beautiful pictures. Beautiful phrases" when she thinks of Mrs. Ramsay. But she must confront the fact that "the human apparatus for painting or for feeling" is "miserable" and "inefficient" and it "always broke down at the critical moment" (TTL 287). Unfortunately, too, visual images can be hackneyed, just as verbal expressions can. The word "marriage," for example, irritates Terence Hewet in *The Voyage Out* because of the stock pictures it prompts his brain to form. He creates several such pictures, first of "two people sitting alone over the fire;

the man was reading; the woman sewing." Another picture follows: "He saw a man jump up, say good-night, leave the company and hasten away with the quiet secret look of one who is stealing to certain happiness." Neither picture pleases him; nor does

> a third picture, of husband and wife and friend; and the married people glancing at each other as though they were content to let something pass unquestioned, being themselves possessed of the deeper truth. Other pictures— . . . they came before him without any conscious effort, like pictures on a sheet—succeeded these. Here were the worn husband and wife sitting with their children round them, very patient, tolerant, and wise. But that, too, was an unpleasant picture. He tried all sorts of pictures, taking them from the lives of friends of his . . . ; but he saw them always, walled up in a warm firelit room (VO 241).

Hewet sees the firelit room as confining. In *The Years*, however, Eleanor sees a similar picture in a positive way: "And a scene came before her; Maggie and Renny sitting over the fire. A happy marriage, she thought . . ." (Y 299).

In *Night and Day*, too, Katharine Hilbery contemplates William Rodney in his firelit room and imagines a pleasant "picture" of herself returning there from a lecture with an armload of scientific books: "It was a picture plucked from her life two or three years hence, when she was married to William" (ND 138). Marriage, she thinks, would give her freedom to pursue her own interests, but her picture of marriage as a firelit room of one's own runs counter to Rodney's view of women as creatures formed to encourage and to glorify men's achievements. Her picture also contrasts sharply with another one her imagination forms of "some magnanimous hero, riding a great horse by the shore of the sea. They rode through forests together, they galloped by the rim of the sea" (ND 107). The visual equivalents for Katharine's relationship with Ralph, as we have seen, are different from either those of firelit rooms or gallops on horseback. They are more tentative, experimental, abstract. They do not suggest conventional stories, as Vanessa Bell's paintings do not.

Woolf wonders in "A Sketch of the Past" if her desire to create representative and enduring "scenes" is the foundation of her writing. Scenes, which she says "are not altogether a literary device," sum up and make "innumerable details visible in one concrete picture" (MB 122). The tendency derives as much from painting as from literature. An example of Woolf's ability, reminiscent in fact of Priest's *Cocaine*, is a memoir description of a gardenhouse beneath a leafless tree on a summer night after Stella Duckworth's death. Inside, Jack Hills grips Virginia's hand and groans out his agony. The skeletal tree symbolizes, she says, the emptiness of Jack's life (MB 121). Woolf's characters also create scenes that resemble a visual artist's productions. Some of the scenes activate the imagination and prompt words, others are the forms memories take; some are amusing, some foolish; some are concrete, others more abstract. In *The Waves*, for instance, Bernard consciously fills his "mind with imaginary pictures," and sketches an encounter with an athletic young woman in a "shabby but distinguished house." The need to go from situation and setting, easy to visualize and set down, to the complexities of human relationships is what Bernard finds difficult, to move from painting to drama (W 79–80). In *Between the Acts* Miss LaTrobe's next play emerges, not from words, but from visual images; but, like Bernard, she does not know initially what her "two figures, half concealed by a rock," will say (BA 210).

Eleanor in *The Years* also creates mental scenes that are much like paintings. Both "words and sights" recur to her, like the image of "old Mrs. Levy, sitting propped up in bed with her white hair in a thick flop like a wig and her face cracked like an old glazed pot" (Y 30). As Eleanor grows older, memories predominate. When North goes to war, "A picture came before her eyes—the picture of a nice cricketing boy smoking a cigar on a terrace." The terrace causes her to remember "another picture. . . . She was sitting on the same terrace; but now the sun was setting; a maid came out and said, 'The soldiers are guarding the line with fixed bayonets!' That was how she had heard of the war—three years ago" (Y 285). North also has a picture-making mind. On the phone he describes Sara as "sitting on the edge of her chair . . . with a smudge on her face, swinging her foot up and down," a "telephone picture" which makes Eleanor smile (Y 324; 365–66). Later, North creates mental scenes out of a card with a woman's name written on it (Y 374, 376). His thoughts, especially in solitude, also generate visual images. The effect is not always positive. Trying to muster sufficient courage to share his ideas with Edward, North admits that "thinking alone bred pictures, foolish pictures" (Y 414).

Woolf's comments on Walter Sickert, then, grew out of her interest in different responses to painting, and in pictures created by words as well as by paint. They also emerge, as the subtitle "A Conversation" indicates, from considerable discussion of art in general and of the relationships between art and literature. Although Virginia Woolf wrote to Ottoline Morrell in 1913 that artists' talk is too "philosophical and religious and profound" (L II 18), most of the time her reaction was more positive. In 1917 she recorded in her diary the substance of a conversation with Roger Fry and Clive Bell on "literature & aesthetics." She also noted her pleasure: "Much no doubt is perfectly vague, not to be taken seriously, but the atmosphere puts ideas into one's head, & instead of trying to curtail them, or expatiate, one can speak them straight out & be understood—indeed disagreed with" (D I 80). In 1918 she wrote that what she liked doing best with Vanessa and Duncan was sitting in their studio and talking about art (D I 120–21). She also talked to Walter Sickert "of painting, & Whistler" at a social gathering in 1923 and concluded, tongue partially in cheek, "There is something indescribably congenial to me in this easy artists talk; the values the same as my own and therefore right; no impediments; life charming, good & interesting; no effort; art brooding calmly over it all; & none of this attachment to mundane things, which I find in Chelsea" (D II 223–24).

Woolf was familiar with Sickert's painting for many years before she wrote *Walter Sickert: A Conversation.* In 1919 she wrote to Vanessa Bell, "Did I tell you how Sickert is a great painter? In fact he's now my ideal painter; I should like to possess his works, for the purpose of describing them" (L II 331). If Virginia wanted to arouse her sister's jealousy by her admiration for another painter's work, as Vanessa perhaps did when she praised Austen or Forster, she did not have much success. Vanessa, in fact, was largely responsible for Virginia's putting her admiration of Sickert's painting into words. In 1933, the sisters attended an exhibition of his work. He had expressed his appreciation of Vanessa's art before, and she of his.[41] Vanessa, when Virginia was impressed, suggested that she write and tell Sickert her reactions. His response indicated the nature of her comments: "I have always been a literary painter, thank goodness, like all the decent painters," he said. "Do be the first to say so."[42] At a dinner arranged by Clive Bell, Sickert again encouraged Woolf to publish her opinions on his art, and in 1934 her pamphlet appeared with Vanessa Bell's cover design.

When the pamphlet produced little response, Woolf decided that she ought to have included an explanation of why she wrote it (D IV 275). She offered several reasons. One was pity: "he is getting very old and is in very bad circumstances" (L V 314). Submissiveness, albeit mocking, is another; her essay, she said, "was written at command of the old tyrant himself, who says no one appreciates him, and has the bailiffs in the basement" (L V 340). In both cases, however, she insisted that she liked his work. In fact, she said to Ethel Smyth that he was "the greatest English painter living" (L V 354). Quentin Bell's remark that "It would have been difficult to choose an approach to the art of painting more completely opposed to that of her sister"[43] implies defiance or self-assertion on Woolf's part. He is correct to the extent that Woolf does defend literary motives and responses to paintings. The essay is, on one level, an imaginary dialogue between painter and writer. Woolf's literary emphases, though, are by no means dogmatic; nor do they exclude the painter's more technical orientation.

Woolf's understanding of the painter's eye is evident in her fiction as well as in her essays, however competitive she might feel. Five years earlier, in "The Lady in the Looking-Glass" (1929), Woolf's narrator, however interested in character, has an eye that sometimes functions without preconceptions and responds, like a modern painter's, primarily to shapes, textures, and colors: "A large black form loomed into the looking-glass; blotted out everything, strewed the table with a packet of marble tablets veined with pink and grey, and was gone. But the picture was entirely altered. For the moment it was unrecognizable and irrational and entirely out of focus. One could not relate these tablets to any human purpose" (HH 90). Then the narrator realizes that the tablets are letters brought by the postman. Even so, the eye responds to color and composition rather than to their practical purpose. The mirror frame, like that of a painting, immobilizes and harmonizes what lies within it.

Sickert's paintings do the same. Woolf's *Walter Sickert* is a dinner conversation that proceeds by questions and attempted answers as well as by association. The unidentified participants in the discussion have both visual and verbal biases. Beginning with some talk of getting around London and the efficacy of colored signal lights, the diners proceed quickly to the possibility that our color sense is destroyed by an association between colors and actions, to the effects upon the senses of other conditions of modern life, and to the perception of color in general. A comment on an insect that takes on the hue of the flower it lights upon prompts the speakers to consider the extent to which human beings revert "to the insect stage of our long life" when they enter picture galleries. Someone talks of entering an exhibition of Walter Sickert's paintings and of becoming "completely and solely an insect—all eye," by responding exclusively to colors.

In "Pictures" Woolf lists Sickert with her sister among the mute painters. In this essay, however, she leans toward other reactions. Some of the diners doubt that one can see color only; they mention other qualities of Sickert's paintings. One speaker calls him "a great biographer" (CE II 235). The painters reject this idea. With pictures of Sickert's portraits in front of them, they examine dispassionately the relationships among the forms and colors and go "into the silent land . . . out of reach of the human voice" (CE II 236). Unable to follow, inclined like most of the English to talk, two members of the group continue their own more literary line of thought. Sickert, one of them says, can do what biographers who use words cannot: He can make "complete and flawless statements" whereas they "are tripped up by those miserable impediments called facts. . . . But Sickert takes his brush, squeezes his tube, looks at the face; and then, cloaked in the divine gift of silence, he paints—lies, paltriness, splendour, depravity, endurance, beauty—it is all there" (CE II 236).

The other speaker thinks Sickert is more a realistic novelist than a biographer. He depicts middle-class people in moments of crisis; his paintings, with titles like "*Rose et Marie*; *Christine buys a house*; *A difficult moment*," recall stories like those by Dickens, Balzac, Gissing, Bennett, and Turgenev. Detailed descriptions of three paintings illustrate this point. Although Woolf does not mention their titles, one is Sickert's *Ennui*[44] (Figure 2.9). Her description, like the one of *Cocaine*, treats the painting as if it were a drama.

> You remember the picture of the old publican, with his glass on the table before him and a cigar gone cold at his lips, looking out of his shrewd little pig's eyes at the intolerable wastes of desola-

2.9. Walter Sickert (1860–1942). *Ennui*, c. 1913–14. Permission of the Tate Gallery, London.

tion in front of him? A fat woman lounges, her arm on a cheap yellow chest of drawers, behind him. It is all over with them, one feels. The accumulated weariness of innumerable days has discharged its burden on them. They are buried under an avalanche of rubbish. In the street beneath, the trams are squeaking, children are shrieking. Even now somebody is tapping his glass impatiently on the bar counter. She will have to bestir herself; to pull her heavy, indolent body together and go and serve him. The grimness of that situation lies in the fact that there is no crisis; dull minutes are mounting, old matches are

> accumulating and dirty glasses and dead cigars; still on they must go; up they must get (CE II 237).

Yet, the first speaker suggests, Sickert does more than evoke characters and plots; he "makes us aware of beauty" and is thus a "true poet" (CE II 240). The scenes he depicts, animated always by human beings, are reminiscent of "Crabbe, Wordsworth, Cowper," poets who have "kept close to the earth, to the house, to the sound of the natural human voice" (CE II 240–41).

Do Woolf's literary conversationalists recognize Sickert as no more than biographer, realistic novelist, and poet? The conclusion to the description of *Ennui* includes the answer. In spite of the unpleasant story of the disillusioned publican and his wife they have created, the writers realize that Sickert's painting is "beautiful, . . . ; satisfactory; complete in some way. Perhaps it is the flash of the stuffed birds in the glass case, or the relation of the chest of drawers to the woman's body; anyhow, there is a quality in that picture which makes me feel that though the publican is done for, and his disillusion complete, still in the other world, of which he is mysteriously a part without knowing it, beauty and order prevail; all is right there . . ." (CE II 237).

At this point the speakers realize that they are on the verge of discussing the painter's art, the way Sickert creates tensions and harmonies between forms and colors and sweeps us into a world free from the difficulties of human life. They avoid discussing paintings in these terms, but they acknowledge the validity of the approach. When they begin to feel that they have pushed the parallel between painting and literature too far, they defend themselves:

> . . . for though they must part in the end, painting and writing have much to tell each other: they have much in common. The novelist after all wants to make us see. . . . And he must often think that to describe a scene is the worst way to show it. It must be done with one word, or with one word in skilful contrast with another. . . . It is a very complex business, the mixing and marrying of words that goes on, probably unconsciously, in the poet's mind to feed the reader's eye. All great writers are great colourists, just as they are musicians into the bargain; they always contrive to make their scenes glow and darken and change to the eye (CE II 241).

These speakers have begun to discuss, not the literary characteristics of Sickert's painting, but the ways in which literature incorporates some of the impact of the visual arts. Literary critics in an age of specialization, they agree, would do well to remember that "the arts are closely united." Returning once more to the paintings themselves and to their formal characteristics, they "admit that there is a great stretch of silent territory in Sickert's pictures," relationships between colors and lines that words cannot duplicate (CE II 242). Precisely because neither painters nor writers can explain these relationships in words, the two speakers "turn back to the sunny margin where the arts flirt and joke and pay each other compliments" (CE II 243). The fact that Sickert considers himself a "literary painter," however, vindicates them. One of the "hybrid" artists who are "always making raids into the lands of others" (CE II 243), he appeals to a diverse group of viewers like those gathered here. They agree that he is "probably the best painter now living in England" (CE II 244).

The cover of *Walter Sickert: A Conversation*, done in a more detailed, representational style than many of Vanessa Bell's others (Figure 2.10) is suitable for an essay in which Woolf recognizes the formal elements of Sickert's art but emphasizes its ability to evoke incident and character. The occasion of the conversation, the dinner, is suggested by a round table top; in the foreground is a napkin dropped into a heap shaped like a mountain with two peaks. These point upward, and a knife and a spoon direct the eye inward to a composition of stemmed glasses, a wine bottle, and a centerpiece of grapes on a plate with a pedestal. If Bell evokes the occasion for the conversation, she does not go so far as to include the participants. In the course of the conversation Woolf describes, the diners' meal is irrelevant; the discussion of Sickert's paintings and the criteria for responding to and evaluating them is the issue. But the table, empty of diners who have gone to fetch photographs of Sickert's paintings, interests Bell more than the talk. Her cover design balances the writer's concern with conversation and reasserts the supremacy of lines and shapes and their arrangements.

In her comments on the visual arts, including those on her sister and on Walter Sickert, Woolf always comes to a similar conclusion. Something in paintings she admires slips her net of words. She deals, therefore, with what she can encompass with her verbal skill, but she acknowledges and respects the silent realm her words cannot pene-

2.10. Vanessa Bell. Cover for *Walter Sickert: A Conversation* (London: Hogarth, 1934) by Virginia Woolf. Courtesy of the Bloomsbury Collection at Washington State University Libraries, Pullman, Washington; permission of the estate of Vanessa Bell and the Hogarth Press.

trate. That realm is the relief from too large doses of its opposite. "I think the art of painting is the art for ones old age," Woolf wrote to her sister in 1938. "I respect it more and more. I adore its severity; its bareness from impurity. All books are now rank with the slimy seaweed of politics; mouldy and mildewed" (L VI 294).

In her remarks at the opening of the Roger Fry Memorial Exhibition in 1935, Woolf once more declared herself a layperson and an outsider in the world of painters and art critics. This time, however, she was certain that her comments were appropriate. Fry, through his books and lectures as well as through the exhibitions he organized, brought art into the domain of the layperson. He made paintings "things we live with, and laugh at, love and discuss."[45] Just as Fry could explain painting to laypeople, including writers like Woolf, so Woolf wanted to explain writing to laypeople, including painters like her sister and Duncan Grant. In "Notes for Reading at Random" (1940), one of Woolf's last comments on the relationship between writing and painting, she contemplates such a work. In *Walter Sickert: A Conversation* a group of people, some with a verbal bias, grapple with painting. In the projected work, the focus would be literature:

> From Duncan & Vanessa yesterday I got this idea. A
> book explaining lit. from our common standpoint, to painters.
> This wd. then be the angle. [*Our*] It would begin
> from the writers angle..That is: we all feel
> the desire to create. The curiosity to know about
> others in the same condition. . . .
> The universality of the creative instinct . . .
> Stone, wool, words paint. discuss words.
> Always keep the writer in the foreground. . . .[46]

Woolf would define the basic link between painting and writing: creativity. In this context, she would use words to discuss not paint, but words themselves. Unfortunately, this counterpart to her earlier essay never materialized.

Virginia Woolf's essays on painting contain her assessment of her sister's visual medium. She deferred to Vanessa Bell's understanding of the visual arts and admired her sister's formal priorities and those of many other modern painters. At the same time she was as intrigued by the efforts of painters to tell stories in paint as she was by her own and other writers' attempts to capture visual beauty in words. And, when she wrote about painting, she found it easier to respond in words to the narrative dimension of a painting than she did to its formal excellence. Without Vanessa at her side or her work in front of her, Virginia sometimes viewed paintings as if they were dramas. Although she ultimately acknowledged the formal dimension, she did so only after having reacted to the paintings in question on her own terms.

Those terms are a writer's. In her introductions and essays, Woolf traces the mental processes, the catechisms of questions and answers, the imaginative flights by which a common viewer, but one with verbal biases and limitations, arrives at conclusions. Or, as in *Walter Sickert: A Conversation*, written at Vanessa's instigation and, in some ways, an imaginary interchange with her, Woolf embodies opposing approaches to a painter's work in dialogue form. The visual medium, which her sister and some of the other painters she knew defined as essentially free of the muddles of human psychology and relationships, is thus put back into the context most familiar to a writer like Woolf, that of a verbalizing human mind. Her own indecision is related to the elusiveness of human beings and to the self-deceptions and misunderstandings that comprise her fictional characters' experiences. Acknowledging both the formal and the literary qualities of painting, Woolf ultimately is most concerned with what a writer can derive from works of visual art and most comfortable with the areas where the two media overlap: painting and writing both sometimes suggest materials for characters and scenes but, more importantly, both arise from a desire to appeal to the eye and an even more fundamental impulse to create overall designs that communicate the moments of delight or truth that the artist experiences.

The "silence" that Virginia Woolf associates with painting has several meanings to her. Human silence causes her to wonder about what people think but intentionally do not say, as well as about sensations and emotions that seem to defy verbal expression. Since Woolf's medium is verbal, she must turn to images, usually visual ones, to embody such experiences. Like words and phrases, particular visual images can be overused. Yet visual images, even if expressed verbally, have another function. They provide Woolf and her characters with an alternate language, one that parallels the painter's. Vanessa Bell's paintings reveal nothing, either about people's inner lives and relationships or about herself. They suggest no stories, prompt no actions, provide no solutions to people's problems. Their silence is inhuman and chilling, and Woolf sometimes associates it with emptiness, loss, and death. She is also attracted by the silence of her sister's kind of painting, just as in her own work the confusions of individual psyches and human relationships alternate with perceptions of impersonal, transcendent realms. Vanessa's silent picture spaces are related not only to Virginia's interest in formal concerns; the objects, rooms, houses, and landscapes, as often as they are linked with people in the sisters' painting and writing, also outlast, dwarf, even obliterate individual pleasures and problems.

3

Criticism and Collaboration

THE SISTERS' RESPONSES TO EACH OTHER'S WORK

Careful to avoid infringing on her sister's rights as a visual artist, Virginia Woolf shrouded her raids on painting in all kinds of apologies and explanations. Consistently she deferred to or incorporated Vanessa Bell's judgments on the visual arts. At the same time, Woolf commented candidly on her sister's work, not just in the two published introductions to exhibitions discussed in the previous chapter but also, less formally, in letters. In most instances, Vanessa took Virginia's conclusions seriously, at least where her own paintings and decorative works were concerned. What emerges from an examination of each sister's informal reactions to the other art medium and its most beloved representative is not only personal and professional rivalry, but also varying degrees of respect, identification, sympathy, and stimulation. In Woolf's case especially there was an abiding fascination with the other medium and its methods. Surrounding herself with Vanessa's paintings and decorations, depending on her for advice and visual sustenance, Virginia manifested another variation of the child/mother relationship to her sister that some of her editors and biographers detect. Often Vanessa's paintings tempted Virginia to create similar works in words. Virginia's stories, which frequently had the same effect upon Vanessa, resulted in striking and appropriate illustrations.

At the same time that she was nourished by Vanessa and her art, Virginia accommodated them to the demands of what she considered her own more inclusive artistic medium. Vanessa, with a similar independence, adamantly applied her primary criterion for art, formal unity, to literature as well as to painting. She resented, however, any attempts to see in painting what she thought were peculiarly literary qualities, like suggestions of stories or characters. Because writers usually paid too little attention to the formal arrangements of the details that interested them, their works, in Vanessa's view, often did not measure up as art. Her responses were of great importance to Virginia as measures of her books' artistic success—perhaps, she sometimes thought, of too great importance. Aware of this fact, Vanessa was under considerable pressure when she had to respond to one of the novels. Whereas Virginia encouraged her sister to produce larger paintings, Vanessa, for a time at least, thought that Virginia's shorter pieces of writing were better than the longer ones. Each may have reacted to traditions in the other's medium, those that anticipated small, pretty paintings by women and long, fact-filled, intricately plotted novels by writers who were predominantly male. Virginia often moved from a formal reaction to the chilly, impersonal silence of her sister's paintings to a more emotional or verbal response; Vanessa's sequence of reactions to one of Virginia's novels often went in the opposite direction: from personal to aesthetic, subjective to objective. Vanessa was so familiar with her sister's materials and with her mind that she had trouble seeing Virginia's books as art. Over the years, however, she concluded that the intense psychological reality which so impressed her was the result of, not the substitute for, Virginia's artistic skill.

In spite of Virginia Woolf's many comments on the visual arts, including the formal introductions to her sister's exhibitions, she deprecated her ability to judge painting when she wrote to Vanessa Bell. "The worst of art," Virginia confessed to her sister in 1917, "is that it appeals solely to the aesthetic faculties, and one's extremely shy and snobbish about giving away ones deficiency or eccentricity about them" (L II 195). Possibly accepting and echoing some of her sister's own estimates, she criticized a "marmoreal chocolate box nymph"[1] Roger Fry had produced for a show and denounced the paintings of both Will Arnold-Forster and Augustus John (L II 469; III 312; IV 47). She also confessed her blunders, like telling Fry his paintings were "literary" or using works done a decade earlier as proof of his great progress as a painter (L II 195, III 340–41). When she did describe visual art works, she often added disclaimers like "I daresay I am saying all the wrong things" or "I see why you laugh at me for writing about painting" (L II 130; III 271). She was certain that Vanessa and Duncan mocked what she said about art; on one occasion she referred to "Duncans flickering adders tongue a-playing round my verbiage" and, on another, to Vanessa's "tooth and Duncans venom sweetly though it is exuded through a stalk of silver." Both, she said, "slightly inhibit my art criticism" (L III 490, 367, cf 499).

These inhibitions had some justification. Vanessa, well aware of her sister's derogatory remarks about painters, sometimes slighted Virginia's art criticism. Shortly after the Woolfs' marriage in 1912, Vanessa wrote to Leonard that she and Roger were painting indoors because of the weather. "How you would cackle at us," she added. "But you havent got the right jargon yet. Tell the Ape [Virginia] his criticisms are not worth notice. I handed them on to Roger who wasnt even amused."[2] Vanessa also wrote to Virginia from Paris that she had just read an article by her sister in the *Nation*. Roger Fry and Duncan Grant, she said, approved of it. Fry, in fact, "thinks it a great advantage to have art criticism written by those who know nothing about it." Vanessa personally "couldn't see any art criticism in it." Fry softened the tone of her comments with an appended note: "This isn't at all what I said but you can read between the lines & allow for Vanessa's artistic distortion."[3] Most of the time, though, Vanessa actively solicited and at least said she appreciated Virginia's comments on art in general and on her own work. "I'm very much pleased by your compliments," Vanessa wrote to her sister around 1914, apparently after having given her a painting. The reactions of people who are "sensitive to art in general," she said, are valuable. She wanted to know that people like Virginia responded to her paintings even though they might not be able to provide detailed analyses of their reactions: "I have a great respect for your judgement as to whether a thing is genuine or not so I hope you mean what you say because if so it gives me great satisfaction."[4]

A decade later Vanessa even wrote from Venice encouraging Virginia Woolf to write art criticism for the *Nation*. "I won't say you're infallible, though Duncan can tell you that . . . I ruminate again & again on your words & wonder if I should recast all my intentions regarding my art in consequence of them—but at least you would be readable."[5] She referred to a letter written six days earlier in which Virginia commented on the paintings her sister had in a London Artists' Association show. On the whole, Woolf was "hugely impressed." She singled out "a divinely lovely landscape . . . of Charleston: one of flashing brilliance, of sunlight crystallised, of diamond durability" as well as a painting of a bridge and a blue boat; she was critical, however, of a large painting "of Angelica etc. in the garden." Woolf thought her sister was defeated by "the problem of empty spaces, and how to model them. . . . There are flat passages, so that the design is not completely comprehended" (L III 270–71). Woolf had just completed Part II of *To the Lighthouse* (D III 88) and, although her struggles with Part III were several months in the future, her observations of her sister's work foreshadow Lily Briscoe's creative process. The scene Lily tries to paint without Mrs. Ramsey becomes "like curves and arabesques flourishing round a centre of complete emptiness" (TTL 266) until the "line there, in the centre" (TTL 310) finally solves her "problem of empty spaces." Virginia also had reservations about a painting Vanessa apparently had done from an "Aunt Julia photograph. It seems to me that when you muffle the singing quality of your tone, and reduce the variety and innumerability of colour . . . to bone, where the frame of the design is prominent, then, now and again, you falter, or somehow flatten" (L III 271).[6] So Lily Briscoe must hold to the "bright violet" and "staring white" she sees and not reproduce the "thinned and faded" tones of Paunceforte's work (TTL 31, 75). When Vanessa Bell replied that she pondered rethinking her artistic motives as a result of her sister's comments, Virginia answered with a typical disclaimer: "I'm much amused you should cast a days thought after my criticism—considering how it was fired off with my feet on the fender in 6 seconds precisely." Fearing too that she had not praised Vanessa's and Duncan's works highly enough, she wrote, "No pictures now painted give me so much pleasure" (L III 274–75).

Although Virginia thought Vanessa had difficulties with "design on a large scale," she still dubbed her "A mistress of the brush" (L III 271). A year later, in 1927, Woolf commented again on problems with overall structure in Bell's painting. This time she associated Vanessa's difficulties with her own: "I think we are now at the same point: both mistresses of our medium as never before: both therefore confronted with entirely new problems of structure." She now used literary (or musical) terminology to describe her sister as a painter, calling her not "mistress of the brush" or even of line or color, but "mistress of the phrase." "All your pictures," she added, "are built up of flying phrases." Woolf singled out a landscape in which "The downs seem to billow; yet the hay cart is perfectly substantial." She praised her sister's "lyricism," her "air of complete spontaneity," and her color. What she wanted to see, however, was "a large, large picture; where everything would be brought perfectly firmly together, yet all half flying off the canvas in rapture" (L III 340–41). Vanessa Bell replied that she was "very much flattered and interested" by her sister's comments. "I dont think I'm by any means 'Mistress of the phrase' as you say—But the large works you require are slowly being provided."[7]

In Angelica Garnett's opinion, the desire to do large works, a result of her mother's admiration for Duncan Grant, caused both uncertainty and "a bigger ratio of failures to successes."[8] Vanessa Bell's tendency to commit herself to projects that were too big may also have had to do with her sister's advice: "the large works you require." "Women," in Germaine Greer's words, "have always excelled in the production of the 'merely' beautiful, remarkable for fineness, elegance, small work taking up little space, much time in its making and no duration in its observation."[9] Working on a large scale requires the confident self-assertion of one who knows her works to be worthwhile and enduring or else does not care. In *To the Lighthouse* Lily Briscoe finally recognizes the importance of the creative process and dismisses the fate of her canvas: "It would be hung in attics, she thought; it would be destroyed. But what did that matter?" (TTL 309–10) Woolf wanted her sister to combine, with confidence, the beautiful with the grand just as, in her own medium, she devoted her greatest energies not to the short story but to the novel redefined in a similar inclusive fashion.

The other portion of Woolf's advice may also have been related to her concurrent work on Lily Briscoe in *To the Lighthouse.* The similarities between Lily's aesthetics and both Woolf's and Fry's are critical commonplaces, and rightly so. Lily says that she wants to embody both evanescence and permanence when she paints: "Beautiful and bright it should be on the surface, feathery and evanescent, one colour melting into another like the colours on a butterfly's wing; but beneath the fabric must be clamped together with bolts of iron. It was to be a thing you could ruffle with your breath; and a thing you could not dislodge with a team of horses" (TTL 255). Woolf does not associate this balance only with painting. "The thing about Proust," she noted in 1925, "is his combination of the utmost sensibility with the utmost tenacity. . . . He is as tough as catgut & as evanescent as a butterfly's bloom" (D III 7). Neither was the goal unfamiliar to Vanessa Bell. In about 1920 she wrote to Fry about the changes she and Duncan Grant had undergone since the first Post-Impressionist Exhibition. Then, their preoccupation with color often caused objects to disintegrate. Now she thought she could combine nuances of color with underlying structure and a sense of form and space.[10] In 1934 Fry praised one of Vanessa's paintings in these terms. "It's wonderful in its weighty quality—so dense so resistant and yet so delicate and subtle."[11] In 1938, Virginia did the same. Eleven years earlier she had defined the biographer's goal as a "perpetual marriage of granite and rainbow" (CE IV 235); now she called one of Vanessa's paintings "complete and entire, firm as marble and ravishing as a rainbow" (L VI 235–36).

Still, Woolf suspected that her comments on the visual arts were "all literary" (L III 483). As we have seen, paintings sometimes stimulated her as a writer to such an extent that she set aside the formal characteristics of the works she reviewed. In 1928, she wrote to her sister, "I am greatly tempted to write 'Variations on a Picture by Vanessa Bell' for Desmonds paper—I should run the three women and the pot of flowers on a chair into one phantasmagoria." Here Woolf admitted again her desire to write iconic prose; but she went further. She attributed to her sister some of the literary qualities she defined in Sickert's work. Not only is Bell "a most remarkable painter," she is also "a satirist, a conveyer of impressions about human life: a short story writer of great wit and able to bring off a situation in a way that rouses my envy. I wonder," she added, "if I could write the Three Women in prose . . ." (L III 498).

Vanessa began the Three Women painting, better known as *The Conversation* (Figure 3.1), in 1913 and reworked it in 1916.[12] The "situation" Woolf admires is three women conversing in front of a flower garden seen through a draped window. The essentially two-dimensional composition anticipates, in a general way, Woolf's use in *The Waves* of the circle as an image of human relationships. None of the women look out from Bell's painting; they look intently at each others' faces, which form a semicircle. The curved lines of their arms, shoulders, and backs as well as the hands of the woman who is speaking lead the eye into the center. Contrasting sharply with the dark colors of the women's dresses, the bright colors of flowers and grass surround the profile of the woman who is speaking. Spalding sees the colorful circular garden as "the visual equivalent to the animated chatter of the three women."[13]

Virginia tried her own hand at being "a satirist, a conveyer of

3.1. Vanessa Bell. *The Conversation*, c. 1917–18. Permission of the Courtauld Institute Galleries, London (Fry Collection).

impressions about human life: a short story writer of great wit." In October of 1919 she said she intended to send Vanessa some stories she had completed and wanted illustrated (L II 393). A year later Virginia reported that she had the title for a volume, *Monday or*

Tuesday (L II 445). The collection appeared in 1921. Both the story, "A Society," and Vanessa Bell's woodcut illustration for it, are closely related to *The Conversation*. The sisters reproduce, each in her own medium, the intimacy of the women, their complete absorption in their discussion, their monumentality, and the unity of the design.

In his Foreword, Leonard Woolf indicates that Virginia chose to omit "A Society" from *A Haunted House*, the volume of her stories they were planning at the time of her death. One reason, perhaps, is its length. Or the Woolfs may have concluded, with Virginia's imaginary *Times* reviewer, that it was "too one sided" (D II 98).[14] One of her more polemical stories, it treats issues similar to those taken up again in *A Room of One's Own* and *Three Guineas*. The story depicts women who, one day at tea, turn from praising men and anticipating marriage to assessing their own goals. They had planned to produce good children, as they had always done, assuming that men would produce good books and continue to civilize the world. A glance at some of the books, however, makes the women decide to form "a society for asking questions." They vow to produce no more children until they are sure that men are keeping their part of the bargain. By methods reminiscent of the Dreadnought Hoax,[15] the women infiltrate the universities, the military, the courts, the Royal Academy, and the concert halls and theaters. Unable to conclude whether men's scientific achievements outweigh their economic and political failures, the women turn to the arts. Again the discussion is inconclusive. After the war, the narrator and one of the other women glance through the minute books of the society. Men's intellect has been their ruin, they decide, but women who have sacrificed everything to foster masculine intelligence are to blame for the proud and condescending creatures they have produced. Men ought to be kept busy with children instead of with their minds, and women ought to be taught to believe not in men but in themselves.

Vanessa Bell portrays some of the women whose observations are the focus of her sister's story (Figure 3.2). This story must have reminded Vanessa of her earlier painting, because again she communicates the women's centrality and cooperation by constructing a semicircle of three faces. Although this time we see little more than the faces, here too the women look intently at each other and draw our eyes into the center of the composition. In the lower center is a stack of books, the manmade objects under scrutiny or perhaps the society's own records; their spines again lead our eyes into the center.

3.2. Vanessa Bell. Illustration for "A Society" in *Monday or Tuesday* (London: Hogarth 1921) by Virginia Woolf. Courtesy of the Bloomsbury Collection at Washington State University Libraries, Pullman, Washington; permission of the estate of Vanessa Bell and the Hogarth Press.

With its bold, simple strokes, the two-dimensional design for "A Society" communicates the serious and thoughtful social criticism at the basis of Woolf's fanciful piece.

"Isn't it odd?" Virginia Woolf wrote to Vanessa Bell in 1927, "perhaps you stimulate the literary sense in me as you say I do your painting sense." She referred to a story about some giant moths at Cassis that Vanessa had told her; Virginia felt compelled to write about it and the story eventually became "The Moths," then *The Waves* (L III 372). Vanessa apparently had a similar effect upon Virginia on social occasions. Roger Fry wrote to Vanessa in 1928 that he wished she were going to be present when he and the Woolfs were scheduled to meet, because Vanessa prompted Virginia to her greatest imaginative flights.[16]

Vanessa Bell's decorative art work also intrigued Virginia Woolf. An interchange occurred in 1918 which proved that Woolf wanted to do more than write variations on her sister's works. Virginia wrote to say that she wanted to describe her feelings about one of Vanessa's paintings; it not only gave her much enjoyment but also altered her "views upon aesthetics" (L II 256). The painting was *The Madonna Lily*, painted in 1915 (Figure 3.3).[17] In two subsequent letters, Vanessa asked her sister to elaborate on these reactions: "I am longing to hear them & it will be too tantalizing if you dont."[18] Virginia finally satisfied her sister's curiosity. She related how she had become increasingly irritated by a chair covered in yellow checks and how Vanessa's picture of "the vase and the long flower. . . . so cool, so harmonious, so exquisitely tinted" caused her to reexamine the relationship between the painting and everything in the room. The results were a series of attempts to cover the chair and considerable perplexity about the significance for her creativity of the whole process: "I came to the conclusion that there is a quality in your picture which though perceptible is at present much beyond me, but that in the main my aesthetic feelings are so undeveloped that I had better begin at the very beginning. But do you think that this semiconscious process of coming to dislike one colour very much and liking a picture better and better points to some sort of live instinct trying to come to existence? I humbly hope so" (L II 259).

Although Virginia Woolf gained some confidence in her abilities to arrange a room as a result of this episode, she consistently represented herself to Vanessa Bell as an inferior decorator. When her sister and Duncan Grant stayed at Monks House in 1923, Woolf

3.3. Vanessa Bell. *The Madonna Lily*, 1915. Private collection. Courtesy of the Anthony d'Offay Gallery, London. Permission of Angelica Garnett.

wrote to ask if the house was "inferior to Charleston" and imagined her guests calling the decorations "ridiculous" (L III 27). Virginia observed Vanessa's decorative projects with interest. In 1933, for example, she went to *Pomona*, a ballet for which her sister had done both costumes and sets, "all very pale & bright—I mean Fra Angelico against a background of Cassis" (D IV 144). She also constantly asked for advice from Vanessa and Duncan about colors, fabrics, and positions for paintings. Frequently she commissioned them to paint panels and to create designs for wallpapers and chair cushions, tiles and furniture, carpets, lampshades, and pottery. In 1927, she wrote to Vanessa that she had "several problems" awaiting her: "I have my own ideas, and my own taste, but its all ineradicably bad" (L III 381). In 1932 a guarantee of money from Virginia for an exhibition of Bell's and Grant's "Music Room" decorations at the Lefevre Gallery yielded a carpet and a mirror framed with an embroidered design by Grant as well as a painted screen by Bell (D VI 131).

These discussions of interior design problems, projects, and purchases had several results. Woolf could encourage her sister and reduce their rivalry by deferring to her superior abilities. In addition, although Vanessa would not always accept payment, Virginia could occasionally help out the larger family. She could also have around her tangible reminders of her sister and her sometimes enviable way of life. "My rooms are all vast panels of moonrises and prima donna's bouquets—the work of Vanessa & Duncan Grant," she wrote proudly to Janet Case in 1924 (L III 97). Later Vanessa provided portraits of her children. Finally, all the discussion these exchanges entailed kept Vanessa's attention turned in her sister's direction.

As Vanessa's paintings and letters tempted Virginia to generate everything from informal remarks to entire works of fiction, so Virginia's writing stimulated Vanessa's creativity. In 1939, for example, she described her reaction to one of Virginia's stories: ". . . it seems to me lovely—only too full of suggestions for pictures almost. They leap into my mind at every turn. Your writing always does that for me to some extent, but I think this one more than usual. I fear I should come a cropper by comparison. I could hardly help doing illustrations."[19] Since Vanessa asks how "Ivimey" is pronounced, the story must be "The Searchlight," unpublished until *The*

Haunted House came out in 1944. It is an intensely visual story. Mrs. Ivimey, standing on a balcony with friends as the airforce searchlights scan the night sky, recalls what she says is the story of her great-grandfather. From a crumbling old tower, he first spied through a telescope her great-grand-mother-to-be wearing "something blue on her head" and kissing a man who, like Mrs. Ivimey herself, remains a mystery. Woolf was delighted with her sister's approval, declared Vanessa "the only person in the world whose opinion can help me," and enjoined her to paint from models and to produce a picture for her.[20] Instead of an illustration for "The Searchlight," Vanessa gave Virginia the painting of Quentin with a book still hanging at Monks House (L VI 381, n. 3).

Vanessa Bell's desire to respond visually to Virginia's works did result in illustrations to several of the shorter pieces of fiction: *Kew Gardens*, "The Mark on the Wall," and four of the stories in *Monday or Tuesday*; Vanessa also illustrated *Flush*. With some exceptions, critics slight Woolf's short works, dismiss them as early experiments that prepared the way for the major novels, or treat them as respites from more serious work. They neglect Vanessa Bell's illustrations almost entirely. The same is true of the cover or dust-jacket designs she provided for most of her sister's other books. While some of the designs appear in books on Woolf or in exhibitions of Bell's art, they are rarely discussed.[21] Like the short stories and *Flush* in the context of Woolf's work as a whole, art historians judge Bell's illustrations and dust-jacket designs to be less significant than her painting and decorative art work. But these works form another nexus in the relationship between the sisters and their art media.

A book illustrator who knew her mother's family and whose work appealed to Vanessa while she was growing up was Frederick Walker. His realistic yet sentimental illustrations appeared in *The Cornhill Magazine*, well represented on Leslie Stephen's bookshelves, and in Anne Thackeray Ritchie's novel *The Village on the Cliff* (Figure 3.4). To "Aunt Anny," Walker seemed able to reproduce exactly what she had imagined. So in *To the Lighthouse* Mr. Ramsay, based on Leslie Stephen, looks "at his wife and son in the window" and sees them "as an illustration, a confirmation of something on the printed page to which one returns, fortified, and satisfied" (TTL 52-53). But just as Lily Briscoe justifies treating this scene in quite another fashion, so Vanessa in a letter to Virginia used Walker and his kind of illustration as an example of the bad taste she had had to get rid

3.4. Frederick Walker. *A "Vacarme."* One of six illustrations for *The Village on the Cliff* (London: Smith, Elder, 1867) by Anne Thackeray Ritchie. Courtesy of the Library of Leonard and Virginia Woolf at Washington State University Libraries, Pullman, Washington.

of.[22] Fry's views were closer to her own. "It seems to me," he wrote in 1927,

> that real illustration in the sense of reinforcing the author's verbal expression by an identical graphic expression is quite impossible. But it may be possible to embroider the author's ideas or rather to execute variations on the author's theme which will not pretend to be one with the text, but rather, as it were, a running commentary, like marginal notes written by a reader. . . . And of all such marginal commentators the draughtsman is

> the most discreet, for he is inaudible, he never puts an actual word into your head which might get confused with the words of the author. He merely starts a vague train of thought by the image which he puts before you in one of those pauses which the author's discursiveness allows.[23]

Henri Matisse, whom Vanessa Bell first met in 1914,[24] had similar views. The illustrator does not complete the text unless it is "inadequate. . . . Writers have no need of painters to explain what they want to say," he insisted. "They should have enough resources of their own to express themselves."[25] The illustrator is subordinate, even unnecessary to a good text, just as a title is unnecessary to a good painting. Illustrations, however, can provide an intriguing, noncompetitive dimension to the reading experience. They can, in their own ways, embellish and ring variations on the writer's words and thoughts.

Fry and Matisse put into words a problem Vanessa Bell had to confront. She generally agreed that text and illustration are not equivalent; they need not even be closely related. In practice, she reveals a sensitivity, conscious or unconscious, to her sister's experiments with point of view. She prefers a few appropriate and versatile images, like flowers and windows, to human figures, yet her apparently simple arrangements of recognizable objects, abstract shapes, lines, and colors convey the fundamental psychological oppositions Woolf, too, tries to harmonize in her writing. A close examination of some of the designs and of their final relation to the texts also reveals the perennial tensions between the sisters and their sister arts. Fruitful collaboration is combined on occasion with subtle and not-so-subtle competitiveness and artistic self-assertion.

Kew Gardens is a good early example of the professional interchange between the two sisters and their art media. Leonard Woolf rightly called this story "a microcosm of all . . . [Virginia's] then unwritten novels,"[26] but she thought it "vague . . . slight & short" (D I 271), "a case of atmosphere" that was not quite a success. Nevertheless, in 1918 she sent a copy to her sister and asked for both criticism and a title page design (L II 257). Vanessa Bell replied that, although she recognized some of the dialogue, she liked the story very much and would be glad to do a drawing for it. She cautioned Woolf that the design might be somewhat remote from the text, but added that she did not consider a close relationship important. The moment in the story which stimulated her visually, she indicated, was the third of the four conversations overheard in the garden. It is between two "elderly women of the lower middle class, one stout and ponderous, the other rosy cheeked and nimble"; their "very complicated dialogue" about people concludes with the repetition of the word, "sugar." The heavy woman, losing interest, stares at the flower bed. This time Vanessa Bell specifically mentions her own painting of three women conversing in front of a window that looks out upon a flower bed (Figure 3.1). Although *The Conversation* would not have served, in any traditional sense, as an illustration, Vanessa still felt that the two scenes were, in essence, the same.[27] Virginia replied that she did not think it mattered whether the illustration was "about the story or not" (L II 258).

The woodcut Vanessa Bell created is closely related, in one important sense, to the story. Within a framework of floral description Woolf juxtaposes the conversations of the people and the observations of a snail in the flower bed. In the conversations themselves, the natural world plays an important role: it triggers memories and provides symbols for difficult-to-express emotional states. In her two-dimensional design, Vanessa Bell reflects this interpenetration of human and natural worlds (Figure 3.5). She also follows the text more closely than her remarks anticipate. The woodcut depicts, from the waists up, a thin woman who looks at a heavy one who looks away. The alternating areas of dark and light that delineate them blend into equally prominent areas of dark and light that recreate the flower bed between and above them. In fact, the lines of the thin woman's hat also form the edge of the flower bed and, in a kind of visual pun, the flowers may be either in the garden or on the hats. In this design, which serves as the frontispiece, Bell suggests not just a specific scene, but an essential theme of the story as a whole.

A scene in *The Voyage Out* resembles this woodcut. Helen, a character with some of Vanessa's traits, observes Hirst's "worried and garrulous" face against "the background of flowering magnolia," flowers which are "so smooth and inarticulate." The shapes of the flowers, leaves, and shade which register upon her mind "half-consciously . . . become part of their talk" (VO 208–9). In *Kew Gardens*, *The Voyage Out*, *The Conversation*, and the frontispiece for *Kew Gardens*, then, the lines between words and visual images, humankind and nature, are blurred. Both sisters give talk a visual dimension.

Woolf praised her sister's *Kew Gardens* design; it is "just in the

3.5. Vanessa Bell. Frontispiece for *Kew Gardens* (London: Hogarth, 1919) by Virginia Woolf. Courtesy of the Bloomsbury Collection at Washington State University Libraries, Pullman, Washington; permission of the estate of Vanessa Bell and the Hogarth Press.

mood I wanted," she said, and "extremely decorative" besides (L II 259). She used the word "decorative," common among the painters involved for several years with interior design through the Omega Workshop, in a complimentary sense. She also used it self-consciously: "You see my language is already tainted," she teased, presumably with terms from the visual arts. Bell, pleased with her sister's approval, indicated that she was working on another design for the story. Although she did not admit to doing so, she also used "tainted" language. She was worried that her design might be "too incoherent" and sent Woolf a revision which she considered less so.[28]

The woodcut discussed in this interchange became the endpiece for the book (Figure 3.6). It is related to the text in a more general way than the frontispiece. The story mentions butterflies, a dragonfly, and a snail; the woodcut includes an earlier stage of the butterfly, a caterpillar, as well as an insect with wings and feelers. If, in her frontispiece, Bell introduces the relationship between humankind and the natural world, in her endpiece she depicts only the life lived at the base of the flower stems and blades of grass. She emphasizes, whether intentionally or not, one of her sister's experiments with point of view: Woolf moves from what the snail "appeared" to be considering and struggling to achieve to the snail's motives, without the filter of a speculative human being. Again Woolf liked the design: "I think the book will be a great success—owing to you:" she said, "and my vision comes out much as I had it, so I suppose, in spite of everything, God made our brains upon the same lines, leaving out 2 or 3 pieces in mine" (L II 289).

Collaboration on *Kew Gardens* required a frequent exchange of letters in which each sister approved and supported the other's work; both felt that they were communicating a similar vision in two different but complementary media. This fruitful interaction, however, threatened to break down in June 1919. Vanessa Bell, disappointed over the quality of the printing of *Kew Gardens*, said she would illustrate no more of Woolf's work. She "went so far," Woolf noted in her diary, "as to doubt the value of the Hogarth Press altogether" and to suggest that an "ordinary printer" could have done the job better. Woolf, "stung & chilled" and "crumpled" (D I 279), made every effort, when a second run of the book became necessary, to give her sister more control over the type and designs. She engaged an "ordinary printer" and wanted Vanessa either to instruct him or approve someone to do so (L II 364–66). But the printer threatened

3.6. Vanessa Bell. Endpiece for *Kew Gardens* (London: Hogarth, 1919) by Virginia Woolf. Courtesy of the Bloomsbury Collection at Washington State University Libraries, Pullman, Washington; permission of the estate of Vanessa Bell and the Hogarth Press.

to charge more if he had to await instructions, so apparently the second edition was done without Vanessa Bell's suggestions. Woolf also reported to her sister that the printer "cut *all* the covers crooked." "A professional printer," she told her, "isn't necessarily infallible as you seem to think" (L II 369).

This altercation was not the first. In 1917 Virginia had suggested to Vanessa that she and Duncan do a series of woodcuts to be published in book form by the Hogarth Press; some difficulties they had had with printing Carrington's woodcuts in their first publication should be solved, Virginia said, by a new machine they had ordered (L II 168). Vanessa, who had asked Roger Fry to contribute some woodcuts to the project, cautioned him to wait before doing the actual cutting of the designs since she was still negotiating with Leonard and Virginia. Vanessa wanted a contract giving her decision-making power over all visual aspects of the book; she would take into account, of course, the Woolfs' budget. Virginia, however, thought such a contract unnecessary, and Leonard would not agree to it. Vanessa reported to Roger that Leonard considered his abilities to make decisions on such matters equal to hers. At this point Virginia, uncomfortable with Leonard's preferences, offered an alternate plan.[29] She suggested that the woodcuts be printed on separate sheets rather than in book form. Then buyers could order any combination or number of each print and hang individual ones on their walls. The prints would also be easier and less expensive for the press to produce than a book would be. Because Vanessa liked the book idea better, neither plan was carried out (L II 178–79).

Virginia also suggested in 1918 that Vanessa do a woodcut for the cover of *Kew Gardens*, a design that again need not have "reference to the story" and that could be used, with a change of title, for subsequent publications. Such a design would be "a tremendous draw," Woolf said (L II 298). Bell's cover finally appeared on a third edition in 1927 (Figure 3.7). The design is roughly symmetrical with curved lines emphasized by stippling in contrasting colors. Although ultimately abstract, various portions suggest an urn, clouds, or vegetation. Within the design, the printing subordinates Vanessa's work to her sister's: "KEW GARDENS" is at the top in the largest letters, "VIRGINIA WOOLF" is in smaller ones, and, at the bottom of the page, "DECORATIONS BY VANESSA BELL" and "THE HOGARTH PRESS" are in the smallest.

In addition to the cover, Bell did twenty-one page designs. Little correspondence remains concerning this edition. It may have been the result of a letter Vanessa wrote to Virginia from Cassis in February of 1927. In it she said that, since she often spent her evenings alone, she would have time to illustrate a story if Virginia would send her one.[30] Virginia, Leonard, or both must have given Vanessa some indication of what part of the text would be on each page since the portions are relatively self-contained. In only one instance does a sentence run from one page onto the next and then there is a natural break; whenever possible the text is broken in

3.7. Vanessa Bell. Cover design for *Kew Gardens* (London: Hogarth, 1927) by Virginia Woolf. Courtesy of the Bloomsbury Collection at Washington State University Libraries, Pullman, Washington; permission of the estate of Vanessa Bell and the Hogarth Press.

strategic places, between descriptions or dialogues. Bell must have produced her designs for these textual units, and then Herbert Reiach, the London printer who did the actual printing and engraving, set the type within each design. If this was the procedure, Vanessa would have known what portion of the text she was illustrating as well as its length, but not exactly how her design would look with the words on the page. Indeed, the text was not always placed in relation to the design very effectively; the writing sometimes fills only half the page, leaving empty space below, or else short lines of dialogue leave space at the right. The printer may have had instructions from Bell or from one or both of the Woolfs. We do know that Vanessa discussed the proofs with Leonard (L III 426), but by then the type would have been set. Otherwise the published and unpublished letters between Bell and the Woolfs do not indicate their exact methods.

Vanessa Bell often worked hard to achieve an appearance of spontaneity and freedom, especially towards the end of *Kew Gardens*.[31] To look at the designs for the book, therefore, is not to seek technical virtuosity and verisimilitude, but to observe the ways in which they are sensitive and vital responses in a visual medium to portions of Woolf's text or to perceptual experiences similar to those Woolf describes. The result is often striking. On half of the pages, the format is relatively consistent: justified left margins and uneven right ones. On the other half, all sorts of variations exist, from blocks of lines arranged to form steps at the top and pedestals at the bottom, to diagonals and curves.[32] Vanessa Bell's visual "running commentary" complements this text in a variety of ways. No longer limited to frontispiece and endpiece, she creates designs even less representational and more spontaneous in their appearance than the earlier woodcuts. Sometimes she decorates the edges of the pages with circles, cross-hatching, stippling, or wiggly lines, some of which have no discernible relationship to the text. About two-thirds of these border designs are roughly symmetrical, but the rest are strikingly asymmetrical, usually to emphasize references to motion, tension, or confusion in the story. Most of Vanessa Bell's designs do relate to the writing by providing simplified visual suggestions of images Woolf introduces on the same page, but in no way is any design a literal translation of the writing into visual terms. Bell, however, continues to reinforce the experiments with point of view in Woolf's story. In the text, human and natural worlds mingle, but in Bell's designs, no people appear. Although a few images suggest objects produced by human hands, most are drawn in such a way that they might be confused with vegetative forms.

In significant instances, trees, flowers, and grasses surround and dwarf the text. The design on the first page, for example, provides simplified visual suggestions of the "heart-shaped or tongue-shaped leaves" and the flower petals Woolf describes (Figure 3.8). In a black-and-white medium, Vanessa Bell cannot use the primary colors her sister mentions in the text, but she can include the "straight bar, . . . slightly clubbed at the end" which projects from the throat of the flower. Larger and darker than the writing, the design dominates this page and the seventh, which describes the snail moving in the flower-bed (Figure 3.9).[33] Vanessa draws neither the snail nor the insect that crosses its path but, rather, the tangle of plant growth the snail sees. Similarly, the thirteenth design, a second response to the passage about the two women, depicts dominant vegetative forms (Figure 3.10). While the two women do not appear this time, the artist suggests visually one woman's state of mind. She stares at the flowers, Woolf says, like a sleeper who, waking, "sees a brass candlestick reflecting the light in an unfamiliar way" and is prompted to look at it again and then to study it. Bell depicts a flower, not the candlestick, but she invests it with a similar significance. Defying the conventional rules of illustration, the flower forces its way through the words on the page.[34] Although both artists are concerned with perception, then, Woolf depicts the perceiver and the act of perception, while Bell asserts, through the size, darkness, and relationship of image to text, the importance of the objects perceived.[35]

Even though none of the people Woolf mentions in the text appear in Bell's designs, she does suggest their qualities or states of mind in subtle, possibly unintentional ways. When, on the ninth page, the couple passing the flower bed consists of two men, the flowing vegetative forms give way to suggestions of rigidity and formality (Figure 3.11). The vertical lines on either side of the text might be read as classical columns and arches with heavy black accents above and below. The reference to the ancients by the elder man on the next page or the couple's traditional education and masculinity may have prompted the columns. The vertical lines also suggest pleated theater curtains with a row of footlights beneath.[36] In this case, the design may evoke the public, formal dimension of men's lives or the sometimes melodramatic roles they are required to

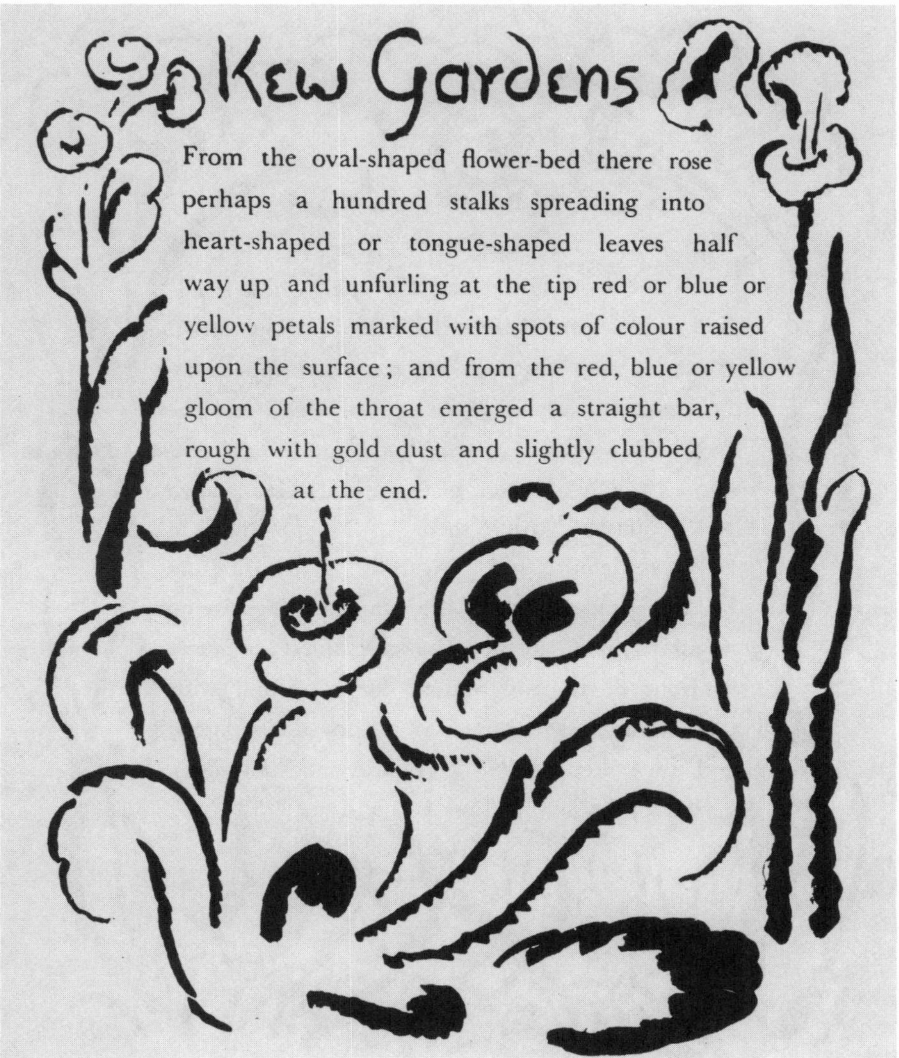

3.8. Vanessa Bell. Illustrated page 1 of *Kew Gardens* (London: Hogarth, 1927) by Virginia Woolf. Courtesy of the Bloomsbury Collection at Washington State University Libraries, Pullman, Washington; permission of the estate of Vanessa Bell and the Hogarth Press.

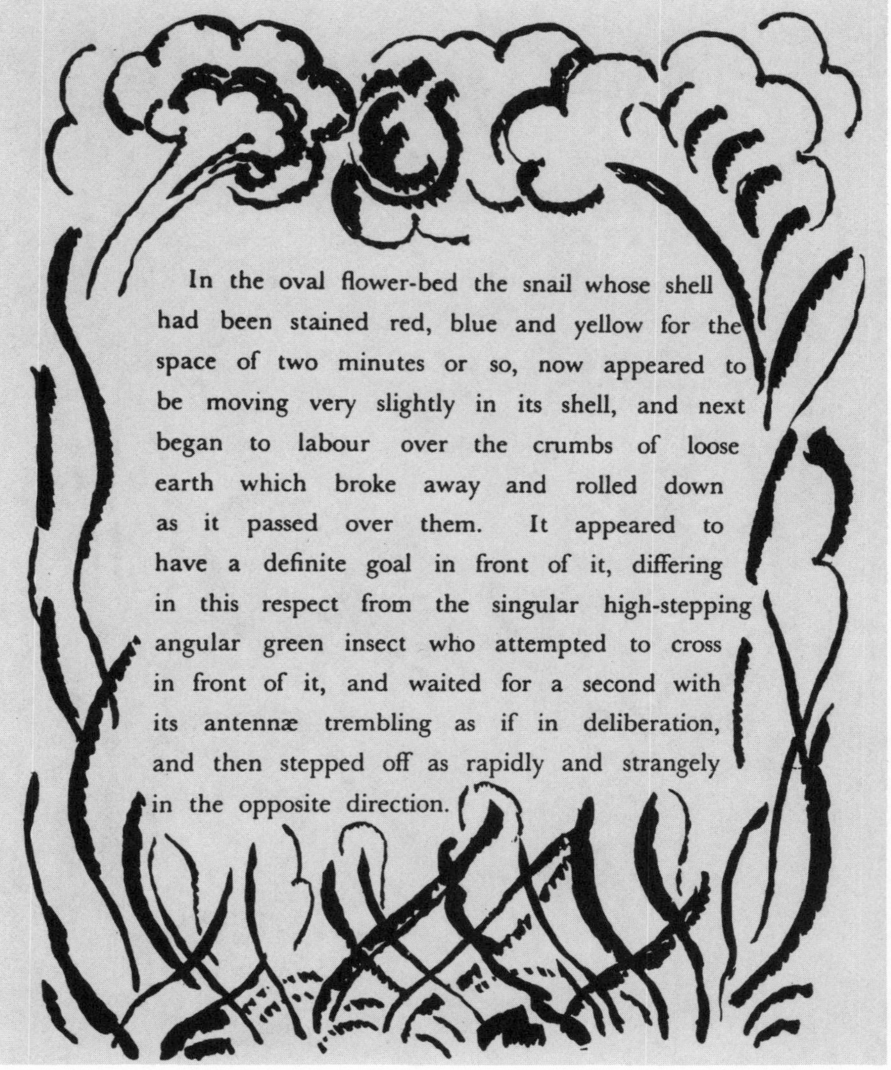
In the oval flower-bed the snail whose shell had been stained red, blue and yellow for the space of two minutes or so, now appeared to be moving very slightly in its shell, and next began to labour over the crumbs of loose earth which broke away and rolled down as it passed over them. It appeared to have a definite goal in front of it, differing in this respect from the singular high-stepping angular green insect who attempted to cross in front of it, and waited for a second with its antennæ trembling as if in deliberation, and then stepped off as rapidly and strangely in the opposite direction.

3.9. Vanessa Bell. Illustrated page 7 of *Kew Gardens* (London: Hogarth, 1927) by Virginia Woolf. Courtesy of the Bloomsbury Collection at Washington State University Libraries, Pullman, Washington; permission of the estate of Vanessa Bell and the Hogarth Press.

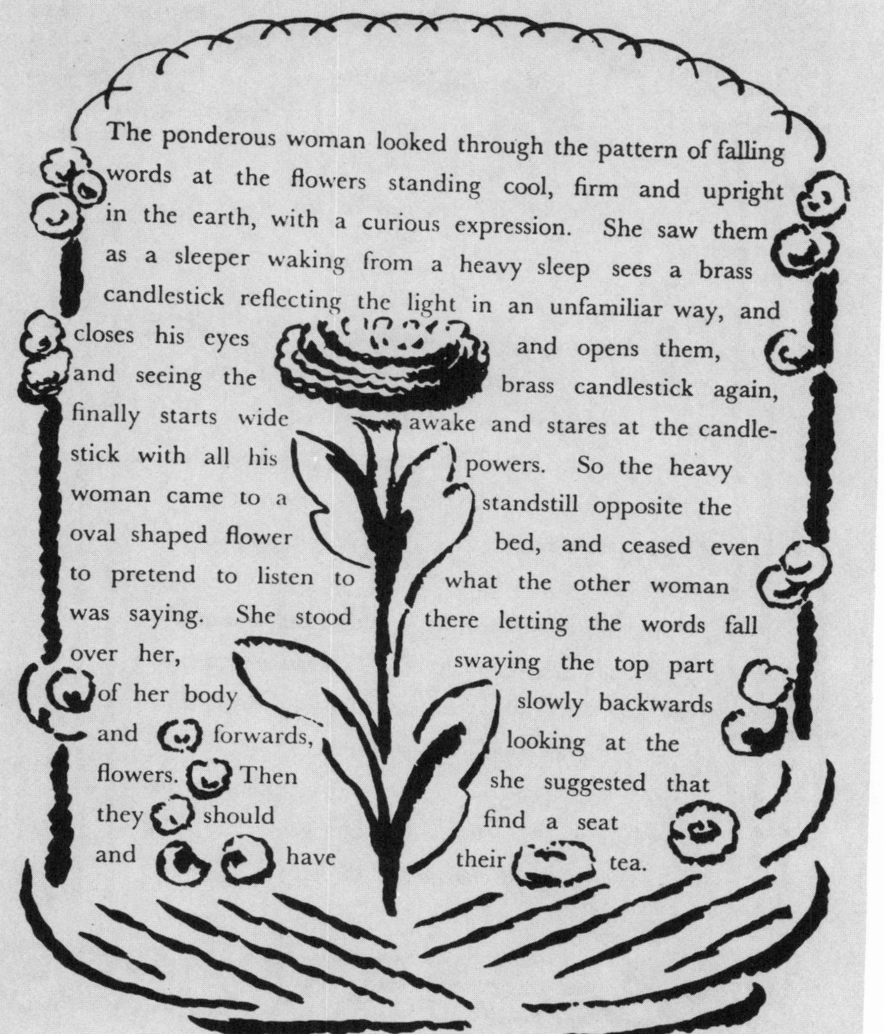

The ponderous woman looked through the pattern of falling words at the flowers standing cool, firm and upright in the earth, with a curious expression. She saw them as a sleeper waking from a heavy sleep sees a brass candlestick reflecting the light in an unfamiliar way, and closes his eyes and opens them, and seeing the brass candlestick again, finally starts wide awake and stares at the candlestick with all his powers. So the heavy woman came to a standstill opposite the oval shaped flower bed, and ceased even to pretend to listen to what the other woman was saying. She stood there letting the words fall over her, swaying the top part of her body slowly backwards and forwards, looking at the flowers. Then she suggested that they should find a seat and have their tea.

3.10. Vanessa Bell. Illustrated page 13 of *Kew Gardens* (London: Hogarth, 1927) by Virginia Woolf. Courtesy of the Bloomsbury Collection at Washington State University Libraries, Pullman, Washington; permission of the estate of Vanessa Bell and the Hogarth Press.

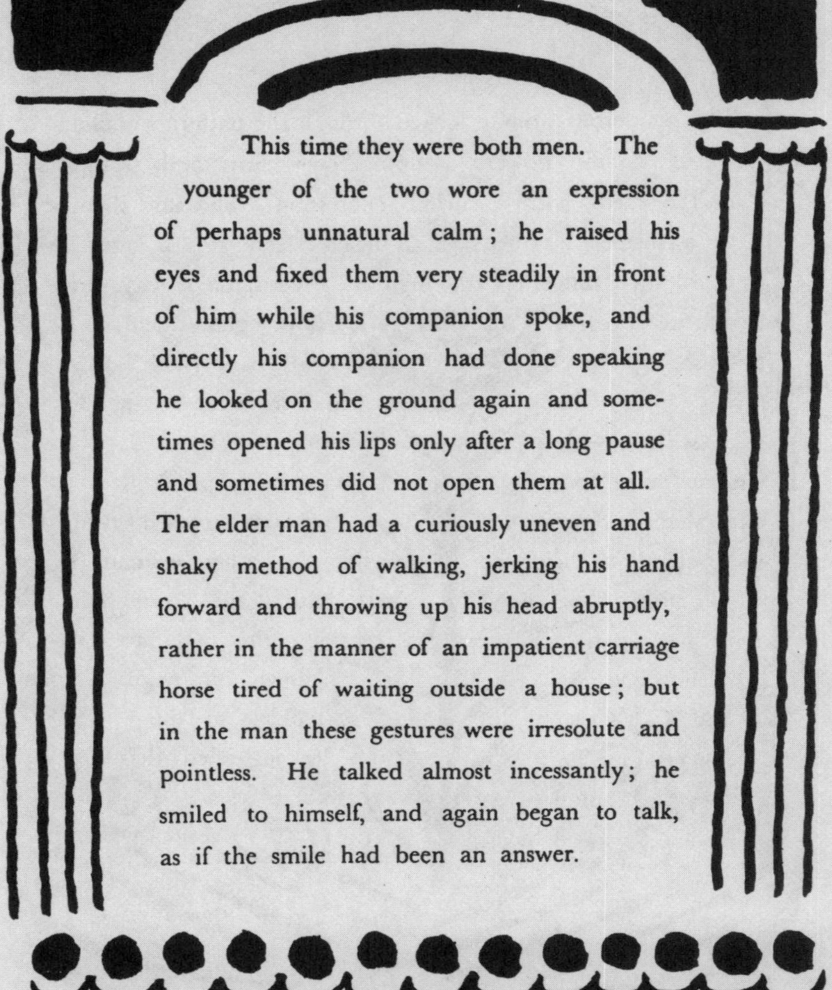
This time they were both men. The younger of the two wore an expression of perhaps unnatural calm; he raised his eyes and fixed them very steadily in front of him while his companion spoke, and directly his companion had done speaking he looked on the ground again and sometimes opened his lips only after a long pause and sometimes did not open them at all. The elder man had a curiously uneven and shaky method of walking, jerking his hand forward and throwing up his head abruptly, rather in the manner of an impatient carriage horse tired of waiting outside a house; but in the man these gestures were irresolute and pointless. He talked almost incessantly; he smiled to himself, and again began to talk, as if the smile had been an answer.

3.11. Vanessa Bell. Illustrated page 9 of *Kew Gardens* (London: Hogarth, 1927) by Virginia Woolf. Courtesy of the Bloomsbury Collection at Washington State University Libraries, Pullman, Washington; permission of the estate of Vanessa Bell and the Hogarth Press.

play. In either case, the general symmetry and rigidity of the design communicates stereotypical masculine characteristics. As the older man's confused thoughts turn to "the forests of Uruguay," beautiful women, and the sea, however, the vegetative, asymmetrical designs return (Figure 3.12).

When the couple consists of the two women, Vanessa Bell draws what look like intertwined tree trunks, curving lines that encircle space (Figure 3.13). This design, like the flower that dominates the page, indicates that Vanessa, like Virginia, knew the artists with dual creative abilities. At least she knew and sometimes echoed the work of William Blake (Figure 3.14).[37] The designs for the two couples, juxtaposed, suggest in a general way the male-female dichotomies which interest Woolf and form the basis of much of her writing. Appropriately, the design that introduces a young, unformed couple, who are compared to buds or butterflies with wings still wet from the cocoon, is neutral or androgynous. It is a combination of intersecting straight lines with loops and arches and a single flower shape.[38]

Sometimes the thoughts and words of the people in Woolf's text become lines and shapes which suggest motion or stasis. In the fourth design, for example, the male half of the first couple remembers his certainty that if a circling dragonfly settled on a particular leaf, "the broad one with the red flower in the middle of it," the woman with him would accept his proposal (Figure 3.15). Instead of the conventional, tender scene between a man and a woman in a garden or the active-passive, projectile-receptacle, male-female dichotomies the man's imagery implies, Bell uses asymmetrical arching and circling lines that suggest wings and flight. She draws two spiral vortices, one purely linear, relating to the motion of the circling dragonfly, the other suggesting the petals of the flower upon the leaf. The following plate, again asymmetrical, concludes the man's memory and includes his wife's enigmatic observation that memories always occur "in a garden with men and women lying under the trees," people who are, in her mind, the ghosts of the past, "all that remains of . . . one's happiness, one's reality" (Figure 3.16). In a few heavy lines, Bell sketches a tree trunk with two horizontal branches that divide groups of lines, again as in Blake's work. At the bottom of the page are three more black horizontal lines which balance those of the branches above and parallel the reference to people lying beneath the trees. To Bell this part of the text, with its comments on past and present and

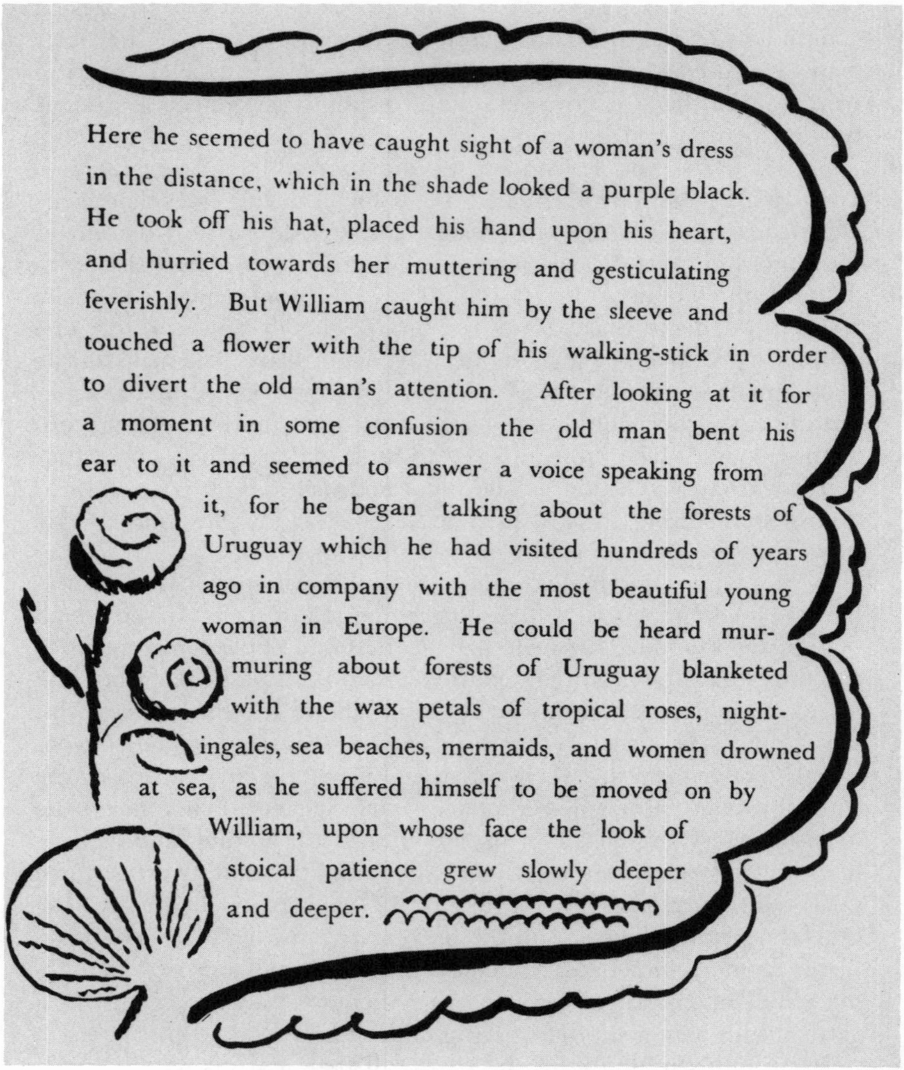

Here he seemed to have caught sight of a woman's dress in the distance, which in the shade looked a purple black. He took off his hat, placed his hand upon his heart, and hurried towards her muttering and gesticulating feverishly. But William caught him by the sleeve and touched a flower with the tip of his walking-stick in order to divert the old man's attention. After looking at it for a moment in some confusion the old man bent his ear to it and seemed to answer a voice speaking from it, for he began talking about the forests of Uruguay which he had visited hundreds of years ago in company with the most beautiful young woman in Europe. He could be heard murmuring about forests of Uruguay blanketed with the wax petals of tropical roses, nightingales, sea beaches, mermaids, and women drowned at sea, as he suffered himself to be moved on by William, upon whose face the look of stoical patience grew slowly deeper and deeper.

3.12. Vanessa Bell. Illustrated page 11 of *Kew Gardens* (London: Hogarth, 1927) by Virginia Woolf. Courtesy of the Bloomsbury Collection at Washington State University Libraries, Pullman, Washington; permission of the estate of Vanessa Bell and the Hogarth Press.

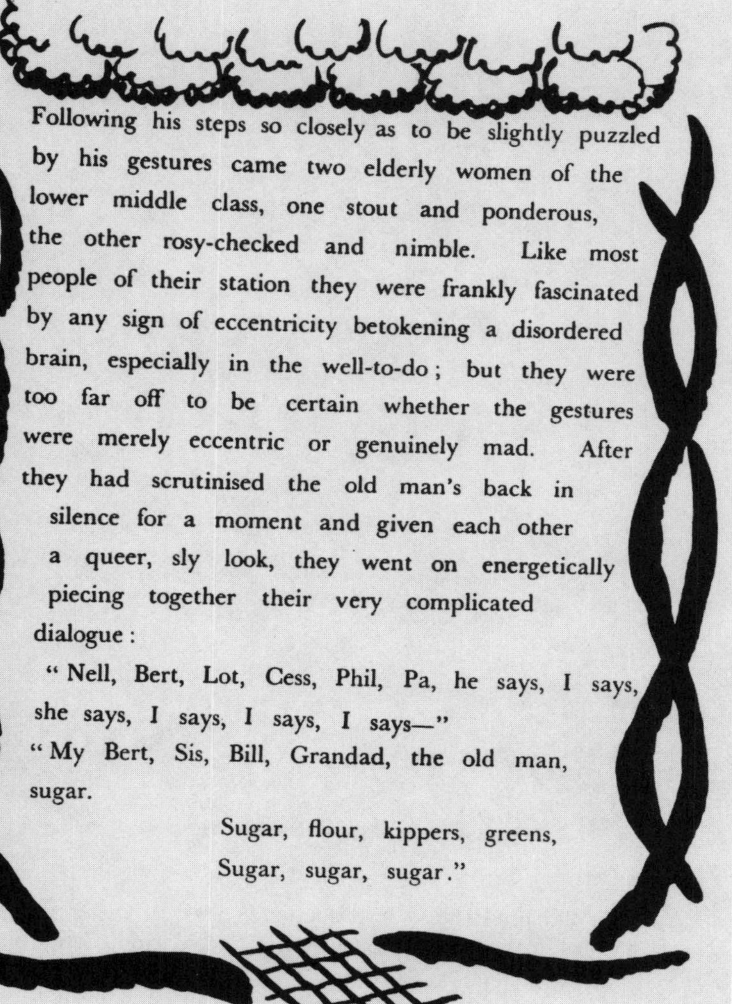

Following his steps so closely as to be slightly puzzled by his gestures came two elderly women of the lower middle class, one stout and ponderous, the other rosy-checked and nimble. Like most people of their station they were frankly fascinated by any sign of eccentricity betokening a disordered brain, especially in the well-to-do; but they were too far off to be certain whether the gestures were merely eccentric or genuinely mad. After they had scrutinised the old man's back in silence for a moment and given each other a queer, sly look, they went on energetically piecing together their very complicated dialogue:

" Nell, Bert, Lot, Cess, Phil, Pa, he says, I says, she says, I says, I says, I says—"

" My Bert, Sis, Bill, Grandad, the old man, sugar.

Sugar, flour, kippers, greens,
Sugar, sugar, sugar."

3.13. Vanessa Bell. Illustrated page 12 of *Kew Gardens* (London: Hogarth, 1927) by Virginia Woolf. Courtesy of the Bloomsbury Collection at Washington State University Libraries, Pullman, Washington; permission of the estate of Vanessa Bell and the Hogarth Press.

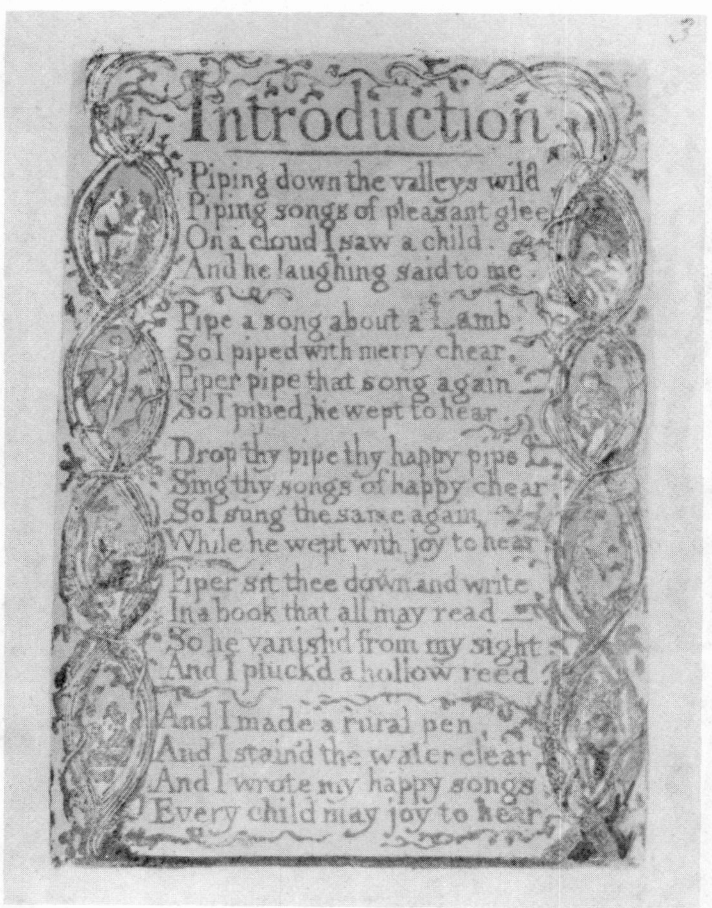

Introduction

Piping down the valleys wild
Piping songs of pleasant glee
On a cloud I saw a child.
And he laughing said to me.

Pipe a song about a Lamb;
So I piped with merry chear,
Piper pipe that song again—
So I piped, he wept to hear.

Drop thy pipe thy happy pipe
Sing thy songs of happy chear,
So I sung the same again
While he wept with joy to hear

Piper sit thee down and write
In a book that all may read—
So he vanish'd from my sight
And I pluck'd a hollow reed.

And I made a rural pen,
And I stain'd the water clear,
And I wrote my happy songs
Every child may joy to hear

3.14. William Blake. "Introduction," *Songs of Innocence*, 1789. Courtesy of the Huntington Library, San Marino, California.

its implications of reality and appearance, prompts verticals and horizontals just as the previous page suggests arches and spirals.

In her frontispiece design for the first edition of *Kew Gardens*, Vanessa Bell visually blends the human and natural worlds. In the endpiece she shifts the focus to the natural world. The later edition goes further in the direction suggested by the endpiece. She draws

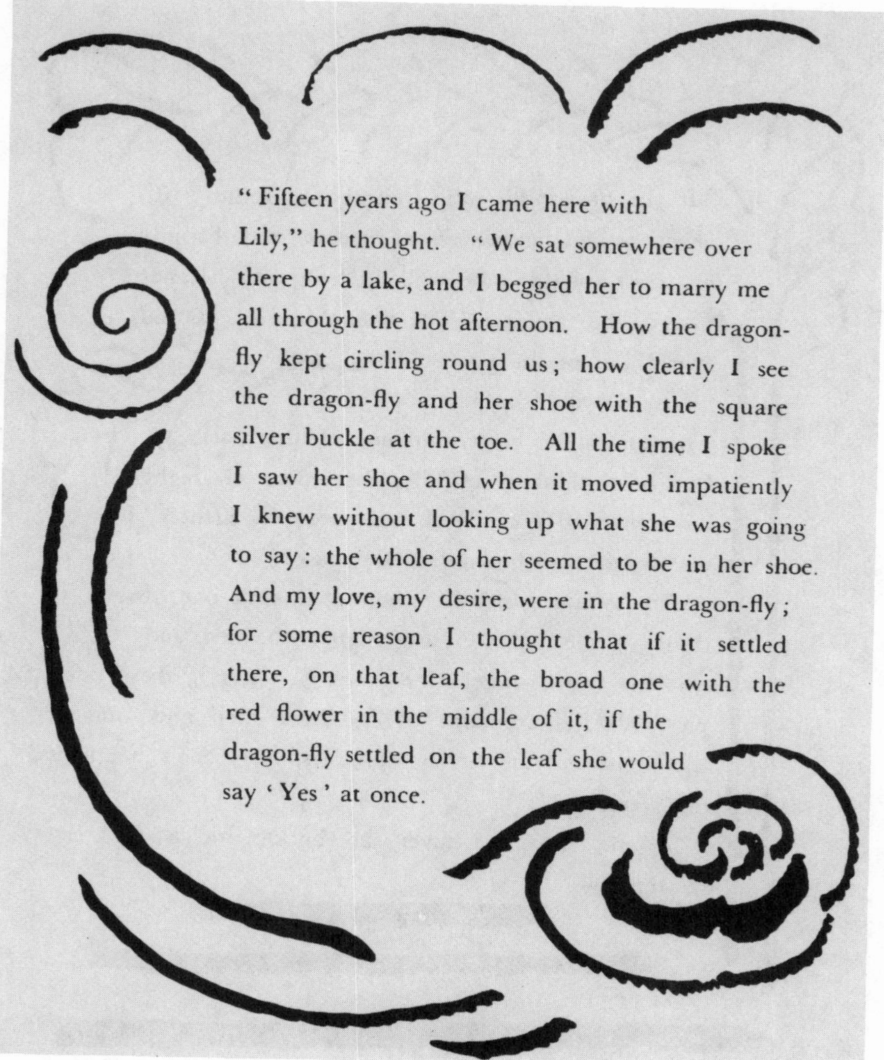

"Fifteen years ago I came here with Lily," he thought. "We sat somewhere over there by a lake, and I begged her to marry me all through the hot afternoon. How the dragon-fly kept circling round us; how clearly I see the dragon-fly and her shoe with the square silver buckle at the toe. All the time I spoke I saw her shoe and when it moved impatiently I knew without looking up what she was going to say: the whole of her seemed to be in her shoe. And my love, my desire, were in the dragon-fly; for some reason I thought that if it settled there, on that leaf, the broad one with the red flower in the middle of it, if the dragon-fly settled on the leaf she would say 'Yes' at once.

3.15. Vanessa Bell. Illustrated page 4 of *Kew Gardens* (London: Hogarth, 1927) by Virginia Woolf. Courtesy of the Bloomsbury Collection at Washington State University Libraries, Pullman, Washington; permission of the estate of Vanessa Bell and the Hogarth Press.

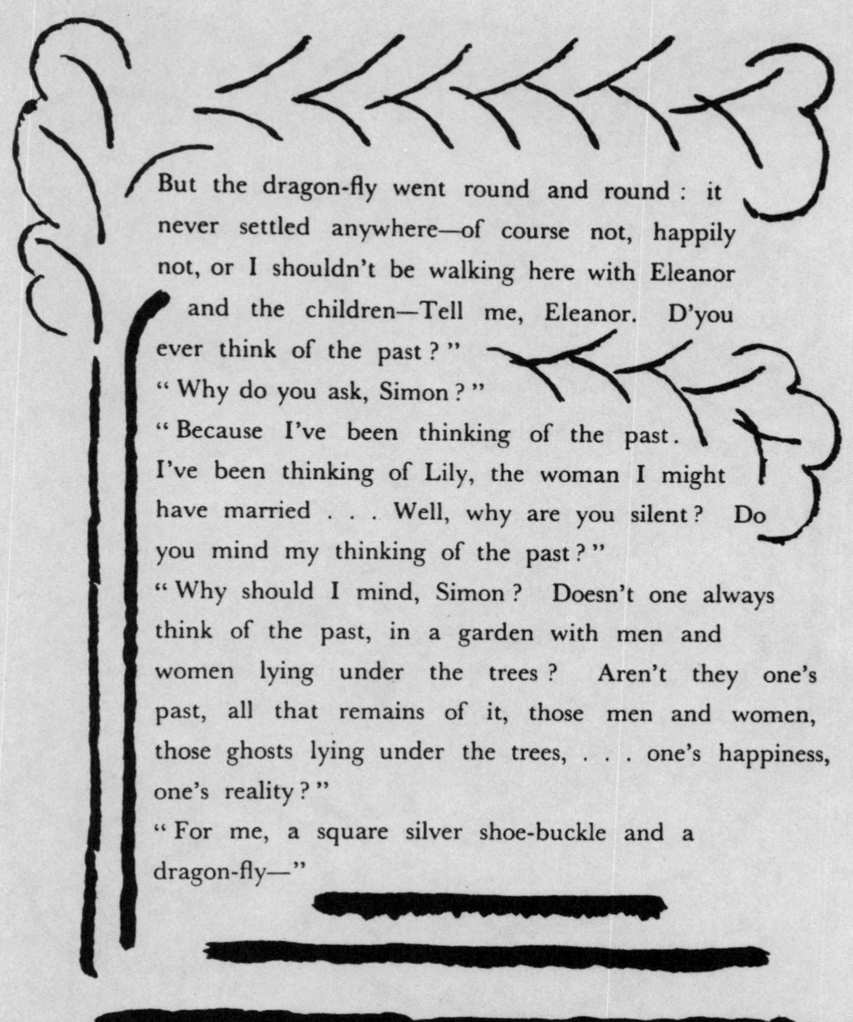

But the dragon-fly went round and round : it never settled anywhere—of course not, happily not, or I shouldn't be walking here with Eleanor and the children—Tell me, Eleanor. D'you ever think of the past ? "

" Why do you ask, Simon ? "

" Because I've been thinking of the past. I've been thinking of Lily, the woman I might have married . . . Well, why are you silent ? Do you mind my thinking of the past ? "

" Why should I mind, Simon ? Doesn't one always think of the past, in a garden with men and women lying under the trees ? Aren't they one's past, all that remains of it, those men and women, those ghosts lying under the trees, . . . one's happiness, one's reality ? "

" For me, a square silver shoe-buckle and a dragon-fly—"

3.16. Vanessa Bell. Illustrated page 5 of *Kew Gardens* (London: Hogarth, 1927) by Virginia Woolf. Courtesy of the Bloomsbury Collection at Washington State University Libraries, Pullman, Washington; permission of the estate of Vanessa Bell and the Hogarth Press.

none of the perceivers in the story, human or mollusk; she presents only the natural and occasionally human-produced objects they perceive. As Virginia Woolf said on several occasions, the visual artist can withdraw into a silent world of objects as well as colors, lines, and shapes; but the verbal artist must remain immersed in the world of people and the ideas and feelings they struggle to communicate to each other (L III 294, CE II 131). Yet just as Woolf describes the mingling of people and the natural world, so Bell, without including human figures in her designs, indicates some of their stereotypical qualities or states of mind through visual imagery as well as through arrangements of lines and shapes. The difference is that Woolf's text can communicate the complex relationship between people and nature without the designs; Bell's designs for the 1927 edition depend upon the juxtaposition with the words to achieve a similar complexity.

Vanessa Bell's variations on Woolf's theme in *Kew Gardens* provide an additional dimension to the reading of that story and a good early example of the sisters' arts. At its worst, collaboration on such projects involved arguments and concessions, hurt feelings and implicit rivalries, as well as some designs that overpower portions of the written text. At its best, collaboration revealed the extent to which they approved of each other's work and saw themselves as communicating in different but complementary media similar fresh and vivid responses to the interrelated human and natural worlds around them.

Between the 1919 and 1927 editions of *Kew Gardens*, Vanessa Bell produced two little-known designs for a second separate, partial edition of "The Mark on the Wall" (1921).[39] A passage from the last paragraph of the story details the narrator's expanding thoughts about wood—trees in different seasons and weather conditions and, finally, their uses. Wood lines rooms like the one where the narrator sits after tea, smoking and contemplating a mark on the wall. Vanessa's illustration, appropriately a woodcut, includes a teacup and saucer near the edge of a round table (Figure 3.17). Above the cup hang two oversized leaves with suggestions of fruits or flowers and an arching trunk or branch. To the left is a meditative woman's face with tilted head bent forward, eyes downcast. Framing her head and shoulders

WOOD is a pleasant thing to think about. It comes from a tree; and trees grow, and we don't know how they grow. For years and years they grow, without paying any attention to us, in meadows, in forests and by the side of rivers - all things one likes to think about. The cows swish their tails beneath thém on hot afternoons; they paint rivers so green that when a moor-hen dives one expects to see its feathers all green when it comes up again. I like to think of the fish balanced against the stream like flags blown out; and of water-beetles slowly raising domes of mud upon the bed of the river. I like to think of the tree itself; first the close dry sensation of being wood; then there is the grinding of the storm; then the slow, delicious ooze of sap. I like to think if it, too ,on winter's nights standing in the empty field with all leaves close-furled, nothing tender exposed to the iron bullets of the moon, a naked mast upon an earth that goes tumbling, tumbling, all night long. The song of birds must sound very loud and strange in June; and how cold the feet of insects must feel upon it, as they make laborious progresses up the creases of the bark or sun themselves upon the thin green awning of the leaves, and look straight in front of them with huge diamond-cut red eyes ... One by one the fibres snap beneath the immense cold pressure of the earth; then the last storm comes and, falling, the highest branches drive deep into the ground again. Even so, life is'nt done with; there are a million patient, watchful, lives still for a tree, all over the world, in bedrooms, in ships, on the pavement, lining rooms where men and women sit after tea, smoking their cigarettes.

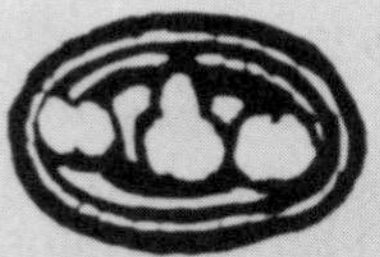

From THE MARK ON THE WALL by VIRGINIA WOOLF
BLOCKS by VANESSA BELL
The Chelsea Book Club Broadside No. I ptd. at 43 BELSIZE PARK GDNS.

3.17. Vanessa Bell. Illustration for *The Mark on the Wall* (London: Chelsea Book Club, 1921) by Virginia Woolf. Courtesy of Richard Outram, Toronto, Canada; permission of Angelica Garnett.

on one side is a rounded chairback. As the natural world fills the narrator's thoughts, so it mingles with the furniture and teacup in the woodcut. Both Woolf and Bell blur the distinction between interior and exterior environments. This theme and the reference to tea are reinforced by a small woodcut of fruit on an oval plate placed beneath the passage from the story.

Monday or Tuesday, a volume of Virginia Woolf's short stories, also appeared in 1921. Printed with Leonard Woolf's help by F. T. McDermott of the Prompt Press, Richmond, the book contains eight stories. The illustration for "A Society," already discussed, was one of four designs Vanessa Bell did for her sister. She also produced a cover. Roughly symmetrical and abstract, it affirms a separate, although similar identity for the visual artist (Figure 3.18). In the center is a large black circle surrounded by a thick white ring; from it project four curled circular shapes, two at the top, and two at the bottom. Each pair has different outlines. At the top Vanessa encloses the title and "VIRGINIA WOOLF" in a horizontal rectangle. At the bottom, in a slightly smaller rectangle, are "WOODCUTS BY" and "VANESSA BELL." This rectangle appears now to recede, now to project, because Bell joins the lower corners to the bottom of the cover with short diagonal lines. That such visual complexity exists around her name is fitting since her appeal is exclusively to the eyes. The similarities and differences between the portions of the design surrounding the two sisters' names are also appropriate, given their habits of competitive collaboration.

The four illustrations for *Monday or Tuesday* appear opposite the first pages of the texts. Unlike the marginal designs for the 1927 edition of *Kew Gardens*, these are not so closely related to specific passages; nor do they compete for attention with the text in any way. Like the woodcuts for the earlier edition of the story, these designs, although pleasing in themselves, acquire greater complexity in conjunction with the stories as well as reinforce some ideas Woolf tries to convey. The first and last designs focus on objects, the other two on people.

"A Haunted House" recreates the peregrinations of a benign, inquisitive, invisible "ghostly couple" who seek some treasure left behind in a house now occupied by people who both sense their presence and are engaged in a similar search. Past and present dwellers meet, in some insubstantial way, at the end of the story. The ghostly couple bends over the two who sleep in safety with "love

3.18. Vanessa Bell. Cover design for *Monday or Tuesday* (London: Hogarth, 1921). Courtesy of the Bloomsbury Collection at Washington State University Libraries, Pullman, Washington; permission of the estate of Vanessa Bell and the Hogarth Press.

upon their lips." Waking, one of them cries, "Oh, is this *your* buried treasure?" The last line of the story does not answer the question; rather it defines the treasure: love, life, "The light in the heart" (HH 4–5).

Vanessa Bell stresses the invisibility of the couple and the importance of the house as the repository of a treasure that is not the property of just the current residents. She sketches, in a few white lines on black, a small portion of an interior scene: a big, empty armchair at lower left, the lower portion of a tied-back curtain at one side of a window at upper right, a portion of the window itself (Figure 3.19). The curved lines of the curtain echo those of the chair. Although the bottom edge of the curtain forms a diagonal which suggests a deeper space, the armchair itself is two-dimensional. As in the later *Kew Gardens* designs, Bell depicts not people, but their surroundings and provides some ballast for a story Woolf fears "may be sentimental" (WD 31).

In her final design for *Monday or Tuesday*, Vanessa again depicts objects: the musical instruments of the story "The String Quartet." She arranges three smaller instruments atop a larger one like the petals of an opened flower. The precise outlines are unclear because of the overlapping and because of a counterpointing of dark and light areas in the spaces around as well as within the outlines. In fact, the dissolution of these perceived objects into the overall black-and-white, almost abstract design suggests the sounds emanating from them. In the story, Woolf counterpoints scraps of conversation with the feelings and corresponding images aroused by music. In both design and text a rhythmic patterning and shifting of dimensions links the visual and verbal arts with another sister, music.

Vanessa Bell illustrates two stories, however, in which people are difficult to avoid: "A Society" and "An Unwritten Novel." As "A Society" is related to *A Room of One's Own* and *Three Guineas*, so "An Unwritten Novel" is related to "Mr. Bennett and Mrs. Brown." Meditating on the things people do not say, the narrator studies five people on a train. Four occupy themselves in some way; the fifth is completely idle. The narrator imagines scenes and alternate plots involving this woman, then concludes that her actions are less important than her emotions and thoughts. These, too, the narrator imagines. The structure of satisfactions and losses she creates, however, topples when the woman leaves the train platform with a man who must be her son. Despairing of the identity of others,

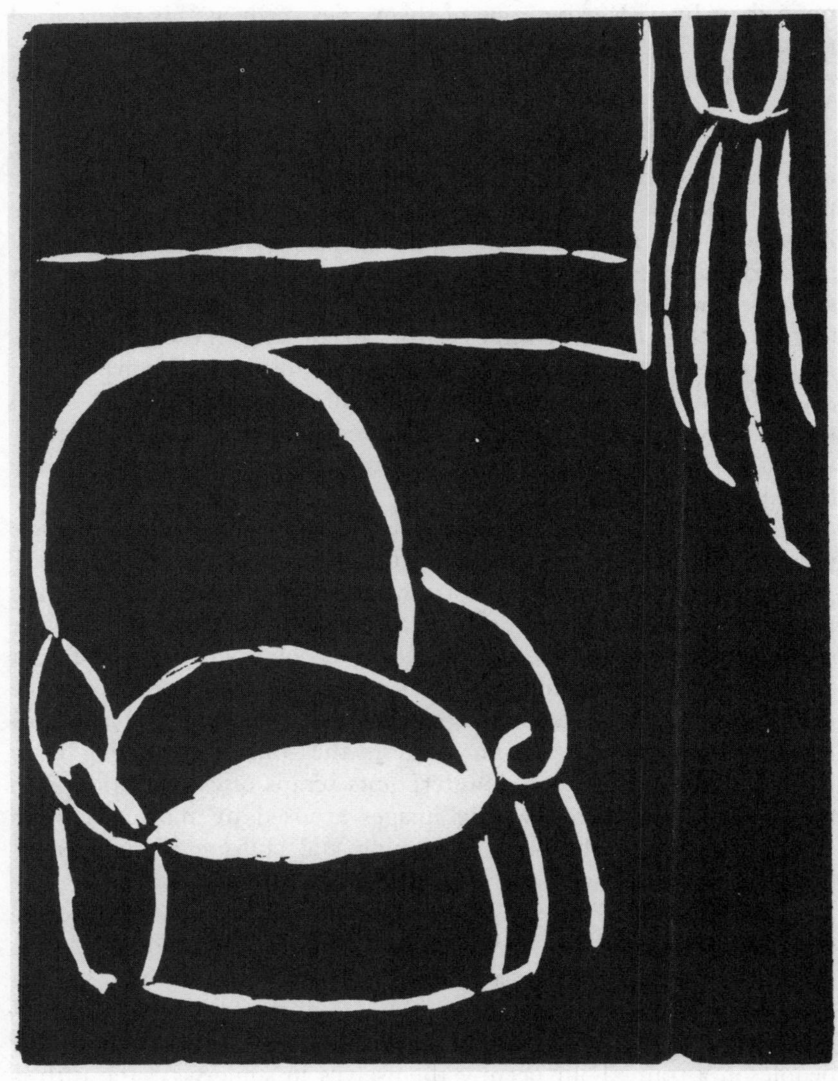

3.19. Vanessa Bell. Illustration for "A Haunted House" in *Monday or Tuesday* (London: Hogarth, 1921) by Virginia Woolf. Courtesy of the Bloomsbury Collection at Washington State University Libraries, Pullman, Washington; permission of the estate of Vanessa Bell and the Hogarth Press.

almost of her own, the narrator is at the same time exhilarated by the elusiveness of human beings.

In her illustration (Figure 3.20), Vanessa again shows her sensitivity to point of view in her sister's story. She depicts two of the people sitting opposite the narrator. At the left of the page is a man with hat and pipe who is preoccupied with a book or newspaper. Black outlined in white, his figure is half on, half off the page. At the right of the design is the woman who does nothing. White outlined in black, she stares ahead, arms crossed at the wrists. No detail about her is startling or distinctive; she is open white spaces for the imagination to fill. If the semicircular structure of the design for "A Society" underscores the cooperative efforts of the women, then the contrasts between the man and woman in the illustration for "An Unwritten Novel" help to emphasize the barriers between people as well as the narrator's speculations and frustrations. Even when her subjects are people, however, Bell interests herself in their formal possibilities. Although her arrangements of blacks and whites, lines and shapes, communicate resolutions and tensions like those among the people in her sister's stories, she leaves the specific complexities of human motivations and relationships to Virginia. "Nessa approves of Monday or Tuesday—mercifully," she wrote in her diary when the book came out, "& thus somewhat redeems it in my eyes" (D II 98).

Vanessa Bell's four illustrations for *Flush: A Biography* (1933), like those for earlier works, reflect Virginia Woolf's experiments with point of view; unlike the other illustrations, they are line drawings, more detailed although loose in style. They supplement six other illustrations, mostly photographic: a picture of a spaniel; a rendition of "Flush's Birthplace;"[40] a photograph of Miss Mitford, Flush's first owner; two photos of Elizabeth Barrett Browning; and one of Robert Browning. Woolf begins *Flush* in the traditional biographical style; she defines the origins of the spaniel family and the conflicting opinions on that subject, then narrows to the spaniel families of England and to Flush's lineage in particular. The point of view, however ironic, is conventional until Miss Mitford brings Flush as a gift to Elizabeth Barrett. Then, although she does not use it with

3.20. Vanessa Bell. Illustration for "An Unwritten Novel" in *Monday or Tuesday* (London: Hogarth, 1921) by Virginia Woolf. Courtesy of the Bloomsbury Collection at Washington State University Libraries, Pullman, Washington; permission of the estate of Vanessa Bell and the Hogarth Press.

complete consistency, Woolf shifts to a dog's-eye view of the surroundings and proceedings.

Vanessa Bell alters the point of view in her designs correspondingly. The first drawing, *Miss Mitford takes Flush for a Walk*, portrays the dog, as in the text, leaping along next to his mistress. *The Back Bedroom* at Wimpole Street, in contrast, is an interior scene drawn from a low angle. The dog no longer appears in the illustration; rather, we see what he sees (Figure 3.21). Bell follows the text to some extent in depicting the room: she includes one of the three busts atop the wardrobe and the bust atop the shelves; she also includes the table and Elizabeth Barrett on her couch. To suit her design, Bell changes other details: for the mirrors and the patterned drapes, she substitutes patterned wallpaper and carpet and adds a vase of flowers to the window ledge. All of these details crowd into the small space visible through an opened door. Elizabeth Barrett on her couch looks to one side, into the room. Whatever Bell's alterations, text and design both communicate enclosure.

Vanessa Bell's third illustration contrasts markedly with the second, as does the situation of Flush and his mistress in Woolf's description (Figure 3.22). No longer repressing their instincts and emotions in a crowded, perfumed Victorian bedroom in London, Flush and Elizabeth Barrett Browning experience vigorous living and loving in Italy. *At Casa Guidi* is, like the previous illustration, from the dog's point of view, but there the resemblance ends. The rectangular door through which we saw Elizabeth Barrett in her cluttered, ornamented space has become a huge window in front of her. No longer looking into an interior space, she now reclines, with the position of her body exactly reversed, upon the one piece of furniture in the large, bare room. Her back to us, she gazes at the book on her lap or out of the window at the city and hills beyond.

Flush is back in the last illustration, *So she knitted and he dozed.* Ignored by Mrs. Browning, the aged dog has gone down to the market woman, guarded her produce, and fallen asleep beside her. "He drowsed off," Woolf writes, "under the shadow of the lilies" (F 147). Bell chooses to make this scene visible through a window; we see the left edge in the foreground and a vase of lilies on the ledge. Shortly after this point in the biography, Woolf shifts briefly to Mrs. Browning's point of view as Flush returns to her room and dies on her couch.

Jean Guiguet notes how Vanessa Bell's drawings, like the text,

3.21. Vanessa Bell. *The Back Bedroom*. Illustration for *Flush* (London: Hogarth, 1933) by Virginia Woolf. Courtesy of the Bloomsbury Collection at Washington State University Libraries, Pullman, Washington; permission of the estate of Vanessa Bell and the Hogarth Press.

3.22. Vanessa Bell. *At Casa Guidi*. Illustration for *Flush* (London: Hogarth, 1933) by Virginia Woolf. Courtesy of the Bloomsbury Collection at Washington State University Libraries, Pullman, Washington; permission of the estate of Vanessa Bell and the Hogarth Press.

"stress the likeness which the spaniel's ears and Elizabeth's ringlets reveal between the two heroes." Still, Guiguet thinks that the drawings do not ultimately solve the difficulties of Woolf's unusual point of view: ". . . the distance between them [the two heroes] remains considerable," he says, "and divides the reader's attention, inflicting a constant strain on his mind as if he were striving not to see more than Flush sees, or beyond what Flush sees."[41] Guiguet is only one of many readers irritated by this kind of imaginative effort. Virginia's feisty friend, Ethel Smyth, confided to Vanessa Bell that the book both bored her and gave her the "Kick-Screams."[42] Virginia Woolf had predicted Ethel's reaction. "How you'll hate it!" she wrote to her in 1932 (L V 108). To Woolf *Flush* was "a little joke" (L V 140) originally intended as a parody of Lytton Strachey's biographies (L V 162) but ultimately "a matter of hints and shades" which few of her readers fully understood (L V 236).

Quentin Bell notes Woolf's well-known tendency to think of herself as an animal in her relationships with other people: "*Flush* is not so much a book by a dog lover as a book by someone who would love to be a dog."[43] Vanessa Bell also played animal roles. Accepting her sister's name for her, Vanessa frequently referred to herself as "Dolphin." In 1910 or 1912, for example, she wrote to Clive Bell, "Dolphin rubs your orange whiskers with her snout and offers her tail to be stroked."[44] Animals, however, can be neglected. Stephen Trombley thinks that *Flush* reflects an actual love triangle. He identifies Elizabeth Barrett with Vanessa, Robert Browning with Clive, and Flush's jealousy of Browning with Virginia's of Clive.[45] Vanessa's own experiences with triangular relationships, including the flirtation between her sister and her husband, prepared her to understand Flush's viewpoint too. Both sisters, after their move to Bloomsbury and travels on the continent, could also sympathize with the break Elizabeth Barrett and her spaniel made with Victorian interiors and values.

Vanessa Bell's illustrations are related to her decorative art work. In the second and third decades of the century, she worked for the Omega Workshops as well as on her own. She designed textiles and dresses, rugs and screens; and she collaborated on entire room designs which included mosaics for floors and murals for walls. The book artist and the mural painter confront similar problems. The latter must suit the subject to the sizes and locations of the panels to be covered, relate each panel to the others, and consider the order in which the viewer will see them. So a book is, as one writer notes, "a room or a contained space into which the reader goes, to be shut off from the noises and interruptions of the world's anarchic experiences. In this contained space he is subjected to a series of stimuli, partly words, partly pictures, all carefully controlled in sequence, content, and so far as possible, emotional impact." To achieve this goal, "an integrated experience for the reader,"[46] the book artist must be attuned to the writer's values. In 1935 Virginia Woolf wrote to Vanessa Bell, "Do you think we have the same pair of eyes, only different spectacles?" (L VI 158). No doubt the question was rhetorical.

Vanessa Bell's illustrations for Virginia Woolf's works represent one kind of professional interchange. There were others, ranging from exchanges of their work to Vanessa's comments on literature. In 1917 Vanessa suggested that Virginia trade daily letters for pictures, not replies.[47] Two months later Virginia wrote, "I enclose a sketch—in fact it's word for word true—of Marny's [Margaret Vaughan's] conversation, as a thank offering for the loan of your picture; and if you think it a fair exchange, we might do traffic on these lines" (L II 199). Over the years, they did. In 1919 Woolf asked her sister to paint a Greek vase in exchange for an advance copy of *Night and Day* (L II 393). In 1927 the sisters again agreed on a picture from Vanessa in exchange for letters from Virginia while she and Leonard were in France and Italy for a month. "Will there be a special allowance," she asked, "for letters written under circumstances of great difficulty? If so, this one must be paid at the rate of 17 inches by 8 ¾: oil: canvas: still life" (L III 360). This letter was written on the ninth of April; long letters followed on the fourteenth and the twenty-first. On the twenty-sixth, Woolf wrote, "You see how hard I work for my picture—or have I the right to exchange for a decoration, or what is my position exactly?" They had better clarify it, she said, "to avoid those fierce broils which may well break our sisterhood before its over." Might Vanessa agree to paint their gramophone? (L III 367) Their sisterhood was threatened, not by the precise terms of the exchange but by what Virginia considered Vanessa's indiscretions. "Damn it all—I'm afraid I shall have to make an end of our agreement and lose my picture," she wrote after her return to London. She had heard that Clive had been amusing people in Paris with stories of her "rhapsodies about Italy" and of her other experiences. Virginia admitted that she had not forbidden Vanessa to share her letters; but she did not see how she could continue to write unself-consciously about anything more than "mere facts or gossip" knowing that other people would read her comments (L III 368). Still, exchanges of one kind or another continued. When Woolf could not find the embroidery design her sister had lent her, she asked to have it repainted in return for a story although, she added, "you dont think much of stories" (L III 415). Two years later, in 1929, Vanessa Bell refused to take any money for her art from her sister because, she said, she had had all the advantages of Virginia's novels for nothing.[48]

Just as Virginia Woolf commented on painting, often to her sister, so Vanessa commented on writing. She also disclaimed any skill as a critic of the other medium. "There is a peculiar mixture of suavity and force in your writing," she wrote to Clive in 1910, "which gives me great pleasure. Theres literary criticism for you!"[49] Her literary tastes, she told Virginia in 1917, were "simple and domestic."[50] Throughout her life, however, Vanessa retained a respect for the written word. Just as she sometimes read while Virginia drew, so Vanessa remembered painting at Hyde Park Gate while Virginia read: "We read most of the Victorian novelists in this way, and I can still hear much of George Eliot and Thackeray in her voice."[51] Later she was amused at Clive's and Lytton's discovery of George Eliot, whose works, she reminded Virginia, they had learned in the nursery.[52] Forced to move her father's library after his death, Vanessa acknowledged to her sister that books were "wonderful things" and that she felt "a great affection for the scrubbiest and most backless volume." She attributed her attitude to having lived "in a book-loving family. I feel happy and content," she concluded, "sitting on the floor in an ocean of calf."[53]

Just as Virginia attended meetings of Vanessa's Friday Club, so Vanessa got involved in the 1920s in a play-reading society instituted by Virginia and Clive.[54] Perhaps she did so because of her repeatedly confessed ignorance of whole eras of literary history. In about 1913 she admitted reading *Antony and Cleopatra* for the first time. Having experienced so much more in her own life, she said in her defense, she appreciated Shakespeare's plays more than she would have at a younger age.[55] In 1921 she saw a production of Sophocles' *Oedipus*. Because she had not read that play either, she had no knowledge of the plot, but again she concluded that her ignorance was an advantage.[56] It certainly did not stop her from pronouncing judgment upon writing, often in letters to Virginia. In 1918, for instance, she listened to Lytton Strachey read portions of *Eminent Victorians* and concluded that "the Strachey mind is purely dramatic & . . . the result in writing biographies is to give a superficial & unreal effect."[57] She noted too "the peculiar mixture of common place banality, snobbishness, . . . & boastfulness" in Mrs. Humphry Ward's writing, qualities which made "her hit the bull's eye of British middle-class taste with such amazing skill each time."[58] She reported to Virginia on one occasion that she was "fascinated" by Harriet Martineau's autobiography, and, on another, that she was "rather absorbed" in a book by Beatrice Webb. She also indicated her plans to read a Hugh Walpole novel and to tell Virginia her reactions.[59]

Vanessa Bell did not allow literary criteria to be used when discussing painting, but she used her criteria for visual art criticism when she evaluated literature. She told Roger Fry that he could appreciate some aspects of Duncan Grant's work better than she because she was "really very dense about this curious fantastic literary thing in his painting."[60] She also told Fry that he and Duncan would have to discuss Giotto's "dramatic sense" with each other, not with her.[61] She faulted Lytton Strachey because "he only feels character & relationships of character" in painting "& has no conception of the form its all being made into." Nor did she agree with Strachey about literature. She wanted human relationships and emotions that had some value, even though she could not define what she meant. In her eyes, Lytton opted for verisimilitude at the expense of significance.[62] Judging from her reaction to Shaw's *Saint Joan*, significance was not a social or political message. Shaw's integrity impressed her, but she refused to call him an artist. "But after all it seems to me hardly any literature is [art] & plenty of writers survive who arent at all artists."[63] An entry in Woolf's diary four years later indicated a reservation which may cast light upon Vanessa Bell's: "Shaw does not visualize" (D IV 163). In contrast, Woolf liked D. H. Lawrence's "sudden visualisation" although she did not like his "explanations of what he sees" or his philosophizing (D IV 126) any more than she liked Aldous Huxley's tendency to make "people into ideas" (D IV 276). Neither literature nor painting, the sisters thought, should imitate the essay.

Vanessa Bell's criteria for "artist" are more clear from her comments on E. M. Forster. When *A Passage to India* came out, she disagreed with Fry about some of its qualities. The somewhat inconclusive ending, she thought, could be defended as appropriate to the overall design of the book. She also liked the actual writing; but, on the whole, she would have liked to see him get "writing & ideas & construction all more of a piece somehow."[64] Virginia Woolf, several years later, also criticized Forster for a tendency to teach and preach as well as to create pure art. As a teacher, his message is elusive. As an artist, he exhibits "an exquisite prose style, an acute sense of comedy, a power of creating characters in a few strokes which live in an atmosphere of their own" (CE I 345). The "double vision" which disconcerts Woolf, however, approaches single vision in *A Passage to India* (CE I 351). Her conclusion, like her sister's, is qualified praise for the overall coherence of the book.

Just as Vanessa thought about Virginia's reactions to her paintings, so Virginia pondered Vanessa's comments on her writing. For her sister's correspondence, Vanessa had high praise. One exception was a letter Virginia wrote from France after her marriage to Leonard Woolf. Her sister pronounced it dull but said that perhaps one must expect such communications from the newly wed.[65] Other exceptions were letters written during the period of recurring mental illness prior to and following the publication of *The Voyage Out*. These Vanessa also thought were dull compared to Virginia's earlier letters and, in addition, she thought they showed signs of mental exhaustion.[66] Early in Virginia's literary career, however, Vanessa liked the letters even better than the fiction. Around the time that Virginia was completing *The Voyage Out*, Vanessa wrote to Roger Fry that her sister's accumulated letters were "extraordinarily amusing. I think really better than her novel. I wish she could have found some form which didnt mean having to concentrate over such a long space," Vanessa added. "When she's giving short accounts of people or talk its amazing."[67] Vanessa may have expressed some variation of this opinion to Virginia. Although she does not limit women to the short story in *A Room of One's Own*, she speculates that their books "should be shorter, more concentrated, than those of men, and framed so that they do not need long hours of steady and uninterrupted work. For interruptions there will always be" (AROO 81).

To Virginia herself, Vanessa certainly praised the letters and solicited them quite as effusively as Virginia solicited Vanessa's. She called Virginia's letters "charming."[68] She also noted the intimate tone. When someone published the letters, she wrote, "people will certainly think that we had a most amourous intercourse. They read more like love-letters than anything else," more so even than Clive's. But she added, "I like love letters—the more passion you put in the better. . . . I am greedy for compliments & passion."[69] Again with posterity in mind, Vanessa wrote, "I purr all down my back when I get such gems of imagery thrown at my feet & reflect how envied I shall be of the world some day when it learns on what terms I was with that great genius. . . ."[70] Nor was such praise confined to Virginia's early letters. Continually Vanessa Bell encouraged her sister to write to her by noting the "admiration and interest" or the "amusement & pleasure" her letters produced.[71]

She would give her sister a description of an exhibition, Virginia wrote to Vanessa in 1918, "since I suppose that there may be the same curious interest in a writer's account of pictures as the other way round. And yet the queer thing is that I accept your or Duncan's view of writing absolutely seriously" (L II 261). When *To the Lighthouse* came out in 1927, Virginia wrote to her sister, "I would like your good opinion, which is more than one can say of most people" (L III 370). Receiving no reply, she wrote a comic dialogue between her sister and Duncan on the subject of having to say something about a novel which neither had yet read: Deciding to write and tell Virginia that she has written "a masterpiece," Vanessa finds the inkpot "full of dead and dying insects" (L III 375–76). Meanwhile, of course, Vanessa had written her praises of the book. Virginia was very pleased: "Why do I attach so much importance to what you and Duncan think?" she queried, "illiterate, simpletons, as you are? I daresay you are qualified however, much more than many of my literary friends to judge of things as a whole, as works of art" (L III 383). So when *Orlando* appeared, she wrote, "I pant for your opinion—the only one that has a grain of sense in it" (L III 546). She even considered, as she wrote *The Waves*, that she was making it "too mystical, too abstract" because she was courting the admiration of the painters, "Nessa & Roger & Duncan & Ethel Sands" (D III 203). Relieved when Vanessa liked the book, she confessed, "Nobody except Leonard matters to me as you matter, and nothing would ever make up for it if you didn't like what I did. So its an amazing relief—I always feel I'm writing more for you than for anybody" (L IV 390). In her diary Woolf noted that her sister's praise of *The Waves* was "the brightest spot" (D IV 49).

Virginia's desire for approval made commenting difficult for Vanessa, who sometimes had reservations about her sister's work. When she had them, as in the case of one of Virginia's early articles, she said that she probably would not agree with everything her sister said, but since she had not read the relevant books, she was "incompetent to judge." Virginia, she knew, would respond, "That means you think it bad."[72] When she wrote about her sister's memoir writing, Vanessa used words like "witty & brilliant" and "masterpiece," but she evaded any "real criticism" because, she said, she could "only talk as do laymen about a portrait & tell you whether I think it like or not."[73] Sometimes Vanessa Bell relied on other people's responses. In 1922 she reported to Clive that a book by Virginia, presumably *Jacob's Room*, had appeared. Not having read it yet, she noted Desmond MacCarthy's conclusion that it was her sister's best work so far, but that it was not sufficiently unified.[74] Sometimes she asked for the opinions of others, like Roger Fry, as she did in 1928 when she returned from France to find *Orlando* the topic of much excited discussion.[75]

Vanessa Bell usually saved her reservations about Virginia's work for Roger Fry or Clive Bell. The first publication of the Hogarth Press, *Two Stories*, with woodcuts by Carrington, is a good example. Vanessa wrote to Fry that "The Mark on the Wall" was "rather good." A short time later she declared it "amazingly good of its kind." Clive, she said, initially proclaimed the story "a work of genius" but later toned down his opinion, blaming Vanessa for his change of mind. She, in turn, thought Mary Hutchinson was to blame: "We had a rather unfortunate discussion which would become an argument as to the comparative merits of Virginia's point of view as an artist & what Mary's own was supposed to be—only that couldnt be said openly. Clive," she added, "is always so down upon Virginia in spite of his temporary admirations of her."[76] To Clive years later Vanessa wrote of *The Waves*, "I cant imagine what the ordinary reader can finally make of it," but added that not having completed it herself, she could not formulate any opinion. Whatever she concluded, she knew that when she wrote to Virginia, it would be "ticklish work saying anything about it."[77]

Although Vanessa Bell consistently looked for form in both painting and literature, other considerations distracted her when she evaluated the writing of people who were close to her. In 1913 she condemned Leonard Woolf's novel, *The Wise Virgins*, a book based on but not identical with his own early experiences with Virginia and Vanessa Stephen. Vanessa pronounced it "superficial & dull & somehow very commonplace, & very badly written." She admitted to Roger Fry, however, that her personal response to the book may have biased her, however hard she had tried to be fair.[78] Virginia had a similar problem, as we have seen, when she evaluated Edmond X. Kapp's drawings of people she had met. Vanessa's personal response also got in the way when she read her sister's books. Her confusion caused her to consider some differences between writing and painting.

When *The Voyage Out* appeared, for example, Vanessa expressed her opinions to Roger Fry. While she thought the book "extraordinarily brilliant," it was "almost too much so at times." Vanessa liked the way her sister presented people and their conversations, but she was not sure individual parts were sufficiently unified. She then launched into a more general discussion of the relationships between the visual arts and literature:

> Novel writing does seem a queer business—at least this kind. If it's art, it seems to me art of quite a different sort from making a picture but I don't think all novel writing is. The quotation from Jane Austen even though its only a sentence seemed to me at once to put one into a different world, one that's the same really that one is in when one looks at a Cézanne. Did you feel it? I suppose it's because one knows the rest of the book and one couldn't feel it from only one sentence. Reading V's book is much more like being with an extraordinarily witty and acute person in life and watching all these things and people with her. But that may be because I have actually done so. I wish I could really get outside it all. As it is I know all the people nearly and how she has come at so much of it which makes it very difficult to be fair.[79]

In chapter 4 of *The Voyage Out*, Rachel Vinrace attempts to discuss women writers and Austen with the Dalloways. Austen is the only woman, Richard declares, who "does not attempt to write like a man." Rachel cannot muster any evidence to contradict him. Clarissa, wishing to "divert" her husband "in an exquisite, quaint, sprightly, and slightly ridiculous world," begins to read from *Persuasion:* "'Sir Walter Elliott, of Kellynch Hall, in Somersetshire, was a man who, for his amusement, never took up any book but the *Baronetage*. . . . There he found occupation for an idle hour, and consolation in a distressed one'" (VO 62). This is the brief passage that Vanessa Bell said "seemed . . . at once to put one into a different world," one like that of a Cézanne painting. She tried to explain what she meant in two ways.

First, she sensed that she responded to more than the sentence or two her sister had quoted. That sentence evoked the entire book, complete and unified. As Woolf herself noted later in "How Should One Read a Book?" (1926) a book, once read through, "will return, but differently. It will float to the top of the mind as a whole. And the book as a whole is different from the book received currently in separate phrases. Details now fit themselves into their places. We see the shape from start to finish; it is a barn, a pigsty, or a cathedral" (CE II 8). Or it is a painting. At the same time that Walter Sickert represents squalid human lives like a realistic novelist, he takes his viewers into another world where "beauty and order prevail," Woolf noted still later (CE II 237). Vanessa Bell suspected that, to respond to a world created in literature as one would to a painting, one had to see it whole.

Second, she admitted that she might not have sufficient distance and objectivity to evaluate her sister's perception and verbal skill. That these two explanations did not entirely satisfy her, however, is evident from a subsequent letter to Roger Fry. In it Vanessa defended her earlier remarks and commented on some he had made. "I suppose its true that she has genius," she said, but added, "I'm not sure I should call it so—Can Stephens produce a genius? I doubt it." She did not mean to suggest that nothing apart from Jane Austen is art, she assured Fry; she only compared her sister's writing with Austen's because Leonard Woolf frequently did so, to his wife's advantage. Still Vanessa insisted that Austen did seem "to use all her observation for another purpose & I dont think Virginia does—But of course she's an artist even though she maynt have produced a work of art."[80]

Vanessa Bell actually may have drawn her conclusion from a 1913 article in which Virginia spoke of an Austen novel as if it were a painting able to transport one into an entirely different, self-contained realm: "More than any other novelist she fills every inch of her canvas with observation, fashions every sentence into meaning, stuffs up every chink and cranny of the fabric until each novel is a little living world, from which you cannot break off a scene or even a sentence without bleeding it of some of its life."[81] Vanessa seemed convinced, however, that in some way her sister's first novel was not such a unified realm in which the formal elements gave at least as much pleasure as the representational. It remained tied both to its creator and to the world in which she moved.

As each of her sister's novels appeared, Vanessa Bell continued to have problems with objectivity. In the case of *Night and Day* she noted to Fry that "one cant help guessing who all the characters are." Not having finished it, however, she mostly quoted Clive's positive responses.[82] The problem was particularly acute, however, with *To the Lighthouse*. In a letter to Clive, she responded to it as representation, not as art: "I was very much excited by Virginia's book. I agree with you & think it her best work, but at first it is difficult for me to know exactly what I think about it as a work of art. It is so fascinating as a portrait of my parents, both of whom seem to me to be given far more completely than they have been by anyone else . . . extraordinarily true."[83]

To Virginia, Vanessa wrote something similar: "So you see as far as portrait painting goes you seem to me to be a supreme artist and it is so shattering to find oneself face to face with those two [her parents] again that I can hardly consider anything else" (L III 572). She tried to do so, however, and concluded, "I know that in spite of all my personal interest I shouldn't have been moved as I was if it hadn't moved me impersonally too, only at the moment I dont feel capable of much analysis. I am excited and thrilled and taken into another world as one only is by a great work of art, only now also it has this curious other interest which I can't help feeling too" (L III 573).

To the Lighthouse even served as inspiration for a tile fireplace Vanessa designed in 1930 for Virginia's room at Monks House (Figure 3.23). In an oval at the top is a seascape. A sailboat in the left foreground balances a spit of land or rock on the right in the background. While the large sail of the boat is brown as in the novel (TTL 254, 270, 286), its outline also suggests the reference to Mrs. Ramsay as a "triangular purple shape."[84] Recalling Lily Briscoe's final "vision," a lighthouse on a rocky island provides a line down the center of Vanessa's painting and unites the two masses. In fact, both lighthouse and sail are vertical accents and a white, irregular shape in the dark water below reflects the building or its beam and extends the

3.23. Vanessa Bell. Lighthouse tile fireplace, 1930. Virginia Woolf's room at Monks House; Rodmell, Sussex. Courtesy of the National Trust; permission of Quentin Bell and Angelica Garnett.

vertical line. In her own way, Vanessa created a version of Lily's painting with its own kind of impersonal artistic coherence.

With the publication of *The Waves*, the book that grew from her own story of giant moths, Vanessa Bell again faced the problem of her personal as opposed to her impersonal response. She wrote to Virginia that the book had moved her profoundly: "For its quite as real an experience as having a baby or anything else, being moved as you have succeeded in moving me—Of course there's the personal side—the feelings you describe on what I must take to be Thoby's [Percival's] death. . . . Even then I know its only because of your art that I am so moved. I think you have made one's human feelings into something less personal" (L IV 390–91, quoted in n. 1).

From being unable to get beyond the personal response, to crediting her sister's art with at least a portion of the impact upon her, Vanessa Bell finally concluded, at least in her letters to Virginia, that her sister's skill did take her into another world and was responsible even for her personal reactions. Just as Woolf had noted earlier their mutual concern with problems of structure, so now Vanessa said that what her sister had done in *The Waves* paralleled what she had been trying to do for two years in a large painting: " . . . if I could only do what I want to—but I can't—it seems to me it would have some sort of analogous meaning to what you've done. How can one explain," she added, "but to me painting a floor covered with toys and keeping them all in relation to each other and the figures and the space of the floor and the light on it means something of the same sort that you seem to me to mean" (L IV 391, quoted in n. 1). Vanessa Bell's attempt to see in her sister's work a creative struggle similar to her own is a new phase in her responses to Virginia's writing.

The large painting Vanessa mentions cannot be found and may have been destroyed during World War II. Spalding, who identifies it as *The Nursery*, painted in the early 1930s, thinks its "nostalgic evocation of motherhood" might have been "inspired" by *To the Lighthouse*.[85] An existing photograph (Figure 3.24) helps to explain the parallels Vanessa sees between her work and *The Waves*. The painting is a successful attempt to define the relationship between adults and children as both intimate and independent.[86] The circle they form and the gazes of the mother and nurse upon the children unite them. The children's nudity and their preoccupation with their toys, however, separates them. The women share an interest in the children, but their roles and responsibilities differ. The children share an interest in the toys, but the fact that the younger child reaches for the horse the elder pulls on a string suggests competition. This counterpointing of harmonies and tensions within the domestic circle parallels the united yet disparate personalities of the characters

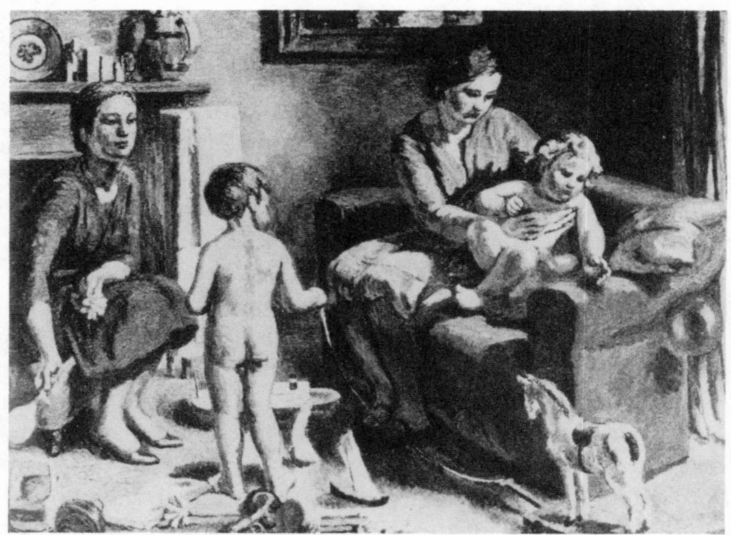

3.24. Vanessa Bell. *The Nursery*, 1930–32. Location unknown. Courtesy of Frances Spalding; permission of Angelica Garnett.

in *The Waves*. As Woolf weaves the lives of her six characters into their surroundings, so Vanessa's four figures and the numerous objects in the room combine to form her overall design. She arranges horse and boats into a line that leads the eye into the center of the domestic group. A small racket and shuttlecock in the mother's hands draw the eye in from the left as the sofa does from the right. Objects clustered on the mantelpiece above echo the groups of objects on the floor in the foreground.

The sisters' awareness of each other as professional artists, then, manifested itself in many ways. Each tried the other's medium and, even when the artistic territories were firmly established, retained an interest in it. Each was stimulated by her sister's work to produce, in her own art, something comparable. The best example so far in this study is the illustrating Vanessa Bell did for Virginia Woolf's work. Responsive to her sister's experiments with point of view, Bell varied her illustrations accordingly. She preferred, however, to emphasize the environments people perceive rather than the people themselves, although she also communicated some of their characteristics and states of mind through combinations of lines and shapes. When she did depict people, her interest remained in the formal problems her sister's stories posed for the visual artist, not in translating or completing the text. On occasion she produced some visual competition, as some of the large, dark illustrations for the 1927 edition of *Kew Gardens* show. That was the only time she had such a page-by-page opportunity. Usually the illustration relates to the story in a more general way, as in the case of the *Monday or Tuesday* designs. There Bell contented herself with visually underscoring on the cover the unity and diversity of writer and illustrator. Valuing the other's criticism, Virginia Woolf and Vanessa Bell each commented, albeit apologetically, on the other art form as well as on her sister's achievements in it.

In the next three chapters my emphasis shifts from such collaboration and commentary to representative aspects of Virginia's writing that recall certain kinds of Vanessa's paintings. Rebecca West's comment in a review of *Jacob's Room* that Woolf was more influenced by painting than by literature has some justification. "She can write supremely well only of what can be painted," West says; "best of all, perhaps, of what has been painted."[87] So, with some qualifications, Clive Bell says that Woolf's "almost painterlike vision . . . is what distinguishes her from all her contemporaries."[88] David Garnett recalls Bloomsbury as "a world of painters" in which everyone was "looking at pictures all the time and listening to discussions of aesthetics which were always devoted to the visual arts rather than to literature." He thinks that Virginia learned "her palette" as a writer by watching and listening to painters.[89] We can test such assertions by examining Vanessa's portrait painting in relation to Virginia's biographies and fictional works. In both sisters' creations, however, people exist in a material world. Comparisons between Vanessa's still life and landscape paintings and Virginia's descriptive writing define best the similarities and differences between the sisters and their arts.

4

Visual and Verbal Portraits

A division of Vanessa Bell's painting into portrait, still life, and landscape is artificial: her human figures merge with their surroundings; portrait and landscape, interior and exterior scenes, still life and landscape mingle. Still, the categories are useful in discussing the relations between her work and Virginia Woolf's. The Stephen family's interest in biographical writing,[1] and Woolf's own, are well known, but its connection in her mind with portrait painting is not.[2] As the sisters discovered, authorized biographers and commissioned portrait painters both confront the problem of achieving a likeness. Woolf and Bell preferred to capture, whether in words or paint, the essence of the individual and to depict people as parts of larger human, natural, and aesthetic patterns.

Vanessa Bell's relatively small canvases depicted her family, friends, acquaintances, and her immediate surroundings. She painted striking likenesses of people, but she also included them, with few if any identifying facial features, as parts of her overall designs. Virginia Woolf also depicted the everyday. She created characters she admitted were inspired, at least initially, by people she knew; she also modified them and created additional characters to suit her overall design. Like her sister, Woolf merged even her fully detailed characters at times into their surroundings. Deprived, like some of the people in Bell's paintings, of facial features, even of words, Woolf's characters are also on one level silent. Individuals are transient, both sisters imply in their art; the patterns they make in the contexts in which they move are not. To make this point, Woolf also includes painted portraits in her characters' environments. When painted, people eventually lose their individuality and exist only as works of art. References to painted portraits help Woolf in a variety of other ways to create characters, some of whom are artists themselves. Both sisters, in fact, create portraits of artists.

The sisters developed parallel theories about how people should be portrayed. Max Friedländer notes that "the job of painting a portrait entails something akin to obsequiousness, against which creative power puts up a fight." Not only is the portrait painter's freedom limited by the necessity of being accurate and objective, but he or she must also submit to the evaluation of a pretentious or vain patron who does not necessarily know anything about painting.[3] In Roger Fry's words, "it becomes almost part of his [the portrait painter's] duty to sacrifice something of aesthetic necessities to non-aesthetic demands."[4] This assessment of the motives and ignorance of the commissioners of portraits is evident from Vanessa Bell's comments on her in-laws' decor. One aspect of it which she particularly disliked, she wrote to Virginia in 1924, was "the family portraits—heads of the children in oil done from photographs by the photographer I should think. . . ."[5]

The extent to which Vanessa Bell was occupied with portrait painting is evident, both from the works remaining and from her letters. Virginia received accounts of her sister's progress with her first commissioned portraits, one of Lady Robert Cecil in 1905 and one of Lord Robert in 1906. In both cases, her great concern was achieving a likeness. Vanessa pleased her clients,[6] but there were limits to what she would do to make money in this field. Turning down a commission, she said that if she had to go and stay with clients in the midlands in winter, she had no desire to be an established portrait painter.[7] Such painting was increasingly unappealing for other reasons. After her son Julian Bell's death in 1937, Vanessa wrote to Virginia that she could not seriously paint portraits. They needed a special kind of concentration, she said, and they mattered to the people painted. She preferred to paint small works that mattered only to herself.[8]

The commissioned portrait painter and the authorized biographer face similar problems. "I think it is a good idea to write biographies," Virginia Woolf noted in her diary in 1931, "to make them use my powers of representation reality accuracy; & to use my novels simply to express the general, the poetic" (D IV 40). In "The Art of

Biography" (1939) she is less positive: "the biographer is tied" not only to facts but also to the desire of the family and friends of the subject for a superficial, flattering picture (CE IV 221–22). The remark reflects her frustration with the biography of Roger Fry. Her subject was dead, unlike those of most portrait painters, but Woolf still had to write under the watchful eyes of Fry's sister and friends. One of Woolf's many problems was how to deal accurately with Vanessa's role in Roger's life; another was how to treat Fry himself. To her sister, Virginia described her difficulties in painter's terms:

> What am I to say about you? Its rather as if you had to paint a portrait using dozens of snapshots in the paint. Either one ought to dash it off freehand, red, green, purple out of ones inner eye; or toil like a fly over a loaf of bread. As it is I'm compromising; and its a muddle; and unreadable; . . . But Roger himself is so magnificent, I'm so in love with him; and see dimly such a masterpiece that can't be painted, that on I go (L VI 285).

Like many modern portrait painters, Woolf recognized the subjectivity of her "inner eye," but she tried to minimize self-portraiture and to be discreet about other people as well.[9]

Although Woolf compared her work to a static, painted portrait, her verbal rendition had to capture Fry at many time periods in his life and create continuity among them. Neither the seven photographs of him included in the book nor a series of portraits done over many years was an equivalent. Woolf used only one of her sister's portraits of Fry, and it is on the cover (Figure 4.1). There Bell depicts Fry in a characteristic pose, with his brush poised above his palette and his eyes staring intently to the left at what must be a work in progress. Although Woolf's portrayal of Fry is more comprehensive, the seriousness and intensity of his expression in the painting parallel characteristics emphasized in the written account. Both sisters understood Fry's own priorities. In Woolf's words, "His painting was beyond comparison more important to him than his criticism" (RF 293).

In "The New Biography" (1927) Woolf had already discussed the compromises twentieth-century biographers negotiate, with varying degrees of success, between fact and fiction. Biographers try to combine them because "the life which is increasingly real to us is

4.1. Vanessa Bell. Dust jacket for *Roger Fry: A Biography* (London: Hogarth, 1940) by Virginia Woolf. Courtesy of Jean Peters; permission of the estate of Vanessa Bell and the Hogarth Press.

the fictitious life" that reveals the private person (CE IV 234). In most of her own biographical writing, Woolf lets fiction overwhelm fact. As early as 1907 she wrote "Friendships Gallery," a comic biography in which Violet Dickinson and Nelly Cecil eventually become sacred princesses who leave "Tokio" on the back of a sea monster.[10] The same tendency caused her to note in her diary in 1922, "One of these days, . . . I shall sketch here, like a grand historical picture, the outlines of all my friends." The portraits, she notes, "should be truthful; but fantastic." She would begin with Gerald Brenan, include Lytton Strachey, Roger Fry, Duncan Grant, Clive Bell, Adrian Stephen, and Vita Sackville-West as "Orlando, a young nobleman" (D III 156–57). Woolf's plans for a grand historical picture resulted in *Orlando* (1928), her mock biography of Vita in which the main character lives through several hundred years and changes from male to female before she emerges in the present century.

Vanessa also wanted to sketch the outlines of her friends both individually and together. In 1933 she planned but never completed a series of caricatures which were to be combined with written versions by Virginia.[11] She did complete a group portrait, however, in about 1943. Because Virginia, Lytton Strachey, and Roger Fry were dead by then, Vanessa had to find an imaginative, yet truthful way to include them. In *The Memoir Club*, portraits by Duncan Grant of Woolf and Strachey and one of Fry by Vanessa herself hang on the wall above an unposed, seated group consisting of Duncan Grant, Leonard Woolf, Vanessa and Clive Bell, David Garnett, Maynard and Lydia Keynes, Desmond and Molly MacCarthy, Quentin Bell, and E. M. Forster (Figure 4.2).[12] Some sit with their backs toward the viewer; some look down, some away. Although the individuals are recognizable, they also blend into a roughly circular group. *The Memoir Club* is Vanessa Bell's grand historical picture. Her friends merge in space although the portraits of the dead evoke a temporal dimension. Virginia's Orlando has multiple selves that merge in time as she occupies country estates and roams city streets. In this case a similar impulse had strikingly different results.

There is a parallel, then, between commissioned portrait painters and authorized biographers. Visual artists who paint people when and as they wish are more like mock biographers or like novelists. Walter

4.2. Vanessa Bell. *The Memoir Club*, c. 1943, Private collection. Permission of Angelica Garnett.

Sickert, Virginia Woolf writes, even when seen as a "great biographer," need not be impeded by too many details. He can communicate the essence of an ordinary person's life (CE II 235) by providing not just one fact after another but, instead, "the creative fact; the fertile fact; the fact that suggests and engenders" (CE IV 228). The question of superficial likeness as opposed to true character dominated Vanessa Bell's reactions to the portraits she painted during the second and third decades of the century, just as it preoccupied Woolf's thoughts about people in general as well as biography and fiction during the same period. A likeness was of primary importance to Bell only when the portrait was commissioned.[13] Otherwise her paintings of people were not noted for their verisimilitude. Some difficulties resulted. For instance, in 1928 Clive Bell complimented her on a portrait of Mary Hutchinson in a recent show. He was annoyed at Roger Fry, however, for putting Mary's name in the catalogue as the title of the painting, since it was neither representational nor flattering.[14] Desmond MacCarthy also noted the nonrepresentational quality of Vanessa's portraits. He wrote to Clive with good-natured mockery that he would bring on his visit the suit appropriate for Vanessa's portrait of him; the fact that it had a hole in the elbow would not matter since exact details did not concern her anyway.[15] Vanessa's correspondence with Roger Fry indicates that she wanted most to convey her subject's essential character. Fry admired her ability to do so without verisimilitude and praised her in print for her "great power of characterisation."[16]

Vanessa Bell also subordinates human figures to her interest in light, color, and overall composition. While her early portrait paintings were relatively conservative,[17] in the second decade of the century she painted people with featureless faces. An example is *The Studio* (1912), a depiction of Duncan Grant and Henri Doucet at their easels (Figure 4.3). Here Vanessa is interested in modulating and balancing browns and grays with whites and flesh tones as well as rectangles with curves. In other paintings, she may suggest human features, but increasingly her concern is brilliant colors and simplified forms, as in the portrait of Lytton Strachey done in 1913 (Figure 4.4). Strachey has yellow in his skin and shirt, orange in his hat band and beard, and a green jacket. He sits in a blue chair and reads a red-covered book.[18] Vanessa's preference for informal, brightly colored, simplified portraits is perhaps a reaction to the early years at Hyde Park Gate. There, she recalls, "darkness and silence" pervaded the house, and "At dinner in the evening faces loomed out of the surrounding shade like Rembrandt portraits. . . ." To these visual impressions she contrasts "the bare plaster walls and faces seen against them" that she encountered in the house of the painter Charles Furse.[19] Like some of her predecessors and contemporaries in France, Bell found human beings interesting, but not necessarily more so than inanimate objects. Both could be worked into striking combinations of color and line in interior as well as exterior settings. Vanessa Bell thus goes beyond the superficially representational portrait in two ways: she attempts to capture her subject's essential character, and she subordinates human figures to her interest in light, color, and overall composition.

Virginia Woolf confronted the problem of representation and

4.3. Vanessa Bell. *The Studio: Duncan Grant and Henri Doucet Painting at Asheham*, 1912. Private collection, U.S.A.; Courtesy of the Anthony d'Offay Gallery, London; permission of Angelica Garnett.

4.4. Vanessa Bell. *Portrait of Lytton Strachey*, c. 1913. Anthony d'Offay Gallery, London. Courtesy of Christie's; permission of Angelica Garnett.

solved it in similar ways. Early in 1919 she too attempted a portrait of Lytton Strachey. Just as Vanessa's earlier painting reveals little interest in the minute details of his appearance, so Virginia's diary "portrait of Lytton" places the emphasis elsewhere. She considers the traits he shares with his relatives and his own more negative qualities, then combines these with his "mental gifts, & gifts of character—honesty, loyalty, intelligence of a spiritual order." She attacks the inadequacies of her portrait, however: "Written down these words are too emphatic and linear; one should see them tempered & combined with all those charming, subtle & brilliant qualities which compose his being in the flesh" (D I 236). Her description of the missing qualities brings to mind Vanessa's colorful painting and suggests that the verbal rendition needs some more sensory counterpart.

Woolf's attempts to get at Strachey's essential character and to see him in larger contexts as well are characteristic of her diary entries; these, her equivalent of the visual artist's sketches, serve in part as exercises for fictional characterizations. In her diary Woolf distinguishes between "portraits to sketch; conversations to write down; & reflections to work in" (D II 114) but, using the term loosely, she calls all three "portraits." The diary entries do include treatments of her friends that are primarily visual. Then she sees people as "detached . . . —cut out, emphatic, seen thus separately compared with the usual way of seeing them in crowds" (D II 126); her friends and visitors become "a gallery of little bright portraits hanging against the wall of my mind" (D II 156) or merely "pictures hung on the wall" (D III 46). One value of her diary, Woolf reminds herself when she is tempted not to write, is that "many portraits are owed to it" (D II 170). Her portraits single out individuals, isolate them under a spotlight either flattering or mocking. Woolf's diary is filled with such glimpses of people's appearances: "Nessa in her spotted feather hat with the pink plume" (D II 6), or "All very gay in French boots, hat, & check skirt; with that queer antique simplicity of surface which I compare to the marble cheeks of a Greek statue" (D II 156); "long fatuous Philip [Morrell] in his leather gaiters, double breasted waistcoat & jewelled buttons to go those lengths" (D II 7); Ottoline Morrell in her "sealing wax green" dress (D II 19); and Mark Gertler with his "tightly buttoned face" (D II 150).

Since her medium is verbal, however, Woolf increasingly turns to her subject's words or to conversations as a more congenial method of portraiture. In spite of the many descriptive passages that writers produce, as Wendy Steiner indicates, "the proper imitative subject of writing can only be speech"[20] or, one might add, that portion of the thought process carried on in words or, finally, more writing. Woolf partly solved her problems with *Roger Fry*, in fact, when she decided to "paint" him primarily through his own words: letters, essays, remembered conversations, many of them about art. "I was certain he would shine by his own light better than through any painted shade of mine," she wrote (L VI 417).[21] So the biography has an element of self-portraiture after all, but Fry is the painter. In this instance, the analogy between biography and painting seems more inhibiting than stimulating. If Woolf has to paint a formal portrait, she would rather deny her skill and abnegate the responsibility. She hands her sitter the brush.

When her speakers are unknown, Woolf is more comfortable. Among her recently published materials are eight or nine short verbal portraits, some or all of which she may have written for "Faces and Voices," the collaborative project she and Vanessa Bell planned in 1937.[22] The group is a compendium of techniques. Perhaps recalling Sickert's paintings of everyday life, Woolf creates a third-person description of the surroundings of Monsieur and Madam Louvois as they notice nothing and wait for the waiter to bring their plate of tripe (CSF 236). In another portrait one character transforms another into a still life reminiscent of a Cézanne painting: "Her face was yellow and red; round too; a fruit on a body; another apple, only not on a plate. Breasts had formed apple-hard under the blouse on her body" (CSF 237). Characters also describe or reveal themselves through interior or dramatic monologues. In one of these, an elderly London gentleman, who says he should be living in an earlier era, comments on painting. Although he loves beauty and thinks he appreciates painting more because he is not a painter himself, he no longer goes to galleries. They are too crowded, he says. Nor would he want to be one of today's painters whose wild lives contrast so markedly to Fra Angelico's devout toil. He thinks he should live in Italy where he has met other people who love beauty, but he either cannot recall their names or never really knew them (CSF 239–40).[23] His words would have amused Vanessa and no doubt were written partly for that purpose.

The people in Woolf's work talk about paintings and people, objects and sights we cannot see. The people in Bell's paintings speak words we cannot hear. She paints people conversing in, for example, *Street Corner Conversation*, *The Conversation*, and *A Conversation Piece*, but she emphasizes figures grouped in a total composition, usually circular, not the talk. The subtitle of Woolf's *Walter Sickert, A Conversation*, recalls several of Vanessa's works. On such occasions, each sister evokes the other's medium and defines the boundaries of her own.

Words, whether about painting or other topics, may reveal character. Unfortunately, Woolf complains in her diary, people usually "don't say things," or else she cannot record them effectively (D II 163, 202). Still she keeps practicing, sometimes in dramatic form (D II 252). Some of the dialogues Woolf records in her diary are with Vanessa. In 1922, for example, Virginia set down a portion of their conversation about Clive and his relationship with Mary Hutchinson (D II 157). In her next entry, Virginia returned to an interchange with Vanessa and tried to define why it was "painful": "Perhaps it is that we both feel that we can exist independently of the other. The door shuts between us, & life flows on again & completely removes the trace." She exaggerates, she realizes, and decides that the real problem is Vanessa's dislike of being back in a country where no one mentions painting. Again Virginia records a bit of their conversation in which they argue about who is more unconventional, Vanessa with her nonbinding relationship with Duncan Grant or Virginia with her childless marriage. Vanessa contrasts her spartan and bohemian existence in Paris with her sister's more stable, comfortable one and leaves Virginia discontented with the whole encounter (D II 159). On other occasions she is more dissatisfied with her efforts to capture the appearance and conversation of her model than she is with the substance of the discussion. After a struggle to portray Violet Dickinson, she despairs: "But this doesn't make a picture, all the same" (D II 165–66). No doubt these many efforts to record conversations account for Virginia Woolf's interest, throughout her career, in what people cannot say or in what they leave unspoken, in the abyss between their thoughts and what they communicate to others, and in what is communicated entirely without words.

Aware of numerous distinctions in characterization in the novel, Woolf attributes them to the writer's historical period, individual temperament, and nationality (CE I 325). She contrasts a stereotypical Edwardian novel, which would present the hypothetical Mrs. Brown by means of multiple facts about her external appearance and surroundings, with another kind of novel, one that captures "human nature" (CE I 330) and ultimately the quality of "life itself" (CE I 337). The difficulty of capturing the truth about people's lives and relationships recurs in Woolf's thoughts about her own fiction as well as in the fiction itself. Considering *Jacob's Room* she asks, "But how far can one convey character without realism?" She admits her inability to produce realistic writing (L II 571) and her desire to get away from "strict representation" (L II 588; 568–69). But even a definition of reality which includes the internal life is elusive. A refrain in *Jacob's Room* is "It is no use trying to sum people up. One must follow hints, not exactly what is said, nor yet entirely what is done" (JR 31). It is easier to grasp a person's appearance than "what was in his mind" (JR 94). Yet that information is what Woolf wants most. So do the artist characters in her novels. "How . . . did one know one thing or another thing about people, sealed as they were?" Lily Briscoe asks, pondering the secret of Mrs. Ramsay in *To the Lighthouse* (TTL 79). Ultimately she has to distance herself, subdue "the impertinences and irrelevances" (TTL 235) and know people by "the outline, not the detail" (TTL 289).

If biography is more tied to representation, Woolf repeats elsewhere in the same year as *To the Lighthouse*, the novel "will give, as poetry does, the outline rather than the detail" (CE II 224–25),[24] will transcend the personal and examine "the relations of man to nature, to fate; his imagination; his dreams" (CE II 226). The novelist will penetrate external facts to reveal what goes on within the characters and also place them in larger psychological, intellectual, social, natural, and aesthetic patterns. Two years later in "Phases of Fiction," Woolf notes that "the most complete novelist" will balance the "close touch with life" with the distance that "the gift of style, arrangement, construction" achieves (CE II 101).

To present a reality so complex, Woolf thinks not only temporally but spatially. When Lily Briscoe in *To the Lighthouse* tries to capture the essence of Mrs. Ramsay, she paints by "tunnelling her way into her picture, into the past" (TTL 258). So Woolf herself had discovered a way to "dig out beautiful caves behind . . . characters." This "tunnelling process" relates "the past by installments," as needed (D II 263, 272). Ultimately all of the caves or tunnels will "connect, & each comes to daylight at the present moment" (D II 263). Such is her method in *Mrs. Dalloway*. The selected contents of several intersecting minds, not sets of external characteristics or even spoken words, form the substance of the novel. In a related sense *The*

Waves is "a gigantic conversation" (D III 285) by means of which Woolf wants to "give in a very few strokes the essential of a person's character." She wants to proceed "boldly, almost as caricature" (D III 300). As in *Mrs. Dalloway*, however, the juxtaposition of the characters' thoughts or soliloquies and the overlapping of their experiences and memories result in connections among the caves or tunnels. The results are individual portraits within a group picture, as in Vanessa Bell's *The Memoir Club*.

In *The Waves* Woolf is still concerned with the problem of knowing people. Bernard, for example, closely observes "an elderly and apparently prosperous man" on the train and tries to imagine what his private and public lives are like. Bernard has a compulsion to fill his mind with facts, "with whatever happens to be the contents of a room or a railway carriage as one fills a fountain-pen in an inkpot" (W 67–68). Jinny too is curious about people and tries to know them through close observation; they "are so soon gone;" she says, "let us catch them." To do so "One must be quick and add facts deftly, like toys to a tree, fixing them with a twist of the fingers" (W 174), and one must "decipher the hieroglyphs written on other people's faces" (W 175). Such methods fulfill certain needs for the observer, but they do not solve the riddles of other people's identities or, for that matter, the observer's own.

Both sisters counter the desire to capture external facts by experimenting with varying degrees of abstraction. Thinking about the "Time Passes" section of *To the Lighthouse*, Virginia Woolf noted that it was "the most difficult abstract piece of writing—I have to give an empty house, no people's characters, the passage of time, all eyeless & featureless with nothing to cling to" (D III 76). Woolf's interest usually is in her characters' inner lives, not in their faces, but in this passage she uses eyes and other features to represent her deviation from the traditional, more representational novelist's methods. Time itself becomes her character and its face has no features. Here abstract writing, for Woolf, is eliminating characterization and restricting her verbal medium to its purely temporal dimension. The experiment creates difficulties and insecurities. For Vanessa Bell, total abstraction is painting without recognizable objects, human or nonhuman, and limiting her visual medium to colors, lines, shapes, and textures. Although she did several such paintings, Vanessa usually sought a lesser degree of abstraction, at least in her renditions of people, by eliminating features from faces.

Woolf not only thinks of sections of her novels as featureless but also creates characters who see themselves and other people that way. Featureless faces, like those in some of her sister's paintings, can suggest a terrifying lack of identity; more often faces rid of features transcend the individual and tap the communal or the eternal. Most representative is *The Waves* (1931).[25] Rhoda particularly thinks of herself as faceless and of her life as merely disconnected moments directed at no goal (W 130). Unlike her friends she has no "children, authority, fame, love, society" and no "attitude" or commitment to give her life coherence; therefore, she thinks, "I have no face" (W 223). She is frightened and alienated. Ottoline Morrell identified Rhoda with Virginia (D IV 73), but clearly Woolf drew upon aspects of her own experience for other characters as well, sometimes with the opposite results. The same experience of becoming featureless, for instance, calms and interests Bernard. It brings him into contact with "this omnipresent, general life": "The surface of my mind slips along like a pale-grey stream reflecting what passes. I cannot remember my past, my nose, or the colour of my eyes, or what my general opinion of myself is. . . . The roar of the traffic, the passage of undifferentiated faces, this way and that way, drugs me into dreams; rubs the features from faces" (W 113). The experience recurs, triggered for a talker like Bernard by silence: "I am dissolved utterly," he says, "and become featureless and scarcely to be distinguished from another" (W 224).

Other people sometimes become featureless to Bernard because they are unimportant or because he has transcended the temporal. He realizes that he can be free, if only at moments, from the inexorable succession of ordinary days. As if he were in front of a painting, he experiences beauty; he sees "two figures standing with their backs to the window . . . against the branches of a spreading tree. With a shock of emotion one feels 'There are figures without features robed in beauty, doomed yet eternal'" (W 271). Even Rhoda, when the featureless faces are those of other people, not herself, is comforted. "When I have passed through this drawing-room flickering with tongues that cut me like knives," she notes, she can look from a balcony at "a world immune from change." There she sees two people "leaning like statues against the sky" and finds "faces rid of features, robed in beauty" (W 106–7). The fact that Bernard and Rhoda have the same experience embodied in almost the same words obliterates their individual features as well and blends them for a moment into one consciousness. In Woolf's fiction, then, the uncertainties of individual identities, the muddles of human relationships, even the inadequacies of language itself become parts of larger concerns and patterns. These she associates with her sister's art, the silent painted portrait.

Both sisters also depart from representation by recognizing the relativity of human perception, but their portraits reveal it in different ways. As Virginia knew, Vanessa and other painters often used the same model at the same time. When they painted Lytton Strachey, for example, Vanessa Bell, Roger Fry, and Duncan Grant placed their easels at alternate distances and angles.[26] Together Vanessa and Duncan painted quite different portraits of Henri Doucet (1912), Iris Tree (1915), Mary Hutchinson (1915), and David Garnett (1915; Figures 4.5 and 4.6).[27] Two members of the group may disagree on a third, Vanessa noted when she wrote her memoir on Bloomsbury in 1951, "yet each view may throw light and make the subject alive." She drew an explicit parallel with painting: "The two portraits of Chocquet by Cézanne and Renoir give very different views of the same man. That only adds to one's knowledge of the original."[28] Woolf's much-discussed multiple points of view in novels like *Mrs. Dalloway*, *To the Lighthouse*, and *The Waves* go even further to communicate relativity. Each character appears through the eyes of several others as well as through his or her own thoughts and sensations. Yet, although each portrait is a composite, it is inevitably incomplete. "Fifty pairs of eyes were not enough," as Lily Briscoe says, to sum up Mrs. Ramsay (TTL 294).

Woolf also communicates the relativity of perception through her characters' comments. *The Waves* is representative. Sitting at a table with his friends, Bernard notes a red carnation in a vase: "A single flower as we sat here waiting, but now a seven-sided flower, many-petalled, red, puce, purple-shaded, stiff with silver-tinted leaves—a whole flower to which every eye brings its own contribution" (W 127). So all of the characters have different visual images of Percival, and Bernard concludes that he himself is multiple. With the loss of Percival, however, the seven-sided flower becomes "six-sided . . .; made of six lives" which are in some mysterious way "One Life" (W 229). Each character perceives only part of the whole in another; each forms part of a whole glimpsed only occasionally.[29]

One reason why everyone perceives the same person or object differently is that emotion colors perception. Tears transform what Betty Flanders sees in *Jacob's Room* (JR 7) and what Orlando sees in

4.5. Vanessa Bell. *Portrait of David Garnett*, 1915. Courtesy of the Anthony d'Offay Gallery, London; permission of Angelica Garnett.

4.6. Duncan Grant. *Portrait of David Garnett*, 1915. Private collection. Courtesy of the Anthony d'Offay Gallery, London; permission of Angelica Garnett.

Orlando (O 286). In *The Years* pleasure affects Peggy's sight: "The stars had softened; they quivered" (Y 362). The presence of a special person also can transform surroundings for others. Virginia thought that Vanessa could alter the room she entered (L II 292). So in *The Waves* Rhoda thinks that when Miss Lambert passes, "everything changes and becomes luminous" (W 45). Percival too has this ability. his "intensity of being," says Neville, causes objects to lose "their normal uses—this knife-blade is only a flash of light, not a thing to cut with. The normal is abolished" (W 119) and the artist's fresh perspective imposed. Without Percival, Neville thinks, "we are silhouettes, hollow phantoms moving mistily without a background" (W 122). Jinny, too, transforms her surroundings and knows it: "When I came in just now," she says, "everything stood still in a pattern" (W 128).

Featureless faces, like those in some of Vanessa's paintings, then, occasionally suggest to Virginia Woolf a lack or a loss of identity which can be terrifying; more often they suggest a transcendence of the individual to the communal and possibly to some eternal principles of order. For most people, an awareness of the patterns they create and those in which they move occurs only at moments, but the artist can communicate such experiences and assure others of their validity.

Each sister portrayed the other numerous times in ways that illustrate the ability of both painter and writer to transform reality into art. These portraits are another way they stimulated each other's creativity. Not all of the ones Vanessa did of Virginia have survived. In 1908, for example, Francis Dodd convinced Virginia to sit for him. Vanessa joined him and recorded painting her sister in a "green and yellow dress against a dark blue background, life size or a very little under[,] down to below her waist sitting with one hand on a table." The pose was not original, Vanessa said, but the color was "rather beautiful." Still she admitted that she was "nervous about doing her [sister] justice."[30] In 1912, Vanessa did several portraits of Virginia that still exist. Through these paintings, Spalding says, Vanessa learned to communicate emotion and personality by capturing a characteristic pose.[31]

In one of these paintings, Virginia reclines in a deck chair

(Figure 4.7). As in many of Vanessa's works from this period, including a self-portrait currently in a private collection, the sitter is faceless, although the shape of the face and the pose suggest Virginia. Her figure almost fills the shallow picture space. Red-stockinged ankle foremost, one leg is crossed over the other beneath the long gray skirt of a dress. The red tie at the throat echoes the red of the stocking, just as the white collar of the dress echoes the white of a book page on the sitter's lap. The brim of a large hat repeats the gray of the dress and the curve of the knee, while the flesh tones of the arm lying atop the book are picked up in the face as well as in an arm-shaped horizontal form behind the sitter at upper right. Virginia leans her head back against the chair with its gold-colored frame. This warm color is combined with the soft green of sunlit grass surrounding the figure. Looking slightly down at the sitter we see none of the sky; above and slightly to the right of the hat, we see only the bottoms of two tree trunks. The picture is a masterful orchestration of neutral and warm colors, of angular and round shapes, of light, and of line.

Another portrait from this period catches Virginia, dressed in subdued shades of green and blue-green, reclining in a deep, orange-colored, wing-backed chair and concentrating on some needlework on her lap (Figure 4.8). Again the marked simplification of this stage in Vanessa Bell's painting is evident; she reduces the sitter to a series of shapes and colors that harmonize with those of the chair and the bluish background; the features of the face are not detailed, although this time they are suggested. Such is not the case with a third portrait done at about the same time (Figure 4.9). Unlike the other two, it does not catch Virginia asleep or occupied; it captures her seemingly in the middle of a word, leaning forward, lips parted, eyes looking off to the viewer's left. Here the focus is the face. The upper body is merely suggested. Flesh tones recur in the prevailing blues and greens of the clothes and background. Leon Edel lists the painting as unfinished, as well it might have been if the sitter had become too uncomfortable under scrutiny.

Because Virginia hated being observed for long periods of time, Vanessa did fewer portraits of her than she otherwise might have done. In 1931 she did a drawing of Virginia in Stephen Tomlin's studio in order to get her to sit for him. Unable to stand the sculptor's probing eyes, however, Virginia refused to go back after only a few brief sessions: "Oh dear, what a terrific hemp strong heather root

4.7. Vanessa Bell. *Virginia Woolf*, 1912. Ivor Braka Ltd., London. Courtesy of Mrs. Trekkie Parsons; permission of Angelica Garnett.

4.8. Vanessa Bell. *Virginia Woolf at Asheham*, 1912. National Portrait Gallery, London. Courtesy of Mrs. Trekkie Parsons; permission of Angelica Garnett.

4.9. Vanessa Bell. *Virginia Woolf*, 1912. Monks House; Rodmell, Sussex (The National Trust). Courtesy of Mrs. Trekkie Parsons; permission of Angelica Garnett.

4.10. Stephen Tomlin. *Virginia Woolf*, 1931. Permission of the National Portrait Gallery, London.

obstinate fountain of furious individuality shoots in me," she wrote in her diary; "—they tampered with it—Nessa & Tommy—pining me there, from 2 to 4 on 6 afternoons, to be looked at" (D IV 36–37). The irony, as Quentin Bell points out, is that the uncompleted bust is one of Tomlin's best works and one of the best likenesses of Woolf (Figure 4.10).[32] Virginia reported that she was sitting for Vanessa in 1932 and again in 1933 and 1934 (L V 22, 30; D IV 191, 200). A portrait, dated 1934, may have been one result (Figure 4.11).[33] It shows Virginia once again in an armchair; this time, however,

4.11. Vanessa Bell. *Virginia Woolf*, 1934. Current location unknown. Permission of Angelica Garnett.

Vanessa clearly represents her sister's facial features. The chair is at a diagonal and Virginia, in three-quarter profile, turns her eyes directly towards the viewer. Her expression is serious. In a dark dress with light sleeves and collar, she sits, legs crossed, and rests her left forearm on one arm of the chair; her right elbow rests on the other. In her right hand is what appears to be a cigarette. She sits in a fully delineated corner of a room with tables stacked with books, a vase of flowers, and bookshelves to her right, a painted mural, wall, or screen behind her, and a patterned carpet beneath her feet. Both the decoration and the carpet are the kinds that Bell and Grant designed.[34]

One of Vanessa Bell's last attempts to portray her sister was on the jacket for *Virginia Woolf and Lytton Strachey: Letters* (1956; Figure 4.12). Against black curving brushstrokes on a cream-colored background are two ornate, oval frames on either side of a single pedestal. Within them are two solid, black profiles facing each other. Lytton's mouth is hidden by mustache and beard, but Virginia's lips are parted. As the design suggests, Virginia Woolf and Lytton Strachey lived in two separate domestic worlds, but they were linked by their pasts, their communications with each other, and their devotion to writing in general. By the time this volume appeared, however, their letters and books as well as the visual and written portraits of them by others were all that remained.

Profiles are appropriate for the cover of the posthumous Woolf/Strachey letters. They provide only a partial view and make the subjects seem aloof, the inhabitants of another world. A full face is more complete in the information it provides and more intimate with the viewer, but it seems immobile. The three-quarter profile is a successful compromise and the one Vanessa Bell uses most frequently in her portraits of Virginia; in the process of turning, the face gives the illusion of vitality. Whether the face, the half, the three-quarter, or the whole figure is represented is also important, since the more of the subject and its environment we see, the more our response is affected by the sitter's social status and profession as well as historical time and place.[35] The 1934 portrait of Virginia, thoroughly ensconced in an environment of books, flowers, furniture, and the decorative arts, is also the one with her facial features most clearly delineated. She sits in a natural pose in her daily milieu. In Vanessa Bell's paintings, Woolf says in the "Foreword" she wrote for the

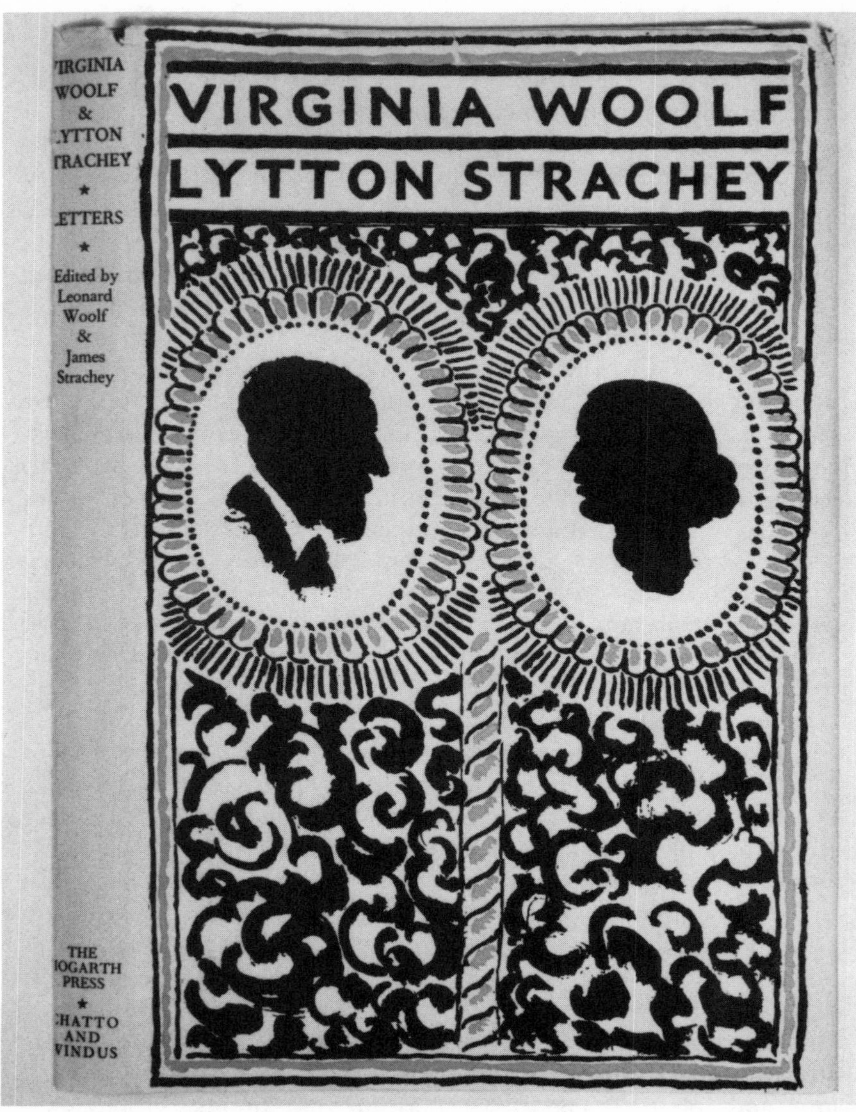

4.12. Vanessa Bell. Dust jacket for *Virginia Woolf and Lytton Strachey: Letters* (London: Hogarth, 1956). Courtesy of Jean Peters; permission of the estate of Vanessa Bell and the Hogarth Press.

exhibition in the same year, 1934, "People's minds have split out of their bodies and become part of their surroundings."[36]

This portrait and the comment on Vanessa's exhibition parallel a method Woolf uses to create characters. Although they seem opposites, figures with featureless faces which form parts of larger patterns and more detailed figures within fully recreated environments have an effect upon the perceiver that is in one respect similar. In both cases the boundaries of the individual fade and the ego fuses with its surroundings. In "The Lady in the Looking Glass," the narrator speculates that Isabella's carpets and furniture seemed to know "more about her than we, who sat on them, wrote at them, and trod on them so carefully, were allowed to know" (HH 89). The fusion of people and places is also the foundation for "Great Men's Houses," one of Woolf's essays on London. Woolf declares that "One hour spent in 5 Cheyne Row" will reveal more about the Carlyles and the way they lived than "all the biographies" can.[37] Similarly, Pepys' diary, Woolf says, presents "a portrait where not only the main figure, but the surroundings, ornaments, and accessories are painted in" (BP 40).

One of Woolf's best-known attempts to portray someone at least in part by means of surroundings is her description of Jacob Flander's room in her third novel. Empty of Jacob, it reveals something about him through his accessories. The furniture is minimal. The slippers are "incredibly shabby, like boats burnt to the water's rim." Decorations include photos of his mother and some "from the Greeks" as well as a Reynolds mezzotint. "Cards from societies with little raised crescents, coats of arms, and initials" suggest social activity and status. Notes and an essay entitled "Does History consist of the Biographies of Great Men?" indicate scholarly interests. Most revealing in this regard is Jacob's eclectic taste in books: literature, philosophy, art, and animals. Pressed flowers coexist with pipes. Jacob's presence permeates the room, yet his absence is also apparent: "Listless is the air in an empty room, just swelling the curtain; the flowers in the jar shift. One fibre in the wicker armchair creaks, though no one sits there" (JR 39). Out of the environment emerges its inhabitant, although his outline is faint and not all of the details are filled in. So, in *Mrs. Dalloway*, Peter Walsh ponders Clarissa's theory that "the unseen part of us, which spreads wide, the unseen might survive, be recovered somehow attached to this person or that, or even haunting certain places after death . . . " (MD 232).

In *To the Lighthouse*, Woolf merges Mrs. Ramsay with her surroundings. She becomes "the thing she looked at." Alone, she leans "to inanimate things; trees, streams, flowers; felt they expressed one; felt they became one; felt they knew one, in a sense were one . . ." (TTL 97). After her death, Mrs. Ramsay survives in Lily's memories but also in mysterious visions. In one, Lily sees her "putting her wreath to her forehead and going unquestioningly with her companion, a shade across the fields" (TTL 270); in another, Mrs. Ramsay sits in the window again, knitting a stocking (TTL 300). Her death creates emptiness, but she also remains part of the lives she touched and the environment she occupied. Orlando also perceives, as she tours the rooms of her house, that her only immortality will be "that her soul would come and go for ever with the reds on the panels and the greens on the sofa" (O 317). Woolf is not so opposed, then, to externals as her denunciation of the "materialists" among novelists in "Modern Fiction" would imply (CE II 104). But she makes clear, in "The Lady in the Looking Glass" and elsewhere, that people's surroundings are not infallible guides to their essential characters.

Neither are people's appearances. Even Vanessa's is deceptive. Although she looks like a "potential peeress," she wants only "paint and turpentine," Virginia says (MB 148–49). Except in *Orlando*, where she parodies such methods, Woolf rarely provides lengthy descriptions of her characters' physical appearances. When she does, usually in her earlier novels, she does so through their own eyes or through the eyes of other characters. The people in her fiction think especially about what they or others wear. Mable Waring suffers agonies in the "pale yellow, idiotically old-fashioned silk dress" that she had hoped would make her charming (HH 48). Peter Walsh admires Clarissa Dalloway "Lolloping on the waves" in her "silver-green mermaid's dress" (MD 264). While clothes reveal something about such wearers and observers, they do not reveal everything. Nor can one strip away people's costumes and discover truth, in spite of observations like the one in *Orlando* that "often it is only the clothes that keep the male or female likeness, while underneath the sex is the very opposite of what it is above" (O 189). The body uncovered, as Sandra Gilbert points out, is merely another costume in most twentieth-century women's writing, another of the multiple selves or dimensions that make up any individual.[38] Woolf does not describe nudity in her fiction. Just as she presents her characters' experience of clothes and not clothes themselves, so, as "Professions for Women" indicates, she wants to present not the body but its "passions." Dealing with her own "experiences as a body" is difficult for her and for women writers, she says, because they are "impeded by the extreme conventionality of the other sex" (CE II 288). Still, even with the restrictions of her own temperament and of society, she frequently writes powerfully of a wide range of physical responses and needs, from the fears of Rachel Vinrace in *The Voyage Out* to the hungers of Miss Kilman in *Mrs. Dalloway*.[39]

In spite of similar restrictions placed on women art students in the recent past, Vanessa Bell did paint nudes, as pictures like *The Bathers* (1911), *The Tub*, (1918), *Interior with Two Women* (1932), and a number of her decorative designs indicate.[40] Her full-length nudes are more likely to be women or children than men, so perhaps some inhibitions remain, yet clearly her interest is less in the fact of nudity than in its compositional possibilities. In *The Tub*, for example, she works with curved forms; in *The Bathers*, *Interior with Two Women*, as well as *The Nursery*, contrasts between figures, some clothed, some unclothed, preoccupy her. Each sister subordinates the body, in ways that suit her own medium, to her main concerns. Woolf presents the life of the body through the mind of a character, Bell the shapes and colors of bodies in the context of other shapes and colors.

Just as Vanessa painted portraits of Virginia, so Virginia recreated Vanessa in her fiction with varying degrees of verisimilitude and thoroughness. Not only did she write a life of Vanessa in 1908 (L I 325), but she also drew upon her for *The Voyage Out*. "Of Helen I cannot trust myself to speak," Clive wrote to Virginia about a draft of the novel, "but I suppose you will make Vanessa believe in herself."[41] Richard Shone says that Vanessa recognized some of her own qualities in Helen Ambrose who, with "apparent calm," sits quietly and embroiders.[42] To Helen, moreover, the eye is all important. She refuses to go for a walk: "'one's only got to use one's eye,'" she says. "'There's everything here—everything,' she repeated in a drowsy tone of voice. 'What will you gain by walking?'" (VO 269–70).

Of Vanessa's role in the creation of Katharine Hilbery in *Night and Day*, Virginia was candid from the beginning. "I am very much interested in your life," she wrote to Vanessa in 1916, "which I think of writing another novel about" (L II 109). Two years later she reported, "I've been writing about you all the morning, and have made you wear a blue dress; you've got to be immensely mysterious and romantic, which of course you are; yes, but its the combination that's so enthralling; to crack through the paving stone and be enveloped in the mist" (L II 232). Paving stone and mist suggest the androgyny Virginia says is essential for the artist; they also recall granite and rainbow and the qualities both sisters insist must be united in a work of art. To Janet Case in 1919, Virginia wrote about *Night and Day*, ". . . try thinking of Katharine [Hilbery] as Vanessa, not me; and suppose her concealing a passion for painting and forced to go into society by George [Duckworth]—that was the beginning of her . . ." (L II 400).

Virginia dedicated the book to her sister in a way that is both personal and impersonal. "But looking for a phrase," she wrote, "I found none to stand beside your name." Vanessa acknowledged her role in the novel's conception. "I am the principal character in it," she wrote to Roger Fry, "& I expect I'm a very priggish & severe young woman but perhaps you'll see what I was like at 18. I think the most interesting character is evidently my mother who is made exactly like Lady Ritchie down to every detail apparently. Everyone will know who it is of course."[43] Her comments imply that she had not yet read the novel, but even if she had, as we have seen, she would likely have had trouble getting beyond a personal response to Virginia's work.

In the novel itself, Katharine Hilbery has the opposite problem. Instead of life obscuring art, art obscures life. She looks at Ralph Denham with her mother's comparison of him to a portrait of Ruskin in her mind. This circumstance

> led her to be more critical of the young man than was fair, for a young man paying a call in a tail-coat is in a different element altogether from a head seized at its climax of expressiveness, gazing immutably from behind a sheet of glass, which was all that remained to her of Mr. Ruskin. He had a singular face—a face built for swiftness and decision rather than for massive contemplation; the forehead broad, the nose long and formidable, the lips clean-shaven and at once dogged and sensitive, the cheeks lean, with a deeply running tide of red blood in them.

> His eyes, expressive now of the usual masculine impersonality and authority, might reveal more subtle emotions under favorable circumstances, for they were large, and of a clear, brown color; they seemed unexpectedly to hesitate and speculate; but Katharine only looked at him to wonder whether his face would not have come nearer the standard of her dead heroes if it had been adorned with sidewhiskers. In his spare build and thin, though healthy, cheeks, she saw tokens of an angular and acrid soul (ND 16–17).

Woolf contains Katharine's limited view within the narrator's more complex one. Ruskin's image in her mind, Katharine not only fixes Ralph in an awkward moment, to his disadvantage, but also draws a simplistic conclusion about his inner life from his external appearance. His complexity is apparent when we add other people's assessments and his own.

The focus of *Night and Day*, however, is Katharine's identity. Her portrait, like Ralph's, is a composite of partial ones. Read on one level, the novel reveals some of Vanessa's characteristics as Virginia, frustrated by her sister's elusiveness, tries to capture her in words. Ralph Denham notes selected physical attributes, especially Katharine's eyes, and speculates about her character:

> She had the quick, impulsive movements of her mother, the lips parting often to speak, and closing again; and the dark oval eyes of her father brimming with light upon a basis of sadness, or, . . . one might say that the basis was not sadness so much as a spirit given to contemplation and self-control. Judging by her hair, her coloring, and the shape of her features, she was striking, if not actually beautiful. Decision and composure stamped her, . . . For the rest, she was tall; her dress was of some quiet color, with old yellow-tinted lace for ornament, to which the spark of an ancient jewel gave its one red gleam (ND 12–13).

Ralph Denham remembers Katharine after this first meeting as "the young woman with the sad, but inwardly ironical eyes" (ND 23) and later he thinks of "those honest sad eyes" (ND 95). He has to adjust his visual image, however. When he sees her in daylight, even her eyes look different: "now they looked bright with the brightness of the sea struck by an unclouded ray" (ND 235). Katharine accuses him of having seen her inaccurately, an accusation Vanessa often leveled at Virginia. Katharine insists that she is not "mysterious" and "romantic," but a "matter-of-fact, prosaic, rather ordinary character." Because Ralph is "very inexperienced and very emotional," he imagines a woman who does not exist and now cannot see the one who does. "You call that, I suppose, being in love," Katharine concludes; "as a matter of fact it's being in delusion" (ND 381).

Ralph is not the only one who sees Katharine inaccurately. To her cousin Henry, she insists that she is not the person most people think her: "In some ways, Henry," she says, "I'm a humbug—I mean, I'm not what you all take me for. I'm not domestic, or very practical or sensible, really" (ND 195). From Henry's point of view, Katharine is somewhat inhuman, a quality he thinks marriage might alleviate. He acknowledges her independence and competence, but he thinks her behavior to William is brutal. He speculates on women's "peculiar blindness to the feelings of men" (ND 203). William also concludes that Katharine is insensitive and resents her making him look foolish (ND 238). He decides that she is a woman of no moods, yet he realizes that "Beneath her steady, exemplary surface ran a vein of passion which seemed to him now perverse, now completely irrational, for it never took the normal channel of glorification of him and his doings" (ND 246). He does not think she wounds him purposely, yet she can't seem to help it: "Was she cold? Was she self-absorbed? He tried to fit her with each of these descriptions, but he had to own that she puzzled him" (ND 281). William perceives, too, that Katharine has an ease more masculine than feminine; the narrator, contrasting her to Cassandra, concurs (ND 341). Some of William's feelings of rejection and perplexity may well be Virginia's own. "William" is a version of "Billy," her own nickname. William also tells Katharine, much as Virginia told Vanessa, that he would rather she approved of his writing "than anyone in the world" (ND 140).

Other characters also remain perplexed. Mrs. Hilbery admires and relies upon her daughter's reserve but remains vaguely dissatisfied with her (ND 214). To Mary Datchet, Katharine is "inscrutable" (ND 175), possibly "maternal" in her relationship to William (ND 174), as well as somewhat irresponsible and unfeeling. "What an egoist, how aloof she was!" Mary thinks. "And yet, not in her words, perhaps, but in her voice, in her face, in her attitude, there were signs of a soft brooding spirit, of a sensibility unblunted and profound, playing over her thoughts and deeds, and investing her manner with an habitual gentleness" (ND 271). Tears in Katharine's eyes surprise Henry and later Cassandra. In the latter case, they are produced by "an emotion so complex in its nature that to express it was impossible" (ND 404). Partly because she reveals her feelings in her face, Ralph suspects that Katharine represses her emotions, a suspicion the narrator confirms.

To these pieces of her character, varying in their accuracy, Katharine adds her ignorance of most bodies of knowledge and her confusion about why she acts the way she does. She admits that "she was rather unobservant of the finer shades of feeling," but rather than charging herself with brutality, she sees her failures to interpret some situations correctly as "proof that she was a practical, abstract-minded person, better fitted to deal with figures than with the feelings of men and women." She realizes, however, that she may be merely echoing William's view of herself (ND 274). What she wants initially is some empty space in her life like Mary and Ralph seem to have, space not muddled with tangled human lives. She also wants time of her own not wasted on her mother's interminable project. What she ultimately gets is a marriage relationship with Ralph Denham that promises to be loneliness and profound independence shared.

Virginia Woolf admitted that unpredictable things happened as she developed Katharine's character. She became perhaps too "chilly." Woolf also subordinated her to the preoccupation with "the things one doesn't say" and the resulting questions: "what effect does that have? and how far do our feelings take their colour from the dive underground? I mean, what is the reality of any feeling?" The character was also affected by Woolf's concentration on "the form, which must sit tight, and perhaps in Night and Day sits too tight; as it was too loose in The Voyage Out" (L II 400). As the novel took shape, then, Vanessa's portrait was transformed by the demands of the work as a whole.

Virginia also drew upon Vanessa in her creation of *To the Lighthouse*. In an early draft Rose, one of the Ramsay daughters, dreams like Vanessa of a less conventional life "in Paris with painters."[44] Duncan Grant, however, thought Vanessa's characteristics and Julia Stephen's had been combined in Mrs. Ramsay; he thought that both had similar emotions.[45] Roger Fry asked in a letter how much Virginia had drawn upon her sister. Woolf admitted in replies to both Fry and Vanessa Bell that, although her sister and her mother were quite separate in her mind, possibly something of Vanessa did get into her portrait of Mrs. Ramsay (L III 383, 386). Fry was amazed at the description of Lily Briscoe and of the problems of a painter. Neither he nor Vanessa, he said, could have described those of a writer so well.[46] Vanessa too was impressed. "By the way," she wrote to Virginia, "surely Lily Briscoe must have been rather a good painter—before her time perhaps, but with great gifts really?" She insisted that "the bits about painting" did not make her laugh as Virginia had predicted, although she was not sure about "covering paints with damp cloths" (L III 573). Roger Fry did not associate the portrait with Vanessa; neither did Vanessa. Nevertheless, Lily's doubts about herself and about her work could very well have been influenced by Vanessa's.

The connection is not commonly made.[47] The links between Lily's theories of painting and Fry's dominate discussions of the novel. But Lily Briscoe is a woman and her awareness of a conflict between her desire to paint and her role as a woman is an important part of Woolf's characterization. Her inferiority feelings have a different source from those a male painter might have, and her limited knowledge of past works in her own medium results no doubt from the inferior education and more limited opportunities for travel that traditionally have been the lot of women. A possible connection between Lily Briscoe and Vanessa Bell is therefore worth exploring.

In *To the Lighthouse* Lily Briscoe contemplates the scene she paints: "The jacmanna was bright violet; the wall staring white. She would not have considered it honest to tamper with the bright violet and the staring white, since she saw them like that, fashionable though it was, since Mr. Paunceforte's visit, to see everything pale, elegant, semitransparent. Then beneath the colour there was the shape." When Lily tries to transfer her vision to her canvas, however, she has trouble. "But this is what I see; this is what I see," she has to keep assuring herself in the face of dwindling self-confidence (TTL 31–32). The ability to hold to one's view of reality and the determination to present it accurately regardless of what is fashionable is a struggle for most artists, but especially for women who are taught that they can neither paint nor write.[48]

Tradition as well as fashion daunts Lily Briscoe. Mr. Bankes tells her about all of the great works he has seen in Amsterdam, Madrid, Rome, and Padua. Lily thinks of the few great works she has seen on her own limited travels and wonders if "perhaps it was better not to see pictures" because "they only made one hopelessly discontented with one's own work." Mr. Bankes cautions her against such an attitude: "we can't all be Titians and we can't all be Darwins," he says, and adds that such giants grow out of a milieu of much artistic and intellectual productivity (TTL 109–10). One master Lily Briscoe is aware of, we discover in the third part of the novel, is Raphael. Lily knows that there is a long tradition in the depiction of mother and child. She explains to Mr. Bankes in Part I that she is not trying to achieve a likeness, nor is she trying to be irreverent towards "objects of universal veneration." She can reverence mother and child, she explains, in "other senses. . . . By a shadow here and a light there, for instance. Her tribute took that form if, as she vaguely supposed, a picture must be a tribute" (TTL 81). Ten years later she recalls the conversation. In Woolf's early draft, Lily remembers having added that the faces can even be "left blank," a comment that links her painting with several of Vanessa's.[49] In the final version Lily recalls having said that "She did not intend to disparage a subject which, they agreed, Raphael had treated divinely. She was not cynical. Quite the contrary" (TTL 262).

Vanessa Bell had considered the same issue and had reached parallel conclusions. In 1912 she wrote to Fry about Giotto's paintings, "I feel if one can have those things to see it doesn't the least matter what one does oneself. It's enough that that should be in the world & one's lucky to see it."[50] In 1923, however, she admitted that seeing masterpieces was "upsetting. . . . In one's youth one's mind was always in such a dither it didn't seem to make much difference, but nowadays its a rare experience and I find rather an overwhelming one."[51] Like Lily Briscoe, Vanessa Bell knew the traditional representations of mother and child and painted similar subjects.[52] Paintings of this kind culminated in a commission with Duncan Grant and Quentin Bell in the early 1940s to decorate St. Michael and All Angels Church at Berwick, Sussex. While Grant painted the climactic events in the life of Christ, Bell chose the subjects that deal with Mary, *The Annunciation* and *The Nativity*. Angelica Garnett says that her mother's choices were unselfconscious and natural. Although no believer, Vanessa would have defended her decoration of a church, Mrs. Garnett says, not only by pointing to her familiarity with the iconography but also by emphasizing the chance it gave her to do large murals, by noting that the Italian masters also "painted their nearest and dearest posing as the Virgin Mary or angels" in whom they probably did not believe either, and by asserting the fundamental irrelevance to a painter of the subject matter.[53]

Neither Lily Briscoe nor Vanessa Bell seems aware of female predecessors. Although Vanessa and Virginia mentioned and even knew quite a few of their contemporaries who were both painters and women, they rarely mentioned women painters of the past. When Vanessa and Duncan decorated a dinner service for Lord Kenneth Clark in the thirties using the theme of famous women, their designs for the forty-eight white Wedgewood plates formed four groups, each identified by a different design for the outer edge. The plates included twelve queens, among them Marie Antoinette, the Queen of Sheba, and Victoria; twelve actresses or dancers like Garbo and Pavlova; twelve beauties ending with Miss 1933; and twelve writers, including Lady Murasaki, Jane Austen, and Charlotte Brontë. Vanessa and Duncan also gave Virginia Woolf a vote of confidence by including her portrait in that company (Figure 4.13). The dinner service "ought to please the feminists," Vanessa wrote,[54] but perhaps not all of them. No women painters were among the numerous plates produced. The only exception was Vanessa herself, since she and Duncan decided to include portraits of the artists.[55] Only in recent decades are some of the women's names in the visual arts being rediscovered and recorded, so perhaps Bell and Grant could not think of twelve names; it may not have occurred to them to try. That the name of their daughter recalls Angelica Kaufmann, the eighteenth-century Swiss painter who resided in London for fifteen years, is due to Virginia. Upon hearing that Vanessa, after long deliberation, had registered the child as Helen Vanessa, Virginia wrote, "I was on the point of wiring to you to call your child Angelica." The name, she said, "has liquidity and music, a hint of green in it, and memories of no one except [Angelica] Kaufmann, who was no doubt a charming character" (L II 339).[56]

While Lily Briscoe's lack of confidence probably reflects Virginia Woolf's own to some extent, there is evidence that Vanessa Bell also underwent severe bouts with self-doubt both in her early years as a painter and throughout her life. One of the themes of her letters to Marjorie Snowden was the conquering of inferiority feelings. In 1904, for instance, she recalled feeling "utterly mean & despicable" among the students at Cope's and admitted that she had had the feeling frequently since then.[57] Lily's determination to paint

4.13. Vanessa Bell and Duncan Grant. Virginia Woolf plate for Lord Kenneth Clark's dinner service (1933). Courtesy of Lady Clark; permission of Angelica Garnett.

what she sees, however, also reflects Vanessa's. During the years when she studied art formally, her teachers were all male: Arthur Cope, then John Macallan Swan, and John Singer Sargent at the Royal Academy Schools, then Henry Tonks, briefly, at the Slade. If Tonks's views were at all typical, Vanessa's reactions need little further explanation. According to his biographer, he believed in and encouraged women students, but only up to a point. In a letter, he wrote that women "do what they are told, [and] if they don't you will generally find they are a bit cracked. If they become offensive it may be a sign of love," he continued. "They improve rapidly from about 16 to 21, then the genius that you have discovered goes off, they begin to take marriage seriously."[58]

Vanessa was not always inclined to do what she was told. In 1905 she decided that her studies were a waste of time and insisted on taking her own direction: "One thing that consoles me always in painting is that I believe all painting is worthwhile so long as one honestly expresses one's own ideas. One needn't be a great genius," she added. "All the second rate people are worth having so long as they're genuine because one always must have something of one's own to say that no one else has been able or will be able to say. . . . " Therefore, while imitating other painters might be valuable for a student, it could also be destructive.[59] She soon distinguished her methods even from those of painters, like Whistler, whom she admired.[60] While the advice of a teacher might be valuable at some stage, too, ultimately Vanessa rejected being taught. She admired Walter Sickert's work and thought she might learn a great deal from him but, she said, "I shouldnt do anything he told me to unless I happened to agree with it"; she admitted to disliking "any kind of teaching."[61]

Angelica Garnett reports that when her mother was before her easel, "she was intensely serious" about what she was doing and about its importance. Away from the easel, however, she "found it difficult to take herself seriously as an artist."[62] The honest expression of her own ideas that she, like Lily Briscoe, valued so highly was threatened by the ideas of others, especially established male teachers, and by the traditional demands of the female role. Even when she was working at her easel, she sometimes had difficulty translating her independent perceptions into forms and colors that pleased her. In 1909, for example, she described the sea for Virginia in a way that anticipated Lily Briscoe's comparison of her work to the fashionable Paunceforte's many years later: "I kept thinking of how various painters would have treated it & decided that they would all have made bad jobs of it & I flattered myself that I saw how it might be treated but I could not do it. A melancholy watercolour of a sunset is my only achievement."[63] Sometimes she merely reported to her correspondents the kinds of paintings she was working on. When she reported her enthusiasm for her work, she often did so apologetically, as if it were misguided, and pointed out that, although she liked an idea or a design, she was no Picasso, nor would Fry approve some aspect of it.[64]

Vanessa Bell's apologetic attitude may be, in part, that of the woman artist who hesitates to draw attention to her work or to expose herself to possible negative criticism by revealing too much commitment to her art. In *To the Lighthouse* Lily Briscoe minimizes her commitment to painting even to William Bankes, one of the few to whom she has the courage to explain her intentions as an artist. When she expresses dissatisfaction with her work and he tries to console her, she utters a "little insincerity." She remarks that "she would always go on painting because it interested her" (TTL 110). As the novel reveals, Lily is not insincere about continuing to paint. She is insincere, however, when she says that painting merely "interests" her. She is far more committed than the word suggests. So was Vanessa Bell who, in an early letter, declared that she was upset when she saw people with ability "neglecting the art of painting and using it only as a half-learned language. It ought to be such a fine thing in itself & there's no excuse for anyone not doing it as well as he can if he does it at all."[65] Vanessa, like Lily Briscoe, hated "playing at painting" (TTL 224).

About her own work Vanessa was often negative without qualification. Like the comments that reflect her self-conscious enthusiasm, many of the pejorative remarks occur in letters to Roger Fry. The abundance of such comments in her letters to him was in part a bid for compliments. She admitted as much: "Is Miss Sands horribly skillful & do you really think I can ever do anything to make up for my complete lack of skill? There's a nice fishing question for you to answer."[66] Another explanation for the abundance of such remarks in letters to Fry was her desire to encourage a painter who was both uncertain about his own work and knew that she did not really like it. For instance, she wrote in 1913 that perhaps her failure with a still-life painting would cheer Fry because he would realize that, even though she currently had more time to paint than he did, the results were no better.[67] Whatever her reason, adjectives like "feeble" and "dull," as well as nouns like "failure," "muddle," or "mess" punctuate her descriptions of her work. Sometimes the project she selected was too difficult; sometimes the overall design eluded her. Often the difficulty was some kind of negotiation between her original plan and what she saw in front of her. She worried when the painting deviated too much from what she saw as well as when it became too "realistic." She defined what she wanted in a letter to Fry in 1916: "unrealistic realistic" paintings.[68]

Vanessa Bell's greatest difficulty with self-confidence arose, however, from her close personal and professional relationship with Duncan Grant. She did not always admire Grant's work without qualification; nor did she always agree with him about art. In 1911, for example, she wrote to Fry that she thought Duncan was on the wrong track, overworking his canvases, but, worse, conceiving paintings that were "sweet & too pretty & small," the typical English malady.[69] More often she confessed how depressed or desperate his work made her about her own. In 1913 she reported how she and Duncan had painted in water colors until she was defeated; he, however, began mixing them with chalk and achieved effects that made her jealous.[70] Being compared to Duncan was depressing,[71] but critics who claimed to see no differences between her work and his were a worse problem. True, she and Duncan often used the same models and still-life arrangements, because doing so saved money and because they worked in the same studio. Yet Vanessa could not see how critics could confuse them. What worried her more, however, was whether Duncan's work had a negative effect on hers; she disclaimed any effect on his.[72] The following year she wrote that they had worked together much less, that Duncan was using a "spotty" technique and she was not, and that critics should no longer get their work confused.[73]

Fry reproached her both for her negative feelings about her painting and for her depressions over her work in comparison with Duncan's. He insisted that her way of structuring a painting was completely unlike Grant's.[74] Vanessa Bell was pleased when the French painter Segonzac thought her works and Duncan's only superficially alike. If Segonzac and Fry could convince other people, she said, she might be saved from "the usual female fate" of having her reputation as an artist swallowed up in a man's.[75] Duncan himself reproached her. Repeatedly he assured her that her negative feelings about her work were absurd, and that he admired both individual paintings and entire shows; he was not sure she would believe him or that he was entirely unbiased, but that people could not tell their work apart he thought ridiculous.[76] Vanessa had long ago defined her inferiority feelings as "quite unreasonable" and noted that she had admired the work of her contemporaries in Paris without getting depressed about her own; sure of her own direction, she could accept the success of those attempting something different. For the same reason she noted that a long conversation about art with Henry Lamb had not left her feeling depressed about her work.[77] Whatever their differences, Vanessa Bell shares with the fictional Lily Briscoe a mixture of doubt and determination. Virginia Woolf could identify with these states of mind and, what is more important, communicate them.

Certain of Vanessa's characteristics, therefore, inspire to a greater or lesser degree a number of her sister's characters. Katharine Hilberry in *Night and Day* is the most consciously and completely created portrait, but Woolf's understanding of her sister and of her creative process also aided her in the creation of Helen Ambrose, Mrs. Ramsay, and Lily Briscoe. One might argue that some of Vanessa's traits also animate Susan in *The Waves*, with her maternal preoccupations and closeness to the rhythms of the natural world. It is certainly true that just as Virginia was aware of Vanessa's repeated attempts to sketch or paint her, so Vanessa thought of Virginia as creating an ongoing portrait of her. After Angelica's birth she wrote that her sister still had "several notes to take" of her as "mother of a daughter. Its quite different," she added, "from being mother of two sons."[78] Each sister, therefore, saw herself in part as material for the other's art.

Like her sister, Virginia altered her models in an attempt to get beyond external appearances to something essential as well as compatible with the overall design of her book. As in Vanessa's portraits of her, where Virginia's features are sometimes obliterated, sometimes suggested, and sometimes presented in considerable detail, so in Virginia's portraits of Vanessa the degree of representation varies depending upon whether the author's view of the complexities of human nature or her artistic design requires the character to be tranquil, maternal, enigmatic, pragmatic, confident, insecure, or any combination of these and other qualities. Whether the subject of the portrait is subsumed in a formal pattern of shapes, lines, and color or in a natural or human environment, the individual ego is transcended. The person who is the subject of the portrait becomes a work of art.

Although both were interested in portraiture, neither Vanessa

Bell nor Virginia Woolf thought she could evaluate a portrait in her sister's medium. Confronted with a written portrait, Vanessa wrote to her sister that she could only evaluate it, like a layperson, on the basis of its verisimilitude.[79] Virginia Woolf also claimed to react to visual portraits in this way. To William Rothenstein, who had sent her drawings of her parents, she wrote politely, "I have the ordinary person's love of a likeness and desire to be reminded by portraits of real people and I have been greatly interested and pleased to find in your pictures a trace of my father and mother. They are more worn and sad than I remembered them. . . . but I am very glad to have these records of them" (L IV 6–7). She reacted to the drawings as repositories of historical facts which evoked memories, not as works of art. Yet Woolf realized that people inspired quite different treatments in painting, as her discussion of Kapp's drawings in "Pictures and Portraits" reveals. So when Ethel Smyth indicated in a letter to Vanessa Bell in December 1933, that she had seen both Virginia and a sketch Vanessa was making of her, she also mentioned that Virginia had instructed her, traditionalist that Ethel was, on how to react to portraits that were not strictly representational.[80]

Rothenstein's drawings of her parents were not the only ones with which Virginia Woolf was familiar. Their home at 22 Hyde Park Gate, she recalls, was decorated in red and black like a room out of a Titian painting. Busts shrined in crimson velvet were part of the decor, and on the walls were portraits of Leslie and Julia Stephen by Watts (MB 142). In the early years of the century, Vanessa also did a painting of her father.[81] As we have seen, she found Virginia's renditions of their parents in *To the Lighthouse* "extraordinarily true" and called her "a supreme artist" in "portrait painting" (L III 572). Woolf insisted, however, that since she was only thirteen when their mother died, that portrait was inevitably inexact.[82] As for their father, she said she had not intended "an exact portrait." "A book makes everything into itself," she explained, "and the portrait became changed to fit it as I wrote" (L VI 517).

The fact that Lily Briscoe, the character trying hardest to sum up Mr. and Mrs. Ramsay, is a painter suggests that Woolf was working with the visual as well as the verbal portrait in mind. To Rothenstein's drawings, Watts's portraits, and even Vanessa's paintings of her parents, Virginia juxtaposed her own attempt in *To the Lighthouse* to capture their essential qualities and relationships to other people. To the extent that she transformed them into works of art, she both gave them immortality and exorcised their ghosts. In 1939 she noted a disagreement with Mark Gertler that is relevant. He "denounced the vulgarity, the inferiority of what he called 'literature'; compared with the integrity of painting. 'For it always deals with Mr and Mrs Brown,'—he said—with the personal, the trivial, that is." Woolf admitted that the criticism stung. "Yet," she added, "if one could give a sense of my mother's personality one would have to be an artist. It would be as difficult to do that, as it should be done, as to paint a Cézanne" (MB 85). One must, she suggests, tap what is beneath or beyond "the trivial." If she were painting a self-portrait, Woolf says in "A Sketch of the Past," she would have to do just that. Some "—rod, shall I say—," would have to stand for her idea that "there is a pattern hid behind the cotton wool" of one's everyday life of talk and action. This pattern makes "the whole world . . . a work of art" and all people parts of it (MB 72–73).

In addition to written portraits or characterizations, Virginia Woolf frequently includes references to painted portraits in her biographies and fiction. As Vanessa Bell does in *The Memoir Club*, where paintings of dead friends hang on the wall, so Virginia creates portraits within portraits. As part of the environments of her characters, they recall family intimacy and identity, tradition and authority within the fields of literature or education. In these capacities, sometimes they console, sometimes they oppress, and sometimes they reproach their viewers. Portraits of people in their youth mock old age and death. Portraits also signify wealth, status, taste, or the absence of these. As such the paintings help to characterize their owners. So does Woolf's tendency to compare her characters to painted portraits or, more subtly, to present verbal descriptions of them reminiscent of the painted portrait tradition. She also uses her characters' attitudes towards painting to help define them, especially if they are painters themselves.

Literary tradition and authority are embodied in the white busts of poets that preside over the room of Elizabeth Barrett in *Flush*. These figures are part of a stereotypical, ornamented Victorian decor that Virginia and Vanessa both disliked.[83] Like Elizabeth Barrett, Orlando compliments her illustrious eighteenth-century literary guests by hanging their pictures on her wall although, careful to give them no cause for rivalry, she hangs them in a circle (O 211). More significant are the literary figures of the past whose portraits dominate the Hilbery home in *Night and Day*. From the dining-room walls, autographed "heads of three famous Victorian writers" oversee the meals (ND 98). The most important portrait in the house of this literary family, however, is that of Katharine Hilbery's grandfather, the famous poet Richard Alardyce. That portrait again inspires Woolf to describe a work of art, although she does so through her characters. Ralph Denham finds that Alardyce's "eyes looked at him out of the mellow pinks and yellows of the paint with divine friendliness, which embraced him, and passed on to contemplate the entire world. The paint had so faded that very little but the beautiful large eyes were left, dark in the surrounding dimness" (ND 15). Katharine Hilbery observes the portrait more closely:

> The artist who had painted it was now out of fashion, but by dint of showing it to visitors, Katharine had almost ceased to see anything but a glow of faintly pleasing pink and brown tints, enclosed within a circular scroll of gilt laurel-leaves. The young man who was her grandfather looked vaguely over her head. The sensual lips were slightly parted, and gave the face an expression of beholding something lovely or miraculous vanishing or just rising upon the rim of the distance. The expression repeated itself curiously upon Katharine's face as she gazed up into his. They were the same age, or very nearly so. She wondered what he was looking for; were there waves beating upon a shore for him, too, she wondered, and heroes riding through leaf-hung forests? For perhaps the first time in her life she thought of him as a man, young, unhappy, tempestuous, full of desires and faults; for the first time she realized him for herself, and not from her mother's memory (ND 319).

To Katharine, reluctantly occupied throughout much of the novel with assisting her mother's futile efforts to write a biography of the great man or with guiding curious visitors among the relics of his life and work, the poet finally becomes something other than a famous literary figure. By means of a painted portrait, he becomes a young person with longings like her own. The painting becomes a mirror for the viewer as, Woolf suggests, it should. The dead, Katharine concludes, want "neither flowers nor regrets, but a share in the life which they had given her, the life which they had lived" (ND 320).

Not all of the ancestors portrayed on the walls of Woolf's books are literary, but they have no less impact. In *A Room of One's Own*, a "portrait of a grandfather by Romney" is an example of "the pathetic devices" people use to assert their superiority over each other (AROO 35). Orlando, roaming her galleries, sees "loom down at her again the dark visage of this Lord Keeper, that Lord Chamberlain among her ancestors" (O 171). They, along with the tapestries and carved wood, remain part of her family tradition and an important part of her identity.[84] In "The Duchess and the Jeweller," ancestral dominance also occurs through a portrait. Oliver Bacon's home has a "picture of an old lady on the mantelpiece." Beneath that picture Bacon, hands in a prayerful gesture, assesses his life as "the richest jeweller in England" (HH 95–96). The old lady is his dead mother who, as a kind of conscience, struggles for his integrity against the influence of an inpecunious Duchess with an attractive daughter. Bacon writes a check for pearls he knows are fakes with "the eyes of the old woman in the picture . . . on him." She warns him to "'Have sense! Don't be a fool,'" but the temptation is too strong. "'Forgive me, oh, my mother!' he sighed, raising his hand as if he asked pardon of the old woman in the picture'" (HH 102).

The dangers of flaunting family values and characteristics are communicated again through portraits in "Lappin and Lapinova." Rosalind, who with her husband, Ernest Thorburn, has created a secret fantasy world in which they are king and queen of a rabbit kingdom, notices at a gathering of his large family how much the living Thorburns are like the "lustrous family portraits" in the drawing room (HH 72). Most disconcerting, however, is that Ernest stands "straight as a ramrod with a nose like all the noses in the family portraits; a nose that never twitched at all" (HH 73). As he loses his ability to transform himself into King Lappin, Rosalind recalls the Thorburn house with the earnest family portraits and the black-and-white severity of the steel engravings; these inevitably triumph over the fantasy world that had vitalized and unified the couple.

Among the later novels, portraits on the walls play important roles in *The Years* and *Between the Acts*. In *The Years* a portrait that preserves the distant past for the present generation hangs in the home of Morris when he marries Celia Chinnery. It is a "pleasant eighteenth-century picture of all the little Chinnerys in long drawers and nankeen trousers standing round their father and mother in the garden" (Y 197).[85] Similarly Kitty Malone grows up in Oxford among "vast cracked canvases" in the dark dining room (Y 76), a portrait in the drawing-room of "The old gentleman who had ruled the college over a hundred years ago" (Y 77), and portraits of Kitty's own "former masters" whose "dark gold-framed faces" are illuminated by candles as the women mount the staircase after dinner (Y 58–59). Kitty's father, "had a frame been set around him, might have hung over the fireplace" with his predecessors (Y 77). In this environment, Kitty feels constrained and oppressed; she dreams of being a farmer. Instead, she marries Lord Lasswade and gets her greatest pleasure from her escapes to their country house in the north.

In the Pargiter house, too, portraits are important. In her mother's sickroom, Delia Pargiter stares "at the yellow drawing of her grandfather with the high light on his nose" (Y 22). She responds only enough to wonder why the artist had "put a dab of white chalk" just there (Y 24). A similar fate eventually befalls the portrait that dominates the novel, that of Mrs. Pargiter. In the front drawing room, over the fireplace, is "the portrait of a red-haired young woman in white muslin holding a basket of flowers on her lap"; it smiles down upon the tea ceremony of the Pargiter daughters (Y 10). A picture of their ailing mother when she was young, it stimulates a variety of reactions. When, lit by candles on the mantelpiece, "The girl in white seemed to be presiding over the protracted affair of her own death-bed with a smiling indifference," it enrages Delia (Y 45). To Martin almost thirty years later, however, "it had ceased to be his mother; it had become a work of art." But it needs cleaning, he thinks, because a blue flower in the grass is no longer visible (Y 149). He points out the fact to Eleanor, who "had not looked at it, so as to see it, for many years" and does not remember the flower (Y 159). Later, however, she tells her niece Peggy that she can barely remember it from her childhood (Y 325). North recalls the portrait when he looks at his sister Peggy's smiling face. She is interested in the painting because she has been told that she resembles her grandmother and, although she does not want to be like her, she has to admit the similarity. She looks to the portrait for answers to questions that bother her, but, as in Martin's mind, the person in the painting "had assumed the immunity of a work of art; she seemed as she sat there, smiling at her roses, to be indifferent to our right and wrong" (Y 327). Portraits, even if the faces have features, ultimately are divorced from the people who sit for them; living people communicate with others, however imperfectly, as well as grow ill and old; ultimately they die and their thoughts are lost. The portraits outlive them as mirrors of their viewers or as painted forms and colors to which the eye responds.

A portrait similar to that of Mrs. Pargiter is painted of Kitty Lasswade when she is young: "Her hair had been very red in those days; she was toying with a basket of roses. Fiery but tender, she looked, emerging from a cloud of white muslin" (Y 256). The reactions to this portrait are hostile. Kitty dislikes the picture, and when Martin calls it a "horrid daub" she says she has forgotten who painted it (Y 262). We are told only that the artist, like the one who painted Richard Alardyce in *Night and Day*, is "fashionable" (Y 249). Martin wonders, ill-temperedly, how people who own a Gainsborough can have such a painting in the house. Clearly the young woman in white holding a basket of flowers is a stereotypical rendition that suggests innocence as well as budding sensuality.[86] So Clarissa goes "all in white . . . about the house with her hands full of flowers" in Sally Seton's memory (MD 287).

Woolf may have had in mind a specific painting of a young woman. In March of 1903 Vanessa visited the Watts (L I 71). In late February of the same year, G. F. Watts had begun a portrait of his adopted daughter against a rock with trailing ivy and a stormy sky (Figure 4.14). A pink-trimmed, white hat frames her red hair. Dressed in a white gown, she holds a large basket of white, pink, and red roses. Watts's *Lilian* was exhibited at the Royal Academy in 1904, the year of his death, and in a posthumous exhibition in the winter of 1905.[87] Almost certainly both Virginia and Vanessa saw the painting at the latter exhibition. Virginia called the show in general "*atrocious*" and wrote that she and her sister had "walked through the rooms almost in tears" because of its "childlike" quality (L I 174). When Virginia wanted portraits of her characters by a fashionable painter of the previous era, then, Watts would naturally have come to mind as he did when she wrote *Freshwater*. In fact, the dates during which both paintings in *The Years* would have been done coincide with those of Watts's career.[88]

Martin also notices in the Lasswades' dining room "pictures with hooded bars of light under them"; he speculates about the identity of "a nobleman with a crimson cloak and a star that hung luminous in front of him" (Y 250, 252). Similarly in *Between the Acts*,

4.14. G. F. Watts. *Lilian*, 1903. Courtesy of the Trustees of the Watts Gallery, Compton, Surrey.

enigmatic portraits in Pointz Hall augment Woolf's concern with interrelated literary, human, and natural history in a world threatened by war. Three are prominent. One is hung on the main staircase: "A length of yellow brocade was visible half-way up; and, as one reached the top, a small powdered face, a great head-dress slung with pearls, came into view." Although the painted woman is referred to as "an ancestress of sorts" (BA 7), Mrs. Swithin tells William Dodge that the "Lengths of yellow satin unfurled . . . on a cracked canvas" are called so only because the family has become used to having the painting in the house. No one really knows who she was or who painted her (BA 68). The portrait is a link with the past, but the figure is also distant, uncommunicative, and mysterious. Like Mrs. Pargiter in *The Years*, the woman in yellow satin is not an individual but a work of art. She has nothing to say to posterity.

In the dining room are two other portraits, one of an actual ancestor "holding his horse by the rein." This man is "a talk producer" (BA 36), an individual with a distinct personality. Both narrator and characters respond to him as Woolf does to Priest's *Cocaine* or Sickert's *Ennui*. The interest is in dramatic scenes, not artistic form:

> He had a name. He held the rein in his hand. He had said to the painter:
>
> "If you want my likeness, dang it sir, take it when the leaves are on the trees." There were leaves on the trees. He had said: "Ain't there room for Colin as well as Buster?" Colin was his famous hound. But there was only room for Buster. It was, he seemed to say, addressing the company not the painter, a damned shame to leave out Colin whom he wished buried at his feet, in the same grave, about 1750; but that skunk the Reverend Whatshisname wouldn't allow it (BA 36).

This portrait with horse and dog characterizes the subject as a bluff, outdoor type. At lunch Bart Oliver tells the same story of the ancestor's wish to have his famous dog buried with him. "I always feel," Lucy Swithin says, that "he's saying: 'Paint my dog'" (BA 48–49). The discussions of the painting suggest the aggravations of someone who commissions his own portrait as well as what the painter must endure.

The other portrait in the dining room has a completely different effect. It is no ancestor whose image recalls family stories; it is simply a picture of a "long lady" that Bart Oliver bought because he liked it (BA 36). The narrator first describes it, along with the portrait of the ancestor, in the empty, silent dining room and, whenever it reappears, it is associated not with talk but, more like the portrait on the staircase, with formal values and with silence: "In her yellow robe, leaning, with a pillar to support her, a silver arrow in her hand, and a feather in her hair, she led the eye up, down, from the curve to the straight, through glades of greenery and shades of silver, dun and rose into silence. The room was empty" (BA 36). Even when the room is full of people, the picture has the same effect. At lunch,

Dodge stares at it and confesses that he did not hear what was said to him. "The picture looked at nobody. The picture drew them down the paths of silence" (BA 45). It has the same effect again: "They all looked at the lady. But she looked over their heads, looked at nothing. She led them down green glades into the heart of silence" (BA 49). Although Mrs. Manressa suggests Reynolds as the painter, Dodge says no. The artist is left a mystery, although the robe, pillar, and arrow suggest the kind of portrait in classical garb characteristic of some eighteenth-century English painters, Reynolds among them. The arrow may mean that the subject is dressed as Diana, goddess of the hunt. If so, in spite of the different effects the paintings have on their viewers, the long lady is an ironically appropriate companion for the ancestor with horse and dog.

Still, the differences dominate and are central to an understanding of the novel. The portraits establish two poles against which to measure the situations and characters in the book. One painting causes the viewers to generate words, the other to be silent. One is associated with everyday life, the other with more formal, aesthetic concerns. The characters in *Between the Acts* go on talking and thinking self-centered trivia or avoid talking and thinking altogether.[89] They prefer to ignore the threats of the larger social/political world and are mostly oblivious to the natural world, which, as Lucy Swithin points out, will "be there . . . when we're not" (BA 53). Like the "ten mins. of present time. Swallows, cows, etc." (BA 179) that Miss LaTrobe wants to try instead of literary parody at the end of her pageant, the portrait of the long lady stands in contrast to the portrait of the voluble ancestor and to the words the characters often use so ineffectively and unthinkingly. In this novel more than any of the previous ones, the inadequacy of words is a theme. They are impotent in a world on the brink of war. Yet Woolf's own skill with words paradoxically creates a whole that includes yet transcends the chatter, unites the fragments, and, like the "long lady," leads us "down green glades into the heart of silence."

One of the portraits is also stereotypically masculine, the other, in a more complex way, feminine.[90] Already in "The Mark on the Wall" Woolf associates certain kinds of paintings with sex roles. Thinking associationally, the narrator contemplates "the masculine point of view which governs our lives" and links it to "Landseer prints" which, along with "mahogany sideboards, . . . Gods and Devils, Hell and so forth," are being "laughed into the dustbin" (HH

4.15. Edwin Landseer (1802–73). *Dignity and Impudence*, 1839. Permission of the Tate Gallery, London.

42). Because the importance of animals to men and men to animals are themes in Landseer's paintings, Woolf may have had his work in mind when she created the ancestor with horse and dog in *Between the Acts*. Vanessa disliked Landseer,[91] and her tastes may have influenced Virginia's. His work, much reproduced during the previous century, included sentimental animal paintings like *The Old Shepherd's Chief Mourner* (1837) in which a dog sadly rests its chin on its master's coffin, and droll ones like *Dignity and Impudence* (1839; Figure 4.15) in which the painter gives human characteristics to two contrasting types of dogs. Landseer also appealed to English sportsmen in the 1840s with paintings like *Stag at Bay* and *Monarch of the Glen*.

Appropriately Miss LaTrobe's pageant encourages members of the audience to look critically at the male-dominated culture that has brought them to the brink of a war that could obliterate what they consider civilization. Her attacks on English values and her experimental techniques alienate and perplex her audience. In her pageant she contrasts feminine and masculine roles, especially when she represents the Victorian Age dominated by Budge and his truncheon. Just as Miss LaTrobe's vignettes parody various literary works, so the descriptions of the portraits are, on one level, parodies within the visual arts tradition. One portrait, like a commissioned biography, is anecdotal; it brings the subject vividly to life, complete with words. The other reveals little about the sitter; she has become, like Mrs. Pargiter in her portrait, a work of art.

Just as Lady Lasswade's wealth and status in *The Years* demand that she have her portrait painted, so do Lady Bradshaw's in *Mrs. Dalloway*. The portrait helps to characterize both her and her husband, the doctor treating Septimus Smith. In Sir William Bradshaw's office "the pictures on the wall" along with "the valuable furniture" are marks of the doctor's success and authority as well as of his insensitivity. Among the pictures is "Lady Bradshaw in ostrich feathers . . . over the mantelpiece." This detail is coupled with a statement of Bradshaw's income and a description of his inability to comprehend the frustrations and despair of patients less secure (MD 153). As Lady Bradshaw presides over his office, so she presides in person over social occasions in his home. In both instances, however, she is dressed, posed, and confined within a frame of her husband's choice. The portrait is a violation of some kind, a symbol of her repression. The narrator refers to "the slow sinking, water-logged, of her will into his," to the falsification of her whole life in deference to his (MD 152). Although, we are told, she has some interests of her own and takes photographs "scarcely to be distinguished from the work of professionals," she does so while she waits for him (MD 143).

Woolf constantly draws upon the visual arts in yet another way to aid her in creating written portraits. Watching Vita Sackville-West with Harold Nicolson's head upon her knee, Woolf noted in her diary in 1927 that her friend "looked like Sappho by Leighton, asleep" (D III 142). It is natural that many of her characters think in similar terms about people and about themselves. In *The Voyage Out*, for example, Rachel Vinrace observes Clarissa Dalloway: "She wore a white dress and a long glittering necklace. What with her clothes, and her arch delicate face, which showed exquisitely pink beneath hair turning grey, she was astonishingly like an eighteenth-century masterpiece—a Reynolds or a Romney. She made Helen and the others look coarse and slovenly beside her" (VO 46–47). The allusion communicates Mrs. Dalloway's refinement and associates her with another era. In this novel Woolf's characters also take on the qualities of statues. At the top of Monte Rosa, Hewet looks at the rest: "He observed how strangely the people standing in a row with their figures bent slightly forward and their clothes plastered by the wind to the shape of their bodies resembled naked statues. On their pedestal of earth," he thinks, "they looked unfamiliar and noble, but in another moment they had broken their rank . . ." (VO 132). Similarly, Hewet likes Helen Ambrose's appearance, "not so much her beauty, but her largeness and simplicity, which made her stand out from the rest like a great stone woman" (VO 135), a primitive goddess of some kind.

Night and Day reveals the same interest in portrait painting and sculpture as methods of characterization. Now Katharine Hilbery's aunts look like eighteenth-century paintings: "Portraits by Romney, seen through glass, have something of their pink, mellow look, their blooming softness, as of apricots hanging upon a red wall in the afternoon sun . . . ," thinks Ralph Denham (ND 148). Through such comparisons Woolf can reveal both the viewer and the person viewed. In Cassandra Otway's eyes, Katharine Hilbery reflected in a mirror becomes a picture: "as she enveloped herself in the blue dress which filled almost the whole of the long looking-glass with blue light and made it the frame of a picture holding not only the slightly moving shape of the beautiful woman, but shapes and colors of objects reflected from the background, Cassandra thought that no sight had ever been quite so romantic" (ND 344). William Rodney also looks like a work of art. Denham sees his appearance as, on the whole, "ridiculous." At rest, however, "his face, with its large nose, thin cheeks and lips expressing the utmost sensibility, somehow recalled a Roman head bound with laurel, cut upon a circle of semi-transparent reddish stone. It had dignity and character" (ND 56).

The same method recurs in the later novels with a similar effect. The people compared to works of art lose their individuality for a moment and gain dignity and immortality. Elizabeth, in *Mrs. Dal-*

loway, rides atop an omnibus "like the figure-head of a ship . . . ; the heat gave her cheeks the pallor of white painted wood; and her fine eyes, . . . gazed ahead, blank, bright, with the staring incredible innocence of sculpture" (MD 206). In *The Pargiters*, Edward's head, we are told, "was much like the head of a Greek boy on a frieze; . . . It was a . . . head, . . . carved in marble, rather than the face looming up in flesh colour from a canvas" (P 64–65). So in *The Years* Sara calls attention to "the old brothers and sisters" who, standing together, "wore a statuesque look for a moment, as if they were carved in stone. Their dresses fell in stiff sculptured folds" (Y 432–33).

Characters with visual orientations see people as parts of visual patterns linking the centuries. Martin, at the Lasswades', observes the resemblance between the women rising from the table and the famous painting by Gainsborough of a lady dressed in "sea green" (Y 255, 252). Watching her brother Morris at court, Eleanor thinks that his wig "gave him a framed look, like a picture." In fact, "all the barristers looked emphatic, cut out, like eighteenth-century portraits hung upon a wall" (Y 109). Woolf again uses the portrait reference to freeze people in their traditional roles. Women rise from tables and reveal their long dresses; men, in their wigs and robes rise from court-room benches to argue and pass judgment. But some patterns vary. Eleanor decides that her sister Rose "was exactly like the picture of old Uncle Pargiter of Pargiter's Horse" (Y 157). Rose as a child plays at being her uncle and as an adult gallops off on a feminist crusade that lands her in prison. The portrait, like the one that reminds Peggy of her likeness to her grandmother, links the generations and reinforces the younger person's identity within a family tradition, but it also presides over change. Some of the women have become more assertive, some of the men less so. North, who shares the tendency to compare people to paintings, says he is "like the picture of a Frenchman holding his hat. . . . And getting fat" (Y 380).

A final example of this mental habit occurs in the earlier of two typescripts of *Between the Acts*. William Dodge, watching "the figures between the trees against the background" during Miss LaTrobe's pageant, is what he calls "staked." It is Dodge's "short-cut word for emotions in front of sights, or pictures ⟨too strong for analysis.⟩ He used it to mark down certain exaltations." Later, when he recalls such an experience, he either tries to "write it down" or he associates it with "a picture—by Degas, Renoir, Cézanne."[92] The tendency to refer an intense experience or merely an impression of people to a specific painting, and a modern one at that, is a variation on a process we have already seen; Woolf and her characters often search for a visual image to embody what words cannot express.

Woolf's characters or her narrators often freeze people into poses reminiscent of paintings or statues without mentioning specific works, artists, or periods. In "The Lady in the Looking-Glass," for instance, a mirror does to Isabella what an etched portrait would: "At once the looking-glass began to pour over her a light that seemed to fix her; that seemed like some acid to bite off the unessential and superficial and to leave only the truth." Divested of all her clothes and personal objects, "She stood naked in that pitiless light," an empty person with an empty life (HH 93). Framed images of people can ruthlessly expose the vacuum at the center of an individual's life. On the other hand, they can reveal depths and inner riches not usually perceptible. A window behind her has a similar framing effect upon Julia Craye as Fanny Wilmot observes her in "Moments of Being" or "Slater's Pins Have No Points." As in a number of portraits of women in Woolf's fiction, Julia is portrayed with a flower. In "a moment of ecstasy," she

> sat there, half turned away from the piano, with her hands clasped in her lap holding the carnation upright, while behind her was the sharp square of the window, uncurtained, purple in the evening, intensely purple after the brilliant electric lights which burnt unshaded in the bare room. Julia Craye, sitting hunched and compact holding her flower, seemed to emerge out of the London night, seemed to fling it like a cloak behind her, it seemed, in its bareness and intensity, the effluence of her spirit, something she had made which surrounded her (HH 110).

Frozen in the window frame during this moment, Julia Craye has the intensity if not the voluptuous beauty of the Pre-Raphaelite painters' women. Similarly, in *The Years* Edward's image of Kitty Malone is reminiscent of the well-known Botticelli painting of Venus. In his mind "a luminous shell formed, a purple fume, from which out stepped a Greek girl; yet she was English" (Y 51).

Imagining themselves painters or writers, Woolf's characters sometimes consciously create mental portraits of each other. Woolf analyzes the portrait-making process within the portraits she creates. Her characters often begin with a "type," as Woolf herself does in her portraits of adults from her childhood and of Jack Hills (MB 103). Then they fill in this general outline with complexities and contradictions. In *The Years* Peggy collects facts about Eleanor for her "portrait of a Victorian spinster." Eleanor, however, refuses to conform to the type. Considering one of her aunt's remarks, Peggy thinks,

> And how does one get *that* right? . . . trying to add another touch to the portrait. "Sentimental" was it? Or, on the contrary, was it good to feel like that . . . natural . . . right? She shook her head. I'm no use at describing people. . . . They're too difficult. . . . She's not like that at all, she said, making a little dash with her hand as if to rub out an outline that she had drawn wrongly (Y 334).

Her experience is related to a recurrent conversation precipitated by Nicholas about how we cannot know other people and how the world cannot be improved until we know ourselves. It is also related to North's constant readjustments of his initial portrait of Lady Lasswade, and to his inability to sum up his Aunt Sara:

> She left the room without looking in the glass. From which we deduce the fact, he said to himself, as if he were writing a novel, that Miss Sara Pargiter has never attracted the love of men. Or had she? He did not know. These little snapshot pictures of people left much to be desired, these little surface pictures that one made, like a fly crawling over a face, and feeling, here's the nose, here's the brow (Y 317).

External portraits, whether painted, photographic, or written, do not capture the complexity of individual human beings. The portrait painter, Woolf says in "Pictures" (1925), "must not say 'This is maternity; that intellect,' the utmost he must do is to tap on the wall of the room, or the glass of the aquarium; he must come very close, but something must always separate us from him."[93] He must not try to sum up, in other words, or he will distort and diminish his subject.

Woolf also uses people's attitudes towards painting in general as a way to communicate something about their self-images and values and thus to supplement written portraits of them. At parties in her fiction, characters often look at pictures on their hosts' walls not out of interest but as an escape from boredom or as a way to hide their self-consciousness. Mabel Waring in "The New Dress" and Prickett Ellis in "The Man Who Loved His Kind" are examples. Clarissa Dalloway, disappointed about her party and her own emotional inadequacies, catches sight of "the gilt rim of the Sir Joshua picture of the little girl with a muff." Perhaps because she associates the painting with her daughter, it reminds her of "Kilman her enemy" and makes her feel strongly both love and hate. "It was enemies one wanted," she concludes, "not friends" (MD 265–66). When Sir William Bradshaw stops to look at a picture at Clarissa's party, however, "He looked in the corner for the engraver's name," presumably for some indication of its value. "Sir William Bradshaw," the narrative voice adds ironically, "was so interested in art" (MD 294). In "The Mark on the Wall" Woolf also uses pictures to communicate values. The narrator hypothesizes that the mark may be a nail hole for "a miniature—the miniature of a lady with white powdered curls, powder-dusted cheeks, and lips like red carnations," the fraudulant type of picture that the previous owners of the house would have chosen to go with their furniture (HH 37–38). Benighted in a different way, the Brownings' servant in *Flush* "maintained her British balance" for a while in Italy: "She still had the conscience to walk out of a picture gallery 'struck back by the indecency of the Venus' " (F 123–24).

In *Night and Day* Woolf uses the visual arts for the purposes of character contrast. Katharine and William disagree about the art they see. She likes the Elgin marbles and finds most of the paintings "very dull." He, who "had kept notebooks; . . . knew a great deal about pictures," and "could compare different examples in different galleries," thinks Katharine's indifference is merely a pose. Nevertheless, he thinks, women have no need for knowledge (ND 174–76). His information as opposed to her indifference is of a piece with his virtuosity in poetic meters as opposed to her boredom with such feats. Again he insists that he expects not a scholarly reaction from her but an emotional one (ND 140).

Other characters in Woolf's fiction do respond to painting in an emotional, personal way. Mary Datchet too goes to look at works of art in *Night and Day*. The Elgin marbles make her think less about art, however, than about Ralph Denham. The statues and the "solitude and chill and silence of the gallery" make her life "solemn and beautiful," sufficiently secure to admit her love for him, and proud of her ability to keep her feeling separate from her daily activities. "Engraved obelisks and winged Assyrian bulls," however, cause her to imagine a future traveling with Ralph (ND 82–83). In a parallel state of mind, Orlando roams his galleries "looking for something among the pictures." A "Dutch snow scene by an unknown artist" triggers thoughts not of the future but of the past. Reminded of the Great Frost and his lost Russian princess, he gives way to "a veritable spasm of sobbing" (O 72).[94] When Clarissa Dalloway "(. . . stopped to look at a Dutch picture)," its subject remains a mystery. As she does so, however, she realizes her anonymity, her lack of individual significance: "She had the oddest sense of being herself invisible; unseen; unknown; there being no more marrying, no more having of children now, but only this . . . being Mrs. Dalloway; not even Clarissa anymore; this being Mrs. Richard Dalloway" (MD 14). The scene recalls the Dutch pictures of bourgeois respectability and materialism that Woolf saw on her travels and in the National Gallery.[95]

Woolf used references to portrait painting, then, in a variety of ways to help her create portraits in her own verbal medium. The sisters were also fond of using their media to create portraits of artists, both painters and writers. Vanessa painted herself as well as Jessie and Frederick Etchels, Duncan Grant, and Roger Fry at their easels or with their palettes; she portrayed writers reading, like her sister and Lytton Strachey, and Leonard Woolf writing at his desk. Artistic and intellectual activity is Bell's subject, more so than the individual artists portrayed. Some of them therefore have faces without features; others, like the portrait of Leonard, are more detailed. All lose some degree of individuality to the larger design as well as to the focus on creativity.

Virginia Woolf often depicted painters and writers in a similar way. Just as a writer like Terence Hewet in *The Voyage Out* wants to write a novel about the silence beyond people's words, so a painter like Lily Briscoe in *To the Lighthouse* combines the verbal and visual. Woolf often makes little distinction between art media because, like her sister, she is most interested in the creative activity itself. One could even say, like Maurice Beebe, that "'the artist' established in fiction is always a literary man"[96] or, as Woolf certainly would have pointed out, a literary woman. As such, Lily Briscoe's struggles to create parallel not only Vanessa Bell's but also Virginia Woolf's:

Lily's dislike of interruptions, her need to lose consciousness of her personality when she creates, her awareness of negative attitudes towards women painters and writers, her remarks on the difficulties of verbal expression, her desire to communicate both the solidity and transiency of life, her tendency to reduce people and objects to essential shapes originate or reappear in Woolf's diaries and essays. The fact that Woolf chooses to portray the painter's struggle to create rather than to describe in a detailed "word-picture" either the painter's appearance at her easel or her finished product is the final reason these many parallels exist. The parallels reveal a difference, however, between Woolf's portraits of artists and her sister's. Although both focus on creative activity, Woolf presents it from within.

Lily's creative process in many ways resembles a writer's. Often she tries to understand another person by means of a visual image, like "the scrubbed kitchen table, symbol of her profound respect for Mr. Ramsay's mind" (TTL 41). Nevertheless, words also inspire her to create both pictures and more words. From a few of Paul's phrases emerge pictures of the Rayleys' married life. The fragments of poetry Mr. Ramsay recites as he strides past become symbolic: "If only she could put them together, she felt, write them out in some sentence, then she would have got at the truth of things" (TTL 219). Lily, much as she may want to do so at times, also does not shut herself away from people as Woolf says the painter does. Like the novelist, her subjects are human relationships and the individual personality, however nonrepresentational her treatment. Because her interest is the essence of Mrs. Ramsay, Lily is perhaps more vulnerable to other people's views of her as both woman and artist than she would be were she able to withdraw for long periods of time with a still-life arrangement.

Just as Charles Tansley indicts women's abilities in both fields, so Lily refers to writing and painting interchangeably. Both are permanent; both have traditions. Lily imagines Mr. Carmichael, the poet, telling her how words and paint will remain after the people who have created them have vanished (TTL 267). Again equating the two media, she realizes that the artist, in creating a work of art, must get behind the already established "Beautiful pictures. Beautiful phrases" (TTL 287). Lily, with her intention to express the truth about people and human relationships, does not paint pictures which suggest historical events or stories. The "truth" does not reside there. It resides in images, shapes which suggest the private, essential Mrs.

Ramsay behind the public, self-abnegating role. Like Woolf, and like her many characters, Lily seeks visual correlatives for emotional states and individual identities. Then she paints these shapes in harmonious arrangements upon a canvas.

Yet Woolf's novel has certain advantages. It includes Lily Briscoe and her painting. To the extent that Lily's struggles to create her painting parallel Woolf's creation of her novel, it can include as part of its content the struggle that went into its own creation. Lily's painting can only demonstrate the fruits of such a struggle, the finished form which denies the effort, frustration, temporary failures, and moments of inspiration behind its achievement. Woolf creates a portrait of Lily Briscoe creating a portrait, however abstract, of Mrs. Ramsay, but she creates her own portrait of Mrs. Ramsay and her own partial self-portrait besides. Like Vanessa Bell's, therefore, Woolf's portraits of artists focus on creative activity, but they include more dimensions of it.

Although she is the most fully realized, Lily Briscoe is not the only painter whose portrait is rendered in Woolf's fiction. Although the others are more like quick sketches than completed paintings, they communicate Woolf's continual awareness of the many varieties of activities and degrees of quality within the other medium. Even *To the Lighthouse* includes mention of Paunceforte, the popular artist who does evanescent beach scenes not to Lily's taste.[97] *Jacob's Room* has several such figures. A predecessor of Paunceforte is Charles Steele, who paints Mrs. Flanders on the beach at the beginning of the novel. In the novel too is Nick Bramham who tries unsuccessfully to capture the fleeting beauty of women. *The Voyage Out* mentions Henry Philips, a painter who, Clarissa Dalloway says approvingly, has none of the affectations of the artist. Mrs. Elliot in the same novel sees her sketching as a substitute, but not a very serious one, for both children and occupation. More committed and confident is Mrs. Flushing, who sees and portrays "things movin" (VO 234).

In *Mrs. Dalloway* painters appear at Clarissa's party. One is Miss Helena Parry, whose memories of India were of "orchids (startling blossoms, never beheld before) which she painted in water-colour" (MD 271). Another is Sir Harry, "who had produced more bad pictures than any other two Academicians in the whole of St. John's Wood (they were always of cattle, standing in sunset pools absorbing moisture, or signifying, for he had a certain range of gesture, by the raising of one foreleg and the toss of the antlers, 'The Approach of the Stranger'—all his activities, dining out, racing, were founded on cattle standing absorbing moisture in sunset pools)" (MD 266).[98] Woolf's mocking view of the Royal Academy, which reflects her sister's opinion as well as Roger Fry's (RF 108), is also evident in "A Society," in which one of the women investigating men's achievements visits this institution. Asked for a report, all she will do is "recite from a pale blue volume" (MT 19). Traditional pictures at the Academy, the woman conveys, are literary; like the poems quoted, they tell stories or point morals, sometimes in the most sentimental way.

Woolf's knowledge of portraiture in the visual arts and of painting in general, then, aids her in characterization. As Steiner notes, written portraits derive from painted ones and the assumptions are traditionally mimetic. To evoke an absent person preserves intimacy or recalls that person's authority.[99] In Woolf's fiction portraits appear as reminders of traditions which various characters reject or adopt, as works of art whose subjects have lost their identities, as indications of status or of values, and as ways of seeing fellow human beings, if only at moments, as parts of larger patterns. To make present a dead person confers a kind of immortality or exorcises a ghost, motives behind Woolf's renditions of dead family members. Some degree of imitation of the subject is necessary for portraits to function in these ways. Imitation can provide historical information as well. Or it can be used to evaluate the subject according to some ideology, a tendency that can result in caricatures or types. The often unacknowledged assumption is that physical characteristics and mannerisms correspond to a person's character, an assumption Woolf explores and challenges.

Neither Woolf nor Bell claimed to understand portraiture in the other's medium; each looked for likenesses. In her own medium, each looked for ways to portray more than superficial external appearances, to incorporate or even substitute for representation what is essential about their human subjects. Yet the essential is often elusive, as two or more paintings of the same person or two or more perceptions of the same character reveal. On the one hand, then, Woolf tries to break the silence represented by her sister's painting with volleys of well-chosen words which do all that portrait painting does and more. On the other hand, like her sister, Woolf places the uncertainties of individual identities and the muddles of human relationships into the context of the silent, transcendent form that she associates with the painted portrait.

5

Still Life in Words and Paint

A shift to the sisters' interest in still life and landscape, where the focus is the material world, raises the question of Virginia Woolf's metaphysics. "Reality" is a word about which she has some reservations. The novel, she says in "Modern Fiction" (1919), must capture "life." She apologizes for being vague, "but we scarcely better the matter by speaking, as critics are prone to do, of reality." Her solution is to refer to "life or spirit, truth or reality, . . . the essential thing." The novelist who finds it looks within at the "myriad impressions" the mind receives from the outside world (CE II 105–6). Then such a writer, as her comments on Dorothy Richardson indicate, must resolve "the flying helter-skelter . . . into a perceptible whole" (CW 121). Several people link Woolf's metaphysics to that of a specific philosopher: Bergson, McTaggart, Russell, Whitehead, or most commonly, G. E. Moore. Balancing idealism and materialism, Moore insists that objects exist apart from our perception of them, but that consciousness is also a reality.[1] Indeed, although the mind must have the external world to respond to, the responses are most important. Among states of mind, certain ones take precedence and are "the *raison d'etre* of virtue"; these, Moore writes in *Principia Ethica*, "may be roughly described as the pleasures of human intercourse and the enjoyment of beautiful objects."[2]

S. P. Rosenbaum argues that Woolf's philosophical realism evolved from listening to conversations about Moore's ideas and from reading his *Principia Ethica* in 1908.[3] She read the book at Clive Bell's urging and to him and others, including Vanessa, she reported her progress in letters (L I 340, 347, 352–53, 357, 364). When she married Leonard Woolf in 1912, he had admired Moore for a decade and had read *Principia Ethica* and other pieces of the philosopher's writing.[4] Moore also stayed with Virginia and Leonard in 1914.[5]

When *The Voyage Out* appeared a year later, we find Helen Ambrose reading Moore's book (VO 74).[6] Leonard, in fact, credits Moore and his "divinely cathartic question . . . 'What do you mean by that?'" with "the clarity, light, absence of humbug in Virginia's literary style and perhaps in Vanessa's painting." Both sisters, he says, follow Moore in "getting rid of 'irrelevant extraneous matter.'"[7]

The case for Moore's influence on Virginia Woolf's ideas and style is strong. Yet it is important to remember that she was an artist theorizing about her own work, not an philosopher in any formal sense. She was, in addition, a woman. Spalding is correct to note that, although Virginia and Vanessa listened to the conversations of the Cambridge young men and were equally impatient with Victorian traditions and restrictions, their orientation was different. They did not have the university educations, career prospects, or political privileges their young male contemporaries enjoyed.[8] In *To the Lighthouse* Mrs. Ramsay and Lily Briscoe reveal some of the complex attitudes of women towards their male-dominated society. Mrs. Ramsay trusts herself to the "admirable fabric of the masculine intelligence" (TTL 159), yet she is aware, as Lily is, of the devouring, priggish, monotonous egotism of male intellectuals writing dissertations on "the influence of something upon somebody" and talking in "ugly academic jargon" (TTL 22). In this novel Mr. Ramsay writes books about "Subject and object and the nature of reality" (TTL 38), a topic Rosenbaum notes was more characteristic of Moore than of Leslie Stephen, upon whom Woolf based her character.[9]

While that is true, Mr. Ramsay's view of the world and his methods of defining it are balanced in the novel by Mrs. Ramsay's. "She knew," the narrator tells us, "without having learnt. Her simplicity fathomed what clever people falsified" although perhaps her means of achieving truth, Lily also thinks, "delighted, eased, sustained—falsely" (TTL 46). There is more than one way, then, of "getting rid of 'irrelevant extraneous matter'" and, as Lily Briscoe's experience in the novel demonstrates, the artist must comprehend Mrs. Ramsay's intuition and creative power as well as Mr. Ramsay's intellect before she can achieve her vision. So Woolf balanced the philosophical statements of university-educated men like G. E. Moore with her observations of painters like her sister who, like Mrs. Ramsay, could make "Life stand still here" (TTL 240).

Quentin Bell does not think Vanessa or the other Bloomsbury painters thought of themselves as disciples of Moore.[10] Certainly they, like the writers, considered the question of reality. Fry, for example, says that the French painters represented in the Second Post-Impressionist Exhibition (1912) "do not seek to give what can, after all, be but a pale reflex of actual appearance, but to arouse the conviction of a new and definite reality. They do not seek to imitate form, but to create form; not to imitate life, but to find an equivalent for life. . . . In fact, they aim not at illusion but at reality."[11] If the painters' interest in such questions is due to Moore, it may be so in an unexpected way. In 1940 Virginia, along with Vanessa and Quentin Bell, looked back at Moore's influence and defined it as "his silences. 'I didn't want to be silent,'" Virginia records him as having said. "'I couldnt think of anything to say. . . .'" Virginia thinks he was "rebutting . . . with some feeling that he'd carried his influence too far—our charge that he had silenced his generation" (D V 286). If Moore's "What do you mean by that?" had inhibited speech, even his own, perhaps that influenced Vanessa most. While Moore's emphasis on precise meanings "may have indirectly encouraged Vanessa's use of elemental shapes and the extreme openness and honesty of her abstract style," as Spalding says, the more direct influence was a reaction against the kind of representational painting that tried to tell sentimental stories or point morals.[12] There were similar influences on Woolf within the literary tradition, as *Freshwater* reveals. Both sisters, whatever they knew of Moore, were also like many other modernist writers and painters who wanted to explore and define the essential elements and boundaries of their media. But whereas Vanessa Bell usually refused to use painting to evoke words, Virginia Woolf tried to use words to evoke silence. Moore, like Fry, articulated for Woolf and perhaps for Bell some of the issues in which both were already interested. Woolf, in fact, had studied Greek in 1902 and 1903 with Janet Case, read the Platonic dialogues (MB 151, 152, 155), and was introduced to some fundamental questions about reality before she ever read any contemporary philosophy.[13]

In one of her reading notebooks Virginia Woolf copied a marginal notation William Blake had made in Crabb Robinson's volume of Wordsworth: "'Natural objects always did & now do weaken, deaden, & obliterate imagination in me.'"[14] The statement intrigued Woolf or she would not have copied it down, but there is no evidence that she or Vanessa Bell would have stated their own views so strongly. Natural objects delighted them both, but it is the delight, not the object per se, that they wished to capture. Solid objects like crockery and furniture or perishable ones like fruits, vegetables, and flowers stimulated rather than obliterated their imaginations. One can argue that Woolf's treatment of objects and the perception of them derives as much from painting, especially her sister's, as from philosophy.

Vanessa Bell's interest in objects is closely related to her commitment to the decorative arts. It is also part of a desire to escape from a realm of muddled human relationships into a more impersonal world of related shapes, lines, colors, and textures, as well as angles of vision and degrees of representation. In Virginia Woolf's work, the preoccupation with objects manifests most of the same concerns. "But how describe the world seen without a self?" Bernard asks in *The Waves*. "There are no words" (W 287). So Woolf usually presents objects through a self with interests in surroundings like her own. Such a character struggles to find words that neither disguise the object nor distract the reader from it.

"She is so splendid as soon as a character is involved," Roger Fry wrote of Virginia Woolf in 1926, ". . . but when she tries to give her impression of inanimate objects, she exaggerates, she underlines, she poeticizes just a little bit."[15] In spite of Fry's reference to poetry, it is when Woolf tries to be most like a painter, to present objects as she sees them without a character as intermediary, that he thinks she falters. One need not agree with his assessment, although he has not been alone in dismissing some of Woolf's descriptive interludes as purple passages. What is more important is that two different kinds of descriptive passages appear in her work: those few rendered by the narrator directly and those more commonly filtered through a character's state of mind. Even in the latter instances, however, Woolf can transcend her individual characters in ways that parallel her sister's work. For them, as for Vanessa Bell, the impersonality of objects provides an escape from the confusions of the human realm; objects also put human life into perspective. Singly and in groups, they not only reflect their owners but also outlive them, comfort them with their resilience, and provide microcosmic realms that charm and calm with their impersonal variety and beauty.

In 1934 Roger Fry introduced an historical exhibition of British painting and noted "the ominous preponderance of the portrait . . .

and, almost equally symptomatic, perhaps, the absence of still-life paintings."[16] An artist who paints still lifes, Fry says, proves to be "so preoccupied with purely visual values that he can dispense with any other *raison d'etre* for his picture."[17] An earlier book on Cézanne explains further: "In any other subject," Fry says, humanity intervenes. . . . In still-life the ideas and emotions associated with the objects represented are, for the most part, so utterly commonplace and insignificant that neither artist nor spectator need consider them."[18] For this reason the artist's own personality is more likely to come through. Traditionally, British artists have forsaken "a visual plastic art" in favor of "a descriptive conceptual art."[19] In the twentieth century, however, partly because of the impact of painters like Cézanne, still lifes are much more prominent. They certainly play a major role in Vanessa Bell's decorative work and in her paintings.

In *Night and Day*, Katharine Hilbery, the character initially inspired by Vanessa, listens to Ralph Denham explain the differences among varieties of trees and flowers in Kew Gardens. She is fascinated by the scientifically defined order of the vegetable world, in contrast to the chaos in the realm of human relationships to which she, because she is female, has been confined (ND 331). In her still-life paintings, as in most of her illustrations and dust jacket designs for her sister's books, Vanessa Bell does emphasize the nonhuman realm of objects that contains and transcends complicated human activities. To her, solid objects as well as fruits and flowers provide endlessly fascinating possibilities for combining shapes, lines, and colors. We see them with the intensity and angle of her vision, to the extent that she was able to translate it into painted forms.

Just as Virginia Woolf was aware of her sister's experiments in painting people, so she noted with interest the still-life works. In 1909 she reported to Violet Dickinson that Vanessa had "a picture in the New English [Art Club exhibition] . . ., and all her friends are envious" (L I 394). The picture was *Iceland Poppies*, an early still life praised by Walter Sickert as well as by Duncan Grant (Figure 5.1).[20] For this painting Bell selected a trio of intriguing objects. Arranged against a backdrop of greenish cloth with three wide, horizontal bands on it are a plain bowl; a larger, urn-shaped, green-and-white receptacle with a cover; and a corked, green glass bottle. In front of these human-made objects, their stems echoing the bands on the cloth, lie one red and two white poppies. The objects in the painting are diverse and seem small within the picture space, but the repeti-

5.1. Vanessa Bell. *Iceland Poppies*, 1908. Private collection. Courtesy of the Anthony d'Offay Gallery, London; permission of Angelica Garnett.

tions of spherical shapes, horizontal lines, and groups of three unify the canvas.[21]

Vanessa continued to paint still lifes, and Virginia continued to express interest and pleasure in them. In a 1917 exhibition she singled out a painting by Vanessa of a brass pot on its side (L II 187). The painting may have been *A Tin Pan* (1913), which Duncan Grant showed her working on in a painting of his own (Figure 5.2).[22] Vanessa worked indoors on such paintings even when, on her travels, interesting new scenes were all around her.[23] Still lifes rested her, she said, after a rush to complete commissioned decorative work, because she could do them for herself and take as long as she liked.[24] Although she was sometimes frustrated with the tendency for still-life paintings to become "dull & realistic," and although she labeled various of her attempts a "stodgy muddle" or "very feeble,"[25] she returned to still-life arrangements again and again.

Fruits and vegetables were favorite subjects in both her painting and her decorative art work. In *Oranges and Lemons* (1914), the backdrop is one of colorful vertical stripes. This time the picture space is almost filled with a large jar containing leafy branches of fruit (Figure 5.3). In *Still Life with Beer Bottle*, as in an earlier painting, *46 Gordon Square* (1908–9), a bowl of fruit sits next to a window, a setting common in Vanessa Bell's paintings and in modernist works in general.[26] Sometimes she alters not the setting for her still life but her vantage point. In *The Pumpkin* (1912–13) she is slightly above and very close to her subject. The yellow-orange pumpkin filling a bluish-white bowl is surrounded by an array of variously colored fruits and vegetables (Figure 5.4). *Pineapple and Candlesticks* (1915), a watercolor work, is a close-up of the fruit surrounded by smaller fruits in a shallow bowl on a round, turquoise-colored tabletop; the pineapple as well as the blue candles on either side in their tall gray holders are cut off at the tops. Again the vantage point is slightly above and close to the subject (Figure 5.5).

At Monks House Virginia and Leonard Woolf had a number of such paintings by Vanessa. Among them were a still life of an egg in a small bowl arranged with a white vase and an array of green and reddish-brown vegetables on a table with a red-and-white cloth (Figure 5.6). Appropriately a harvest of fruits and vegetables arranged with wine glasses, pitcher, and pedestal plate was Vanessa's design for the 1924 Autumn Announcements of the Hogarth Press

5.2. Duncan Grant. *Vanessa Bell Painting*, 1913. Permission of the National Galleries of Scotland, Edinburgh, and of Angelica Garnett.

5.3. Vanessa Bell. *Oranges and Lemons*, 1913–14. Mr. and Mrs. Milnes Gaskell. Courtesy of the Anthony d'Offay Gallery, London; permission of Angelica Garnett.

5.4. Vanessa Bell. *The Pumpkin*, c. 1912–13. Private collection. Courtesy of the Anthony d'Offay Gallery, London; permission of Angelica Garnett.

(Figure 5.7). Living with them, Virginia knew her sister's still-life propensities well.

In 1918 Virginia described to Vanessa the beginning of a story for which she hoped her sister might eventually "do a picture" (L II 299). "Solid Objects" appeared in 1920. Like many of Woolf's later characters, the one in this story has a visual artist's eye. Fascinated by the shape and color of a chunk of glass worn smooth by the sea, he begins to collect visually interesting objects. His obsession with pieces of broken china and other refuse causes him to neglect his political career. "People gave up visiting him," we are told. "He was too silent to be worth asking to dinner" (HH 85). This story, told from the point of view of an omniscient narrator, does not judge the

5.5. Vanessa Bell. *Pineapple and Candlesticks*, c. 1915. Courtesy of the Anthony d'Offay Gallery, London; permission of Angelica Garnett.

main character. It does communicate both his enthusiasm and other people's irritation and perplexity when they confront him. The story reflects Woolf's own sensitivity to the world of objects around her. As she wrote to Vanessa in 1918, "I shall have to write a novel entirely about carpets, old silver, cut glass and furniture" (L II 284). In her biography of Roger Fry, she suggests one attraction of the material world. Discussing Fry's lessons in making pottery, she says, "It seemed a natural division of labour—while his brain spun theories his hands busied themselves with solid objects" (RF 197). Physical activity balances mental, granite balances rainbow, and some kind of wholeness is achieved. The story also reflects Woolf's ambivalent view of a sister who was visually preoccupied, frequently silent, and likely to find beauty in unexpected places. The sometimes annoying aloofness of painters, she said in 1926, is due to their "ascendancy . . . over all objects of daily use" (L III 294). Virginia Woolf had some of the same ascendancy. Clive Bell recalls her "feeling for textures and the relations of textures. She would pick up a feather in the fields and set it in an appropriate wine-glass against a piece of stuff carelessly pinned to the wall, with the taste and 'rightness' of a Klee, if not a Picasso."[27]

5.6. Vanessa Bell. Still life of egg, white vase, vegetables. Monks House. Courtesy of the National Trust; permission of Quentin Bell and Angelica Garnett.

As Virginia Woolf wrote in her diary, "only pictures that appeal to my plastic sense of words make me want to have them for still life in my novel" (D I 168). Painted objects or paintings themselves that prompt her to respond to the artist's mastery of the medium also stimulate Woolf to use her own art in a parallel fashion and for similar ends. Like Vanessa Bell she "paints" everyday objects from a variety of angles and with different degrees of verisimilitude. Woolf uses the objects that accumulate around people to help characterize them, but she uses objects in yet another way. Like traditional portraits that render their subjects immune to change and more experimental paintings with featureless faces, objects and interiors of houses communicate an impersonal dimension which can be terri-

5.7. Vanessa Bell. Drawing for Autumn Announcements (London: Hogarth, 1924). Courtesy of the Bloomsbury Collection at Washington State University Libraries, Pullman, Washington; permission of the estate of Vanessa Bell and the Hogarth Press.

fying but can also provide a context for and a source of relief from human activity.

Isolated and framed, solid objects are impersonal, transcendent, and, as such, reassuring. In "The Mark on the Wall," the narrator enjoys contemplating the spot mentioned in the title as "something definite, something real." Similarly, when "waking from a midnight dream of horror, one hastily turns on the light and lies quiescent, worshipping the chest of drawers, worshipping solidity, worshipping reality, worshipping the impersonal world which is a proof of some existence other than ours. That is what one wants to be sure of. . . ." (HH 44–45). To lose one's certainty of the inert external world, as the characterization of Septimus Smith in *Mrs. Dalloway* proves, is madness:

> He began, very cautiously, to open his eyes, to see whether a gramophone was really there. But real things—real things were too exciting. He must be cautious. He would not go mad. First he looked at the fashion papers on the lower shelf, then, gradually, at the gramophone with the green trumpet. Nothing could be more exact. And so, gathering courage, he looked at the sideboard; the plate of bananas; the engraving of Queen Victoria and the Prince Consort; at the mantelpiece, with the jar of roses. . . . All were still; all were real (MD 215).

Objects are real even if no one perceives them. In the center section of *To the Lighthouse*, which Woolf calls "all eyeless & featureless with nothing to cling to" (D III 76), the narrator describes the garden urns near the deserted house. Unattended, they still produce flowers in the spring: "But the stillness and the brightness of the day were as strange as the chaos and tumult of night, with the trees standing there, and the flowers standing there, looking before them, looking up, yet beholding nothing, eyeless, and so terrible" (TTL 203). Woolf's personification of the eyeless trees and flowers, seeing nothing, also seen by no one, anticipates Rhoda's precarious identity, signified by a featureless face, in *The Waves*. In "Time Passes," however, Mrs. McNab comes to relieve the terror. She picks some of the flowers to take home (TTL 203). Nature may exist apart from individuals and outlast them, but it also depends upon people for significance.

A contrasting scene makes this point. To Mr. Ramsay, years earlier, the garden urns, along with the hedge and his wife and child, stand for and even facilitate the verbal processes of his mind: "He slipped, . . . seeing again the urns with the trailing red geraniums which had so often decorated processes of thought, and bore, written up among their leaves, as if they were scraps of paper on which one scribbles notes in the rush of reading—he slipped, seeing all this, smoothly into speculation. . ." (TTL 66–67). Mrs. Ramsay does not think he notices flowers and views (TTL 107) and, in a way, he does not. Their familiarity merely provides the secure foundation for the workings of his mind, which Lily Briscoe imagines as a solid object, "a kitchen table, one of those scrubbed board tables, grained and knotted, whose virtue seems to have been laid bare by years of muscular integrity" (TTL 38). Objects stimulate the mind; at the same time the mind is like an object. Woolf reflects the interdependence of internal and external realities in both content and style.

Later, in *The Waves* and *The Years*, Woolf's characters tend to isolate and contemplate objects more for their own sakes. For example, Bernard, relinquishing phrases, turns to things. Like painted portraits they are silent: "How much better is silence; the coffee-cup, the table. . . . Let me sit here for ever with bare things, this coffee-cup, this knife, this fork, things in themselves, myself being myself" (W 295). The essential reality of things parallels the essence of the individual. Bernard, although he is a writer, uses his eyes to tap what is real.

Many such scenes occur at tables. In *A Room of One's Own* the narrator compares the luncheon at Oxbridge with its colorful parade of foods and wines to a Van Dyck scene (AROO 11). In *The Years* Maggie sits with a group of people drinking and talking. First she contrasts the faces of her companions, then she lies "back in her chair. Behind their heads rose the curve of the mahogany chair back. And behind the curve of the chair back was a crinkled glass with a red lip; then there was the straight line of the mantelpiece with little black-and-white squares on it; and then three rods ending in soft yellow plumes. She ran her eye from thing to thing. In and out it went, collecting, gathering, summing up into one whole . . ." (Y 349). Her vantage point, looking up from her chair, is like Vanessa Bell's in a painting of some boxes and paper flowers entitled *Still Life on Corner of a Mantelpiece* (1914; Figure 5.8). The synthesizing movements of Maggie's eyes are like those of a painter or of a viewer responding to the relationships of objects in such a still-life painting.

Virginia Woolf remains fond of describing arrangements of objects on the dinner tables themselves. We have seen Vanessa Bell's similar interest on the cover for *Walter Sickert*. In *Night and Day* Woolf describes briefly but vividly the dinner table at the Hilbery's: "There

5.8. Vanessa Bell. *Still Life on Corner of a Mantelpiece*, 1914. Permission of the Tate Gallery, London.

was no cloth upon the table, and the china made regular circles of deep blue upon the shining brown wood. In the middle there was a bowl of tawny red and yellow chrysanthemums, and one of pure white, so fresh that the narrow petals were curved backwards into a firm white ball" (ND 98). Later in the novel, the dining room scene through Cassandra's eyes is "one of magical brilliancy. The pattern of the soup-plates, the stiff folds of the napkins, which rose by the side of each plate in the shape of arum lilies, the long sticks of bread tied with pink ribbon, the silver dishes and the sea-colored champagne glasses, with the flakes of gold congealed in their stems" exhilarate her (ND 345). The first of these descriptions, presented as it is by the narrative voice, is less characteristic of Woolf's writing than the second, in which the objects described are the cause or the effect of one of the character's states of mind.

One of the best and most familiar descriptions of this latter sort occurs in *To the Lighthouse* when Mrs. Ramsay looks at her dinner table. The candle light unifies the diners by obscuring what it does not illuminate as Woolf practices a version of the traditional painter's chiaroscuro. The candles also illuminate, in the middle of the table,

> a yellow and purple dish of fruit. . . . Rose's arrangements of the grapes and pears, of the horny pink-lined shell, of the bananas, made her think of a trophy fetched from the bottom of the sea, of Neptune's banquet, Bacchus (in some picture), among the leopard skins and the torches lolloping red and gold. . . . Thus brought up suddenly into the light it seemed possessed of great size and depth, was like a world in which one could take one's staff and climb hills, she thought, and go down into valleys . . . (TTL 146).

The centerpiece reminds her of a painting. It is also a miniature world for Mrs. Ramsay's eyes to travel through. So still lifes become landscapes in Woolf's writing but—as a subsequent passage shows—landscapes closely related to mental states. Throughout the dinner, Mrs. Ramsay unconsciously protects the dish of fruit "jealously, hoping that nobody would touch it. Her eyes had been going in and out among the curves and shadows of the fruit, among the rich purples of the lowland grapes, then over the horny ridge of the shell, putting a yellow against a purple, a curved shape against a round shape. . . ." The eye's involuntary movement within the world of the centerpiece is, for Mrs. Ramsay, a kind of tranquilizer (TTL 163). Like Maggie's in the passage mentioned above, her eye unconsciously works like a visual artist's. She experiences a disinterested pleasure that is a response to the formal properties of objects, not to their practical, everyday uses.

Virginia Woolf must have known the substance of the lecture Vanessa Bell gave at Leighton Park School early in 1925. In the talk she emphasized the visual artist's inability to get bored: "Even a kitchen coal scuttle may become the most exciting continuation of curves and hollows, deep shadows and silver edges, instead of a tiresome thing to be filled with coal, or a half worn out thing that will soon need renewal." Mold on fruit, dust on furniture and drapes, meat in butcher's shops, the most unlikely things and places, she says, please her.[28] If the "enjoyment of beautiful objects" is a valuable state of mind, then G. E. Moore and Vanessa Bell agree, provided that she can define "beautiful" in her own way.

Woolf may be more interested in the "pleasures of human intercourse," the other valuable state of mind Moore mentions. Still, Bernard in *The Waves* has an eye like Vanessa's for beauty in unusual places, even though he is a writer. Imagining how his child sees the world, he goes outside: "To see things without attachment, from the outside, and to realize their beauty in itself—how strange!" (W 263) The experience makes him light-hearted and causes him to think of painting. He actually goes to a picture gallery to prolong his sense of "freedom" and "immunity" from suffering (W 264). Later, again overcoming his doubt about what is real by experiencing objects afresh, free from preconceptions about their value, Bernard retreats into his "serene head," and enjoys the table before him: ". . . how beautiful are even the crumbled relics of bread! What shapely spirals the peelings of pears make—how thin, and mottled like some seabird's egg. Even the forks laid straight side by side appear lucid, logical, exact; and the horns of the rolls which we have left are glazed, yellow-plated, hard" (W 290).[29]

In *The Years* North, like Bernard, looks at the remnants of fruit and finds comparisons to describe their quality. He watches Sara help herself: "She began peeling a banana, as if she were unsheathing some soft glove. He took an apple and peeled it. The curl of apple-skin lay on his plate, coiled up like a snake's skin, he thought; and the banana-skin was like the finger of a glove that had been ripped open" (Y 322–23). Maggie, too, likes to look at fruit. Before she leaves a party, she turns once more to the "cheap lodginghouse room" and notes the relationships among shapes and colors: "On the dinner table lay the dish of fruit; the heavy sensual apples lay side by side with the yellow spotted bananas. It was an odd combination—the round and the tapering, the rosy and the yellow." When she turns off the light "only the outlines showed; ghostly apples, ghostly bananas, and the spectre of a chair," but her eyes adjust and their color gradually returns (Y 350).

In an early essay on Charlotte Brontë and Haworth, Woolf

marvels at the fact that personal relics of Charlotte, like her dresses and shoes, have survived her (BP 168). *The Years* contains a number of solid objects that impress both characters and readers in a similar way. Some are of interest for their own sakes. Others reappear and both unify the novel and provide continuity to human experience, even transcend it. On Eleanor's writing table, for example, sits a walrus, its bristles stained with ink. Contemplating it, she thinks, "That solid object might survive them all. If she threw it away it would still exist somewhere or other." Although Eleanor does not throw it away "because it was part of other things—her mother for example" (Y 91), someone does. Eleanor concludes that rooms and people in general, if not individuals, do outlast such objects (Y 426–27). We know, however, that Crosby, who has been concerned with "all the solid objects that . . . [she] dusted and polished every day" for the Pargiters (Y 35), has found the walrus. It reappears in her new room, along with other relics, after the Abercorn Terrace household is broken up (Y 218).

Similarly, in the hall of Digby and Eugénie Pargiter's house is "a great crimson chair with gilt claws" (Y 128). As chairs, empty and occupied, recur in Vanessa's illustrations and paintings, so this one reappears throughout her sister's novel as a link between past and present, human and nonhuman. Rose is relieved to see the chair in Sara and Maggie's cheap rooms (Y 165). When Eleanor, dining with Maggie and Renny, sees it, her perceptions are slightly blurred by wine and thoughts of war: "Things seemed to have lost their skins; to be freed from some surface hardness; even the chair with gilt claws, at which she was looking, seemed porous; it seemed to radiate out some warmth, some glamour, as she looked at it" and she recalls Eugénie (Y 287). Solid objects, then, are freed from quotidian associations and viewed as shapes and colors that, juxtaposed, make pleasing wholes. They also outlast their owners, link generations, and provide enduring contexts for human relationships and activities.

More complex is the sisters' love of flowers. Vanessa Bell frequently uses them in her paintings and decorations; appropriately, she incorporates them into many of her dust jacket designs for Virginia Woolf's books. Woolf uses flowers as metaphors and similes for people or for their moments of intense perception, as indices of their characters or states of mind, and as parts of the natural cycles which contain people's lives. She elaborates on the tradition of contradictory associations between women and flowers, especially roses: virginity and fecundity, pleasure and pain, abundant life and inevitable death. The recurrence of the floral motif in both sisters' art suggests that they were aware of the usual connotations and of their appropriateness; neither, however, produced "symbolic" flowers in any restricting or consistent sense. Both drawn to paradox, to opposing forces which vitalize as well as balance each other, the sisters produced visual and verbal art works with an often remarkable, albeit general similarity of purpose.

Among the works by Vanessa Bell with which Virginia Woolf surrounded herself were also several that featured flowers. As we have seen, she complimented her sister in 1918 on the painting of a vase with a flower that she said changed her ideas about aesthetics (L II 259), and in 1928 she indicated her approval of a pot of flowers on a chair (L III 498). At Monks House one of Vanessa's floral still lifes still hangs. It shows two pink roses in a wine glass next to a pottery vase filled with pink and rose colored flowers, possibly daisies, chrysanthemums, and roses (Figure 5.9). Painted in the early 1930s, it appeared in the exhibition at the Lefevre Galleries for which Virginia wrote the introduction in 1934. Vanessa's use of flowers in her decorative work is also evident at Monks House. The blue, green, and yellow tile fireplace with lilies on the sides and other flowers in a bowl at the top (Figure 5.10) done in about 1931 is probably Vanessa's work.[30] Nearby, her own house, Charleston, has numerous whimsical floral decorations painted on doors, on tile tables, and around windows.

In 1930 Vanessa reported to Roger Fry that she was painting flowers again because she could not resist doing so.[31] Some of Bell's painted flowers are done in a fairly representational style but many, like her portraits, are not. Her blooms are often stylized, "fantastic," as Richard Morphet notes, and botanically "impossible."[32] Vanessa rarely suffered from Matisse's confessed tendency to transform an "unconscious grouping" of blooms into a "conscious arrangement, the result of remembered bouquets long since dead." Perhaps, like Renoir, she arranged a bouquet, then walked around to the other side before she painted or drew it.[33] Whatever her method, her bouquets are usually vital and interesting. She uses flowers, in fact, as examples when she wants to caution artists against mechanical renditions, however skilled:

5.9. Vanessa Bell. Floral still life, early 1930s. Monks House. Courtesy of the National Trust; permission of Quentin Bell and Angelica Garnett.

Suppose you are drawing a flower. If you are capable of seeing that flower with all its subtleties of form, the way its edges recede or are sharp against the space behind you have to try to express your feeling about those things in line. It must be sensitive, everywhere—nowhere must it become mechanical. . . .

5.10. Vanessa Bell. Floral tile fireplace, c. 1931. Monks House. Courtesy of the National Trust; permission of Quentin Bell and Angelica Garnett.

when art is on the downward grade, skill tends to get the upper hand.[34]

Like Vanessa, Virginia is fond of flowers. In her fiction she uses them in many ways, but they are almost always associated with people, rarely presented in isolation. Like her sister, Woolf's characters often treat flowers in whimsical, unconventional ways that surprise other people. Sally Seton in *Mrs. Dalloway*, for example, does not put them into "still little vases all the way down the table"; instead she picks "all sorts of flowers that had never been seen together—cut their heads off, and made them swim on the top of water in bowls." Clarissa recalls the effect as "extraordinary—coming in to dinner in the sunset." Aunt Helena, in contrast, considers it "wicked to treat flowers like that" (MD 49–50). Delia, in *The Years*, also treats flowers in an unusual way that would have appalled Aunt Helena and perhaps even Sally Seton with her more artistic touch. All the tables at Delia's party are "strewn with flowers, frilled with flowers. Carnations, roses, daisies, were flung down higgledy-piggledy" (Y 397–98). When Kitty says that they will die without water, Delia simply notes how cheaply they can be bought, how beautiful they are, and, somehow because of them, how rich England is (Y 399). When Nicholas contemplates "the strewn flowers; the white, waxy flowers, the pale, semi-transparent flowers, the crimson flowers that were so full-blown that the gold heart showed, and the petals had fallen and lay among the hired knives and forks, the cheap tumblers on the table," he wants to make a speech of gratitude (Y 415, 426).

Other characters in Woolf's fiction create more conventional floral arrangements. The emphasis is not on their conventionality, however, but on the creative process of juxtaposing colors and shapes and on the significance of such activity for human relationships. In *The Years*, for instance, Maggie arranges "blue, white and purple" flowers in an earthenware pot before Rose comes to luncheon (Y 163). Then while she talks to her cousin, she rearranges them "as if to arrange flowers," Rose thinks, "to put the white by the blue, were the most important thing in the world" (Y 167–68). Arranging the flowers serves perhaps as an outlet for Maggie's nervousness in addition to one for her creativity. When Elizabeth Barrett arranges flowers in *Flush*, however, her similar preoccupation has to do with the giver of the flowers and with her spaniel's jealousy of Browning. Part of Flush's punishment for biting the suitor is to be ignored, as Virginia may have felt ignored by Vanessa when she was absorbed in other people or in a painting at her easel. "'This rose is from him,'" Elizabeth Barrett appears to say as she arranges the blooms, "'and this carnation. Let the red lie there—.' And, setting one flower with another, she stood back to gaze at them as if he were before her—the man in the yellow gloves—a mass of brilliant flowers" (F 72).

Flowers also serve, in Woolf's writing, as figures of speech which link the human and natural worlds. In *Night and Day*, for example, she notes that spring produces both "little white and violet flowers in the more sheltered corners of woods and gardens" as well as "thoughts and desires comparable to those faintly colored and sweetly scented petals in the minds of men and women" (ND 304). She also compares the opening of London shop doors in the spring to the opening of flowers:

> London, in the first days of spring, has buds that open and flowers that suddenly shake their petals—white, purple, or crimson—in competition with the display in the garden beds, although these city flowers are merely so many doors flung wide in Bond Street and the neighborhood, inviting you to look at a picture, or hear a symphony, or merely crowd and crush yourself among all sorts of vocal, excitable, brightly coloured human beings (ND 364).

More often Woolf uses flowers, as she uses references to painted portraits, to characterize people. In "Moments of Being," the carnation that Julia Craye tries to pin on her pupil, Fanny Wilmot, is "crushed . . . , Fanny felt, voluptuously in her smooth veined hands stuck about with water-coloured rings set in pearls." The hands enhance the beauty of the flower. At the same time Fanny senses "a perpetual frustration" in her teacher. Julia holds the flower without being able to "possess it, enjoy it, not entirely and altogether" (HH 106). Fanny imagines a similar frustration in Julia in her youth, with "her rose flowering with chaste passion in the bosom of her muslin dress" (HH 107), a description that links yet another character to the portraits in Woolf's fiction of young women and roses. Julia's favorite flowers, however, are crocuses. She plans her days carefully in order to visit Hampton Court when "those glossy bright flowers" which bloom in the cold spring are at their best (HH 109). In all of these instances, the flowers emphasize Julia's contradictory nature; she is passionate yet highly disciplined or, perhaps more accurately, inhibited. In contrast, when Abel Pargiter in *The Years* brings Eugénie, his sister-in-law, a camellia, she puts the stalk between her lips before she puts it in her dress. The flower suits some exotic quality in her (Y 119, 121).

Sometimes the variety and abundance of flowers interest Woolf most; sometimes her focus narrows to an intense experience of an individual flower. Flowers mark rites of passage and enliven other gatherings of people. So Woolf describes the funeral flowers in the hall when Rose Pargiter dies in *The Years* (Y 83). Similarly, in the flower shop the morning of her party, Mrs. Dalloway marvels at the abundance and remembers the gardens of her youth. There, in spite of the plentitude, "every flower seems to burn by itself, softly, purely in the misty beds" (MD 18). Appropriately, as in the case of Julia Craye, one of Clarissa Dalloway's intense moments of truth is described as "a match burning in a crocus" (MD 47), heat and light in a cold spring flower. Elsewhere too Woolf associates these experiences, during which an individual has an intense perception of some transcendent reality, with individual flowers. Already in "The Mark on the Wall," a single flower and then a plethora of blooms convey the experience of some kind of immortality:

> But after life. The slow pulling down of thick green stalks so that the cup of the flower, as it turns over, deluges one with purple and red light. Why, after all, should one not be born there as one is born here, helpless, speechless, unable to focus one's eyesight, groping at the roots of the grass, at the toes of the Giants? . . . There will be nothing but spaces of light and dark, intersected by thick stalks, and rather higher up perhaps, rose-shaped blots of an indistinct colour—dim pinks and blues—which will, as time goes on, become more definite, become—I don't know what . . . (HH 39).

To North in *The Years* flowers become entire worlds that lead his mind into an impersonal, silent realm. Half asleep, he detaches himself from the talk around him and, eyes half closed, looks at unidentified "hands holding flowers." As when Mrs. Ramsay loses herself in contemplation of the bowl of fruit with the shell, so here still life becomes landscape. In North's case, the flowers become "Blue mountains with violet shadows," then falling petals of various colors. One of the roses the hands pick has "violet valleys in its petals." Then North's attention returns to the petals that have fallen: "There they lay, violet and yellow, little shallops, boats on a river. And he was floating, and drifting, in a shallop, in a petal, down a river into silence, into solitude . . ." (Y 424). The experience is like that produced by a visual art work; Woolf uses similar words to describe the experience of the "long lady" portrait in *Between the Acts.*

Because of their individual short lives, flowers also help Woolf to convey human mortality. In *Jacob's Room* the narrator contrasts artificial and real flowers and concludes that "real flowers can never be dispensed with. If they could, human life would be a different affair altogether. For flowers fade" (JR 83), although some fade faster than others. "*The bud has flowered; the flower has fallen*" occurs appropriately in Miss LaTrobe's pageant right after the Elizabethan segment (BA 95). That the carpe-diem theme is equally suitable for the present, between the acts, is indicated by its reappearance near the end of the novel. Sitting in a chair by a window "in the shell of the room," Isa Oliver "watched the pageant fade. The flowers flashed before they faded. She watched them flash." The play recedes in her memory and the flowers become a metaphor for that recession. Their fading also parallels the fading of the day and the onset of a darker period in human history. Isa recalls the newspaper passage about the girl attacked by troopers. Then, when she "looked at the flowers again, the flowers had faded" (BA 216). They have accumulated among their meanings, the fragility of human dignity, life, and civilization itself.

The passage about the girl attacked by troopers isolates another set of traditional floral associations in Woolf's art, ones closely related to her portraits of women in white holding roses: flowers suggest both feminine virginity and fertility or sensuality. In a short story called "The Introduction," she compares a young girl's realization of womanhood primarily to a butterfly coming out of the chrysalis, but she also compares that emergence to a flower opening. Appropriately, the girl's name is Lily. Yet here Woolf alters the tradition. Lily realizes that her role is "to air and embellish this orderly life where all was done already" by men (MDP 40). The essay she has just had praised, along with herself, are to be offered to a man like "a cloak for him to trample on, . . . a rose for him to rifle" (MDP 41). So an older but equally virginal Lily in *To the Lighthouse* winces under Tansley's words, women "can't paint, can't write" (TTL 137). While neither Lily is a fatally sensitive plant, the male world appears an unaccommodating place for women with ambition and ability. In *Orlando* Woolf parodies the Elizabethan age when "the poets sang beautifully how roses fade and petals fall. The moment is brief they sang; the moment is over." Young men applied the poems to their lives: "Girls were roses and their seasons were short as the flowers'. Plucked they must be before nightfall" (O 27). To be rifled and plucked, women are objects, anything but solid and invulnerable. While Woolf links flowers with ephemeral feminine youth and sexuality in her other fiction, she does it more subtly. Mrs. Dalloway, for example, sees her seventeen-year-old daughter as "a hyacinth, sheathed in glossy green, with buds just tinted, a hyacinth which has had no sun" (MD 186).

Men also associate women with flowers both in *Mrs. Dalloway* and *To the Lighthouse*, but in different ways. Mr. Dalloway, "bearing his flowers like a weapon" through the streets, expresses his somewhat aloof love for his wife with an appropriate combination of red and white roses (MD 174, 176). Less conventionally, Septimus Smith sees his wife, Rezia, as a "flowering tree; and through her branches looked out the face of a lawgiver, who had reached a sanctuary where she feared no one" (MD 224). Her potential fecundity and the power it gives her threaten him. Mrs. Ramsay in *To the Lighthouse* is also compared to a flowering tree. Here, although the woman is powerful, the male is the threat. To her son, Mrs. Ramsay rises "in a rosy-flowered fruit tree laid with leaves and dancing boughs into which the beak of brass, the arid scimitar of his father, the egotistical man, plunged and smote, demanding sympathy." Having given it abundantly, Mrs. Ramsay "seemed to fold herself together, one petal closed in another, and the whole fabric fell in exhaustion upon itself . . ." (TTL 60–61). Flowers are associated with feminine power, inviolability, and fertility but also with the usual self-abnegating woman's role. The flower blooms and quickly fades, Woolf indicates as she rings variations on the tradition, not just because that is its nature but because few can resist trying to pluck and possess it.

Of all the flowers in Woolf's fiction, roses dominate; but the book most rose-filled is *The Years*. "Go search the valleys, . . . pluck up every rose," sings Sara about the ephemeral beauties of life (Y 163, 172). The Ramsays in *To the Lighthouse* have a child named Rose, and two women in *The Years* bear the name.[35] Sara responds to her red-haired cousin Rose by chanting traditional associations: "Red hair; red Rose. . . . Rose of the flaming heart; Rose of the burning breast; Rose of the weary world—red, red Rose!" (Y 164) or, at several intervals, variations of "withered Rose, spiky Rose, tawny Rose, thorny Rose" (Y 188, 231, 419). Negative in a different way from "withered," "spiky," and "thorny," are the "florid red roses" on

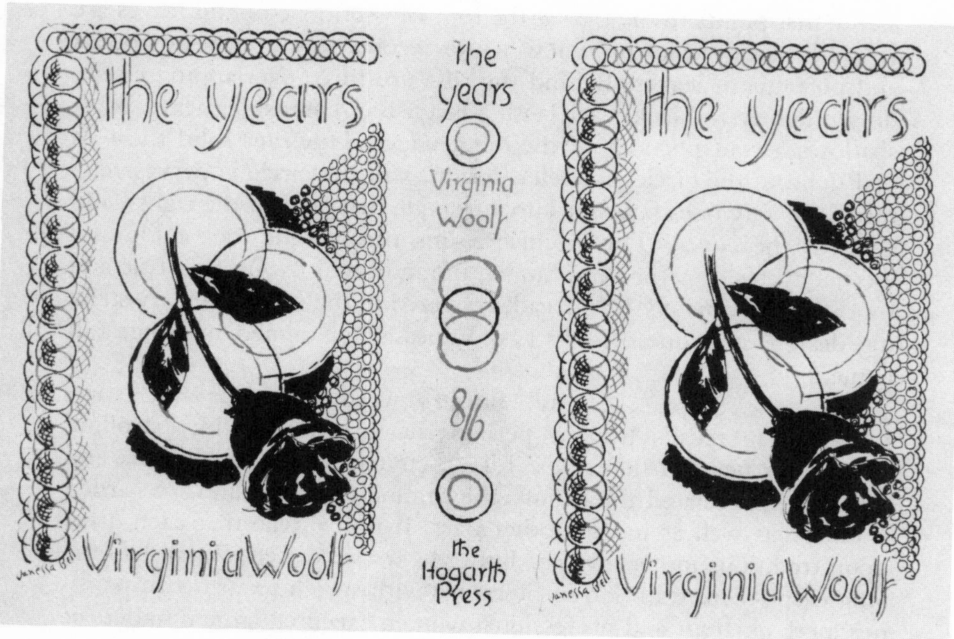

5.11. Vanessa Bell. Dust jacket for *The Years* (London: Hogarth, 1937) by Virginia Woolf. Courtesy of the Bloomsbury Collection at Washington State University Libraries, Pullman, Washington; permission of the estate of Vanessa Bell and the Hogarth Press.

the cheap china owned by the Robsons (Y 68). Roses thus have multiple suggestions: the pleasures of life which must be plucked; passion and pain, innocence and beauty. But the image can be mass-produced, sentimentalized. Roses also suggest mortality. The young Kitty is painted, as we have seen, holding a basket of roses (Y 256). "I don't like to see your roses fade," Kitty's mother tells her as she sends her to bed, then turns her thoughts to the death of the older Rose Pargiter (Y 82), whose youthful image survives in a similar portrait.

Recalling Virginia's own rose bookplate of three decades earlier, a large, partially opened rose dominates Vanessa Bell's dust jacket design for both front and back of *The Years* (Figure 5.11). In Vanessa's version, however, the flower is upside down; its stem forms a curving diagonal line up through the center; two leaves near the end form an arrow that points to the title at the top. Blossom, stem, and leaves are all solid black except for a few white accents on the edges of petals and portions of leaves. Behind the rose are three overlapping circles drawn lightly in black, each with a reddish circle inside; heavy black shadows accent portions of the outer edges. However solid the rose and delicate the circles in Bell's design, still the circle is pervasive; a mosaic of tiny ones fans out into a triangle that ends at the right-hand edge of the cover. The circular forms parallel the inexorable and eternal cycles of nature and human life indicated by Woolf's title and by the approximately five decades covered in the novel itself. A striking design, it is one of only two Vanessa Bell signed with her full name.[36]

In the Stephen family, flowers were Julia's province, not Leslie's. He recalls her, as perhaps her daughters did, "strolling among her beloved flowers."[37] Like their mother, both Virginia and Vanessa appreciated the beauty they found close at hand, in garden or house as well as in each other's art. It is also true that each drew upon traditions in her own medium. As we have seen, Woolf had the long carpe-diem tradition in literature with which to work. In painting, both amateur and professional women executed large numbers of floral studies.[38] Floral still lifes are also close to the decorative arts, which have been historically the province of women.[39] However, Vanessa Bell also follows the Impressionist painters who, whether male or female, took floral still-life painting seriously.[40]

When Vanessa Bell designed dust jackets for her sister's books, the fondness of both for still-life arrangements was evident. Leonard Woolf said that he and Virginia were not very interested in the visual dimension of the books they published. While they wanted their books to "look nice," they were not concerned with "fine printing and fine building" or with the "refinement and preciosity" associated with some of the well-known private presses. They were "interested primarily in the immaterial inside of a book, what the author had to say and how he said it."[41] Still, Vanessa's cover designs, in ways even more general than some of her illustrations, embody in a complementary medium the preoccupations of visual and verbal artists alike. Both are interested in the ways opposites vitalize each other; both also try to bring such tensions into harmony. For these reasons it is worth looking at a few more of the dust jackets and their relationships to particular texts as another example of the sisters' professional collaboration.

In 1936 Woolf inquired about one of Ethel Smyth's books: "And how did the dust cover settle itself? I believe a plain sheet would be best—but its an indifferent matter anyhow" (L VI 23). One wonders whether Virginia was equally indifferent to the dust jackets for her own books. After the founding of the Hogarth Press in 1917, most jackets were designed by Vanessa, who continued to do the covers for collections of her sister's stories and essays after Virginia's death in 1941.[42] No doubt Woolf felt that the jacket, while not so important as the text itself, added to the overall impact of the publication. Her letters contain general responses to some of Vanessa's designs. The one for *To the Lighthouse*, for example, is "lovely"; the style is "unique; because so truthful; and therefore it upsets one completely" (L III 391). A later comment too indicates Woolf's awareness and appreciation of the dust jackets. "Many thanks for the jacket," she wrote in 1938 about Vanessa's design for the American edition of *Three Guineas*. "I think it is one of the best you ever did—quite lovely, and also practical . . ." (L VI 251). In the designs for these two books, as in most of the others, Bell combines abstract elements with images suggested by the titles, yet she unites them in ways pleasing in themselves.

Vanessa's achievement is impressive considering the conditions under which she worked. Sometimes she had time to do many sketches before settling on an appropriate design for a Hogarth Press book; sometimes she had to work very rapidly, judging from the fact that in 1929 she asked her sister for more than a few days' notice when a dust jacket was needed.[43] Often she knew relatively little about the book for which she was designing the cover. In a letter tentatively dated August 1932, Vanessa Bell wrote to John Lehmann, possibly about *The Common Reader: Second Series*, which appeared in October of that year, that she had not read it and that Virginia had given her only "the vaguest description of it and of what she wants me to do. . . ." Vanessa added, irritably, that such "has always been the case with the jackets I have done for her."[44] She may have exaggerated. Unfortunately, there is no way to recreate any brief outlines of her books that Virginia might have provided or any of her suggestions for the dust jackets. As Vanessa indicates, however, they often were not much help.

Sometimes Virginia and Leonard offered suggestions of a practical nature about a dust jacket design. Leonard, for example, suggested that the lettering on the *Jacob's Room* jacket "isn't plain enough, and the effect is rather too dazzling. Could you make the r of Room into a Capital?" he had Virginia ask. "And could the lettering be picked out in some colour which would make it bolder?" Virginia did not want their suggestions to "spoil the design;" nevertheless, she returned it in case her sister "could alter it" (L II 543). In 1924 Virginia asked Vanessa if she could enlarge the *Common Reader* design for the American edition (L III 152). When the book came out in April of 1925, Virginia was obviously amused by some negative criticism and, with Vanessa to share it, more sanguine than usual about it. She wrote to her sister, "The Star has a whole column about your decorations of the Common R: and says I try to live up to them by being as revolutionary and nonsensical—a very good advertisement" (L III 182). What the reviewer had said of the jacket design is that "only a conscious artist could have done it so badly" (D III 16, quoted in n. 4). However negative the assessment, the reviewer was right to link the "decorations" with the text. Whether or not she knew the specifics of each work, she certainly knew the experimental bent of her sister's thinking and writing and, because of similarities in her own, could often respond with strikingly appropriate visual variations on Woolf's basic themes.

Vanessa's designs did not add to the initial sales of Virginia's books. Leonard Woolf recalls the "conservatism" of the booksellers:

> The reception of *Jacob's Room* was characteristic. It was the first book for which we had a jacket designed by Vanessa. It is, I think, a very good jacket and today no bookseller would feel his hackles or his temperature rise at sight of it. But it did not represent a desirable female or even Jacob or his room, and it was what in 1923 many people would have called reproachfully post-impressionist. It was almost universally condemned by the booksellers, and several of the buyers laughed at it.[45]

Perhaps because they considered the covers relatively unimportant, as well as appropriate for their often experimental publications, Leonard and Virginia Woolf made no effort to make their books more appealing to the booksellers' tastes.[46] In fact, in the case of *Walter*

Sickert: A Conversation, the Woolfs raised the price because they liked Vanessa's cover so much (L V 327). As Leonard observed, time has vindicated their perseverance.[47]

The cover for *Jacob's Room* frames a title of black letters with rust-colored curtains and includes the recurrent floral motif (Figure 5.12). Below the title a rust-colored bowl with a pedestal sits near the corner of a table. As in *Iceland Poppies*, Bell uses a triad of flowers. Two black-centered ones balance on the left and right edges of the bowl. A third flower, which has fallen to the table, as well as the empty center of the bowl evoke the absence and loss that are among the preoccupations of the book. The window in the design recurs not only in Vanessa's paintings but also in Virginia's novel. In it people frequently look out of and into windows; rooms are occupied and empty. Although the table in Jacob's room is round and the flowers are in a jar, the cover design still suggests Woolf's description: "Listless is the air in an empty room, just swelling the curtain; the flowers in the jar shift" (JR 39). Windows and flowers—with their suggestions of interpenetrating interiors and exteriors, of human individuality asserted in domestic surroundings and lost beyond those artificial boundaries, and of the beauty and fragility of human life—recur in both Vanessa Bell's visual art and in Virginia Woolf's verbal creations.

Vanessa created her dust-jacket designs, like her illustrations, with a very limited palette, often no more than black with white or buff. Sometimes she substituted one color for black or white; in very few instances she used two colors with white. Most of the time she added one color to the black-and-white combination. Such limitations, probably due to the cost of color printing, might have been frustrating instead of challenging had it not been for Vanessa's decorative work. Even the paintings done prior to the time she began her illustrative assignments for the Hogarth Press reveal a limited palette and sharp contrasts among a few colors. Black or some other dark color often figures prominently in the overall design. The dark clothing of her portrait subjects, for example, frequently contrasts with light skin tones and with a limited number of vivid colors.[48] Compositions in which the identities of the figures are of little or no concern have a similar impact.[49]

In the work of the book artist, black usually is a given. It can be, as Matisse points out, an advantage. "Black is a force," he says. "I depend on black to simplify the construction. . . ." To Matisse black

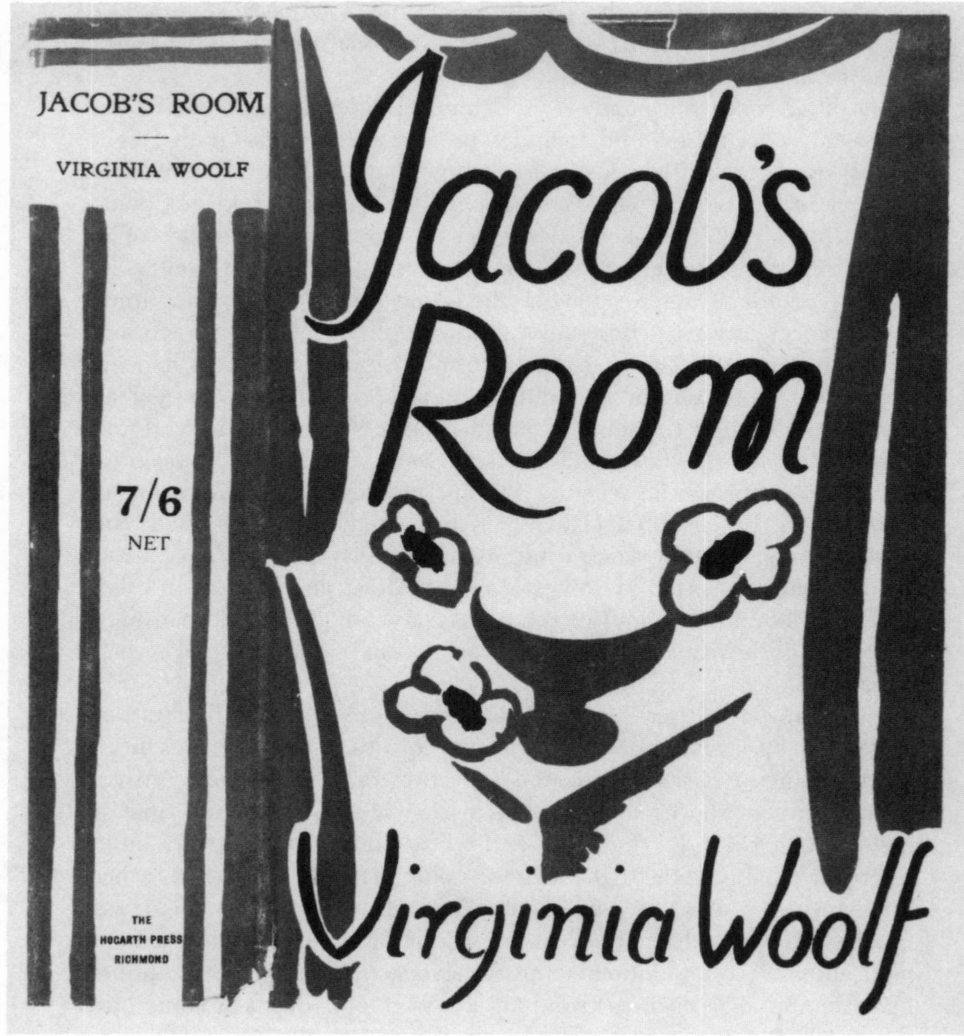

5.12. Vanessa Bell. Dust jacket for *Jacob's Room* (London: Hogarth, 1922) by Virginia Woolf. Courtesy of the Bloomsbury Collection at Washington State University Libraries, Pullman, Washington; permission of the estate of Vanessa Bell and the Hogarth Press.

was a color like any other, just as it had been for the Japanese and the Impressionists.[50] The graphic artist, faced with the necessity of using black, must discover its potential, the way it can lend dignity to a design, activate the viewer's imagination, enhance light areas, and make colors more brilliant.[51] Virginia Woolf and Vanessa Bell might have agreed, although in different ways, that just as an awareness of death gives intensity to life, so black vitalizes the colors juxtaposed to it. The realization of such paradoxes permeates Woolf's *Mrs. Dalloway* as it does so much of her writing and, combined with the selection of appropriate images, it dominates many of Vanessa Bell's dust jacket designs as well.

The most striking examples are Vanessa's black flowers, or her light flowers juxtaposed to black areas. Not peculiar to any period of her artistic development, these designs occur alike in the twenties and in the fifties, on dust jackets for Virginia's novels and on those for collections of her sister's essays. To Vanessa Bell, the floral motif and the color black produced all sorts of interesting tensions with other elements of the design. In addition to the black rose design for *The Years* discussed earlier, four of her other dust jackets are worth examining in this context: *Mrs. Dalloway*, *The Captain's Death Bed*, *A Writer's Diary*, and *Granite and Rainbow*. Although only the designs for the novels appeared during Woolf's lifetime, in all of them Bell combines black and white or buff with one additional color and a floral motif. In all instances, whether or not Vanessa had read the book in advance, the jacket suits the text.

The design for *Mrs. Dalloway* (1925) combines black and white with yellow accents (Figure 5.13). As in the *Jacob's Room* design, what appear to be curtains, scalloped this time, frame the title and a floral motif. At the bottom is a fan spreading out towards us, its handle below the stems of a bouquet of six unopened, yellow flowers wrapped in a cornucopia of white paper. The angle of the fan leads the eye into the center of the design which is solid black except for the white lettering and a large, horizontal white shape slightly above the center. Somewhat more curved on top than on the bottom, this abstract shape cuts across the entire center of the black area. The white surface is broken and related to the rest of the page, however, by five solid, black ovals graduated so that the largest is in the center.[52] A design in which first the white, then the black dominates, the cover anticipates, if only in a general way, the alternating exhila-

5.13. Vanessa Bell. Dust jacket for *Mrs. Dalloway* (London: Hogarth, 1925) by Virginia Woolf. Courtesy of the Bloomsbury Collection at Washington State University Libraries, Pullman, Washington; permission of the estate of Vanessa Bell and the Hogarth Press.

ration and fear, sanity and insanity, as well as life and death which pervade the book.

These black and white contrasts appear in the novel itself where they help to define the emotional complexities of human relationships as well as the precariousness of the human condition. Mrs. Dalloway thinks of Miss Kilman, for example, as one of the "dominators and tyrants"; but realizes that "with another throw of the dice, had the black been uppermost and not the white, she would have loved Miss Kilman!" (MD 16–17) The death of Septimus Smith, reported at the party, causes Mrs. Dalloway to imagine his reaction to the male counterpart of Miss Kilman, Dr. Bradshaw, and also to imagine Septimus' death as "a suffocation of blackness" (MD 280). The flowers Mrs. Dalloway sets out to buy for her party in the first sentence of the book and the fan which no doubt forms part of her party regalia at the end are the ephemera juxtaposed to oppression and death, valued because of that juxtaposition. Love and hate; life and death; white and black; flowers, fans, and windows: by selecting and arranging a few colors, shapes, and images, Vanessa Bell conveys the essence of her sister's novel perhaps only because, in some fundamental artistic sense, their brains were made, as Virginia says, "upon the same lines" (L II 289).

On the jacket for *The Captain's Death Bed and Other Essays*, twenty-five years later, again a bouquet of six flowers appears: three blooms have ruffled petals, three are smooth (Figure 5.14). Filling the center of the cover this time, the flowers project from the mere suggestion of a vase. Bell draws them in black ink upon a white page, but a golden yellow fills the background behind half of the blooms. Black areas of different sizes and shapes appear in two corners, and different-sized, cross-hatched yellow squares appear in the opposite two. Asymmetrical, yet harmonized and balanced, the components of the design form a satisfying whole. Here the title essay, published originally in 1935, suggested the design. Woolf begins with a description of the room in which the dying Captain Marryat lies and of the bouquet of flowers, "three pinks and three roses" (CE I 173) just brought him by his daughter. In this context both the fragile flowers and the sharp contrast between the black areas and the yellow and white ones parallel the tension and the transition between life and death in the essay. The jacket for *A Writer's Diary* (1953) is similarly harmonious and striking (Figure 5.15). Abstract except for a relatively small bouquet of six narcissus in the lower center, the design

5.14. Vanessa Bell. Dust jacket for *The Captain's Death Bed* (London: Hogarth, 1950) by Virginia Woolf. Courtesy of the Bloomsbury Collection at Washington State University Libraries, Pullman, Washington; permission of the estate of Vanessa Bell and the Hogarth Press.

5.15. Vanessa Bell. Dust jacket for *A Writer's Diary* (London: Hogarth, 1953) by Virginia Woolf. Courtesy of the Bloomsbury Collection at Washington State University Libraries, Pullman, Washington; permission of the estate of Vanessa Bell and the Hogarth Press.

balances triads of black and red, straight and curved lines, scallops and circles. The harmony Vanessa Bell achieves on the cover is an appropriate introduction in another medium to the wholeness that Virginia Woolf repeatedly struggled to define in the passages Leonard Woolf selected for this book.

Instead of a bouquet, sometimes a single bloom appears as a representational element in a largely abstract design, as on *The Years* cover. On the *Granite and Rainbow* dust jacket, Vanessa Bell placed a single, all-white flower at the top, two-thirds of it against a black background (Figure 5.16). The curved lower edge of this black area lies adjacent to a narrow, white area that arches across the design like the rainbow of the title. The design, like many of the others, is a union of opposites: dark and light, abstract and representational, solid blocks of color with linear open-work. As such it is again suitable for the book, at least as defined by its title. The "granite and rainbow" images appear in "The New Biography" in which Woolf concludes that no biographer yet exists who is "subtle and bold enough to present that queer amalgamation of dream and reality, that perpetual marriage of granite and rainbow" (CE IV 234–35). The search for that marriage is continual in the art of both sisters.

These are not the only dust jacket designs in which the floral motif appears, but they are among the most memorable. One of Vanessa Bell's other prominent uses of flowers is on the cover of *The Moment and Other Essays* (1948), a design that is interesting because, like the cover for *Walter Sickert*, it has the quality of a pen-and-ink sketch and because it is one of two in which black is combined with pink; no other colors are used (Figure 5.17).[53] In her design for *The Moment*, Vanessa fills the center with a variety of erect and drooping flowers in a vase with a pedestal; these appear against a rectangular black background bordered on the right and left by a kind of basket-weave design. The title of the volume again may have suggested the basic human paradox: intense life and inevitable death. The title essay of the collection, "The Moment: Summer's Night," deals with a related paradox: exhilaration and fear. In it Woolf imagines an exciting but at the same time terrifying, identity-threatening flight, united with nature and the wind. Cut and placed in a vase as Bell draws them, the flowers seem related both to the secure interiors of life and to its precariousness.

Vanessa Bell's use of black and the floral motif for her sister's last novel, *Between the Acts* (1941), is equally striking (Figure 5.18). A

5.16. Vanessa Bell. Dust jacket for *Granite and Rainbow* (London: Hogarth, 1958) by Virginia Woolf. Courtesy of the Bloomsbury Collection at Washington State University Libraries, Pullman, Washington; permission of the estate of Vanessa Bell and the Hogarth Press.

5.17. Vanessa Bell. Dust jacket for *The Moment and Other Essays* (London: Hogarth, 1948) by Virginia Woolf. Courtesy of the Bloomsbury Collection at Washington State University Libraries, Pullman, Washington; permission of the estate of Vanessa Bell and the Hogarth Press.

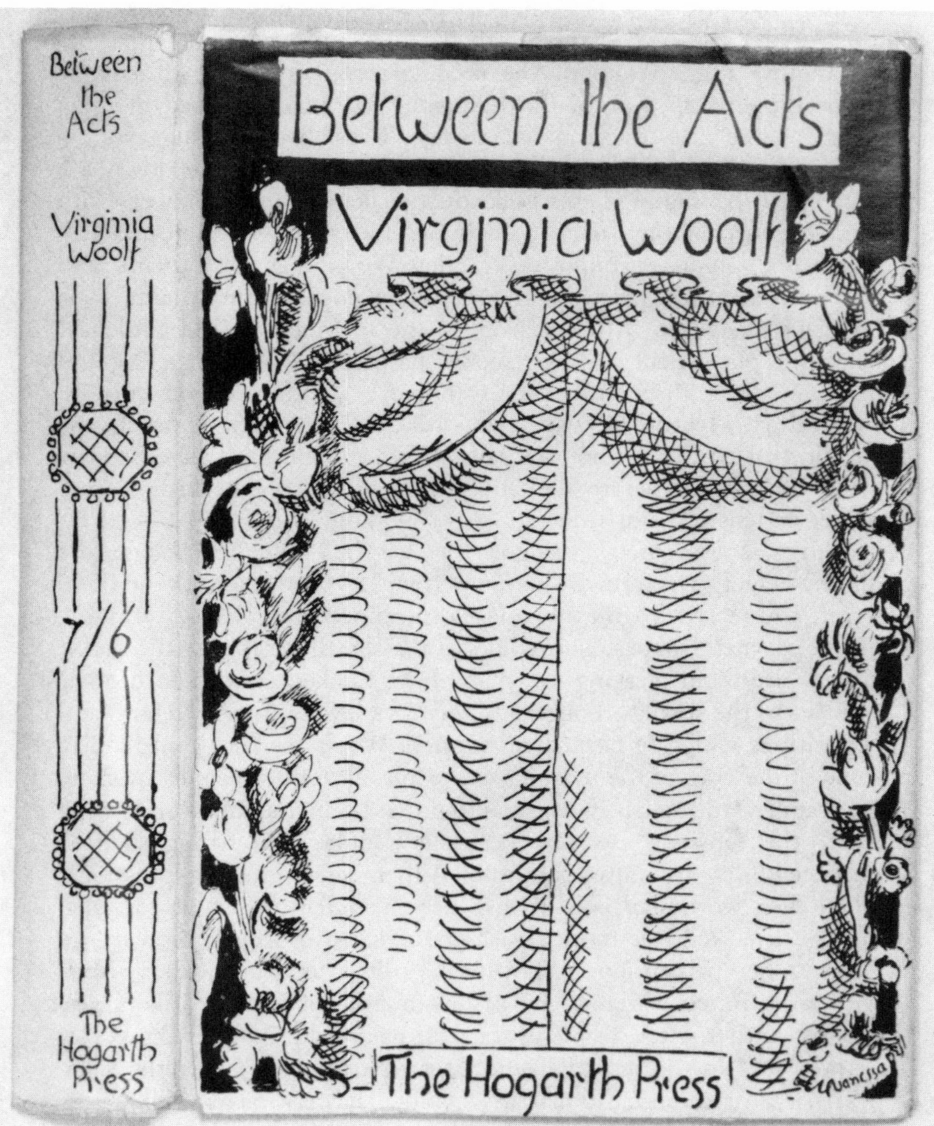

5.18. Vanessa Bell. Dust jacket for *Between the Acts* (London: Hogarth, 1941) by Virginia Woolf. Courtesy of Jean Peters; permission of the estate of Vanessa Bell and the Hogarth Press.

column made up of several kinds of flowers rises on each side against a dark outer curtain. At the top the title and author's name appear in rectangles. The bottom of the rectangle containing Woolf's name forms the edge of a drape bordering the top of a curtained window or, given the title of the novel, a stage. Cross-hatching suggests the loops and pleats of the inner curtain and a vertical line down the center, its opening. Vanessa Bell's dust jacket juxtaposes flowers with human constructions, dark with light, and solid with linear areas. Again the union of opposites carries Woolf's general theme and generates a design pleasing in itself. The novel counterpoints Miss LaTrobe's pageant with the lives of the members of the audience, balancing permanent and ephemeral, natural and human, living and dead. Vanessa Bell confronts us, however, with a closed curtain. Between two words, between two strokes of the pencil or brush, the curtain falls. It divides not just actors from audience but also, because of Woolf's death before the publication of this book, author from reader and sister from sister.

In Vanessa Bell's designs for Virginia Woolf's books, the tensions emerge from black juxtaposed with white, color, or the floral motif, and from recognizable images combined with abstract arrangements of lines, shapes, and colors. Like the illustrations, the jacket designs are often pleasing by themselves. Looked at with each other and with the texts, though, the covers evoke the psychological oppositions which so fascinated Virginia Woolf. In her novels and in some of the essays, the tensions are primarily within people aware of the fragility and mystery of the individual human identity and of life itself; the tensions are also between people who struggle, often unsuccessfully, to know each other. When conventional expressions, when even words fail, Woolf, like her characters who turn to visual images, uses solid or more perishable objects, especially flowers, to embody her perceptions. They provide her, as they do her sister, with an infinitely variable and resonant series of images. Like G. E. Moore, neither sister dismisses the external world. Neither, however, is interested in the material object for its own sake or for the sake, primarily, of any traditional associations it may have. Bell paints objects as she perceives them. Woolf usually portrays the inner lives of characters, their perceptions of objects, even their perceptions of perception. She recreates the ecstatic moments during which the external world and the self unite in a stasis that is like a still-life painting.

6

Landscapes of the Mind and Eye

Virginia Woolf and Vanessa Bell delighted not only in everyday objects but also in the relationships between indoor and outdoor spaces and between people and the places they inhabit. Depicting the external world, both sisters tried to capture their emotional responses to scenes viewed from many different vantage points. Like certain modern French painters, both were interested in light and color and how they affect one's perception—how, indeed, they seem to constitute the visible world. Whether they worked with paint or words, both women revealed a highly developed color sense. When they discussed painting and writing, however, the sisters detected differences in their uses of color. Woolf is more interested in the perceiver of color, Bell in its minute variations. Like her still lifes, Bell's landscapes and indoor-outdoor settings place no intermediary between the viewer and the scene but the painter herself; her scenes, or portions of them, serve no function apart from the aesthetic unity of the painting. Woolf, on the other hand, creates at least two kinds of landscapes in her writing, just as she creates two kinds of still lifes. Although anonymous narrators introduce portions of *The Waves* and *The Years*, most of the pictures in Woolf's fiction would not exist without her characters' consciousnesses. Their responses to the external world increase our understanding of their states of mind, and reveal their awareness of something inviolable in other people as well as their consciousness of time passing.

Both sisters realized that color occupies space. Virginia observed in Vanessa's painting in 1926 "the problem of empty spaces, and how to model them." It is a matter of comprehending "design on a large scale" (L III 270–71), granite as well as rainbow. It is also a matter of locating people, if they are included, within spaces that sometimes reflect them and sometimes are independent of them. Like

Vanessa, Virginia sees spaces within spaces: individuals live in rooms; rooms exist within houses; houses exist within city or landscapes. As in her sister's paintings, windows and doors in Woolf's novels connect inner spaces with outer. Light and weather from outside penetrate interiors; lighted windows cast their glows upon exterior landscapes but, more important, people look at the views outside.

Woolf, however, rarely confines herself to a purely visual response to people's surroundings. In settings perceived by her characters as well as in the anonymous descriptive passages, she incorporates sounds, smells, and movements both of the viewer's eye and of portions of the scene. Sometimes she also includes allusions to paintings, unusual points of view, personification, or other figures of speech. Landscapes and interiors frequently provide her with the imagery she needs to depict inner spaces. While actual places represented in detail were neither sister's purpose, Virginia Woolf goes further than Vanessa Bell towards creating landscapes of the mind and mental rooms.

Prior to 1912 when Virginia took Asheham House in the country, Vanessa did little landscape painting.[1] That year at the second Post-Impressionist Exhibition she showed four works. One was a figure painting entitled *The Spanish Model*; two were still lifes: *Nosegay* and *The Mantelpiece*; and one was a painting of Asheham house and its grounds (Figure 6.1). It revealed her tendency, as Richard Shone says, "to cube her shapes, to draw them towards an overall geometric conception."[2] That Vanessa should have painted landscapes at all is curious, at least on the surface, since she was not inclined to work out-of-doors.[3] Her own response to a scene was more important to her than verisimilitude. She thought it ironic, in fact, that she, who considered herself an "impressionist" interested primarily in light, preferred to paint scenes from her imagination or from quick sketches while Fry, the "pre- or post-impressionist," required nature in front of him.[4] In 1921 she explained to Fry that she could not go on painting expeditions because she was responsible for children and servants. She decided that "as a rule" she should paint inside. "I dont think I'm nearly as enterprising as you (or Duncan) about painting anything I dont find at my door," she said.[5] Disliking hurry and

6.1. Vanessa Bell. *Asheham House*, 1912. Private collection. Permission of Angelica Garnett.

discomfort, she chose to work in her studio at Charleston.[6] When she moved her easel to a protected spot in her garden, as she did now and then, the constant weather changes frustrated her. The pond at Charleston appears frequently in her work, as in *Tilton from the Pond, Charleston*, because her only preference was for landscapes with water in them (Figure 6.2).[7] "My tastes are tame as regards scenery," she wrote; "one views as good as another." She was willing to do some "small quick sketches from nature," but no more,[8] at least not in England. The French countryside, on the other hand, gave her "all kinds of different ideas about space & colour."[9] She commented many times how foolish painters were to spend winters in England

6.2. Vanessa Bell. *Tilton from the Pond* (Charleston), 1937. Private collection. Courtesy of the Anthony d'Offay Gallery, London; permission of Angelica Garnett.

when the conditions in France were so much better for landscape painting.[10] Still, wherever she was, Vanessa Bell did paint outdoor scenes. What she prepared for a show in 1922, she said, were primarily still lifes and landscapes, and her letters over the years mention various such projects.[11]

English painters, Virginia Woolf wrote to Vanessa in 1918 after a visit to the National Gallery, "are far best at landscape." She singled out Cox and Constable: "I like pictures of Norfolk heaths with windmills against the sky." She also found a Turner sketch "very beautiful." Another painting that pleased her was "a very dark amber coloured landscape with one red cow in it" called *The Return of the Ark* by the seventeenth-century French painter, Bourdon (L II 260, n. 3). Woolf was equally aware of her sister's landscape paintings. In 1921 she complimented Vanessa on a "snow scene" (L II 469), in 1924 on a landscape of Charleston and a painting of a bridge and a blue boat (L III 270–71), in 1927 on a painting of a hay cart and downs (L III 341), and, in the 1930 exhibition for which Woolf wrote the introduction, on paintings of a bare hillside and of a little boy standing in the sea. She also owned some of Vanessa's work in this genre. At Monks House there is, for example, a painting of Newhaven Harbour dated 1916 (Figure 6.3). The strong vertical accents created by the posts of the quay in the foreground echo the masts of boats in middle and background. Primarily blue and brown, the painting reveals Vanessa's ability to vary and echo colors subtly as her brush moves from quay to boats, water to sky.

Virginia also seems to have shared her sister's attitudes toward landscape painting. Lacking the time, energy, and tolerance of discomfort, and frustrated with rapidly changing light, Vanessa preferred landscapes constructed with the help of sketches and her imagination. Detailed representation was not her goal. Woolf's similar attitude toward both painted and written renditions of the natural world appeared early in her essays. Considering two attempts to place writers and their works into precise geographical contexts, Woolf concluded in 1905 that the part of the world with which a writer is most familiar is not necessarily recreated in detail in his or her art: "A writer's country is a territory within his own brain," she says, and it is more "real" than any tangible place (BP 161). Therefore, she noted in 1917 that although Keats "wrote some of the most beautiful descriptions in the language," still, "in spite of many famous and exact passages the best descriptions are the least accurate, and represent what the poet saw with his eyes shut when the landscape had melted indistinguishably into the mood." Drawing an explicit parallel with painting, she contrasts this kind of description with Tennyson's, whose "method of sifting words until the exact shade and shape of the flower or the cloud had its equivalent phrase has produced many wonderful examples of minute skill, much like the birds' nests and blades of grass of the pre-Raphaelite painters." Tennyson may have described autumn most exactly, but "for the whole spirit of autumn we go to Keats. He has the mood and not the detail" (BP 164).

6.3. Vanessa Bell. *Newhaven Harbour*, 1916. Monks House. Courtesy of the National Trust; permission of Quentin Bell and Angelica Garnett.

Pursuing this distinction in a review written in 1919, Woolf contrasts "schoolboy attempts at landscape" with "the natural mood of feeling that beauty is better not expressed" (BP 93). Two other reviews, in 1920 and 1921, expand upon this observation. No doubt drawing upon experiences like those reflected in her early travel diaries, Woolf says that beginning writers devote entire notebooks to descriptions of landscapes. Like Vanessa Bell, however, they are frustrated by continual changes in the scene:

> Words must be found for a moon-lit sky, for a stream, for plane-trees after rain. They "must" be found. For the plane-tree dries

> very quickly, and if the look as of a sea-lion sleek from a plunge is gone, and nothing found to record it better than those words, the wet plane-tree does not properly exist. Nothing can exist unless it is properly described. Therefore the young writer is perpetually on the stretch to get the thing expressed before it is over and the end of the day finds him with a larder full of maimed objects—half-realized trees, streams that are paralytic in their flow, and leaves that obstinately refuse to have that particular—what was the look of them against the sky, or, more difficult still to express, how did the tree erect its tent of green layers above you as you lay flat on the ground beneath? (BP 63).

A little older, writers despair of such precision; accurate descriptions do not constitute truth (BP 63).[12] What does? The function of the description in the work of literature itself, or the way the passage reveals the writer or other people. Artistic form and, again, human beings take precedence. Wordsworth's descriptions are, Woolf thinks, often unsuccessful because he accepts nature "as something in herself so desirable that description can be used in flat stretches without concentration" (BP 36). Tennyson's marvels of verisimilitude are impressive as craft but no better as poetry. Hardy, in contrast, uses nature properly "so that she neither satiates nor serves as a curious toy, but appears at the right moment to heighten, charm, or terrify, because the necessary fusion" with other elements in the work "has already taken place" (BP 37).

Woolf mentions Hardy more than once as an example of a writer whose subordination of the natural world to human concerns impresses her. His early novels, she says, again drawing a parallel with painting, promise that he "may well develop into one of our English landscape painters, whose pictures are all of cottage gardens and old peasant women, who lingers to collect and preserve from oblivion the old-fashioned ways and words which are rapidly falling into disuse" (CE I 257). In his maturity, however, Hardy is more than a recorder. He can make vivid the natural world, but Woolf realizes that he does so to convey "the sense that the little prospect of man's existence is ringed by a landscape which, while it exists apart, yet confers a deep and solemn beauty upon his drama" (CE I 259). Woolf's use of landscape has a similar effect.

She admires the descriptive abilities of writers other than Hardy. As an example of the Brontës' facility, Woolf cites the storm at the end of *Villette* which helps "to describe a state of mind which could not otherwise be expressed" (CE I 188). Woolf carries this technique, the "pathetic fallacy," to well-known fantastic lengths in *Orlando* when she identifies changes in the landscape with changes in Orlando's state of mind, literary style, and way of life in general.[13] Less obtrusively, in *To the Lighthouse*, Cam "felt herself overcast" as landscapes sometimes are "when a cloud falls on a green hillside and gravity descends" (TTL 250). So in *The Years* Delia's agitation over her mother's relapse sends her to the window: "Dark clouds were moving across the sky; the branches were tossing up and down in the light of the street lamps. Something in her was tossing up and down too" (Y 37). The Brontës, and Woolf after them, do not describe nature accurately or in detail; their descriptions are designed to "carry on the emotion and light up the meaning of the book" (CE I 188). Mrs. Radcliffe's "beautiful sense of landscape" also impresses Woolf (L III 414). "Her landscapes are sublime," she says, and notes that Austen might have learned something from her (L III 418). Woolf's over-riding opinion, however, is that passages of beautiful descriptive prose suitable for anthology excerpts are not the test of a good writer (BP 16–17). The inner lives of people are the novelist's priority.

In one of her earliest essays (1906), Woolf even talks of landscapes as if they were portraits. They should be easy to paint, she says: "The sitter reclines perpetually in an attitude of complete repose outside the drawing-room windows; he is there whenever you want him; he submits to any amount of scrutiny and analysis; and, moreover, there is no need to trouble about his soul." She notes, however, that writers have not had "encouraging results" with such personifications. Even maps often convey the "character of a place" more effectively. Words fail, she concludes, because landscapes are complex, filled with associations for each viewer. For English scenes one needs the detachment of a visitor like Henry James.[14]

When she visited another country herself, however, Woolf still found portraits of places difficult to write. "Blessed are the painters with their brushes, paints, and canvases," she wrote in "To Spain" in 1923. "But words are flimsy things. They turn tail at the first approach of visual beauty" (CE IV 190). Roger Fry, however, considered her essay successful, and for the same reason she thought Keats succeeded in his poetry; Fry thought she had captured the mood most succinctly: "You really needn't want to paint when you can do a landscape like that over the mountains," he said; "it's astonishing how much of the whole atmosphere you get into a few words." Her verbal landscapes convey "what the Germans call *stimmung*" even better than painting can. "There are landscapes in Proust," he added, "which do certain things painting can't."[15]

Virginia Woolf's later diaries, like the early ones kept on trips, show that she was not entirely convinced of her ability. Constantly the beauty of the landscape invited, even demanded a response. But in a 1924 entry Woolf noted, "I dont often trouble now to describe cornfields & groups of harvesting women in loose blues & reds & little staring yellow frocked girls. But thats not my eyes' fault." They responded as always. She described how a scene the previous night on the way back from Charleston had made her nerves stand "upright, flushed, electrified (whats the word?) with the sheer beauty." She did not try a lengthy description, however, because she could not catch or hold such a moment, an incapacity she "almost resents" (D II 311). At times she still seemed to think the painter's response more appropriate. "It is five o'clock on a fine evening," Woolf wrote to Quentin Bell in 1930, "and if I were a painter I should take my colours to the window and do a brilliant little panel of the clouds over the hotel; how I should like bowling them round and filling them in with a fiery white and bluish grey" (L IV 142). But she was not a painter, and her verbal substitutes both tempted and failed her. Ultimately, Woolf said, she wrote description in her diary for practical reasons. In Greece in 1932 she described scenes "to avoid that demon" which demanded she record their itinerary and other factual material (D IV 94). Another reason was to gather pictures both to use in her writing and to recall for her own pleasure once the trip was over (D IV 96, 100). By 1935, however, she offered another reason for not writing landscape description. On a trip to France she concluded that the perfection of a beautiful seascape "no longer makes me feel for my pen—Its too easy" (D IV 314). Yet the attempts continue through the last volume of her diary (e.g., D V 352).

Trying descriptions of scenery in her diary was one thing; writing them in letters was another. Woolf felt especially self-conscious about such passages when she wrote to her sister. In 1938, for instance, she wrote that, although the painters would not believe her, the Isle of Skye equals "Italy, Greece or Florence." Since "descriptions are your abhorrence," she continued, "I cant run on, did you wish it." She proceeded, however, to do just that (L VI 243–44). A letter from Vanessa already in 1910 indicated that the sisters had discussed Virginia's descriptive writing. "Yes I do prefer your description of humans to those of scenery," Vanessa wrote, "but I might have both I think. Anyhow those of humans give me great pleasure & encourage my hopes of you as a novelist."[16] As usual, Vanessa associated novel writing with human concerns. Virginia apparently never forgot this comment or others like it. "Thats all the description you need skip," she wrote in another letter to Vanessa Bell (L VI 249). She even anticipated the irritation of other correspondents when she included landscape descriptions in her letters. "Do you like descriptions of nature?" she asked Ethel Smyth, "or do you skip?" (L VI 247).

In "Street Haunting" (1930), Woolf reveals additional reservations about descriptions of beautiful sights and, like Vanessa, she distinguishes between them and human concerns. When one leaves home, she says, one leaves behind "the shell-like covering which our souls have excreted to house themselves," and all that is left is "a central oyster of perceptiveness, an enormous eye." Again she anticipates the possibility mentioned in *Walter Sickert* that one's visual sense can obliterate everything else. She is not concerned with the felicities of Emerson's "transparent eyeball;" in "Street Haunting" her interest is the limitations of the ordinary sense of sight. "The eye is not a miner, not a diver, not a seeker after buried treasure," she writes. "It floats us smoothly down a stream; resting, pausing, the brain sleeps perhaps as it looks" (CE IV 156). The eye delights in the beauties of the dark winter street with its lamps forming "islands of light" through which people move; when the mind awakens and turns to the characteristics and situations of individual people, however, it is "in danger of digging deeper than the eye approves." The eye, Woolf says in this piece, is superficial, interested only in "surfaces," resting "only on beauty." It cannot even arrange and order the beauties it perceives in any meaningful way. Consequently, "after a prolonged diet of this simple, sugary fare, of beauty pure and uncomposed, we become conscious of satiety" and turn to individual human beings with all their imperfections. Woolf admits, however, that the reaction she describes is that of the "average unprofessional eye" (CE IV 156–57), an eye like Peter Walsh's. In *Mrs. Dalloway* he walks through London to Clarissa's party. Ultimately "The cold stream of visual impressions failed him . . . as if the eye were a cup that overflowed and let the rest run down its china walls unrecorded." As the body relinquishes its predominance, the brain awakens and Peter prepares himself for contact with human beings once again (MD 250).

Woolf understands the satiety of the lay person's eye. Like Peter Walsh, she turns from beautiful but lifeless surfaces to the complexities of people's inner lives and relationships with each other; her satiated eye activates her brain, a function painting served for her. Woolf also understands the preoccupations of a professional eye like her sister's. The latter, as implied in "Street Haunting," can find unexpected vantage points and beauty in unusual places and can remain an enormous eye much longer; then, because this kind of eye can perceive relationships among beautiful sights, it can arrange them into pleasing wholes (CE IV 157).

Unlike Vanessa Bell, Virginia Woolf is forced by her medium to use, not colored pigments with their more direct appeal, but words to stand for colors and for colored shapes. The sisters discussed other differences between color in writing and painting. In 1909 already Vanessa wrote to Virginia, "I dont see how you use colors in writing, but probably you can do it with art. The mere words gold or yellow or gray mean nothing to me unless I can see the exact quality of the colors, but I suppose if you do it well you convey that. But I don't see how you even can count on the reader getting just the right impression as you can in a painting, when it comes to describing the looks of things. Perhaps you dont really describe the looks but only the impression the looks made upon you."[17]

With the addition of "or one of your characters," Vanessa's last sentence does define her sister's use of color reasonably well. Throughout her creative process, Virginia is more concerned with the consciousness of color than with color per se, while color to Vanessa is a more impersonal matter. She observes and executes in paint its gradations and variations, with less interest than Virginia in communicating states of mind, with the exception of her own delight, or in eliciting traditional associations.

In 1925, in the lecture she gave at the Leighton Park School, Vanessa Bell returned to the differences between writers and painters.[18] She could define such a contrast, she said, because she had always lived among writers. The one she used as her example was her sister, specifically as the author of "Mr. Bennett and Mrs. Brown."

This essay depicts not only Virginia Woolf's view of an old woman in a train but also the different views of several other writers. Although Vanessa mentions the others, she is more concerned with generalizations about writers than with distinctions among them. All writers, she says, notice visual detail, but none of them see it as she does. They observe details rich with what she calls "social and human significance." Color is one example. If writers say about the woman they describe that her hair is gray, they do so to indicate her age; similarly if they note that her gloves are mended or that she wears a particular kind of head gear, they do so to indicate something of social or economic importance. The painter, on the other hand, does not intentionally go beyond the visual: gray hair means a particular shade or variation of the color and no more, "perhaps a grey with silver lights and warm shadows, perhaps an opaque cold grey, but a grey as different from other greys as one chord in music is different from others."[19]

Vanessa Bell's interest in color has been the subject of considerable discussion among both her contemporaries and more recent critics. "What a poet you are in colour," Virginia Woolf said in 1940, complimenting Vanessa on a portrait of Quentin (L VI 381). Woolf's remark is casual. Whether she associated color in painting with specific techniques in poetry or, what is more likely, referred to a general ability to give form to emotion is not clear. Obviously she liked to use her writer's vocabulary to describe her sister's painting, just as she liked to use metaphors from the visual arts to describe writing. Roger Fry wrote more straightforwardly in 1922 that he did not think any living English painter equaled Bell as "a colourist."[20] She has found, he said, "that the secret of colour lies not in vehemence but in maintaining the pitch throughout. She never puts in a touch of merely non-committal or non-descript colour."[21] Duncan Grant called her "the purest colourist he knew."[22] More recently, Frances Spalding describes Bell as "a leading colourist of the [World War I] period."[23] A number of other art historians also trace Vanessa Bell's development as a painter by means of her color sense. Her early low-key palette changed, with a new freedom and exhilaration, to bright colors and then, in the twenties, to more controlled, harmonious tones.[24]

Colors fascinated Virginia Woolf as much as they did Vanessa Bell. "In Duncan's highlands," Woolf wrote to her sister in 1938, "the colours in a perfectly still deep blue lake of green and purple trees reflected in the middle of the water which was enclosed with green reeds, and yellow flags, and the whole sky and a purple hill—well enough. One should be a painter. As a writer," she added, "I feel the beauty, which is almost entirely colour, very subtle, very changeable, running over my pen, as if you poured a large jug of champagne over a hairpin" (L VI 243–44). Painters, she concludes on this occasion, can capture the beauty that is color far better than writers. That did not mean, however, that she did not try to compete.

When G. E. Moore distinguishes between "the object of consciousness" on the one hand and "consciousness" on the other, he illustrates his contention with the colors blue and green: "blue is one object of sensation and green is another, and consciousness, which both sensations have in common, is different from either." Consciousness, however, is elusive, and philosophical materialists do not even recognize its existence.[25] For a similar lack of recognition, Virginia Woolf faults the materialists among novelists and tries herself to convey consciousness, that which the sensations of blue and green have in common.[26] In her writing the precise colors the philosopher uses in his illustration recur.

Moore, however, was not the only stimulus for Woolf's interest in color and the perception of it. She watched her sister and the painters she knew applying color to canvas. In 1912 she mocked the "furious excitement" of the painters "over their pieces of canvas coloured green and blue" (L II 15). In 1918 she watched Vanessa Bell and Roger Fry scrutinize a Cézanne painting and struggle to determine whether he had used "pure paint or mixed; if pure which color: emerald or veridian" (D I 140). Woolf laughs at these concerns, but she also shares them. As she tried to approximate in *Mrs. Dalloway* the simultaneity Raverat reserved for painters, so she tried on occasion to show that she could use words to communicate sensations of even subtle variations of color.

One of the brief pieces in *Monday or Tuesday* (1921), in fact, is entitled "Blue & Green." The two paragraphs, one headed "Green" and one "Blue," associate these colors with day and night, land and sea. In the first, Woolf describes "ten fingers" of glass hanging down and, with the light upon them, reflecting green upon a marble surface. Also green are parakeet feathers and palm fronds. As night falls, however, what was green becomes blue: "The green's out." In the second paragraph, Woolf describes the "blue beads" of water blown from the nostrils of a "snub-nosed monster," the "metallic blue" lines and scales on the monster's hide, and the blue ribs of the remains of a boat on the beach. In the final sentence she contrasts these blues to that within the "different, cold, incense laden" atmosphere of a cathedral. This space is "faint blue with the veils of madonnas" (MT 66–67). She tries to capture the ability of consciousness to perceive one color, whether blue or green, modulating into another and varying in shade and even connotation according to circumstances.[27]

Vanessa said that she supposed writers could "use colors in writing" in ways comparable to painting if they did it "with art." The "art" Virginia employs in "Blue and Green" to evoke precise shades of color is primarily figurative language, but she recognizes the difficulties a descriptive writer confronts. "All great writers are great colourists," she says in *Walter Sickert* (CE II 241); nevertheless in *Orlando* her young character has trouble writing because "Green in nature is one thing, green in literature another. . . . The shade of green Orlando now saw spoilt his rhyme and split his metre" (0 17). Both simple, factual statements like "The sky is blue, . . . the grass is green" and descriptions filled with figurative language seem to him "utterly false" (0 102). Woolf herself tries figures of speech or, as in "Moments of Being" (1928) when she describes Julia Craye as "not so much dressed as cased, like a beetle compactly in its sheath, blue in winter, green in summer" (HH 103), she embeds her favorite simple color words in a simile. On other occasions, she tries more direct, factual statements. Sometimes blue and green are not characteristic of alternating seasons as in "Moments of Being"; rather they blend as part of a landscape of earth and sky. In "The Searchlight" Mrs. Ivimey describes a boy, supposedly her great-grandfather, bored on an endless summer day: "The whole world stretched before him. The moor rising and falling; the sky meeting the moor; green and blue, green and blue, for ever and ever" (HH 123). So "a merry little old tune" on Miss LaTrobe's gramophone in *Between the Act* asks, "What pleasure lies in dreaming / When blue and green's the day?" (BA 124). Eliciting not boredom in this case but exhilaration, the colors are the same, but the mind that perceives them is not. In Woolf's fiction the consciousness of a character is usually the decisive factor.

Throughout her career Woolf retains her early perceptions, reinforced by G. E. Moore but especially by her sister and the other painters, that color is elusive, subjective, and, while fascinating, especially problematic for the writer. Still, as she indicates in *Flush*, our language has a better vocabulary for describing colors with their variations than it has for what the other senses register. Smells, for example, are even more difficult to describe. To do so, Woolf resorts to color words. Flush, who relates to the world with his nose, "devoured whole bunches of ripe grapes largely because of their purple smell" and stayed away from "goat and macaroni" which were "raucous smells, crimson smells" (F 139).

Actual colors can augment words in communicating ideas, Woolf suggests fancifully to Vita Sackville-West in 1941: "I must buy some shaded inks—lavenders, pinks violets—to shade my meanings. I see I gave you many wrong meanings, using only black ink" (L VI 461). The comment is the culmination of a witty view of color evident as early as 1907, when Woolf typed her mock biographical sketch of Violet Dickinson with a violet typewriter ribbon and bound the book in violet leather.[28] Woolf also puts her associations between words and colors to more serious artistic use. Words affect readers as colors affect viewers; a writer can use color words, therefore, to suggest the effect of words upon the mind. Having read T. S. Eliot's *Murder in the Cathedral*, Woolf noted that she had "tested her colour sense" (D IV 323). In fact, she wrote in one of her reading notebooks that when reading poetry "the *Colour* Sense is first touched: roused."[29] If her sister is a "poet in color," then Eliot must be a colorist in words; both artists are able to use their media to create beauty for viewer or reader.

Color similes and metaphors also appear in Woolf's fiction to communicate the experiences of reading and speaking. When Mrs. Ramsay reads poetry in *To the Lighthouse*, "words, like little shaded lights, one red, one blue, one yellow, lit up in the dark of her mind." As she reads, "she felt that she was climbing backwards, upwards, shoving her way up under petals that curved over her, so that she only knew this is white, or this is red. She did not know at first what the words meant at all" (TTL 178–79). Mrs. Ramsay's response to the written word parallels the artistic response of a painter like Vanessa Bell to the world around her: neither focuses on meaning or subject; both, actually or metaphorically, perceive color; and both perceive works of art as separate worlds that, like the natural world, elicit such responses. The nurses pushing perambulators in *Between the Acts* speak rather than read colored words. The narrator describes them as "talking—not shaping pellets of information or handing ideas from one to another, but rolling words, like sweets on their tongues;

which, as they thinned to transparency, gave off pink, green, and sweetness" (BA 10).

In a world made of color, Virginia Woolf and Vanessa Bell both tried to capture some of its manifestations in outdoor scenes by using colored pigments and words with the impact of colors. An eclipse she witnessed with a group of friends in Yorkshire in 1927 especially tempted Woolf to describe her sensations of color. The progress of the eclipse, she wrote in her diary, was one of "colour . . . going out," of clouds "turning pale; a reddish black colour" reflected below in "an extraordinary scumble of red & black," then fading and disappearing altogether. "The earth was dead," Woolf noted. Then the colors returned. In the margin of her diary entry she compared the process to painting; she noted that the returning color "was of the most lovely kind—fresh, various . . . as if washed over & repainted" (D III 143). A year later Woolf elaborated on this thought and the other visual details in a descriptive essay entitled "The Sun and the Fish." As the light returned, she wrote,

> so light and frail and strange the colour was, sprinkled rainbow-like in a hoop of colour, that it seemed as if the earth could never live decked out in such frail tints. It hung beneath us, like a cage, like a hoop, like a globe of glass. It might be blown out; it might be stove in. But steadily and surely our relief broadened and our confidence established itself as the great paint-brush washed in woods dark on the valley, and massed hills blue above them. The world became more and more solid. . . . But still the memory endured that the earth we stand on is made of colour; colour can be blown out; and then we stand on a dead leaf; and we who tread the earth securely now have seen it dead (CE IV 181).

Woolf's equation of the world with color is close to the view of modern painters like her sister and like Cézanne. In the early twenties, Vanessa Bell noted how, after the Post-Impressionist Exhibition of 1910, "there was a great deal of excitement about colour . . . which perhaps has rather quieted down now. I suppose it was the result of trying first to change everything into colour. It certainly made me inclined also to destroy the solidity of objects but," she added, "I wonder whether now one couldnt get more of that sort of intensity of colour without losing solidity of objects and space."[30]

Likewise "Cézanne sees colour and is at pains to find its locus, to hedge it round;" says Max Friedländer, whereas "the Old Masters saw forms and endued them with the appropriate colours."[31]

The experience of the eclipse and the perception of the world as color recur with variations and further elaboration in *The Waves*. Bernard watches the scene wither. "How then," he asks, "does light return to the world after the eclipse of the sun?" His answer includes more color words, incorporates some of the essay's images and comparisons and adds new ones. The light, he says, returns

> "Miraculously. Frailly. In thin stripes. It hangs like a glass cage. It is a hoop to be fractured by a tiny jar. There is a spark there. Next moment a flush of dun. Then a vapour as if earth were breathing in and out, once, twice, for the first time. Then under the dullness someone walks with a green light. Then off twists a white wraith. The woods throb blue and green, and gradually the fields drink in red, gold, brown. Suddenly a river snatches a blue light. The earth absorbs colour like a sponge slowly drinking water. It puts on weight; rounds itself; hangs pendent; settles and swings beneath our feet.
>
> So the landscape returned to me; so I saw fields rolling in waves of colour beneath me. . . ." (W 286)

Bernard notes, however, that he exists only as a perceiver in this "new world." He has become, like the narrator in "Street Haunting," "an enormous eye" (CE IV 156). The identity he has had in his own eyes and in those of other people has vanished. He looks about like a child, innocently, without preconceptions, without his usual plethora of phrases to describe what he sees.[32] The freshness soon fades, but while Bernard maintains his innocent perception, he finds that even the most simple descriptive words, color words, are inadequate: "Blue, red—even they distract, even they hide with thickness instead of letting the light through" (W 287).

Virginia Woolf often gives us the world through the eyes and other faculties of those whose responses have not yet become habitual or whose education, vocabulary, and contacts with a variety of ideas and experiences have been limited: children, women of all ages, and people with artistic potential whose perceptions contrast markedly with those of formally educated or traditional men.[33] Rachel Vinrace confronts a new world in *The Voyage Out*. In *To the Lighthouse* young James reacts to the world around him and to his parents, Mrs. Ramsay retains a similar freshness of perception, and Lily Briscoe struggles to keep the visions of other painters from obliterating her own immediate responses. The early portions of *The Waves* portray the characters as children and adolescents confronting spontaneously their world and each other. Later portions reveal adults, like Bernard, recapturing at moments this freshness of perception. One more example is young George in *Between the Acts* who can lose himself totally in wonder at a flower; his experience, as so often is the case in both sisters' work, begins with color: "Membrane after membrane was torn. It blazed a soft yellow, a lambent light under a film of velvet; it filled the caverns behind the eyes with light. All that inner darkness became a hall, leaf smelling, of yellow light. And the tree was beyond the flower; the grass, the flower and the tree were entire. Down on his knees grubbing he held the flower complete" (BA 11).

In some instances, Woolf counterpoints the adult's and the child's states of mind, as when old Bart Oliver destroys George's awed immersion in the natural world. Woolf's work also embodies in a larger sense a childlike response to people and places.[34] The freshness of her vision, her desire to devise ways to capture it that suit and do not distort the immediate intense experience, are part of this quality in her writing as they are in Vanessa Bell's painting.

Both Virginia and Vanessa, even as adults, could comprehend the views of children and the significance of their everyday activities. Virginia identified especially with her nephews and niece, although her reasons for doing so were complex. As Nigel Nicolson points out, her intimacy with Vanessa's children "was not only a compensation for her own childlessness. She was one of them. She shared Vanessa with them" (L II xxi). Similarly Vanessa, Isabelle Anscombe says, "had a remarkable talent for seeing things from their [her children's] level: this in turn added a richness to her own perceptions."[35] Her paintings, whatever the subjects, communicate at their best a fresh, intense response to visual beauty. Although Vanessa did not want to deal, in her art, with the muddles of the human psyche, she valued the striking images which perception imprinted upon her own brain and tried to capture them with her visual vocabulary, just as her sister tried to capture in words her own perceptions or those of her characters. Woolf does not confine herself to this one aspect of the inner life; nevertheless, in her writing such intense moments play an important role.

In part because both sisters valued new responses to the everyday world and the artistic forms that best communicated them, they associated themselves, or have been associated by others, with modern French painting.[36] When Vanessa painted landscapes or looked out of windows at the external world, she said light was her primary interest.[37] She called herself an "impressionist,"[38] but admitted, as we have seen, that she was as concerned with underlying structure as with surface effects of light. Therefore her label for herself is not entirely accurate. Unlike Vanessa, Virginia did not label herself an Impressionist.[39] She did talk in "Modern Fiction" about the "myriad impressions" that fall upon the mind like "an incessant shower of innumerable atoms" (CE II 106). "Let us record the atoms," she says, "as they fall upon the mind in the order in which they fall" (CE II 107). She also stressed the need to reconsider the priorities reflected in the novel. However, she did not dispense with artistic selection and arrangement of the atoms, as her remark might suggest; nor was Vanessa content to capture only the surface effects of light. Both sisters looked for formal structures that gave coherence to seemingly chaotic and continual change, whether in the natural world or in the mind.

Just as Woolf alluded in her writing to actual portrait paintings and painters, so she used what she knew of landscape painting preceding, including, and succeeding that of the Impressionists. When Mrs. Dalloway boards the Euphrosyne in *The Voyage Out*, for example, she looks at the coast and exclaims, "It's so like Whistler!" Rachel responds with a hurried glance "at the grey hills on one side of her" (VO 40–41). Woolf's reference indicates some knowledge of that painter's work, probably derived from Vanessa, whose early painting was influenced for a time by his subdued palette.[40]

Woolf's awareness of some of the favorite scenes and techniques of modern French painting is also evident in her writing, early as well as late. In "Mrs. Dalloway in Bond Street," Clarissa notices approvingly the frontispiece by "Sir Joshua perhaps or Romney" in an open book in a shop window. When she passes "the picture dealer's," however, she sees "one of the odd French pictures . . . , as if people had thrown confetti—pink and blue—for a joke. If you had lived with pictures (and it's the same with books and music) thought

Clarissa, passing the Aeolian Hall, you can't be taken in by a joke" (MDP 23–24). Her response is like that of the majority of the British public to Roger Fry's Post-Impressionist Exhibition in 1910: "The pictures were a joke, and a joke at their expense," is the way Woolf describes it elsewhere (RF 153–54). She is also aware of the subjects favored by the French Impressionists. In "A Sketch of the Past," begun in 1939, she produces a generalized verbal landscape of the bay near Talland House. The changing color, "deep blue; emerald; green; purple; silver," fascinates her as do the varieties of boats that appear. Regatta Day, "what with its little flags and its little boats and its movement and people dotted on the sand and on the water and the music coming over the water," reminds her "of a French picture" (MB 112–13).

Woolf's awareness of the French and the British painters whose emphasis is changing light and color is also evident in numerous descriptive passages in her fiction. In Woolf's case, however, the perceiver of the natural world is usually identifiable and significant, although the figures of speech and carefully chosen verbs often indicate less their skill than her own. Seas, gardens, and skies especially prompt such descriptions. Light and color effects appear in *Jacob's Room*, for instance, when Jacob swims among the Scilly Isles. These "were turning bluish; and suddenly blue, purple, and green flushed the sea; left it grey; struck a stripe which vanished." Before long, "the whole floor of the waves was blue and white, rippling and crisp, though now and again a broad purple mark appeared, like a bruise; or there floated an entire emerald tinged with yellow" (JR 48). In *To the Lighthouse* the sea again prompts Woolf to describe light and, in addition, the intermingling of water and sky which often occurs in paintings by Monet. Lily Briscoe watches the boat with Mr. Ramsay, Cam, and James in it:

> So fine was the morning except for a streak of wind here and there that the sea and sky looked all one fabric; as if sails were stuck high up in the sky, or the clouds had dropped down into the sea. A steamer far out at sea had drawn in the air a great scroll of smoke which stayed there curving and circling decoratively, as if the air were a fine gauze which held things and kept them softly in its mesh, only gently swaying them this way and that. And as happens sometimes when the weather is very fine, the cliffs looked as if they were conscious of the ships, and the

> ships looked as if they were conscious of the cliffs, as if they signalled to each other some message of their own. For sometimes quite close to the shore, the Lighthouse looked this morning in the haze an enormous distance away (TTL 271).

Other descriptions that recall Impressionist paintings occur in Woolf's fiction. In *The Waves* Bernard recalls throwing up the window "and all the drops are sparkling, trembling, as if the garden were a splintered mosaic, vanishing, twinkling; not yet formed into one whole" (W 247). And, in *The Years*, Eleanor thinks of the calm evening sky as "made of innumerable grey-blue atoms the colour of an Italian officer's cloak; until it reached the horizon where there was a long bar of pure green." As the light fades, individual leaves of the trees blend into masses and downs blend into sky (Y 205).

The pleasant light effects and leisure-time subjects similar to those of the Impressionist painters, however, sometimes become more serious, intense, and brilliant like some paintings by Turner, the Fauves, the Expressionists, or Vanessa Bell during her period of brilliant color. Mrs. Flanders in *Jacob's Room*, for example, is sensitive to the movement and changing light around her as a storm approaches. She is uneasy about "the earth displayed so luridly, with sudden sparks of light from greenhouses in gardens, with a sort of yellow and black mutability, against this blazing sunset, this astonishing agitation and vitality of colour . . ." (JR 11).

Woolf's awareness of the changing effects not only of light but also of wind animating the natural world is evident in a reverie called "In the Orchard" published in 1923. This piece of writing follows the imaginings and sensations of Miranda, dozing and waking "in a long chair beneath the apple-tree" (BP 3). The description details the fluctuating colors of the opals on her hand as the sun's rays touch them, the blowing of her purple dress, and the motion of the grasses as the breeze takes them. Woolf's Miranda (her Shakespearian name is appropriate) feels as though she is at the bottom of a huge sea-like space; all sounds and sights filter down to her. Beginning with a picture, Woolf also ends the reverie with one. If the first is of changing colors and shapes, the last combines change with an underlying structure. Tree branches and movements of insects and birds form lines which balance and stabilize "the uprush of the trees." Orchard walls contain the scene. Moreover, "miles beneath the earth was clamped together" (BP 5), just as Woolf's description is structured

6.4. Vanessa Bell. *Angelica in a Hammock*, c. 1929. Courtesy of Mrs. Trekkie Parsons; permission of Angelica Garnett.

by a number of repetitions and refrains like "Miranda slept in the orchard" (BP 3–5).

Virginia Woolf owned a painting done later by Vanessa, in about 1929, of Angelica Bell lying in a hammock beneath the trees (Figure 6.4). This young woman, too, is at the bottom of the space. The vantage point of the viewer and painter, however, is above and to one side of her. We cannot see through her eyes as we can in Woolf's reverie. Still, the overall effect is similar. Dappled with shadows made by the leaves above, the girl reclines, gazing, eyes half-closed, before her. She is covered from the waist down by a mound of white and deep red fabric which hangs over the edge of the hammock and almost brushes the shadowed grass below. Behind her are swirls of tree trunks, branches, and leaves which encircle one small spot of blue sky. The effect is one of movement and change on the surface of an enclosed, structured space.[41]

In spite of paintings like this one, as Roger Fry noted in 1922, "It is curious how little the human figure makes its appearance in Vanessa Bell's work; her rooms are empty and her landscapes lonely."[42] Similarly, one of the attractions and, occasionally, one of the terrors of the natural world to Virginia Woolf was its apparent permanence, its independence of human beings. In *Jacob's Room*, for example, the narrator notes how nature continues its various activities "unseen by any one" (JR 98). Beautiful scenes remind us of human transciency in the face of the eternal natural forces and the many other human beings who have preceded us. For this reason the "loveliness" of the Cornish hills "is infernally sad" (JR 49). In "The Searchlight" too the group looking at the stars sees them as "very permanent, very unchanging. . . . A hundred years seemed nothing" (HH 122). So Orlando, completing her poem, realizes that if she were dead, the world "would be just the same!" (O 271–72).

Woolf's characters are sometimes tempted to lose themselves in this vast timelessness. In these instances, the experience is positive. The eyes become the dominant senses. Tired of life, Orlando decides to merge with the natural world, to fall upon the moor, gaze at earth and sky, and become "nature's bride" (O 248). Her marriage to nature personified, however, is short-lived and humorously undercut as the heart she imagines beating deep within the earth proves to be the galloping horse of Marmaduke Bonthrop Shelmerdine, Esquire. Kitty Lasswade's union in *The Years* is similar: the same frustration and the same solution. In this case, however, the personification is more subtle and the bride is uninterrupted. Escaping from the city and her social obligations, Kitty takes the train north, then goes for a vigorous walk to the top of a hill.

> Her body seemed to shrink; her eyes to widen. She threw herself on the ground, and looked over the billowing land that went rising and falling, away and away, until somewhere far off it reached the sea. Uncultivated, uninhabited, existing by itself, for itself, without towns or houses it looked from this height. Dark wedges of shadow, bright breadths of light lay side by

> side. Then, as she watched, light moved and dark moved; light and shadow went travelling over the hills and over the valleys. A deep murmur sang in her ears—the land itself, singing to itself, a chorus, alone. She lay there listening. She was happy, completely. Time had ceased (Y 277–78).

With a heart that beats and a voice that sings, the earth is a spouse who makes no demands. It has a life independent of human beings. During moments when they identify with that life, people can transcend their circumscribed existences.

Bernard in his summing up in *The Waves* also considers "that which is beyond and outside our own predicament," permanence suggested by three visual images: "The willow grows on the turf by the river. The gardeners sweep with great brooms and the lady sits writing" (W 248). Natural objects like the willow and impersonal scenes like the unidentified gardeners and the anonymous woman putting down her thoughts survive the rush of individualized, transient details. These symbols, however, are those of childhood and are qualified by the mature realization of "what is unescapable in our lot; death; the knowledge of limitations; how life is more obdurate than one had thought it" (W 269).

In her last novel Woolf's description of the lily pond near Poinz Hall recalls her sister's renditions of the pond at Charleston and suggests again that the natural world exists independent of individual human lives: "There had always been lilies there, self-sown from wind-dropped seed, floating red and white on the green plates of their leaves. Water, for hundreds of years, had silted down into the hollow, and lay there four or five feet deep over a black cushion of mud. Under the thick place of green water, glazed in their self-centered world, fish swam—gold, splashed with white, streaked with black or silver" (BA 43). Spiders move on the surface of the water; petals fall, float, then sink; the fish hesitate, "then with a waver of undulation off they flashed" (BA 44). The world of the pond is self-contained and timeless, a microcosm of the natural world as a whole.

Like Vanessa Bell, Virginia Woolf is fond of views, but she usually filters them through the consciousness of human beings. Her characters often find that views communicate their emotions. Like Orlando and Kitty Lasswade, they personify the natural world, give it, in this case, a voice and a language. In *The Years* Eleanor watches the changing scene and thinks, "It seemed to take what she was feeling and to express it broadly and simply, as if another voice were speaking in another language" (Y 299). Similarly "the view from the window" as Eleanor and Peggy observe it "served, like another voice speaking, to fill up the pause" (Y 328). To Bernard in *The Waves* "Visual impressions often communicate thus briefly statements we shall in time to come uncover and coax into words" (W 189). To the narrator of *Between the Acts* views also speak. The gramophone plays a tune the words of which describe an idyllic pastoral evening and

> The view repeated in its own way what the tune was saying. The sun was sinking; the colours were merging; and the view was saying how after toil men rest from their labours; how coolness comes; reason prevails; and having unharnessed the team from the plough, neighbours dig in cottage gardens and lean over cottage gates.
>
> The cows, making a step forward, then standing still, were saying the same thing to perfection (BA 134).

The "triple melody" of song, words, and view holds the audience's attention. That views should speak for and to people links the natural and the human realms.

This fusion occurs in other ways. In Woolf's fiction exterior and interior places mingle. Light and wind penetrate houses and rooms. In "The Shooting Party," light is a presence in the draughty room of the Rashleigh sisters: "On the carpet lay panels of green and yellow, where the sun rested, and then the sun moved and pointed a finger as if in mockery at a hole in the carpet and stopped. And then on it went, the sun's feeble but impartial finger, and lay upon the coat of arms over the fireplace—gently illumined—the shield, the pendant grapes, the mermaid, and the spears" (HH 59). Here and in "The Lady in the Looking Glass," breezes join lights to animate the room. Instead of the sun's finger, we have "shy creatures, lights and shadows, curtains blowing, petals falling" which the narrator likens to cranes, flamingoes, or peacocks: "They came pirouetting across the floor, stepping delicately with high-lifted feet and spread tails and pecking allusive beaks . . ." (HH 87). She adds two more similes: "And there were obscure flushes and darkenings too, as if a cuttlefish had suddenly suffused the air with purple; and the room had its passions and rages and envies and sorrows coming over it and clouding it, like a human being" (HH 88). This animated scene opposes another. What the Italian looking-glass accurately reflects "lay still in the trance of immortality" (HH 88). The mirror freezes the scene and, as views through window-frames and paintings do, captures some transcendent truth. So, in the "Time Passes" section of *To the Lighthouse*, "certain airs" fumble, nose, rub, sigh, and lament through the house (TTL 190–91), but in spite of the occasional motion, "Loveliness and stillness," personified, unite to make "the shape of loveliness itself, a form from which life had parted" (TTL 195). Motion and stasis, life and death coexist, each defining the other.

Just as Woolf's characters withdraw from the complexities and obligations of human relationships into the world of nature so they withdraw into interior spaces. These sanctuaries are often upper rooms connected with lower ones by stairways. Although houses are central images in most of Woolf's novels, the movement up and down staircases, from one kind of interior space to another, is exemplified well in *Night and Day* and *Mrs. Dalloway*. In *Night and Day* Katharine Hilbery takes her letters up to her room to avoid her mother's curiosity. There she thinks of her life, cluttered with other people's destinies, in contrast to the lives of Ralph Denham and Mary Datchet who have "empty space before them" (ND 106). She also likes the "shabby comfort" (ND 136) of William Rodney's rooms and imagines herself married to him, free to pursue her own interests in the space he has created (ND 138). His rooms are not the haven Katharine seeks, however, and Ralph Denham has less inviolable space in his life than she thinks. Although his "cheerless" room is "up a great many flights of stairs" (ND 25), he is still interrupted by family members who resent "his wish for privacy" (ND 27). Mary Datchet is more successful. In her flat "High in the air," she is very much in her element: "She was robbing no one of anything, and yet, to get so much pleasure from simple things, such as eating one's breakfast alone in a room which had nice colors in it, clean from the skirting of the boards to the corners of the ceiling, seemed to suit her so thoroughly that she used at first to hunt about for some one to apologize to, or for some flaw in the situation" (ND 77).

Withdrawing from the demands of human relationships, if only briefly, to a room of one's own has, for Woolf, both negative and positive connotations. Mrs. Dalloway withdraws "like a nun" to her narrow, virginal bed in the attic (MD 45). Septimus Smith, whose similar inability to achieve intimacy with other people terrifies him, leaps from the window of his room rather than let his solitude be violated by a professional advice-giver like Dr. Holmes. Mrs. Dalloway's room and the one from which Septimus jumps reflect both a desire for privacy and an incapacity for intimacy. Withdrawal can suggest self-denial or a rejection of certain dimensions of life; it can also result in self-assertion and self-affirmation. It promotes changes of perspective. In their own spaces, many of Woolf's characters work to define themselves as separate individuals. While they scrutinize themselves more closely, they also gaze upon other people from a distance; appropriately, these rooms at the tops of stairways have windows out of which their inhabitants look dispassionately upon the world they have left behind. Woolf's descriptions of rooms and their meanings to her characters parallel her dual view both of paintings like Vanessa Bell's and of Vanessa herself. Woolf is intrigued by the aloofness from human concerns of the modern visual arts and by her sister's more detached, undemonstrative demeanor; at the same time she finds them cold. Ultimately rooms, like Jacob's in *Jacob's Room*, are empty; houses, like the one in *To the Lighthouse*, are deserted. Their inhabitants are dead or gone, indistinguishable from their environments. Woolf's characters find and lose themselves in the same spaces.

Vanessa Bell was also intrigued by spaces within spaces, as were many painters in the twenties. She frequently combined indoor and outdoor scenes by showing painted views from windows or balconies or else interior scenes combined with views through windows. In about 1920, for example, she reported her work on a painting which showed part of the sitting room and part of the garden as seen through the window.[43] Two works from the thirties are typical. In *Charleston Garden* (1933), Bell paints a young woman sitting and sewing in a chair in front of the studio door. Through it we see a table with a vase of flowers on it, a walkway, and the garden trees, shrubs, and flowers.[44] In *The Garden Door, Charleston* (c. 1936) part of a chair, empty this time, appears in front of a window that opens onto the garden (Figure 6.5). In a number of Bell's dust-jacket designs for her sister's books we also glimpse interior spaces through win-

6.5. Vanessa Bell. *The Garden Door, Charleston*, c. 1936. Private collection. Courtesy of the Anthony d'Offay Gallery, London; permission of Angelica Garnett.

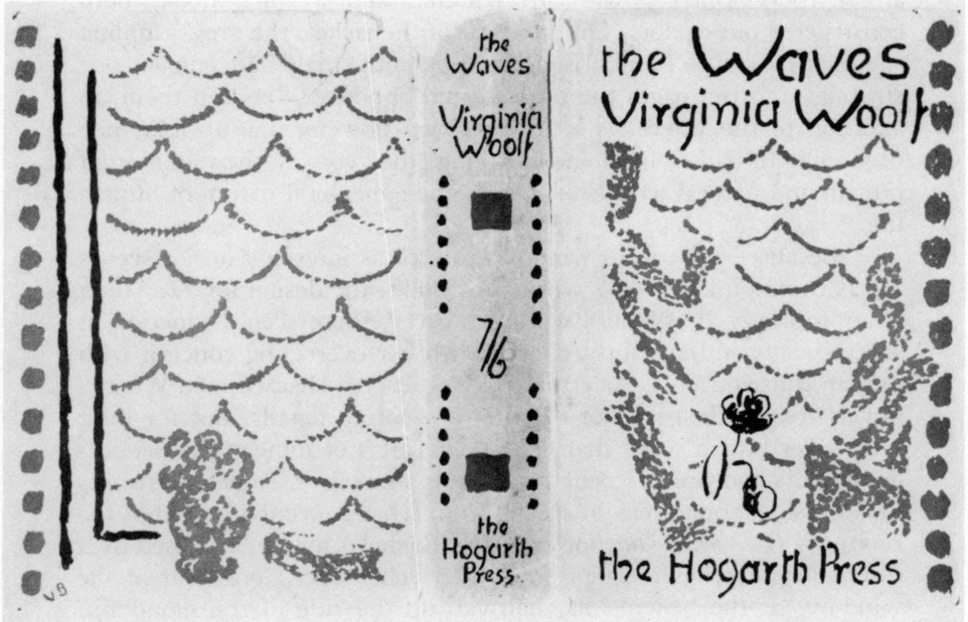

6.6. Vanessa Bell. Dust jacket for *The Waves* (London: Hogarth, 1931) by Virginia Woolf. Courtesy of the Bloomsbury Collection at Washington State University Libraries, Pullman, Washington; permission of the estate of Vanessa Bell and the Hogarth Press.

dows; in others, we look out from inside. In some of these, windows combine with flowers, a motif common, as we have seen, in both sisters' work. Examples of the combination in Bell's dust-jacket designs are *Jacob's Room*, *A Haunted House and Other Stories*, *The Common Reader*, and *The Waves*.[45] An examination of one of these again reveals the sisters' similar values and world views.

For *The Waves* Vanessa Bell designed not only the front and spine of the jacket but also the back (Figure 6.6). Taking her image, as she often did, directly from the title, Bell covers both parts of the jacket with stippled grey lines which form scallops suggesting waves. On the back, however, the waves appear through a window. Two vertical lines on the left, one of which turns at a right angle towards the lower center, suggest the window frame. In front of the corner are a flower-filled bowl with pedestal and a thick book, both constructed out of dots. On the front of the jacket, the grey stippling suggests halves of human figures, apparently male and female, one striding onto the page, the other seated opposite. Between them, in addition to the waves, is a leaf and two flowers, one upright, one drooping. In darker lines and stippling, they convey the mingling of human and natural worlds as well as the ephemeral nature of human life.

Because views from windows as well as interior-exterior scenes are as common in Woolf's work as in Bell's, the design for *The Waves* is appropriate. In Woolf's work, however, these scenes function in several ways and are always fused with her overriding concern with human consciousness. As critics have observed, characters in Woolf's novels frequently gaze out of windows noting details, not for their own sakes but in ways that echo their states of mind.[46] Just as outdoor lights and breezes penetrate Woolf's interiors, so her characters look outside, sometimes to escape from what is occurring within the room. In *The Voyage Out*, for example, Rachel Vinrace, confused by a discussion of religion and by her own vehemence, looks out of the window "at their own villa, halfway up the side of the mountain. The most familiar view seen framed through glass has a certain unfamiliar distinction, and she grew calm as she gazed" (VO 233). Rachel's experience of a framed scene not only reveals her mental state but also suggests the experience of a painting; human concerns become irrelevant.

Similarly, Katharine Hilbery in *Night and Day* habitually and "instinctively" (ND 85) looks out of windows as an escape from the difficulties of various interior scenes and people into a realm less personal and complex. Tired of a conversation with her mother and Aunt Celia about her cousin Cyril's mistress and illegitimate children, Katharine "turned to the window, and stood among the folds of the curtain, pressing close to the window-pane, and gazing disconsolately at the river much in the attitude of a child depressed by the meaningless talk of its elders" (ND 123). Likewise, faced with William's welcome and at the same time discomfiting attraction to Cassandra, Katharine "looked out of the window, sternly determined to forget private misfortunes, to forget herself, to forget individual lives." The voices in the room behind her seem to come "from people in another world, . . . ; it was as if, lately dead, she heard the living talking." Life seems to her a dream, an unreal existence confined to "four walls . . . beyond which lay nothing, or nothing more than darkness" (ND 352). In *The Waves* Susan also flees an oppressive life, the "regimented, unreal existence" of school, by gazing out of the window at "a blue view" (W 125).

Similar scenes, however, affect people differently. To Eleanor in *The Years* the view of the night sky from a window suggests something impersonal that calms her: "She had a sense of immensity and peace—as if something had been consumed . . ." (Y 298). At the party which concludes the novel, however, Peggy looks outside at the night sky and cannot feel what Eleanor does: "Then the stars. Inscrutable, eternal, indifferent—those were the words; the right words. But I don't feel it, she said, looking at the stars. So why pretend to?" (Y 360) The significance of the night sky resides in the perceiver. So does the significance of the view from Pointz Hall in *Between the Acts*. To Mrs. Manressa the scene is unpleasant: "The flat fields glared green yellow, blue yellow, red yellow, then blue again. The repetition was senseless, hideous, stupefying" (BA 67). To Mrs. Swithin, however, the view is both "sad" and "beautiful" because "'It'll be there,' she nodded at the strip of gauze laid upon the distant fields, 'when we're not'" (BA 53).

Equally often Woolf's characters look through windows not at the sky above or off into the distance but at the view directly below them. The effects, however, are similar. Peggy and Eleanor in *The Years* look down at the street and feel detached from what they see: "It was queer to see cabs turning corners, going round this street and down the other, and not to hear the sound they made. It was like a map of London; a section laid beneath them" (Y 328). When Kitty Lasswade looks out of a window during one of her parties, the change in perspective creates similar distancing. In the square below "there was a spatter of leaf-shadow and lamplight on the pavement; the usual policeman was balancing himself as he patrolled; the usual little men and women, foreshortened from this height, hurried along by the railings" (Y 258). A comparable change in perspective exists in *Between the Acts* when Mrs. Swithin and William Dodge watch cars arriving from an upper window: "Their narrow black roofs were laid together like the blocks of a floor." From their doors emerge varieties of shoes and legs (BA 72). These people attain the visual artist's perspective and perceive patterns freed from the complexities of individual human identities and relationships.

Views from windows in Woolf's fiction help to convey states of mind other than the confusion, frustration, or even mere curiosity which result in an experience of a realm beyond human turmoil. A view from a window in *The Years* emphasizes Sara's solitude (Y 132–34). Boredom causes some of Woolf's characters to gaze out of windows, as when Orlando's traditional biographer can think of nothing to do while his subject persists in writing. Noting birds and their activities, servants and theirs, clouds and their movements, then the meaning of life, his thoughts move from concrete to abstract (O 269–71). When Orlando reaches the present day, however, her "favourite station" at the window is not the result of boredom; rather she observes the astonishing inventions of modern life, and thus notes the passage of time (O 297). A view through a window serves a similar purpose in an interior/exterior scene in *Jacob's Room*. The time frame, however, is much smaller. Jacob sits at dinner and looks between and behind the women sitting opposite him at "the grey-green garden, and among the pear-shaped leaves of the escallonia fishing-boats seemed caught and suspended. A sailing ship slowly drew past the women's backs. . . . The dinner would never end, Jacob thought, and he did not wish it to end, though the ship had sailed from one corner of the window-frame to the other, and a light marked the end of the pier" (JR 57–58).[47] In *The Years* views from windows are used again to mark the passage of time as Edward, in Oxford, leans out of his window and notes the passing of evening into night (Y 48, 50). In most of these instances individuals again become parts of larger patterns.

Sometimes in Woolf's fiction two people look through a window together, or else one person watches another gazing out. Often the experience is not one of communion. People realize their remoteness from each other but, paradoxically, the experience elicits a bond of respect or affection. It does so when Mary Datchet and Katharine Hilbery look out of Mary's window in *Night and Day*. First they look "up at the hard silver moon, stationary among a hurry of little grey-blue clouds, and then down upon the roofs of London, with all their upright chimneys, and then below them at the empty moonlit pavement of the street, upon which the joint of each paving-stone was clearly marked out." Then Mary watches Katharine concentrate on the moon "as though she were setting that moon against the moon of other nights, held in memory" (ND 60).

A parallel scene involves Katharine and Ralph Denham. He wants her to appreciate the view of the city from the window of his room. Like Mary, he watches her looking out (ND 380). When she leaves, he stands where she stood, looks at what she saw, and realizes his love for her (ND 386). Later he looks out of a window at her house. "Outside," he thinks, "were truth and freedom, and the immensity only to be apprehended by the mind in loneliness, and never communicated to another. What worse sacrilege was there than to attempt to violate what he perceived by seeking to impart it?" Katharine joins him at the window and, although she seems "distant," still "her presence by his side transformed the world." Ralph imagines himself accomplishing great things. He does not demand, however, that she share her thoughts any more than he wishes to share his own (ND 473–74). Views in Woolf's fiction, then, speak for and to people. They provide escapes into realms which in their impersonality transcend human muddle or oppression; in so doing, views sometimes generate sadness or fear, but more often they calm. They can reflect inner turmoil, consciousness of time passing, or loneliness. Even when people look at a view together, they cannot fully share it, but they can recognize and respect one another's essential solitude.

Characters in Woolf's works look through windows up at the sky or down at the street or yard. Occasionally she describes or has a character view a scene from a more unusual angle. With a vantage point like the snail's in *Kew Gardens*, Jacob in *Jacob's Room* lies in a meadow, "gilt with buttercups," in grass that "stood juicy and thick. Looking up, backwards, he saw the legs of children deep in the grass, and the legs of cows. . . . In front of him two white butterflies circled higher and higher round the elm tree" (JR 37). Some of Woolf's characters are also sensitive to composition and, as their eyes move, they create pictures. As Martin sits by Maggie in Kew Gardens in *The Years*, for example, he defines the view as "admirably composed. There was the white figure of Queen Victoria against a green bank; beyond, was the red brick of the old palace; the phantom church raised its spire, and the Round Pond made a pool of blue. A race of yachts was going forward. The boats leant on their sides so that the sails touched the water" (Y 244). Just as the vantage point is crucial in one descriptive passage so the positioning of elements in the scene is important in the other. Woolf's awareness of both is part of her sympathy with the visual arts.

Virginia Woolf's ability to see spaces within spaces moves in the opposite direction as well. Individuals exist within rooms, buildings, and the world outside; spaces also exist within individuals. Just as painting provides Woolf with metaphors for writing and writing provides her with metaphors for painting, so each space, as we have begun to see, provides metaphors for the others. Rooms and landscapes have moods and voices. So people have within them rooms, houses, and landscapes. "But I like going from one lighted room to another," Woolf noted in her diary in 1924, "such is my brain to me; lighted rooms; & the walks in the fields are corridors . . ." (D II 310). On other occasions she thinks of works of literature, the psychological experiences that prompted them, and the emotional states they produce in the reader, as landscapes. In "Together and Apart" Miss Anning's mention of Canterbury "touched the spring" in Mr. Serle's mind. "Fields and flowers and grey buildings dripped down into his mind, formed silver drops on the gaunt, dark walls of his mind and dripped down. With such an image his poems often began" (HH 138). The reader, in turn, creates a landscape, maps the emotional peaks and valleys as he or she reads (BP 97). Eventually the poem or, in another instance, Dostoevsky's books, become part of the "furniture of our minds" (BP 116). The exterior world provides similar metaphors for the interior in "The Lady in the Looking Glass." The narrator imagines that Isabella's "mind was like her room, in which lights advanced and retreated, . . . and then her whole being was suffused, like the room again, with a cloud of some profound knowledge, some unspoken regret, and then she was full of locked drawers, stuffed with letters, like her cabinets" (HH 92).

Interiors and landscapes provide analogies for personalities and states of mind as palpable to a writer like Virginia Woolf as actual rooms and outdoor scenes are to a painter like Vanessa Bell. In *The Voyage Out* Helen compares Rachel's mind "to the sliding of a river, quick, quicker, quicker still, as it races to a waterfall" (VO 222). "Her mind," the narrator says of Rachel, "was as the landscape outside when dark beneath clouds and straitly lashed by wind and hail" and, since she had no sense of consequences when considering her feelings for Terence, the narrator concludes that "Helen's image of the river sliding on to the waterfall had a great likeness to the facts" (VO 223). Woolf, however, does not limit herself to the stream metaphor for consciousness.[48] Her conception of the mind and its workings is frequently more spatial. Even in *The Voyage Out* Rachel, increasingly ill, moves about restlessly, "in and out of rooms, in and out of peoples' minds, seeking she knew not what" (VO 259).

Although of a vaguer kind, minds are also spaces in *Night and Day*. Ralph, who has persuaded Katharine to utter "a broken statement" in summation of her feelings for him, feels as if he "had stepped over the threshold into the faintly lit vastness of another mind, stirring with shapes, so large, so dim, unveiling themselves only in flashes, and moving away again into the darkness, engulfed by it." In Ralph's mind, Katharine takes on "such strange shapes" (ND 504).

In *To the Lighthouse* and elsewhere Woolf compares human minds to "mirrors, . . . pools of uneasy water, in which clouds for ever turn and shadows form" (TTL 198). After listing sights on the beach in "Time Passes," the narrative voice marvels "how beauty outside mirrored beauty within" (TTL 201). Mirrors, pools, and clouds reappear. In *Orlando* the biographer tells us that Orlando loves night, "in which the reflections in the dark pool of the mind shine more clearly than by day." The dark pool is memory upon which pictures of the past are reflected. It is also her imagination, creator of scenes never seen (O 327). In *Between the Acts* Miss LaTrobe's pageant hangs "in the sky of the mind—moving, diminishing, but still there." The main characters observe it, each seeing something different. "In another moment it would be beneath the horizon, gone to join the other plays. . . . It was drifting away to join the other clouds: becoming invisible" (BA 212–13). Minds in Woolf's fiction are lighted rooms with furniture, dim rooms animated by ambiguous shapes as well as landscapes with mountains, valleys, sliding rivers, deep pools, and cloudy skies. Movement is usually contained within a definite space, however limited or vast. These landscapes of the mind are what Woolf usually paints.

Virginia Woolf often considered how she would represent interiors and landscapes were she a painter herself, but she concluded that the medium would limit her too severely. People's responses to the physical spaces within which they move as well as their mental spaces interested her more, but there was another reason. Late in her life, in "A Sketch of the Past," she tried to describe her childhood memories of her nursery at Talland House. Thinking initially, as she so often does, in terms of colors and then of shapes occupying space, she translates her memory into an idea for a painting:

> If I were a painter I should paint these first impressions in pale yellow, silver, and green. There was the pale yellow blind; the green sea; and the silver of the passion flowers. I should make a picture that was globular; semi-transparent. I should make a picture of curved petals; of shells; of things that were semi-transparent; I should make curved shapes, showing the light through, but not giving a clear outline. Everything would be large and dim (MB 66).

Sounds, however, would play an equally important role. When Woolf looks at paintings, as the references to squeaking trams and shrieking children in her description of Sickert's *Ennui* show (CE II 237), visual images often suggest sounds. In "A Sketch of the Past," however, she forgets this fact. Sounds are such a crucial part of her memories that, she concludes, "pictures is not the right word" to describe them (MB 67).

Woolf's visual descriptions frequently incorporate or conclude with sounds. In *The Years* we see the Robsons and their house through Kitty's eyes; her awareness of the brightly lighted room, too full of objects marked by poverty or lack of taste, and of a garden outside without flowers includes "the sound of hammering" from a shed (Y 68). Later she looks down from her box at the interior of an opera house. The description incorporates some figurative language and evokes smells as well as sounds and sights. In addition, the passage is alive with movement more like a movie scene than a painting:

> People were passing to their seats; they were sitting down and getting up again; they were taking off their cloaks and signalling to friends. They were like birds settling on a field. In the boxes white figures were appearing here and there; white arms rested on the ledges of boxes; white shirt-fronts shone beside them. The whole house glowed—red, gold, cream-coloured, and smelt of clothes and flowers, and echoed with the squeaks and trills of the instruments and with the buzz and hum of voices (Y 181–82).

So the barn, decorated for refreshments between the acts of Miss LaTrobe's play in Woolf's last novel, has not only its "shaft of light like a yellow banner" but also its active mice, swallows, insects, and dogs, its sounds and smells (BA 99–100).

Woolf's interest in landscape description is especially evident in *The Waves*. Here each portion of the life cycle of the six characters is introduced by an italicized descriptive passage that begins by defining the position of the sun in its daily cycle. Clive Bell called these sections "purple passages" and confessed that he did not like them.[49] Later readers, however, have defended and explained them as verbal equivalents of Impressionist paintings.[50] It is true that they capture the light and color of different moments of the day and together form a series parallel to Monet's successive representations of Rouen Cathedral or of a haystack. Woolf's descriptions, however, are neither wholly visual nor static. The first such passage, like the rendition of the eclipse discussed earlier, describes a time before dawn when the blended sea and sky become visually distinct and, as the light increases, vivid colors emerge among the neutral tones. Edges of objects become more distinct; shadows and reflections intensify. As the sun sets, further changes occur until once again sea and sky blend in neutral tones. Characteristic of all the scenes, however, is not only light coloring sea and sky but also the movement of light rays and waves as well as the sounds of the sea and the chirping of birds.

Hardly objective catalogues of facts, Woolf's descriptions are also filled with similes, metaphors, personifications, and sound repetitions. A portion of the first passage provides a good example:

> *Gradually the dark bar on the horizon became clear as if the sediment in an old wine-bottle had sunk and left the glass green. Behind it, too, the sky cleared as if the white sediment there had sunk, or as if the arm of a woman couched beneath the horizon had raised a lamp and flat bars of white, green and yellow, spread across the sky like the blades of a fan. Then she raised her lamp higher and the air seemed to become fibrous and to tear away from the green surface flickering and flaming in red and yellow fibres like the smoky fire that roars from a bonfire. Gradually the fibres of the burning bonfire were fused into one haze, one incandescence which lifted the weight of the woollen grey sky on top of it and turned it to a million atoms of soft blue. The surface of the sea slowly became transparent and lay rippling and sparkling until the dark stripes were almost rubbed out. Slowly the arm that held the lamp raised it higher and then higher until a broad flame became visible; an arc of fire burnt on the rim of the horizon, and all round it the sea blazed gold* (W 7–8).

However visual her initial inspiration may have been, Woolf also worked within the traditions of literary description. Still, in the context of her knowledge of painting, she examines those traditions critically. As she has Orlando consider, color in nature and color in literature differ; both figures of speech and simple denotative labels may be false. *The Waves* also incorporates criticisms of image-making along with considerable indulgence in it. Bernard, like Orlando, is adept at inventing figures of speech. Neville listens to him talk: "Up they bubble—images. 'Like a camel,' . . . 'a vulture.' The camel is a vulture; the vulture a camel." His "foolish comparisons" buoy up his listeners until his power fails and they come back down to earth (W 38).

Comparisons are too seductive, however, for Woolf or for some of her characters to avoid. When Bart Oliver, Mrs. Swithin, and the others in *Between the Acts* observe the changing weather, striking figurative language conveys a landscape made, as in *The Waves*, of color. As in "Blue and Green," Woolf is still interested in conveying consciousness by means of color:

> Here came the sun—an illimitable rapture of joy, embracing every flower, every leaf. Then in compassion it withdrew, covering its face, as if it forebore to look on human suffering. There was a fecklessness, a lack of symmetry and order in the clouds, as they thinned and thickened. Was it their own law, or no law, they obeyed? Some were wisps of white hair merely. One, high up, very distant, had hardened to golden alabaster; was made of immortal marble. Beyond that was blue, pure blue, black blue; blue that had never filtered down; that had escaped registration. It never fell as sun, shadow, or rain upon the world, but disregarded the little coloured ball of earth entirely. No flower felt it; no field; no garden (BA 23).

To make her descriptive passages even less static, Woolf shifts the vantage point. After she introduces the sun in *The Waves* and compares it to a woman with a lamp, she follows its rays as they illuminate not only sea, horizon, and shoreline, but also the garden, the house, and the objects it falls upon through windows.[51] Each introductory passage, in short, includes at least one shift in viewpoint and at least two different scenes. Still life and landscape mingle. The third such introduction, for example, begins with the seashore where the sun shines upon an "eaten-out boat," moves to the sounds and activities of birds and a cat in the garden, takes the birds'-eye-view of the dark underside of all of this vitality: the decay ongoing at the base of the flowers, and finally, follows the sun through the window and onto the furniture, a mirror, and a flower on the sill (W 73–75).

Vanessa Bell, in her paintings of houses or people within natural settings, of unpeopled landscapes or rooms, and of views through windows, also experiments with a number of vantage points. Occasionally she tries more than one within a single painting.[52] As we have seen, she also painted the same subject as Grant or Fry from a different angle and produced, with them, multiple points of view. Bell, however, refused to incorporate the methods of earlier artists who depicted personified seasons or times of day in ways comparable to some of her sister's figures of speech.

Although color was central to both sisters when they looked at the world around them, they agreed that writers and painters use color differently. Painters, according to Vanessa, capture the looks of things and are interested in variations and exact qualities of colors for their own sakes. Writers, she says, are more interested in the impression the color makes upon them or, judging from what her sister says in "Mr. Bennett and Mrs. Brown," in the human significance of the visible world. Virginia thought a great deal about the extent to which the writer can appeal to the reader's sight. She concluded that, although color words are more abundant in our language than words to describe the reactions of the other senses, the writer still has trouble. As Vanessa said, Virginia is more interested in the impressions color makes upon the mind than in the precise shade of the color itself. She recognized the tendency to become an enormous eye. She also tried to rival the painters in "Blue and Green" and elsewhere with her subtle color distinctions. In most of her writing, though, the visible world is subordinated to overall structure or characterization. Both sisters drew their inspiration from the visible world but despaired of exact renditions and drew upon their imaginations too.

Virginia Woolf and Vanessa Bell tried to capture the freshest possible responses to the world around them, to regain the child's innocent perception, free of preconceptions. Both of them succeeded to some extent; each looked for material of artistic interest in her immediate vicinity, in people, objects, and scenes traditionally considered not worth a painter's or a writer's attention. Vanessa's own visual shocks are evident in her paintings. Virginia captures hers in a variety of ways, often as parts of her characterizations, but even when she depicts minds filled with preconceptions, she does so with her own childlike curiosity and delight. Although this innocence, as well as the interest in the quotidian and the definition of the world as color, are characteristic of Impressionist painting, that label does not sum up the work of either sister. Both knew something about Impressionism and about previous and subsequent developments in French and English art. Certain passages in Woolf's writing do suggest the Impressionists, as certain paintings by Vanessa reveal her concern with shifting light effects. Other passages and paintings, however, suggest other interests. Both sisters were ultimately more intrigued, like the Post-Impressionists, with the structure underlying changing surfaces, and Woolf was concerned as well with the invisible world of the mind within the visible person.

Spaces surrounding people preoccupied both sisters. Both perceived landscapes that rendered people insignificant or that did not include them at all. Woolf's characters lose themselves in the timeless world that goes on without people, willingly escape from the confusions of their transient lives into a transcendent realm. Bell's paintings capture that realm. Both sisters were interested in interpenetrating spaces and combined indoor and outdoor scenes. Like Vanessa Bell's paintings, views through windows in Woolf's writing serve to distance, freeze, and provide escapes from the tangles of human relationships. Important perceptions stop time, become like paintings, reveal permanence in the midst of change, calm in the midst of confusion. Rooms too are spaces into which people can escape from the aggravations of their lives with other people. Such escapes, however, are pleasant or unpleasant, life affirming or life denying, depending upon the character and the situation. In Woolf's writing outside spaces ultimately are metaphors for spaces inside and the enormous eye that one becomes is related to the loss of self, the loss of language, the silence that she experiences so consistently in her sister's painting.

Conclusion

DESTRUCTION AND CREATION

In Virginia Woolf's *Orlando*, changes in writing as well as in sculpture, painting, and the decorative arts mark the difference between the nineteenth and twentieth centuries. In the Victorian era, walls and windows, floors and furniture are covered; rooms are dark and cluttered with artificial decorations. A hideous conglomeration of disparate objects and treatments forming some kind of monument on the present site of Victoria's statue drives Orlando to "profound dismay" (O 232). In the twentieth century, however, "the walls were bare so that new brilliantly coloured pictures of real things like streets, umbrellas, apples, were hung in frames, or painted upon the wood" (O 297–98). The description recalls French artists like Monet, Renoir, and Cézanne as well as the British Impressionist and Post-Impressionist painters and decorators like Vanessa Bell who capture the visual excitement of the everyday world. So Orlando's one enduring poem is "a voice answering a voice" that sings to her from the forests and farms, fields and gardens of her daily life (O 325).

Virginia Woolf did not have a comprehensive knowledge of the visual arts, but she knew the major tendencies of her time and she put them, and whatever else she knew, to good, varied, and constant use. Her awareness of traditional and modern portrait, still-life, and landscape painting emerges from a relationship with Vanessa Bell in which professional artistic activity was an important dimension. The sisters, as we have seen, stimulated and inspired each other as artists. Sometimes the comments of one suggested to the other a work in her own artistic medium or even a work she had in progress or had already completed. Sometimes similar perceptions grew out of or led to collaboration on specific projects. Each sister often denied any knowledge of the other's medium, defended her own, and even at times doubted the other's genius. At the same time, combining rivalry with admiration, polite compliments with genuine enthusiasm, each criticized, praised, and learned from the other's work.

Always aware of the visual arts, Woolf continually thought of and described her books as drawings, paintings, and statues. "I'm not sure," she wrote to Roger Fry in 1918, "that a perverted plastic sense doesn't somehow work itself out in words for me" (L II 285). *Night and Day* is her effort to "copy from plaster casts, partly to tranquillise, partly to learn anatomy" (L IV 231), while *Jacob's Room* is her attempt to break "with complete representation" (L VI 501). Retyping *Mrs. Dalloway* is an effective process "as thus one works with a wet brush over the whole, & joins parts separately composed & gone dry" (D II 323). *Orlando* too needs editing because she has "scrambled & splashed, & the canvas shows through in a thousand places" (D III 176). *The Waves* is "a mosaic" of lives (D III 298); when those lives take shape, she has got her "statues against the sky" (D III 300). Revising the novel again is "like sweeping over an entire canvas with a wet brush" (D IV 25). Although *The Years* is an attempt to combine representation of external reality with the truth of the inner life (D IV 142, 245, 274), Woolf felt that she had "muffed the proportions: which should have given a round, not a thin line" (L VI 116).

About her last novel, *Between the Acts*, she observes with relief that she is only "covering . . . a small canvas" (D V 336). As planes overhead remind the inhabitants and visitors at Pointz Hall, with its pageant and its paintings, that England and all civilization are vulnerable, so Woolf worked on this novel while the bombs actually fell. As many have noted, she faced World War II with despair for a variety of reasons. One of them involved her professional relationship with her sister. In September of 1940, bombs damaged the Woolfs' Mecklenburgh Square house in London. Shortly afterwards, Virginia and Vanessa were at odds over Helen Anrep. Vanessa favored Helen's taking refuge in Rodmell; Virginia, thinking the move permanent and fearing the intrusion of the Anrep family, opposed it (L VI 433, 434, 436). On September 26, 1940, Virginia recorded in her diary "a rather strained talk" on the telephone with her sister. Virginia felt defeated in the interchange, however, by Vanessa's "trump card," her announcement that her studio and Duncan's had "'been destroyed. The roofs fallen in. Still burning. Pictures burnt.' So I had to pipe low. My fallen ceilings a trifle. Helen a mares nest" (D V 325).

As Quentin Bell says, the sisters' "old competition . . . was, in the strangest way, renewed" by the wartime destruction.[1] In October of 1940, four bombs dropped near Rodmell, and Virginia reported the event with her own brand of hyperbole to her niece, Angelica: "I had the great delight of seeing the smoke and being within an inch of Heaven. This is a great score over Nessa" (L VI 442). Actually, Virginia's own reactions to the damage at Mecklenburgh Square had been ambivalent. They included, on the one hand, regret (". . . at times I want my books & chairs & carpets & beds—How I worked to buy them—one by one—And the pictures") and, on the other, relief and "exhilaration at losing possessions" (D V 331; cf D V 343). She could identify therefore with Vanessa's loss and simultaneously reproach herself for materialism and acquisitiveness. She also seems to have resented the fact that her sister's losses appeared to be greater than her own, only "a statue & frigidaire" having been saved from the studio (D V 326; cf L VI 435, 439). Because some of Vanessa's pictures were on exhibition elsewhere, and many other possessions had already been transferred to Charleston, her losses were not so devastating,[2] but Vanessa may have exaggerated her plight for her sister's benefit. In October the Woolfs' former residence at Tavistock Square was destroyed by the bombs: "I cd just see a piece of my studio wall standing: otherwise rubble where I wrote so many books," Virginia recorded in her diary (D V 331). In a letter she reported that she could also see her "drawing room panels suspended over the rubble," panels of "garlands and fruit and horns of plenty" that Vanessa and Duncan had painted for her in 1924 (L VI 449 and n. 1).[3] Now her losses more nearly equaled Vanessa's, both of them having been deprived professionally by the war. Writing and painting and the civilization they represented clearly were under seige.

Virginia and Vanessa were barred from the rooms in London where they had painted and written so effectively. Rooms of their own, so hard-won for women artists, were no refuge from a world at war. Individual books and paintings often could not survive it. Could individual artists? Virginia herself could not; Vanessa could. If their competition extended this far, it would be impossible to say who triumphed. Vanessa's last letter to Virginia, written on March 20, 1941, urged her to be "sensible" and to accept Vanessa's judgment, and Leonard's, about her health. "What shall we do when we're invaded," Vanessa worried, "if you are a helpless invalid—what should I have done all these last 3 years if you hadnt been able to keep me alive and cheerful. You dont know how much I depend on you" (L VI 485, quoted in n. 2). Three days later Virginia replied, in the last letter she ever wrote to her sister, that she had "loved" what Vanessa had said, but that she felt incapable of recovering this time from the impending madness. Vanessa was to assure Leonard of his goodness and of their previous happiness, help him to go on alone, and remember how important she and her children had been to Virginia (L VI 485). At the very last, as this letter indicates, Virginia was thinking of Vanessa as sister, sister-in-law, and mother, not as painter. A month earlier, in fact, Virginia had described tea at Charleston: "Clive is digging a trench; Nessa feeding fowls; Duncan painting Christ; Quentin driving a tractor—all as it was in 1917" (L VI 472). Here Vanessa played out the timeless domestic role with which Virginia often associated her, one which another wartime era seemed to demand of women.

Virginia Woolf thought a great deal about artists, women, and war in the final years of her life. She had been laboring over her biography of Roger Fry and worrying over the approval of his family and friends, including Vanessa. Once the book appeared she found that she had to defend Fry against charges like Benedict Nicolson's that "He shut himself out from all disagreeable actualities and allowed the spirit of Nazism to grow without taking any steps to check it" (quoted in L VI 413). On the contrary, she said, Fry spent "half his life, not in a tower, but travelling about England addressing masses of people" and making them understand and enjoy painting. "And wasn't that the best way of checking Nazism?" she asked (L VI 414). As an artist who also wrote about art, Woolf felt under attack for some of the same reasons. She maintained that, like Roger, she had done her "best to . . . reach a far wider circle than a little private circle of exquisite and cultivated people," and so had the other members of so-called "Bloomsbury" (L VI 420).

When the accusations came from within the circle, however, her defense was different. In February 1941 she countered Desmond MacCarthy's charges of elitism by hurling the accusation back at him: "*I* never sat on top of a tower! Compare my wretched little £150 education with yours, with Lytton's, with Leonard's. Did Eton and Cambridge make no difference to you? . . . I assure you, my tower was a mere toadstool, about six inches high." As a woman she was far better able than he, therefore, to identify and communicate with less privileged people (L VI 467). So while she thought of Vanessa, feeding barnyard fowl while Duncan painted Christ, she was closer to her than to any of their male counterparts. Vanessa too had little formal education; she also spent her time not seeking social status or awards but trying to communicate, as honestly and directly as possible, her sense of the valuable in life: the beauty of the everyday world and the creative acts that make others experience it anew. But can one create without readers and perceivers who feel sufficiently safe to attend? War made Woolf feel she was writing in a vacuum, without an audience (L VI 430). Moreover, can creation keep pace with destruction? "I lost several pages of PH ["Pointz Hall"/*Between the Acts*]," she noted in her diary in January 1941. "I say to Nessa, Do you find painting gets slower? Yes" (D V 354).

In *To the Lighthouse* Lily Briscoe concludes that "nothing stays; all changes; but not words, not paint." She is not talking about actual works of art. Her painting might be a "scrawl" that is never hung, but the creative effort it represents is permanent (TTL 267). Art "is indeed the instinct of self preservation," Woolf notes in a version of "Anon," one of the last essays she wrote: "Only when we put two and two together—two pencil strokes, two written words, two bricks (notes) do we overcome dissolution and set up some stake against oblivion." Again, the completed work of art is not her emphasis: "The passion with which we seek out these creations and attempt endlessly, perpetually, to make them is of a piece with the instinct that sets us preserving our bodies, with clothes, food, roofs, from destruction."[4] Perishable themselves, like their paintings and books in a world at war, Virginia Woolf and Vanessa Bell are of the species "artist"; their creative acts, Virginia combining words, Vanessa combining pencil or brush strokes, are immortal. Such creative acts will continue, as the conclusion of *Between the Acts* suggests, even if barbarism reigns.

But Virginia Woolf had no more confidence that she could contribute to this ongoing creative process, or that her words would do any good in the midst of all the shouting of hackneyed slogans. In the past she had defended madness, apart from its horrors, as a fallow time during which her brain could somehow rejuvenate itself, become "fertilised" for future productivity (D III 254). Similarly, the silent realm of the visual arts had ultimately awakened and stimulated her brain and caused it to generate new words and phrases. Although she did not want to remain in either realm, both provided some stimulus for her art and helped to prepare her for new verbal struggles with the difficulties of human individuality and community. But just as she was certain she could not recover once more from the madness that was threatening her and, in another sense, her world, so possibly she could no longer find sufficient stimulation in Vanessa's silent art. Or perhaps the destructive invasions of England distracted her from her own creative artistic raids. For whatever reason, "I've lost all power over words," she wrote (L VI 456). *Between the Acts* did not satisfy her. In that novel, the long lady whose individuality is lost in the silent realm of her portrait hangs beside the man with horse and dog whose assertive egotism, contentiousness, and volubility seem more in keeping with the world between the acts of Miss LaTrobe's pageant.

Instead of going to natural and artistic beauty to gather materials for her own art, more and more Woolf seemed inclined to lose herself in it. When a bomb hit the river near Monks House and forced water into an adjoining field, she expressed her delight in the "indescribable beauty" of this "island sea" and wrote how she loved "this savage medieval water moved, all floating tree trunks and flocks of birds and a man in an old punt, and myself so eliminated of human feature you might take me for a stake walking" (L VI 444). It is as if she imagined herself part of a painting, one like Vanessa's in which people's faces have no features. In January of 1941, she could not resist one more attempt to describe "the downs in snow. . . . And I cant help even now turning to look at Asheham down, red, purple, dove blue grey, with the cross so melodramatically against it." This time she did not become part of the picture; she remained a perceiver but one with death on her mind: "What is the phrase I always remember—or forget. Look your last on all things lovely," a line from Walter de la Mare's *Fare Well* (D V 351 and n. 2). Like the speakers of Keats's odes, she found beauty a refuge from an ugly, strife-torn world.

Vanessa continued to practice her silent art after her sister's suicide. As we have seen, she did the dust jackets for the posthumous volumes and collections of Virginia's work. The sisters' competition, inspiration, and collaboration had ended, but while it lasted Virginia thought that, in spite of differences in media, they created with similar brains and similar eyes. In the final entry of her diary on March 24, 1941, four days before her drowning, Virginia's thoughts were of Vanessa. "I am imagining," she wrote, "how it would be if we could infuse souls" (D V 359). Had they done so in one sense, Vanessa might have become a modern, female version of "Michael Angelo. Leonardo. Blake. Rossetti," the artists who represent "The connection between seeing & writing" that Woolf contemplated once more near the end of her life.[5] Instead, the sisters were united in another sense. Like Rachel's and Terence's in *The Voyage Out*, their relationship was frozen by death. Virginia arrested it at a stage when Vanessa declared herself dependent upon her sister and prior to one when their roles might be reversed.

In a strange way too their relationship was frozen by art. Virginia entered a silent realm like that on Keats's urn or in one of her sister's paintings, a realm that now attracted far more than it repelled. The silence of paintings, as Virginia described them a decade earlier, "is hollow and vast as that of a cathedral dome. . . . Let us wash the roofs of our eyes in colour," she said then, "let us dive till the deep seas close above our heads."[6] We dwarf and drown ourselves in paintings as in great architectural or natural spaces. Noisy individual egos vanish. Life itself is, as Rachel Vinrace realizes in *The Voyage Out*, merely a "short season between two silences" (VO 82). Words having failed more profoundly than ever before, in her short season and that of civilization in general, Virginia Woolf left her books to a better fate than she could foresee and chose the ultimate silence.

Notes

INTRODUCTION—RAIDING AND WRITING

1. See. for example, J. K. Johnstone, *The Bloomsbury Group: A Study of E. M. Forster, Lytton Strachey, Virginia Woolf, and Their Circle* (New York: Noonday, 1954); and Allen McLaurin, *Virginia Woolf: The Echoes Enslaved* (Cambridge: Cambridge University Press, 1973). Jean Alexander too notes in *The Venture of Form in the Novels of Virginia Woolf* (Port Washington, N.Y.: Kennikat, 1974), p. 222, that Woolf's vocabulary, syntax, and structure are all related to the visual arts. A number of articles on specific novels, especially *To the Lighthouse*, link Woolf's work with painting.

2. Vanessa Bell to Virginia Woolf, April 13, 1908; NYPL.

3. *Burlington Magazine*. July 1922. Quoted in Richard Shone, *Bloomsbury Portraits: Vanessa Bell, Duncan Grant, and Their Circle* (Oxford: Phaidon, 1976), pp. 129, 218.

4. Jane Novak, in *The Razor Edge of Balance: A Study of Virginia Woolf* (Coral Gables, Florida: University of Miami Press, 1975), p. 19, makes a similar observation, although her discussion focuses primarily upon the relationships between Woolf's and Fry's theories and practices.

5. Richard Shone's *Bloomsbury Portraits* has been instrumental in the reassessment of her work, as has Isabelle Anscombe's *Omega and After: Bloomsbury and the Decorative Arts* (London: Thames and Hudson, 1982). There have been three recent exhibitions, two in England in 1979 and one in New York in 1980. Frances Spalding's biography, *Vanessa Bell* (London: Weidenfeld and Nicolson, 1983) was recently published, and Angelica Garnett has completed a memoir of her mother's life called *Deceived With Kindness: A Bloomsbury Childhood* (London: Chatto and Windus; Hogarth, 1984).

6. May Sinclair says that critics have treated Charlotte Brontë this way. See *The Three Brontës* (London: Hutchinson, 1912), p. 72.

7. Vanessa Bell to Roger Fry, March 2, 1922, KCL.

8. See, for example, Richard Shone's *Bloomsbury Portraits*, Raymond Mortimer's *Duncan Grant* (Penguin, 1948), and Shone's "Introduction" to an exhibition catalog called *Duncan Grant and Bloomsbury* (Edinburgh: The Fine Art Society, 1975).

9. See, for example, Richard Morphet, "The Art of Vanessa Bell" in *Vanessa Bell: Paintings and Drawings* (London: Anthony d'Offay, 1970); Nancy Topping Bazin, *Virginia Woolf and the Androgynous Vision* (New Brunswick, N.J.: Rutgers University

Press, 1973), pp. 43–45; Jane Novak, *The Razor Edge of Balance*, p. 93; Leon Edel, *Bloomsbury: A House of Lions* (Philadelphia: J. B. Lippincott, 1979), p. 264; Jack F. Stewart, "Impressionism in the Early Novels of Virginia Woolf," *Journal of Modern Literature* 9, no. 2 (1982): 240, 243, 259; and David Dowling, *Bloomsbury Aesthetics and the Novels of Forster and Woolf* (New York: St. Martin's, 1985). Henry R. Harrington begins to draw more specific parallels in "The Central Line Down the Middle of *To the Lighthouse*," *Contemporary Literature* 21 (1980): 364, 371–76. Marianna Torgovnick's recent study, *The Visual Arts, Pictorialism, and the Novel: James, Lawrence, and Woolf* (Princeton, N.J.: Princeton University Press, 1985), contains an insightful although brief chapter on Virginia Woolf and Vanessa Bell. Because her book appeared after my study was complete, I incorporate only a few references to her work in these introductory remarks.

10. See, for example, Edel, *Bloomsbury*, as well as Quentin Bell, *Virginia Woolf: A Biography*, 2 vols. (London: Hogarth, 1973); Jean O. Love, *Virginia Woolf: Sources of Madness and Art* (Berkeley: University of California Press, 1977); Roger Poole, *The Unknown Virginia Woolf* (Cambridge: Cambridge University Press, 1978); Stephen Trombley, *All That Summer She Was Mad: Virginia Woolf: Female Victim of Male Medicine* (New York: Continuum, 1982). One artistic link Trombley notes between Virginia Woolf and Vanessa Bell is the designation as insane of the kind of experimental art both produced. See Trombley's chapter, "The Madness of Art: T. B. Hyslop." Toni A. H. McNaron, in "Billy Goat to Dolphin: Letters of Virginia Woolf to Her Sister, Vanessa Bell" in *The Sister Bond: A Feminist View of a Timeless Connection*, ed. Toni A. H. McNaron (New York: Pergamon, 1985), pp. 93–103, emphasizes Virginia's "incestuous" bond with Vanessa (p. 95) and mentions but does not elaborate upon their relationship as artists.

11. Jean Hagstrum, *The Sister Arts: The Tradition of Literary Pictorialism and English Poetry from Dryden to Gray* (Chicago: University of Chicago Press, 1958). Torgovnick, also unable to resist the pun, calls her chapter on Virginia Woolf and Vanessa Bell "The Sisters' Arts."

12. None of the Muses represents painting or sculpture. Ulrich Weisstein, in "Literature and the Visual Arts," *Interrelations of Literature*, ed. Jean-Pierre Barricelli and Joseph Gibaldi (New York: Modern Language Association, 1982), pp. 251–52, attributes this "gap in the aesthetic pantheon of the Greeks" to the low esteem in which the visual arts were held. Germaine Greer points out, however, that "Painting is allegorically presented always as a female and the legend of the birth of the graphic arts attributes their invention to Kora, the virgin of Corinth, also known as Callirhoe, who seeing her beloved's profile cast upon the wall by the firelight seized a spent coal and drew an outline around it" (*The Obstacle Race: The Fortunes of Women Painters and Their Work* [New York: Farrar Straus Giroux, 1979], p. 2). For an insightful discussion of women artists and their muses, see Carolyn G. Heilbrun, *Reinventing Womanhood* (New York: W. W. Norton, 1979), pp. 163–70.

13. Elaine Showalter, "Feminist Criticism in the Wilderness," *Writing and Sexual Difference*, ed. Elizabeth Abel (Chicago: University of Chicago Press, 1982), pp. 30–31.

14. Ibid., p. 33.

15. Jane Marcus observes in "Liberty, Sorority, Misogyny," in *The Representa-*

tion of Women in Fiction: Selected Papers from the English Institute, 1981, ed. Carolyn G. Heilbrun and Margaret R. Higonnet (Baltimore: Johns Hopkins University Press, 1983), p. 87, that Woolf encouraged women writers not only "to think back through their mothers" but also "to think sideways through their sisters." It is also worth pointing out that, on occasion, Virginia and Vanessa "sistered" the thinking of their male contemporaries. "Art schools do nothing but harm," Clive Bell says, for example, in *Art* (1913). "Art is . . . not to be taught. All that the drawing-master can teach is the craft of imitation . . . . Art schools must go" (p. 168). Having attended none himself, he probably drew upon Vanessa's experiences and the kinds of conclusions that, as we shall see, she expressed in her letters. Another example is Virginia's decision, upon reading Roger Fry's letters in 1938, that, although he had "found his method . . . this wasn't lasting." He was "swayed too much" by Vanessa (D V 172).

16. Vanessa Bell to Roger Fry, January 7, 1913, KCL.

17. Louise Bernikow, in *Among Women* (New York: Harper, 1981), pp. 92–104, for example, emphasizes aspects of this dualism, although she acknowledges the intimacy of the sisters as well. Bernikow says little, however, about the actual art works the sisters produced. Elizabeth Fishel in *Sisters: Love and Rivalry Inside the Family and Beyond* (New York: William Morrow, 1979) declares her interest in how artistic sisters "make a mark on each other's work" (p. 252), but her brief, general treatment of Virginia Woolf and Vanessa Bell mentions only one work of art, Woolf's *To the Lighthouse*.

18. Vanessa Bell, "Notes on Virginia's Childhood," ed. Richard F. Schaubeck, Jr. (New York: F. Hallman, 1974), unpaginated.

19. Vanessa Bell, "Notes on Bloomsbury," in *The Bloomsbury Group*, ed. S. P. Rosenbaum (Toronto: University of Toronto Press, 1975), p. 82.

20. Similarly false is the importance created by wigs, robes, and the other trappings of male-established hierarchies that Woolf satirizes in the text and photographic illustrations of *Three Guineas* (1938).

21. Beverly Ann Schlack, in *Continuing Presences: Virginia Woolf's Use of Literary Allusion* (University Park, Pa.: Pennsylvania State University Press, 1979), demonstrates the importance of Woolf's literary allusions, as do others in articles on the individual novels. Cheryl Mares, in "'Another Space of Time': The Dominion of Painting in Proust and Woolf" (Ph.D. diss. Princeton University, 1982), deals with some of the references to paintings, especially portraits, in her chapters on Woolf.

22. Hagstrum, *The Sister Arts*, p. 152.

23. An understanding of the convergence of the sisters' artistic orientations and productions does not depend upon a definition of "impressionism" in painting and literature, although chapter 6 deals, in part, with the sisters' knowledge of this movement in the visual arts. Among numerous studies of various writers as "impressionists," Peter Stowell's *Literary Impressionism, James and Chekhov* (Athens: University of Georgia Press, 1980) provides a workable summary of the literary tendencies in relation to the painterly. For a discussion of Woolf in this context see Jack F. Stewart, "Impressionism in the Early Novels of Virginia Woolf." Nor is the controversy over the possibility of "spatial form" in literature central to this study. This well-known discussion originated with Joseph Frank's "Spatial Form in Modern Literature," *Sewanee Review* 53 (1945): 221–40; 433–56; 643–53. *Critical Inquiry* 4 (1977–78)

devotes several essays to this issue. Joseph Frank comments further in *Critical Inquiry* 5, no. 2 (Winter 1978). See also Wendy Steiner, "The Temporal versus the Spatial Arts" in *The Colors of Rhetoric: Problems in the Relation between Modern Literature and Painting* (Chicago: University of Chicago Press, 1982), pp. 33–50. Several writers on Woolf have approached her fiction spatially, among them Ian Gregor, "Spaces: To the Lighthouse," in *The Author in His Work: Essays on a Problem in Criticism*, ed. Louis L. Martz and Aubrey Williams (New Haven: Yale University Press, 1978), p. 377. See also McLaurin, *Virginia Woolf*, pp. 85–94.

24. Hagstrum's *The Sister Arts* reveals as much. See also Elizabeth Abel, "Redefining The Sister Arts: Baudelaire's Response to the Art of Delacroix," in *The Language of Images*, ed. W. J. T. Mitchell (Chicago: University of Chicago Press, 1980), p. 38.

25. Abel, pp. 39–47. Weisstein, in "Literature and the Visual Arts," pp. 259–61, lists sixteen kinds of interrelations between the arts that are helpful to scholars of literature. Those relevant, to some extent, to this study include iconic writing, attempts to stimulate a reader's visual sense, attempts to parallel in writing the style of a movement in painting, common motives and values among painters and writers, artist figures in literature, common motifs and themes, book illustration, and multiple talent. See also Susanne K. Langer, "Deceptive Analogies: Specious and Real Relationships Among the Arts," in *Problems of Art: Ten Philosophical Lectures* (New York: Scribner's, 1957), pp. 75–89. Laura Rice-Sayre and Henry M. Sayre, in "Autonomy and Affinity: Toward a Theory for Comparing the Arts," *The Arts and Their Interrelations, Bucknell Review* 24, no. 2 (Fall 1978): 86–103, distinguish among several degrees and types of relationships that critics detect between works in different media. Among them are intentional collaboration, works from "a common creative milieu," works drawn together by a critic, works which reflect a common theme, and works that recreate or illustrate other works. Malcolm Bradbury, in "Putting in the Person: Character and Abstraction in Current Writing and Painting," *The Contemporary English Novel*, ed. Malcolm Bradbury and David Palmer, Stratford-Upon-Avon Studies 18 (New York: Holmes and Meier, 1979), pp. 181–208, traces relationships between the two media and corresponding views of reality from the eighteenth century to the present.

26. W. J. T. Mitchell, "Introduction: The Language of Images," in *The Language of Images*, p. 1; Joshua C. Taylor, "Two Visual Excursions," in *The Language of Images*, p. 31. See also Whistler's "Ten O'Clock Lecture" in *The Gentle Art of Making Enemies* (New York: Dover, 1967), pp. 146–47. Whistler delivered this talk several times in 1885, including once at Cambridge University. Another manifesto of this type is Ezra Pound's *Gaudier-Brzeska: A Memoir* (London: Marvell, 1960; first published 1916). Among the many discussions of the kinds of "literary" painting Whistler, Pound, and others reacted against are Quentin Bell, *Victorian Artists* (Cambridge: Harvard University Press, 1967); Raymond Lister, *Victorian Narrative Paintings* (New York: Clarkson N. Potter, 1966); and Sacheverell Sitwell, *Narrative Pictures: A Survey of English Genre and Its Painters* (London: B. T. Batsford, 1969).

27. In Mitchell, ed., *The Language of Images*, p. 9.

28. Giulio Carlo Argan, "Ideology and Iconology," in Mitchell, ed., *The Language of Images*, pp. 21–22.

29. Mitchell, *The Language of Images*, p. 1.

30. Taylor, in Mitchell, ed., *The Language of Images*, p. 33.

31. Dennis Farr, *English Art: 1870–1940* (Oxford: Clarendon, 1978), p. 3. Lee McKay Johnson, in *The Metaphor of Painting: Essays on Baudelaire, Ruskin, Proust, and Pater* (Ann Arbor, Mich.: UMI Research Press, 1980), p. 3, emphasizes "tangible language and simultaneous form" as the contributions of the Symbolists to modern thinking about visual-verbal analogues.

32. Abel, in Mitchell, ed., *The Language of Images*, p. 37.

33. Torgovnick, *The Visual Arts*, pp. 13–23. One might develop a similar continuum for the influence of literature upon a visual artist's work. Torgovnick suggests, and the point is debatable, that in much modern literature the more sophisticated and central the use of the visual arts, the more successful the novel (p. 12). In much modern painting, however, works revealing the most superficial contacts with literature are perhaps more successful than those in which the link is easier to define, but the assessment depends upon the kind of literature that is influential as well as a definition of "success."

34. See, for example, the essays by Irving Howe, Stephen Spender, and Lionel Trilling in *The Idea of the Modern in Literature and the Arts*, ed. Irving Howe (New York: Horizon, 1967); Spender's *The Struggle of the Modern* (Berkeley: University of California Press, 1963); Frank Kermode's *Modern Essays* (London: Collins, 1971) and *The Sense of an Ending: Studies in the Theory of Fiction* (New York: Oxford University Press, 1967); and the essays in *Modernism: 1890–1930*, ed. Malcolm Bradbury and James McFarlane (Sussex: Harvester, 1978).

35. Malcolm Bradbury and James McFarlane, "The Name and Nature of Modernism," in *Modernism*, p. 25. See also Charles Harrison, *English Art and Modernism: 1900–1939* (London: Allen Lane, 1981). "Modernist art," Harrison says, "is seen as restless, self-critical, self-determining" (p. 18).

36. Bradbury and McFarlane, in *Modernism*, p. 26.

37. Bradbury, "Putting in the Person," in Bradbury and Palmer, eds., *The Contemporary English Novel*, pp. 198–200.

38. Clive Bell, *Art* (New York: Capricorn, 1958; first published, 1913), p. 139.

39. Vanessa Bell, unpublished memoir of Roger Fry; AG.

40. Clive Bell, *Art*, p. 162.

41. José Ortega y Gasset, *The Dehumanization of Art* (Princeton: Princeton University Press, 1948). The quoted passage is reprinted in Howe, ed., *The Idea of the Modern*, pp. 85–86.

42. Bradbury and McFarlane, in *Modernism*, p. 50.

43. See my "Political Aesthetics: Virginia Woolf and Dorothy Richardson," *Virginia Woolf: A Feminist Slant*, ed. Jane Marcus (Lincoln: University of Nebraska Press, 1983), pp. 132–51.

44. "Our Vortex," *Blast* 1–2 (1914–15): 151–52. May Sinclair also links avant-garde literature and the suffrage movement in her novel *The Tree of Heaven* (1917). Woolf was not associated with the Vorticists; when she allied herself briefly with the suffrage movement, it was with the nonmilitants, some of whom she presents none too favorably in *Night and Day*.

45. Judith Gardiner, "On Female Identity and Writing by Women," *Writing*

and Sexual Difference, pp. 185, 187, 189. See also Sandra Gilbert, "Costumes of the Mind: Transvestism as Metaphor in Modern Literature," *Critical Inquiry* 7 (Winter 1980): 405, 410–11.

46. Virginia Woolf, *To the Lighthouse: The Original Holograph Draft*, ed. Susan Dick (Toronto: University of Toronto Press, 1982), p. 295.

47. Dorothy Richardson, "Continuous Performance: The Film Gone Male," *Close-Up* 9, no. 1 (March 1932): 36–37.

48. "The Reader," ed. Brenda Silver, *Twentieth Century Literature* 25, 3/4 (Fall/Winter 1979): 433.

49. Virginia Woolf and Vanessa Bell are both good examples of certain of the mental processes Rudolf Arnheim describes in *Visual Thinking* (Berkeley: University of California Press, 1969).

1—DUAL CREATIVITY

1. "Anon," ed. Brenda Silver, *Twentieth Century Literature* 25, 3/4 (Fall/Winter 1979): 413–14, note 47.

2. A number of Leslie Stephen's sketches are in the books Woolf inherited from him; these are now in WSUL. A selection is reproduced in the *Virginia Woolf Miscellany* 22 (Spring 1984): 2, 4, 7, 8. Just as the sisters' literary father (with whom Virginia in some ways identified) drew as well as wrote, so their mother (with whom Vanessa identified) wrote. As Noel Annan observes, "Virginia Woolf inherited from her mother much of her sensibility and even an echo of her style." Julia Stephen's publication, *Notes from Sick Rooms*, combines "irony, detachment and common sense." See Noel Annan, *Leslie Stephen: His Thought and Character in Relation to His Time* London: MacGibbon and Kee, 1951), pp. 100–101. Julia Stephen also wrote the *Dictionary of National Biography* entry on Julia Margaret Cameron, according to Charles W. Mann, Jr., "Your Loving Auntie and God Mama, Julia Cameron," *History of Photography* 7, 1 (January 1983), 73–74. Virginia Woolf's mother wrote, however, material only recently published, among it three essays and several stories for children. A note by Leslie Stephen on one of the latter indicates that some of his animal drawings might have been used as illustrations had Julia not died. WSUL owns the originals of these manuscripts. See *Julia Duckworth Stephen: Stories for Children, Essays for Adults*, edited by Diane F. Gillespie and Elizabeth Steele (Syracuse: Syracuse University Press, 1987). See also Alex Zwerdling, "Julia Stephen, Mrs. Ramsay, and the Sense of Vocation," *Virginia Woolf Miscellany* 22 (Spring 1984): 4.

3. Thoby's rendition of "the back view of God Almighty" predates G. K. Chesterton's observation in *G. F. Watts* (London: Duckworth, 1906), that even Watts, who made the "magnificent discovery of the artistic effect of the human back" (p. 136), probably would not "dare to paint" God from behind (p. 139). A drawing of eagles by Thoby from one of the books in Virginia Woolf's library, WSUL, is reproduced in the *Virginia Woolf Miscellany* 22 (Spring 1984): 7.

4. The originals of the letters Violet Dickinson typed are in the Berg Collection at the NYPL. The copies, including the drawings, are in Quentin Bell's possession (L VI 89, note 3).

5. Quentin Bell, *Virginia Woolf: A Biography*, 2 vols. (London: Hogarth, 1973), 1:94.

6. A similar figure of Morpheus appears, more stylized and brightly colored, on a headboard Duncan Grant painted in about 1915; the bed was in Vanessa Bell's room at Charleston, where she lived from 1916 on.

7. Georgiana Burne-Jones' *Memorials of Edward Burne-Jones* was published in London by Macmillan in 1904. Neither of the two volumes is among the books from Leonard and Virginia Woolf's library either at WSUL or the HRHRC. But, because of Julia Stephen's family connections and because she was the model for Burne-Jones' *Annunciation* (1879), these recently published volumes are likely to have been in the Stephen house.

8. "Notes for Reading at Random," ed. Brenda Silver, *Twentieth Century Literature* 25, 3/4 (Fall/Winter 1979): 377.

9. WSUL. These bookplates are exceptional. Most of Virginia's books have commercially printed ones, ranging from a heraldic design similar to the Duckworth brothers' to small, plain squares, rectangles, circles, and diamonds. The initials "AVS" or "Virginia Stephen" or "Virginia Woolf" appear, commercially or hand lettered, sometimes with a date.

10. The edition, published in London by Macmillan, is dated 1903. Woolf's interest in the carpe diem theme had sources in addition to Fitzgerald. For a more complete discussion of the floral motif in Woolf's work see chapter 5.

11. Two additional drawings exist in books bought at around this time and marked with Adeline Virginia Stephen's initials. Both are at the WSUL. In the front of the third volume of *The Athenian Drama*, which is devoted to the works of Euripides, is a bookplate done, to all appearances, by the same method as the rose and the death mask. The same intertwined initials appear on the plate. Unfortunately, the one copy I have seen has been partially torn out of the book. All that remains are portions of what appears to be a partly nude female torso. Finally, inside the covers of Virginia Stephen's volume of *The Complete Poetical Works of William Wordsworth* (London: Macmillan, 1902), are some rough designs. Within the front cover is a geometrical abstraction in blue and green with "AVS 1903" in the center. Inside the back cover is another drawing in what looks like a combination of blue and green, mauve and yellow crayons or colored chalks combined with pencil. On the left is what may be part of a house with suggestions of a roof and a window. Above it seem to be tree branches fanning out; another tree is suggested further back and a third to the right. Whether these trees grow up behind a hedge or whether the line which divides the page is a horizon is difficult to determine. It is interesting to speculate, however, that Woolf may have experimented with balancing shapes and forms originally suggested by the natural world as Lily Briscoe does in *To the Lighthouse*.

A rough drawing of a woman on the back of p. 69 of the first volume of the holograph of *The Voyage Out* (NYPL) may also be by Woolf. See *Bulletin of Research in the Humanities* 82, 3 (Autumn 1979): 273. So may be a quick sketch of a woman's head and a parrot at the top of the typescript of "The Widow and the Parrot." The entire page is reproduced in *Redbook*, July 1982, p. 91.

12. Vanessa Bell to Virginia Woolf, August 31, 1915; NYPL.

13. Vanessa Bell to Clive Bell, November 3, 1906; KCL.

14. Diane Filby Gillespie, "Vanessa Bell, Virginia Woolf, and Duncan Grant: Conversation with Angelica Garnett," *Modernist Studies* 3, 3 (1979): 153. Frances Spalding says, however, that Clive Bell's *Art* provided the theories that Vanessa held throughout her life. See *Vanessa Bell* (London: Weidenfeld & Nicolson, 1983), p. 115. Discussions of the changes in Fry's views over the years or of the similarities and differences between his theories and Clive Bell's are beyond the scope of this study. See Solomon Fishman, *The Interpretation of Art: Essays on the Art Criticism of John Ruskin, Walter Pater, Clive Bell, Roger Fry, and Herbert Read* (Berkeley: University of California Press, 1963), pp. 77, 107–8, 115, 118–42. See also Jan Heinemann, "The Revolt Against Language: A Critical Note on Twentieth-Century Irrationalism with Special Reference to the Aesthetico-Philosophical Views of Virginia Woolf and Clive Bell," *Orbis Litterarum* 32 (1977): 212–28.

15. David Garnett, *The Flowers of the Forest* (New York: Harcourt, Brace, 1955), p. 26.

16. Kenneth Clark, *Another Part of the Wood: A Self-Portrait* (London: John Murray, 1974), pp. 248–49.

17. Vanessa Bell to Marjorie Snowden, October 9 and 21, 1908; March 5, 1922; KCL.

18. Leon Edel, *Bloomsbury: A House of Lions* (Philadelphia: J. B. Lippincott, 1979), p.129.

19. Quentin Bell, *Virginia Woolf*, 1:102.

20. Spalding, *Vanessa Bell*, p. 55.

21. Vanessa Bell, "Notes on Bloomsbury" in *The Bloomsbury Group*, ed. S. P. Rosenbaum (Toronto: University of Toronto Press, 1975), p. 77.

22. *Notes on Virginia's Childhood*, ed. Richard F. Schaubeck, Jr. (New York: F. Hallman, 1974), unpaginated.

23. Vanessa Bell to Virginia Woolf, April 18, 1906; NYPL.

24. Quentin Bell, *Virginia Woolf*, 1:97–98.

25. Ibid., 1:120–21.

26. Vanessa Bell to Virginia Woolf, August 1, 1908; NYPL.

27. Vanessa Bell to Roger Fry, November 19, 1928; KCL. Curiously, in 1917, the proposed list of members for a social group called the "Omega Club" includes many nonpainters but excludes Leonard and Virginia Woolf. The invitation to Mary Hutchinson and the list of members are in the HRHRC.

28. Richard Shone, *Bloomsbury Portraits: Vanessa Bell, Duncan Grant and Their Circle* (Oxford: Phaidon, 1976), p. 26.

29. Quentin Bell, *Virginia Woolf*, 1:105; see also Shone, *Bloomsbury Portraits*, p. 26.

30. Isabelle Anscombe, *Omega and After: Bloomsbury and the Decorative Arts* (London: Thames and Hudson, 1982), p. 14. According to Spalding, the Club included three other women students from the Royal Academy Schools, both men and women from the Slade, Henry Lamb, as well as nonpainter friends and relatives. *Vanessa Bell*, p. 56.

31. Vanessa Bell, "Memories of Roger Fry," October 1934, unpublished typescript; AG.

32. Anscombe, p. 36. Judith Collins indicates, however, in *The Omega Workshops* (Chicago: University of Chicago Press, 1984) that unlike Vanessa Bell, who was

one of the directors, most of the women Fry hired executed designs rather than created them (p. 64), or worked "with textiles, an area almost exclusively reserved for the female employees" (p. 76).

33. Vanessa Bell to Marjorie Snowden, early April? 1904?; KCL. Spalding says that Vanessa usually adopted the view of art of the person she felt close to, in this instance, Thoby (*Vanessa Bell*, p. 66). The tendency is there, but should not be exaggerated. Vanessa also struggled to define herself independently of those people with whom she was most intimate.

34. Shone, *Bloomsbury Portraits*, p. 23.

35. Vanessa Bell to Marjorie Snowden, January 11, 1905; KCL.

36. Vanessa Bell to Clive Bell, 1910 or 1912; October 9, 1910; KCL.

37. Vanessa Bell to Virginia Woolf, February 6, 1913; NYPL.

38. Vanessa Bell to Leonard Woolf, January 22, 1913; USL. Frances Spalding quotes part of this letter and discusses Vanessa Bell's reactions to abstract painting. *Vanessa Bell*, p. 126.

39. Vanessa Bell to Roger Fry, September 23, 1926; September 29, 1930; KCL.

40. Vanessa Bell to Julian Bell, December 13, 19??; KCL.

41. Vanessa Bell to Roger Fry, June 23, 1911; October 17, 1912; August 30, 1920; KCL. Fry attributed Vanessa Bell's disagreements with him to her falling out of love with him (Spalding, *Vanessa Bell*, p. 129).

42. Vanessa Bell to Roger Fry, June 1911 and November 23, 1911; KCL.

43. Vanessa Bell to Roger Fry, April 29, 1920; [month and day unknown] 1920; KCL. Roger Fry to Vanessa Bell, May 10, 1920; KCL and *Letters of Roger Fry*, ed. Denys Sutton, 2 vols. (London: Chatto and Windus, 1972), 2:509.

44. Vanessa Bell to Roger Fry, January 29, 1929; KCL.

45. Vanessa Bell to Roger Fry, December 28, 1913?; KCL.

46. Vanessa Bell to Clive Bell, 1914; October 23, post-1928; KCL.

47. Vanessa Bell to Virginia Woolf, May 17, 1927; NYPL.

48. Vanessa Bell to Roger Fry, November 2, 1912; KCL.

49. Vanessa Bell to Roger Fry, February 2, 1929; KCL.

50. Vanessa Bell to Clive Bell, 1914; KCL.

51. Vanessa Bell to Roger Fry, June 22, 1916; KCL. As Jacqueline V. Falkenheim points out, there is a gap in Fry's own work between his theories and his practice. See *Roger Fry and the Beginnings of Formalist Art Criticism* (Ann Arbor, Mich.: UMI Research Press, 1980), p. 91.

52. Vanessa Bell, "Memories of Roger Fry."

53. Typescripts of Virginia Stephen's travel journals written in Greece (1906), Siena and Perugia (1908), and Florence (1909) are in the Monks House Papers A7, USL.

54. Vanessa Bell to Marjorie Snowden, April 25? 1904; September 18, 1908; KCL.

55. Quoted in Quentin Bell, *Virginia Woolf*, 1:138.

56. Spalding notes Vanessa's presence. *Vanessa Bell*, p. 37. See chapter 6 for more discussion of the sisters in the context of the other artistic movements of their time.

57. Quoted in Louise DeSalvo, "1897: Virginia Woolf at Fifteen," *Virginia*

Woolf: A Feminist Slant, ed. Jane Marcus (Lincoln: University of Nebraska Press, 1983), p. 81.

58. Allen McLaurin, *Virginia Woolf: The Echoes Enslaved* (Cambridge: Cambridge University Press, 1973), p. 44.

59. For some of Fry's views, see McLaurin, *Virginia Woolf*, p. 91 and J. K. Johnstone, *The Bloomsbury Group: A Study of E. M. Forster, Lytton Strachey, Virginia Woolf, and Their Circle* (New York: Farrar, Straus, 1963), p. 61.

60. See Quentin Bell, *Virginia Woolf*, 2:107.

61. Leonard Woolf, *The Wise Virgins: A Story of Words, Opinions, and a Few Emotions* (London: Edward Arnold, 1941), p. 44.

62. "Lecture given at Leighton Park," 1925, unpublished typescript; AG.

63. Virginia Woolf to Julian Bell, June 20, 1936; KCL.

64. As Quentin Bell notes, part of Virginia's irritation was "on Leonard's behalf." Employed part-time by the Grafton Galleries, he had to cope with the outraged or amused public. *Virginia Woolf*, 2:7.

65. Quentin Bell, for example, mentions the sisters' "tacit competition" in art and life in *Virginia Woolf*, 2:147, and Leon Edel states, in *Bloomsbury: A House of Lions*, p. 265, that Virginia "always felt herself in competition with the painters."

66. Vanessa Bell to Virginia Woolf, March 11, 1909; August 27, 1909; NYPL.

67. Vanessa Bell to Virginia Woolf, Christmas Day, 1909; December 29, 1909; December 30, 1909; NYPL.

68. Vanessa Bell to Virginia Woolf, April 16, 1927; NYPL.

69. Vanessa Bell to Virginia Woolf, May 27, 1929; NYPL.

70. Vanessa Bell, *Notes on Virginia's Childhood.*

71. Vanessa Bell to Virginia Woolf, August 23, 1912; NYPL.

72. Virginia Woolf's untitled account book, July 1928–July 1937, is in WSUL. "An Unpublished Account Book" in Catalogue 42 of Serendipity Books (Berkeley, California) is a detailed description of the record and of its significance in Woolf's life. For Leonard Woolf's description of their new financial arrangement, see *Downhill All the Way: An Autobiography of the Years 1919 to 1939* (New York: Harcourt Brace Jovanovich, 1967), p. 142. Leonard's indications of Virginia's earnings are close to her own, although his bookkeeping methods are more scrupulous.

73. Vanessa Bell to Virginia Woolf, March? 1908 and August 11, 1908; NYPL.

74. Vanessa Bell, "Notes on Bloomsbury," in Rosenbaum, *The Bloomsbury Group*, p. 74.

75. Vanessa Bell to Marjorie Snowden, April 21, 1904; September 12, 1908; KCL.

76. Vanessa Bell to Clive Bell, 1912; August 16, 1914; c. 1914; KCL.

77. Vanessa Bell to Virginia Woolf, October 24, 1904; NYPL.

78. Vanessa Bell to Virginia Woolf, August 8, 1908; see also August 8, 1909; NYPL.

79. Vanessa Bell to Virginia Woolf, August 27, 1908; NYPL.

80. Vanessa Bell to Virginia Woolf, August 10, 1909; NYPL.

81. Quentin Bell, *Virginia Woolf*, 1:133. Until Virginia's flirtation with Clive, Spalding notes in *Vanessa Bell* (p. 72), the sisters had been exceptionally intimate, each needing the other about equally to stimulate her creative life.

82. Vanessa Bell to Virginia Woolf, July 30, 1907; NYPL.

83. Vanessa Bell to Virginia Woolf, May 9, 1909; May 11, 1909; June 24, 1910; December 25, 1927; April 26, 1924; NYPL. David Garnett points out that Vanessa Bell "was the only woman that any of us knew who could join in the talk of a group of men and allow them to forget that she was a woman, forgetting it herself." *Flowers of the Forest*, p. 26. Vanessa's comment to Virginia indicates, however, that she did not always forget that she was a woman among men.

84. Vanessa Bell to Virginia Woolf, August 26, 1908; August 27, 1908; NYPL. Thirty years later Woolf's short story, "The Shooting Party," presents sportsmen from a woman's point of view; the old sisters of the story, in fact, are identified with the birds upon whom the men and dogs prey.

85. Vanessa Bell to Virginia Woolf, April 19, 1908; NYPL.

86. Vanessa Bell to Virginia Woolf, May 3, 1927.

87. Vanessa Bell to Roger Fry, July 6, 1911; KCL.

88. Vanessa Bell to Virginia Woolf, June/July, 1921; NYPL.

89. Vanessa Bell to Virginia Woolf, May 19, 1927; NYPL.

90. Leonard Woolf, *Downhill All the Way*, p. 115. Spalding identifies this crisis as a "tale concerning a mad servant," *Vanessa Bell*, p. 181. The Memoir Club began its meetings in 1920.

91. Vanessa Bell, *Notes on Virginia's Childhood*, unpaginated.

92. Angelica Garnett, *Deceived with Kindness: A Bloomsbury Childhood* (London: Chatto and Windus; Hogarth, 1984), p. 107.

93. Vanessa Bell to Roger Fry, July 3, 1911; KCL. With the important men in her life, however, she may have behaved much as she did with Virginia. As Anscombe notes, "It was as though she had used the two men [Clive Bell and Roger Fry] at times of crisis, only to shrug them off when, with their support, her troubles had been overcome. More likely she found that, in order to return love, she had to sacrifice the independence which, after the responsibilities she had had in her teens, was vital to her emotional security." See Isabelle Anscombe, *Omega and After*, p. 56. Anscombe adds, in considering Bell's relationship with Grant, that "emotionally she attached herself to her painting rather than to relationships" (p. 164).

94. Vanessa Bell, "Memories of Roger Fry."

95. Ibid., p. 14. Vanessa's description of this incident is quoted in Spalding, *Vanessa Bell*, p. 96.

96. Vanessa Bell, *Notes on Virginia's Childhood*, and "Life at Hyde Park Gate," unpublished typescript; AG. The latter memoir also includes accounts of Vanessa's household record keeping, her relationship with her bereaved father, her escape into the art school environment, and George Duckworth's attempts to introduce her into society.

97. Vanessa Bell, "Memories of Roger Fry."

98. Vanessa Bell to Virginia Woolf, August 31, 1915; NYPL.

99. Clive Bell to Vanessa Bell, October 1938; KCL.

100. Janie Bussy to Vanessa Bell, December 29, 1939; KCL.

101. Roger Fry to Vanessa Bell, July 24, 1927; April 29, 1932; KCL.

102. Vanessa Bell to Marjorie Snowden, April 9, 1904; December 21, 1905; September 18, 1908; February 13, 1910; August 20, 1912; February 26, 1919; KCL. For an account of the Dreadnought Hoax, see Quentin Bell, *Virginia Woolf*, 1:157–

61. In 1910 Virginia, among others, impersonated the Court of Abyssinia and boarded the H.M.S. Dreadnought.

103. Vanessa wrote that she knew the gossip, but that she did not think it was her friend's concern. Asserting her indifference to public opinion, particularly when it was judgmental about people's actions at the expense of their intrinsic worth, Vanessa insisted that Madge accept her as she was. In a subsequent letter, Vanessa added that Madge had no reason to think that she was doing anything without Clive's knowledge and that, in her experience, traditional homes were not inevitably the happiest or the best for the people involved. Vanessa Bell to Madge Vaughan, March 10, 16, 1920; KCL.

104. Vanessa Bell to Madge Vaughan, October 28, 1904?; KCL.

105. Vanessa Bell to Marjorie Snowden, September 6, 1906; KCL.

106. Vanessa Bell to Roger Fry, September 8, 1926; KCL. Another example is her comment that her son would no doubt "become a Primitive Methodist and forgive me graciously for my wickedness—at least I try to prepare myself for such ignominy." Vanessa Bell to Madge Vaughan, June 5, 1910; KCL.

107. David Garnett, *The Flowers of the Forest*, p. 26. Spalding sees the bawdiness as one form the sisters' feminism, which had few outlets, took. *Vanessa Bell*, pp. 64, 66.

108. Vanessa Bell to Roger Fry, May 27, 1915; KCL.

109. Vanessa Bell to Clive Bell, June 25, 1910; KCL.

110. Vanessa Bell to Roger Fry, July 6, 1911; KCL.

111. Vanessa Bell to Roger Fry, September 16, 1912; 1915; 1916; KCL.

112. Spalding, *Vanessa Bell*, p. 263. Although the review is signed E. V., Spalding identifies it as Vanessa's.

113. Quentin Bell, *Virginia Woolf*, 1:142.

114. Denys Sutton, ed., *Letters of Roger Fry*, 2:532.

115. Vanessa Bell to Roger Fry, September 10, 1914; KCL.

116. Vanessa Bell to Clive Bell, c. 1914; KCL.

117. Clive Bell, *Art* (New York: G. P. Putnam, 1958), p. 9.

118. Vanessa Bell to Virginia Woolf, January 21, 1938; NYPL. Julian Bell's *Essays, Poems, and Letters*, ed. Quentin Bell, was published in 1938. Vanessa also encouraged other people to write. In about 1915 she wrote to Roger Fry that he ought to write not only art criticism but also works of literature. Vanessa Bell to Roger Fry, 1915?; KCL. Some of his attempts, not very successful, are in the KCL.

2—THE COMMON VIEWER

1. The painting is reproduced in G. K. Chesterton, *G. F. Watts* (London: Duckworth, 1906). An oil study (1882–83) is in the Watts Gallery, Compton, near Guildford, Surrey. The large painting (1884–85) is in the Tate Gallery, London. The oil study differs in two ways: the figure on the left is less clearly female, and Mammon's feet are more in evidence; the man's arm is behind one of the feet, rather than in front of it as in the Tate version. According to the London *Daily Express* (September 10, 1904), Watts may have used the face of John D. Rockefeller as his model for

Mammon. Richard Jefferies of the Watts Gallery called my attention to the parallel (conversation, August 1983; letter, July 1984).

M. S. Watts, in *George Frederick Watts: The Annals of an Artist's Life*, 3 vols. (New York: George H. Doran, n.d.), describes how Watts, "Jonah-like . . . would often preach against Mammon worship, and the hypocritical veiling of the daily sacrifice made to this deity. 'Holy Mammon—Divine Respectability—Sacred Dividend,' he said once in this Jonah-mood." Watts wanted an English sculptor "to make a statue of Mammon, that it might be set up in Hyde Park, where he hoped his worshippers would be at least honest enough to bow the knee publicly to him" (2:149).

2. See M. S. Watts, *George Frederick Watts*, 2:137, for the origin of the motto, "The Utmost for the Highest" and 3:19–21, 29, and 35 for some of Watts's denunciations of particular facts as opposed to general aspirations or ideas. See also Vanessa Bell to Marjorie Snowden, 1902/1903, KCL. This reconstruction of Watts's comments for her friend, however, included ideas that Vanessa must have thought seriously about, even though she would have applied them in ways different from Watts. "The great mistake of modern art is that they try to make things too real," Watts said. He advised knowing only the fundamentals of anatomy and not working from models; too much knowledge can mislead the artist. He also suggested using large circles as structural principles and warm colors.

3. Quentin Bell, *Virginia Woolf: A Biography*, 2 vols. (London: Hogarth, 1973) 1:95.

4. Frances Spalding, *Vanessa Bell* (London: Weidenfeld and Nicolson, 1983), p. 46; Duncan Grant, "Virginia Woolf," *The Bloomsbury Group: A Collection of Memoirs, Commentary and Criticism*, ed. S. P. Rosenbaum (Toronto: University of Toronto Press, 1975), p. 65.

5. Beverly Ann Schlack, *Continuing Presences: Virginia Woolf's Use of Literary Allusion* (University Park, Pa.: Pennsylvania State University Press, 1979), p. x.

6. Ibid., pp. 8, 31.

7. For a brief account of Vanessa Bell's decorating, see Frances Spalding, *Vanessa Bell, 1879–1961: An Exhibition to Mark the Centenary of Her Birth* (Sheffield City Art Galleries, 1979), p. 2. For a brief assessment of Mrs. Cameron, see Quentin Bell, *Virginia Woolf*, 1:16. In her introduction to *Victorian Photographs of Famous Men and Fair Women* by Julia Margaret Cameron (London: Hogarth, 1926), Woolf presents her aunt with some irony but with more sympathy than she does in *Freshwater*. She sees Julia Cameron as something of a rebel against verisimilitude because she blurred her pictures slightly (p. 6), and as an artist who appealed to both painters and writers (p. 7).

8. G. K. Chesterton, *G. F. Watts*, p. 77. Chesterton says that Tennyson was probably "the greatest and most intimate" of Watts's friends (p. 73).

9. Vanessa Bell to Clive Bell, January 31, 1930, KCL.

10. Virginia Wolf, *Recent Paintings by Vanessa Bell* (The London Artists' Association, 1930), reprinted in S. P. Rosenbaum, ed., *The Bloomsbury Group*, p. 170.

11. Diane Filby Gillespie, "Vanessa Bell, Virginia Woolf, and Duncan Grant: Conversation with Angelica Garnett," *Modernist Studies* 3, no. 3 (1979): 154.

12. In this quotation from Mitchell Leaska's edition of *The Pargiters: The Novel-Essay Portion of "The Years,"* I have retained Leaska's editorial symbols: [*word*] = a deletion editorially restored; ⟨word⟩ = an insertion made by Virginia Woolf.

13. Sidney C. Hutchison in *The History of the Royal Academy: 1768–1968* (New York: Taplinger, 1968), p. 143, notes the "problems of co-education in the Victorian age" and the opposition by women students to being deprived of nude male models. In 1893, according to the R. A. Annual Report, they were allowed such models but only if draped "about the loins" in a carefully defined manner. Hutchison concludes, however, that "never was there such a diaper."

14. Vanessa Bell to Virginia Woolf, February 13, 1918; NYPL. Several times during her life, Vanessa had illnesses which may have been nervous in origin or in effect. One was in 1906, when she was worried about Virginia's mental difficulties and about Clive's marriage proposal. Another was in 1911, when traveling and a miscarriage precipitated a physical and mental breakdown. On that occasion it took her two years to recover completely (Spalding, *Vanessa Bell*, pp. 59, 96). Angelica Garnett in *Deceived with Kindness: A Bloomsbury Childhood* (London: Chatto and Windus; Hogarth, 1984), p. 32, says that "Vanessa was a prey to intermittent but crippling bouts of lethargy lasting over a couple of years, suggesting that she suffered from a severe depression, different in effect but not perhaps unrelated to Virginia's instability."

15. Vanessa Bell, "Notes on Bloomsbury," in S. P. Rosenbaum, ed., *The Bloomsbury Group*, p. 76.

16. Vanessa Bell to Angelica Bell, November 24, 1941. See also Vanessa's sympathetic comments on Janie Bussy's situation (Spalding, *Vanessa Bell*, p. 357).

17. Woolf, *Recent Paintings by Vanessa Bell*, in S. P. Rosenbaum, ed., *The Bloomsbury Group*, p. 171. The present location of the paintings Woolf mentions is unknown. Shone (letter, September 9, 1981) tentatively identifies a few of them from the catalogue as follows: the silent group of women may be *Dieppe in the Eighties* (26); the boy standing in the sea, *Wading* (15); and one of several others not included in the portion of the introduction quoted, *Urn* (9).

18. Woolf makes a similar statement in "Craftsmanship": "But has any writer, who is not a typewriter, succeeded in being wholly impersonal? Always, inevitably, we know them as well as their books." Woolf attributes this phenomenon to the writer's medium: words with their "suggestive power" (CE II, 248). She does not mean, however, that we learn specific facts about an author's life. In her Introduction to George Gissing's *By the Ionian Sea: Notes of a Ramble in Southern Italy* (London: Jonathan Cape, 1933; first published 1901), she associates knowledge of the author with his inadequacy: "For Gissing is one of those imperfect novelists through whose books one sees the life of the author faintly covered by the lives of fictitious people. With such writers we establish a personal rather than an artistic relationship" (p. 7). As Louise DeSalvo's *Virginia Woolf's First Voyage: A Novel in the Making* (Totowa, N.J.: Rowman and Littlefield, 1980) documents, Woolf wrestled with the problem of autobiography in her own first novel, reworking over the years a pastiche of revelation and disguise.

19. Woolf, *Recent Paintings by Vanessa Bell*, in S. P. Rosenbaum, ed., *The Bloomsbury Group*, pp. 172–73. In "The Aesthetic Hypothesis," the first chapter of *Art* (1913), Clive Bell distinguishes between aesthetic emotions and the emotions of life; paintings should arouse the former, not the latter. Woolf's reference to morality in paintings recalls, perhaps, G. K. Chesterton's discussion of this issue in *G. F. Watts* (pp. 120–21). All art, Chesterton insists, is allegorical in some way: "Thus Mr.

Whistler when he drops a spark of perfect yellow or violet into some glooming pool of the nocturnal Thames is, in all probability, enunciating some sharp and wholesome comment." Even the Impressionists may be "a very original and sincere race of stern young moralists."

See also Jacqueline Falkenheim, *Roger Fry and the Beginnings of Formalist Art Criticism* (Ann Arbor, Mich.: UMI Research Press, 1980), p. 88.

20. A number of writers discuss Woolf as a literary critic. Michael Rosenthal, "Literary Criticism," in *Virginia Woolf* (London: Routledge and Kegan Paul, 1979), pp. 244–60, notes rightly that too many people base their conclusions about Woolf's literary criticism on only two essays, "Modern Fiction" and "Mr. Bennett and Mrs. Brown" (p. 252).

21. Quoted in Quentin Bell, *Virginia Woolf*, 1:138.

22. Beverly Schlack mentions several instances of Woolf's familiarity with Keats's work in *Continuing Presences.* Vanessa Bell, in 1921, proposed to illustrate some of Keats's poems. Virginia replied that the idea was "a very brilliant one. There would be no difficulty about printing some lines on every page," a fact Leonard verified (L II 491). Nothing must have come of this plan, however.

23. Virginia Woolf, "Pictures and Portraits," *The Athenaeum* I (January 9, 1920): 46.

24. Ibid.

25. Frances Spalding notes the pervasiveness of the circle in Bell's decorative work (*Vanessa Bell*, p. 171). For a discussion of the globe image in Woolf's work, see Dorothy Brewster, "Fiction: Shaping the Globe" in *Virginia Woolf*, (Westport, Conn.: Greenwood, 1979), pp. 79–161.

26. Ten years later, still trying to capture the essence of Mrs. Ramsay, Lily feels "as if a door had opened, and one went in and stood gazing silently about in a high cathedral-like place, very dark, very solemn," separate from the outside world (TTL 264). The dome is a favorite visual shape of Woolf's. In a memoir, she recalls her mother, upon whom Mrs. Ramsay is based, "in the very centre of that great Cathedral space which was childhood" (MB 81). In *A Room of One's Own*, Woolf lists the dome among the different shapes suggested by the overall structures of novels (AROO 74).

27. Virginia Woolf, "Pictures and Portraits," p. 47.

28. Richard Outram of Toronto, Canada, kindly provided me with a copy of Woolf's Foreword. A draft of her remarks, dated February 23, 1934, is in the Berg Collection at the New York Public Library. Here Woolf refers to her sister by name. As in the final version, however, she disclaims any skill as a critic of the visual arts and focuses on the responses of a lay viewer. The painter's reduction of objects to basic elements in an intellectually controlled design initially demands a like reaction. But there is a second level of response. Vanessa Bell is not interested in the ideas or feelings her pictures elicit; still, some associations arise. Woolf concludes once again that words cannot describe an art which puts viewers into a world that transcends words. One can only purchase fragments of that world and hang them on the wall.

29. In 1938, four years later, there was some talk of Virginia Woolf's contributing an introduction to an exhibition of Vanessa Bell's and Duncan Grant's paintings in Chicago. Woolf demurred and suggested, instead, that two of Fry's articles be used. "They would only need a little introducing—And this would relieve me of the

crime and discomfort of Nepotism. . . ." Apparently neither the introduction nor the show materialized (L VI 265).

30. Jean Hagstrum, *The Sister Arts: The Tradition of Literary Pictorialism and English Poetry from Dryden to Gray* (Chicago: University of Chicago Press, 1958), pp. 29–31. Raymond Lister, in *Victorian Narrative Paintings* (New York: Clarkson N. Potter, 1966), notes the influence of novel illustration on the paintings of the mid-nineteenth century. "The narrative picture's main *raison d'etre* is anecdote; it is, in fact, visual literature, and many of its themes were derived from literary sources" (p. 15).

31. The pictures Woolf describes in most detail are No. 306, *The Wonders of the Deep*, by John R. Reid (1851–1926) and No. 248, *Cocaine*, by Alfred Priest (1874–1929). The *Royal Academy Illustrated* of 1919 contains a reproduction of *Cocaine*, but I could not discover the present location of either painting. See also Brenda R. Silver, *Virginia Woolf's Reading Notebooks* (Princeton, N.J.: Princeton University Press, 1983), p. 18 (XLIV B.13) and p. 208.

32. Vanessa Bell to Marjorie Snowden, April 9, 1904, KCL.

33. Hagstrum, *The Sister Arts*, p. 30. Roger Fry often talked of writing as if it had tactile qualities, "texture." See Denys Sutton, ed., *Letters of Roger Fry*, 2 vols. (London: Chatto and Windus, 1972), 2:486, 529, 555.

34. Woolf's linking of psychology and painting recalls the phrase "psychological volumes" which Charles Mauron said exist in literature where they correspond to the plastic volumes in painting. Roger Fry translated Mauron's essay for the Hogarth Press in 1926. See J. K. Johnstone, *The Bloomsbury Group: A Study of E. M. Forster, Lytton Strachey, Virginia Woolf, and Their Circle* (New York: Noonday, 1963), pp. 58–59, and Allen McLaurin, *Virginia Woolf: The Echoes Enslaved* (Cambridge: Cambridge University Press, 1973), pp. 79, 84.

35. Virginia Woolf, "Pictures," in *The Moment and Other Essays* (London: Hogarth, 1947), p. 142.

36. Ibid., pp. 142–43.

37. The painting by Vanessa Bell entitled *Red-Hot Pokers* (1921), as well as one with the same title by Duncan Grant (exhibited 1924) in the Manchester City Art Gallery, are reproduced in *Concise Catalogue of British Paintings* vol. 2 (Manchester: Manchester City Art Gallery, 1978), pp. 16, 95.

38. *To the Lighthouse: The Original Holograph Draft*, ed. Susan Dick (Toronto: University of Toronto Press, 1982), pp. 38, 112–13.

39. Virginia Woolf, "Pictures," p. 143.

40. In some respects "Three Pictures" is a reworking, in terms of the visual arts, of "An Unwritten Novel." The narrator's speculations about Minnie Marsh in that story prove equally false.

41. Quentin Bell records the series of events in *Virginia Woolf*, 2:173–74. Also see Shone, *Bloomsbury Portraits: Vanessa Bell, Duncan Grant, and Their Circle* (Oxford: Phaidon, 1976), pp. 66, 89. Vanessa Bell was not always positive about Sickert. In 1930, for instance, she went to a show which she saw as having no coherence or direction. See Vanessa Bell to Clive Bell, June 3, 1930; KCL. Vanessa liked, however, a Sickert painting of two women which Maynard Keynes bought. See Vanessa Bell to Roger Fry, October 3, 1922; KCL. Virginia Woolf was not always pleased with Sickert either. A review he wrote of Duncan Grant's show in 1929 offended her (L IV 25).

42. Quoted in Bell, *Virginia Woolf*, 2:174.

43. Ibid.

44. Wendy Baron identifies the painting in *Sickert* (London: Phaidon, 1973), p. 142. Woolf's assessment of Sickert is at least partially valid. Baron indicates that both the subject and the technical concerns of painting were important to him. He echoed his comment that he was a literary painter on many occasions. Although he insisted that good paintings are illustrations, his "method of working was the reverse of that of the illustrative artist." He began, not with a story, but with a formal problem, like the tension between two figures; often he tried in many drawings and paintings to solve the same problem. At some later stage, he added anecdotal titles and details.

Denys Sutton in *Walter Sickert: A Biography* (London: Michael Joseph, 1976), pp. 149–50, notes Virginia Woolf's ability to appreciate both "theme" and "visual qualities" in Sickert's work.

45. The exhibition opening was at the Bristol Museum and Art Gallery on Friday, July 12, 1935. See "Roger Fry" in Virginia Woolf, *The Moment*, p. 84.

46. "Notes for Reading at Random," ed. Brenda Silver. *Twentieth Century Literature* 25, 3/4 (Fall/Winter 1979): 375.

3 — CRITICISM AND COLLABORATION

1. Possibly both sisters knew T. E. Hulme's comment in *The New Age* in 1914 on Fry's landscape painting: "He . . . accomplishes the extraordinary feat of adapting the austere Cézanne into something quite fitted for chocolate boxes." Quoted in Judith Collins, *The Omega Workshops* (Chicago: University of Chicago Press, 1984), p. 93.

2. Vanessa Bell to Leonard Woolf, August 29, 1912; USL.

3. Vanessa Bell to Virginia Woolf, October 20, 1911; NYPL. Since Woolf's articles for the *Nation* appeared mostly in the twenties, this letter may be misdated. Vanessa was in Paris with Clive in October of 1911; Roger Fry and Duncan Grant were also traveling in France. Vanessa was in Paris with Grant and Fry in May of 1925. Since there is no record of an article by Woolf in the *Nation* in 1911, Vanessa Bell's reference may be to "Pictures," published in that periodical in April of 1925.

4. Vanessa Bell to Virginia Woolf, 1914? NYPL.

5. Vanessa Bell to Virginia Woolf, June 8, 1926; NYPL.

6. The paintings to which Woolf refers are difficult to identify and possibly no longer exist. Frances Spalding (letter, August 9, 1981) thinks that the painting of the bridge and blue boat might be a small canvas now at the Fitzwilliam Museum in Cambridge. Richard Shone (letter, September 9, 1981), however, thinks it may be one of several quay-side scenes Bell did in the early twenties. Shone thinks the Cameron photo may have been one of Julia Stephen; he notes that Duncan Grant did a painting from a similar photo in the thirties and, around the same time, used a Cameron photo for a painting of the violinist, Joachim. Leslie Stephen in his *Mausoleum Book* (Oxford: Clarendon, 1977), p. 97, refers to "a photograph by Mrs. Cameron" of Julia Stephen that he gave Vanessa on her birthday and that, he thinks, "shows her mother's beauty better than any other." Vanessa Bell's *Portrait of the Artist's Mother* now hangs in the Royal Pavilion Art Gallery, Brighton, England.

7. Vanessa Bell to Virginia Woolf, March 17, 1927, NYPL. I have not identified the painting with the hay cart.

8. Diane Gillespie, "Virginia Woolf, Vanessa Bell, and Duncan Grant: Conversation with Angelica Garnett," *Modernist Studies* 3, no. 3 (1979): 156. According to Isabelle Anscombe, in *Omega and After: Bloomsbury and the Decorative Arts* (London: Thames and Hudson, 1981), p. 112, Duncan Grant's influence on Vanessa Bell was, in general, negative, "for there is ample indication that she was the stronger painter. . . . But Vanessa was influenced by his lightness of touch into partly abandoning her more serious and considered stance and she lost much of the compelling gravity of her early work, or at least failed to develop it satisfactorily in her later paintings." In Frances Spalding's opinion, Roger Fry was the one who encouraged Vanessa Bell to do large-scale works. See *Vanessa Bell, 1879–1961: An Exhibition to Mark the Centenary of Her Birth* (Sheffield City Art Galleries, 1979), p. 9. Judith Collins, *The Omega Workshops*, p. 127, attributes Bell's large paintings to "the chance to work on a large scale on decorative projects for the Omega."

9. Germaine Greer, *The Obstacle Race: The Fortunes of Women Painters and Their Work* (New York: Farrar Straus Giroux, 1979), p. 108.

10. Vanessa Bell to Roger Fry, September 19, 1920 or 1922. KCL.

11. Roger Fry to Vanessa Bell, April 19, 1934; KCL.

12. See Frances Spalding, *Vanessa Bell* (London: Weidenfeld & Nicolson, 1983), p. 153. The painting of the pot of flowers on a chair is probably *Arum Lilies* (1920–21). Both paintings were exhibited at the London Group Retrospective (1928) and are now in the Courtauld Galleries of the University of London.

13. Spalding, *Vanessa Bell*, pp. 153–54.

14. Jane Marcus in "Thinking Back through Our Mothers," *New Feminist Essays on Virginia Woolf*, ed. Jane Marcus (Lincoln: University of Nebraska Press, 1981), p. 2, suggests that Desmond MacCarthy's negative reaction to the story was a reason for not reprinting it. Quentin Bell in "Virginia Woolf, Her Politics," *Virginia Woolf Miscellany* 20 (Spring 1983): 2, disagrees. See also Marcus' "Liberty, Sorority, Misogyny," in Carolyn Heilbrun and Margaret Higgonet, eds., *The Representation of Women in Fiction: Selected Papers from the English Institute, 1981* (Baltimore: Johns Hopkins University Press, 1983), pp. 60–97; and Sandra M. Gilbert, "The Battle of the Books/The Battle of the Sexes: Virginia Woolf's *Vita Nuova*," *Michigan Quarterly Review* 23, no. 2 (Spring, 1984): 171–95.

15. Virginia Stephen and five men impersonated the Court of Abyssinia and boarded the H.M.S. Dreadnought on February 10, 1910. See Quentin Bell, *Virginia Woolf: A Biography*, 2 vols. (New York: Harcourt Brace Jovanovich, 1972), 1:157–60.

16. Roger Fry to Vanessa Bell, March 21, 1928; KCL.

17. Frances Spalding (letter, August 9, 1982) and Richard Shone (letter, September 9, 1981) both think this painting is the one to which Woolf referred. It is reproduced in the catalogue to an exhibition Anthony d'Offay held in 1973. Roger Fry painted the flower at the same time.

18. Vanessa Bell to Virginia Woolf, July 3, 1918, NYPL.

19. Vanessa Bell to Virginia Woolf, May 31, 1939, NYPL.

20. Woolf's previously unpublished letter is quoted in Spalding, *Vanessa Bell*, p. 309.

21. Richard Shone's *Bloomsbury Portraits: Vanessa Bell, Duncan Grant, and Their*

Circle (Oxford: Phaidon, 1976) includes neither reproductions nor discussions of any of the designs for Virginia Woolf's books. George Spater and Ian Parsons include a reproduction of a Bell design used for several of the Hogarth Essays including "Mr. Bennett and Mrs. Brown" in *A Marriage of True Minds: An Intimate Portrait of Leonard and Virginia Woolf* (New York: Harcourt Brace Jovanovich, 1977), p. 111. Jean Peters in "Publishers' Imprints," *Collectible Books: Some New Paths*, ed. Jean Peters (New York: R. R. Bowker, 1979), reproduces this same design as well as the dust jackets for *Jacob's Room* and *Mrs. Dalloway*. J. Howard Woolmer reproduces the dust jacket for *Three Guineas* in *A Checklist of the Hogarth Press* (Andes, N.Y.: Woolmer/Brotherson, 1976). John Lehmann, in *Virginia Woolf and Her World* (New York: Harcourt Brace Jovanovich, 1975), reproduces, without comment, three covers or dust jackets, three earlier drawings for dust jackets, and two illustrations from *Flush*. Lola L. Szladits includes one of the *Flush* illustrations, too, in "The Life, Character and Opinions of Flush the Spaniel," *Bulletin of the New York Public Library* 74 (1970): 211–18. One illustration for the 1927 edition of *Kew Gardens* appears without discussion in the *Virginia Woolf Miscellany* 13 (Christmas 1979): 8. One for the 1919 edition of *Kew Gardens* is in B. J. Kirkpatrick, *A Bibliography of Virginia Woolf* (London: Rupert Hart-Davis, 1957); the cover for *Monday or Tuesday* is also reproduced in this book. Bell's cover for Woolf's *The Years* is in the *Bulletin of the New York Public Library* 80, no. 2 (Winter 1977): 159, again without commentary. Also without analyzing them, Isabelle Anscombe includes several of Bell's dust jackets for Woolf's books in *Omega and After*, p. 110 and figures 57–62.

Some of Bell's designs for Woolf's books have been exhibited. Frances Spalding comments briefly and generally on the illustrations for *Kew Gardens* in her introduction to *Vanessa Bell; 1879–1961; An Exhibition to Celebrate the Centenary of the Artist's Birth* (Sheffield City Art Galleries, 1979), p. 8. The exhibit included eleven of Bell's dust jackets for Woolf's books. See also Spalding's *Vanessa Bell*, pp. 165–66, 221. The biography includes reproductions of the frontispiece to "Kew Gardens" (1919), two decorated pages of *Kew Gardens* (1927), and six of Bell's dust-jacket designs for Woolf's books. An exhibit entitled *Vanessa Bell; 1879–1961; A Retrospective Exhibition* (New York: Davis and Long, 1980) included eight of these designs.

While this list is not complete, it is safe to say that only about half of the cover and dust-jacket designs have been reproduced and, to my knowledge, only a half dozen of the thirty-one illustrations (if one counts all twenty-one of the page decorations for the 1927 edition of *Kew Gardens*). Although Spalding's comments on *Kew Gardens* mark a beginning, in no instance is any detailed commentary included on the designs themselves or on their relationship to Woolf's texts.

22. Walker's connection with Julia Stephen's family is mentioned by M. S. Watts in *George Frederick Watts: The Annals of an Artist's Life*, 3 vols. (New York: George H. Doran, n.d.), 1:265. See also Frances Spalding, *Vanessa Bell*, pp. 34–35, and Vanessa Bell to Virginia Woolf, May 11, 1927; NYPL. James Thorpe's *English Illustration: The Nineties* (New York: Hacker, 1975) provides some understanding of the tradition of book illustration in England. Frederick Walker is mentioned as an illustrator more characteristic of the 1860s.

23. Roger Fry, "Book Illustration and a Modern Example," *Transformations: Critical and Speculative Essays on Art* (Freeport, N.Y.: Books for Libraries, 1968; first published, 1927), p. 158–59. Beginning in 1915 Fry and the Omega Workshops

produced three illustrated books and one of woodcuts without text. See Collins, *The Omega Workshops*, pp. 116–20.

24. Richard Shone, *Bloomsbury Portraits*, pp. 135, 196.

25. "Interview with Charbonnier" (1951), in Jack D. Flam's *Matisse on Art* (London: Phaidon, 1973), p. 141. The French led in book illustration and design during the early twentieth century. See Eleanor M. Garvey and Peter A. Wick, *The Art of the French Book: 1900–1965* (Dallas, Texas: Southern Methodist University Press, 1967).

26. Leonard Woolf, *Downhill All the Way: An Autobiography of the Years 1919 to 1939* (New York: Harcourt, Brace Jovanovich, 1975), p. 60.

27. Vanessa Bell to Virginia Woolf, July 3, 1918, NYPL.

28. Vanessa Bell to Virginia Woolf, Nov. 11, 1918 and Nov. 15?, 1918, NYPL.

29. Vanessa Bell to Roger Fry, 1917; KCL.

30. Vanessa Bell to Virginia Woolf, Feb. 5, 1927, NYPL.

31. Spalding, *Vanessa Bell*, p. 221.

32. The indentations and variations in line length do not create some equivalent of seventeenth-century patterned poetry, nor in most cases do they separate or group words or ideas as poetry does. In most cases, the indentations and line divisions merely create variety.

33. According to Hugh Williamson, "Illustration," *Methods of Book Design: The Practice of an Industrial Craft* (London: Oxford University Press, 1956), "whether the style of the illustrations is similar to or contrasted with that of the book's typography, there should be a planned relation between the two. The printer can do best with illustrations which in area and in thickness of line conform to the text. . . . Given a suitable paper, however, a good printer can print dissimilar areas of text and illustration together without spoiling either" (p. 263).

34. "Pictures should never be allowed to interfere with legibility, whether by dividing a line of text into two parts, or by encroaching on the type itself" (Williamson, *Methods of Book Design*, p. 272).

35. A scene in *Night and Day* anticipates Vanessa Bell's emphasis on the natural world in her later designs for *Kew Gardens*. Katharine Hilbery, a character inspired by Vanessa Bell (See chapter 4), is intrigued by Ralph Denham's scientific explanation of the differences among trees and flowers. She likes the order of the natural world in contrast to the disorder of the realm of human relationships to which, because she is a woman, she has been confined. In her 1927 designs for her sister's story, Bell does emphasize the nonhuman realm that contains and transcends muddled human activities.

36. I owe this suggestion to S. P. Rosenbaum.

37. See especially Blake's *The Songs of Innocence and Experience*. Blake was well known in Vanessa Bell's circle. Virginia, as we have seen, copied some of his drawings out of books that presumably were at one time in the Stephen home. Blake was also likely to have been a topic of conversation between Vanessa Bell and Madge Vaughan, whose letters in 1914/15 discuss her efforts to write about his life and work. In one letter, Madge reminds Vanessa of a trip they took to the British Museum to learn more about Blake (Madge Vaughan to Vanessa Bell; KCL). In 1918 Vanessa wrote to Roger Fry that she wanted to go to Christie's to see some of Blake's works

(Vanessa Bell to Roger Fry, March 5, 1918; KCL). Duncan Grant was impressed by this exhibition of Blake's illustrations of Dante (Spalding, *Vanessa Bell*, p. 174). While Vanessa Bell knew Blake's work, she did not admire it without qualification. According to Angelica Garnett (conversation, January 1981), her mother considered much of it the inept copying of greater artists.

38. Spalding, *Vanessa Bell*, p. 222, rightly notes a contrast between the "slashing and bold" style of the designs for the earlier pages and the "carefully decorative" style of the later ones.

39. Published by the Chelsea Book Club in 1921, this excerpt differs very slightly from the others. I saw this version through the courtesy of Richard Outram of Toronto, Canada.

40. The photo is possibly of one of Vita Sackville-West's spaniels (L V 35, n. 2), although the "character" of Flush is based on the Woolfs' spaniel, Pinka (L V 167, 187, n. 1). *Flush's Birthplace* is an unsigned engraving from the nineteenth century identified by a Mr. Horne, Virginia Woolf says, as a "working man's cottage" (L V 231).

41. Jean Guiguet, *Virginia Woolf and Her Works*, trans. Jean Stewart (London: Hogarth, 1965), pp. 346–47.

42. Ethel Smyth to Vanessa Bell, October 6 and October 23, 1933?; KCL.

43. Quentin Bell, *Virginia Woolf: A Biography*, 2 vols. (London: Hogarth, 1973), 2:175. Lola L. Szladits, in "The Life, Character and Opinions of Flush the Spaniel," offers additional reasons for Woolf's interest in Elizabeth Barrett Browning and Flush: Woolf identified with the poet's illnesses, her problems with her father, her study of Greek and travel to Greece, and her relationship with Robert Browning.

44. Vanessa Bell to Clive Bell, 1910 or 1912; KCL.

45. Stephen Trombley, *All That Summer She Was Mad: Virginia Woolf: Female Victim of Male Medicine* (New York: Continuum, 1982), p. 279.

46. Lynd Ward, "The Illustrator and the Book," in *Graphic Forms: The Arts as Related to the Book* (Cambridge: Harvard University Press, 1949), pp. 59–60.

47. Vanessa Bell to Virginia Woolf, December 4, 1917; NYPL.

48. Vanessa Bell to Virginia Woolf, April 17, 1929; NYPL.

49. Vanessa Bell to Clive Bell, August 30, 1910; KCL.

50. Vanessa Bell to Virginia Woolf, June 5, 1917; NYPL.

51. Vanessa Bell, *Notes on Virginia's Childhood*, unpaginated.

52. Vanessa Bell to Virginia Woolf, August 12, 1908; NYPL.

53. Vanessa Bell to Virginia Woolf, 1904; NYPL.

54. Vanessa Bell to Roger Fry, February 18, 1921; KCL.

55. Vanessa Bell to Roger Fry, 1913?; KCL.

56. Vanessa Bell to Roger Fry, 1921; KCL.

57. Vanessa Bell to Virginia Woolf, April 19, 1918; NYPL.

58. Vanessa Bell to Virginia Woolf, December 19, 1918; NYPL.

59. Vanessa Bell to Virginia Woolf, February 13, 1918; May 14, 1926; April 17, 1929; NYPL.

60. Vanessa Bell to Roger Fry, November 29, 1918; KCL.

61. Vanessa Bell to Roger Fry, June 1, 1926; KCL.

62. Vanessa Bell to Roger Fry, 1916; KCL.

63. Vanessa Bell to Roger Fry, April 1929; KCL.

64. Vanessa Bell to Roger Fry, July 6, 1922; KCL. The date of this letter must be inaccurate, since Forster's novel appeared in 1924.

65. Vanessa Bell to Clive Bell, 1912; KCL.

66. Vanessa Bell to Roger Fry, June 25, 1915; KCL.

67. Vanessa Bell to Roger Fry, June 9, 1914; KCL.

68. Vanessa Bell to Virginia Woolf, August 21, 1907; NYPL.

69. Vanessa Bell to Virginia Woolf, August 25, 1908; NYPL.

70. Vanessa Bell to Virginia Woolf, August 11, 1908; NYPL.

71. Vanessa Bell to Virginia Woolf, December 4, 1917; February 5, 1927; NYPL.

72. Vanessa Bell to Virginia Woolf, August 27, 1909; NYPL.

73. Vanessa Bell to Virginia Woolf, April 11, 19, 20, 1908; NYPL.

74. Vanessa Bell to Clive Bell, 1922; KCL.

75. Vanessa Bell to Roger Fry, October 27, 1928; KCL.

76. Vanessa Bell to Roger Fry, July 20, 1917; 1917; KCL. Mary Hutchinson reported the conversation to Lytton Strachey in a letter dated August 3, 1917 (HRHRC). According to her, the people at Charleston had described Virginia Woolf as isolated and aloof, studying the troubles of the world. Mary had countered that the true artist must be immersed in the world and humble before its manifestations.

77. Vanessa Bell to Clive Bell, October 10, 1931; KCL.

78. Vanessa Bell to Roger Fry, December 25, 1913; KCL. See also Vanessa Bell to Leonard Woolf, January 14, 1914, USL. In this letter she warns Leonard that, when he copies people from real life so exactly, he risks damaging his relationships with those people.

79. Vanessa Bell to Roger Fry, 1915; KCL.

80. Vanessa Bell to Roger Fry, 1915; KCL. Vanessa Bell and Leonard Woolf were not the only readers who pondered the relationships between Virginia Woolf's novels and Jane Austen's. Reviewers of Woolf's early novels noted a similar satirical bent and limited scope, a similar appreciation of human diversity, and a similar gentility. See some of the reviews of *Night and Day* reprinted in *Virginia Woolf: The Critical Heritage*, ed. Robin Majumdar and Allen McLaurin (London: Routledge and Kegan Paul, 1975).

81. "Jane Austen," *TLS*, May 8, 1913, pp. 189–90. Woolf herself thought a good deal about Austen's work in relation to her own, as numerous references in her letters, diaries, and essays show.

82. Vanessa Bell to Roger Fry, October 24, 1919; KCL. Woolf's use of her sister as the basis for Katharine Hilbery will be discussed in chapter 4.

83. Vanessa Bell to Clive Bell, May 20, 1927; KCL.

84. See Avrom Fleishman, *Virginia Woolf: A Critical Reading* (Baltimore: Johns Hopkins University Press, 1975), pp. 133–34, and Allen McLaurin, "A Note on Lily Briscoe's Painting in *To the Lighthouse*," *Notes and Queries* 26 (August 1979): 338–40.

85. Spalding, *Vanessa Bell*, pp. 250–51.

86. Spalding, *Vanessa Bell*, p. 251, rightly makes this point.

87. Rebecca West, review in the *New Statesman*, November 4, 1922, p. 142, reprinted in Robin Majumdar and Allen McLaurin, eds., *Virginia Woolf: The Critical Heritage*, p. 101.

88. Clive Bell, article in the *Dial*, December 1924, pp. 451–65, reprinted in Majumdar and McLaurin, p. 144.

89. David Garnett, "Virginia Woolf," *The American Scholar* (Summer 1965): 380–81.

4—VISUAL AND VERBAL PORTRAITS

1. Leslie Stephen edited the first twenty-six volumes of the *Dictionary of National Biography* and wrote a number of the entries himself. Less well known is the fact that Julia Stephen did the entry for Julia Margaret Cameron. See Charles W. Mann, Jr., "Your Loving Auntie and God Mama, Julia Cameron," *History of Photography* 7, no. 1 (January 1983): 73–74. In Leonard and Virginia Woolf's library, now in WSUL, are books on biography by Sidney Lee inscribed by the author to Leslie Stephen and to Virginia Stephen.

2. Richard Wendorf discusses some parallels between the two arts in Restoration and eighteenth-century England in "Ut Pictura Biographia: Biography and Portrait Painting as Sister Arts," *Articulate Images: The Sister Arts from Hogarth to Tennyson*, ed. Richard Wendorf (Minneapolis: University of Minnesota Press, 1983), pp. 98–124. For a recent treatment of Woolf's biographical interests and writings, apart from portrait painting, see Thomas S. W. Lewis, "Combining 'The Advantages of Fact and Fiction': Virginia Woolf's Biographies of Vita Sackville-West, Flush, and Roger Fry," *Virginia Woolf: Centennial Essays*, ed. Elaine K. Ginsberg and Laura Moss Gottlieb (Troy, N.Y.: Whitston, 1983), pp. 295–324. Robert Kiely in "*Jacob's Room* and *Roger Fry*: Two Studies in Still Life," in *Modernism Reconsidered*, ed. Robert Kiely (Cambridge: Harvard University Press, 1983), pp. 147–66, deals with Woolf's novel and her biography not as portraits but as still lifes.

3. Max J. Friedländer, *Landscape, Portrait, Still-Life: Their Origin and Development* (New York: Schocken, 1965), p. 232. For women's contributions to this category of painting, see Germaine Greer, "The Portraitists," in *The Obstacle Race: The Fortunes of Women Painters and Their Work* (New York: Farrar Straus Giroux, 1979), pp. 250–79, and Ann Sutherland Harris and Linda Nochlin, *Women Artists: 1550–1950* (New York: Knopf, 1976), pp. 41–43, 46.

4. Roger Fry, *Reflections on British Painting* (Freeport, N.Y.: Books for Libraries, 1969; first published, 1934), p. 25.

5. Vanessa Bell to Virginia Woolf, April 26, 1924; NYPL. Vanessa photographed her own children for use in her paintings but with different motives and results. Although she painted many accurate portraits of them, equally often they served as models for works not intended to be likenesses. See Quentin Bell and Angelica Garnett, eds., *Vanessa Bell's Family Album* (London: Jill Norman and Hobhouse, 1981), p. 10.

6. A photograph of Vanessa Bell painting Nelly Cecil is in Richard Shone, *Bloomsbury Portraits: Vanessa Bell, Duncan Grant, and Their Circle* (Oxford: Phaidon, 1976), p. 25, figure 4. Vanessa's comments to Virginia are in letters dated April 13, 16, and 18, 1906; NYPL. A restrospective comment about the difficulty of achieving a likeness is in a letter to Roger Fry, August 18, 1932?; KCL. The portrait of Nelly Cecil is reproduced in Frances Spalding, *Vanessa Bell* (London: Weidenfeld & Nicolson, 1983).

7. Vanessa Bell to Julian Bell, December 13, 19??; KCL.

8. Vanessa Bell to Virginia Woolf, September 9, 1937; NYPL.

9. Virginia probably remembered her sister's discomfort when a biography of their father was impending. Vanessa wrote to Virginia that the thought of a third party reading letters meant for only one other person was "horrible." She suspected, however, that people with literary bents would not agree with her. Vanessa Bell to Virginia Woolf, October 31, 1904; NYPL. Quentin Bell recounts Woolf's discomforts with the Fry biography from its inception. *Virginia Woolf: A Biography* (N.Y.: Harcourt Brace Jovanovich, 1973), 2:181–83. Stephen Spender says in "The Modern as Vision of the Whole," *The Idea of the Modern in Literature and the Arts*, ed. Irving Howe (New York: Horizon, 1967), p. 56, that a modern portrait painter fuses "the image of the model" with "an image of himself" and distorts his or her subject. The distortion, however, is a matter of degree. A traditional portrait painter, as José Ortega y Gasset notes in a portion of *The Dehumanization of Art* reprinted in *The Idea of the Modern*, p. 91, selects some details and excludes others but still claims to present the truth. The modern portrait painter more often consciously paints "not the real person but his own idea, his pattern, of the person." Robert Kiely, in "*Jacob's Room* and *Roger Fry*," concludes that when Woolf excludes "her personal voice" from her biography, she virtually eliminates Fry as well (p. 157).

10. Virginia Woolf, "Friendships Gallery," *Twentieth Century Literature* 25, 3/4 (Autumn/Winter 1979): 270–302. Ellen Hawkes discusses this work briefly in "Woolf's 'Magical Garden of Women'" in *New Feminist Essays on Virginia Woolf*, ed. Jane Marcus (Lincoln: University of Nebraska Press, 1981), pp. 31–60.

11. Richard Shone, in *Bloomsbury Portraits: Vanessa Bell, Duncan Grant, and Their Circle* (Oxford: Phaidon, 1976), p. 94, n. 3, notes that Vanessa made sketches of Roger Fry and Bertrand Russell and planned ones of Lydia Lopokova and David Garnett.

12. The people depicted in *The Memoir Club* are identified in Richard Shone, *Vanessa Bell, 1879–1961: A Retrospective Exhibition* (New York: Davis and Long, 1980), p. 35. Roger Fry contemplated a similar project in 1922. See Roger Fry to Mary Hutchinson, August 5, 1922; HRHRC.

13. Shone, *Bloomsbury Portraits*, pp. 77–78.

14. Clive Bell to Vanessa Bell, May 20, 1928; KCL. See the portrait of Mary Hutchinson in Shone, *Bloomsbury Portraits*, p. 175.

15. Desmond MacCarthy to Clive Bell, February 13, 1945; KCL.

16. Roger Fry to Vanessa Bell, January 28, 1917; KCL and "Vanessa Bell and Othon Friesz," *The New Statesman* 19, June 3, 1922, p. 238. On other occasions, however, he marveled at her ability to get a likeness (*Letters of Roger Fry*, ed. Denys Sutton, 2 vols. [London: Chatto and Windus, 1972], 2:423) or remarked that she had failed to capture her sitter's character (Roger Fry to Vanessa Bell, January 3, 1926; KCL.)

17. Shone, *Bloomsbury Portraits*, p. 32. Frances Spalding also notes the remarkable change in Bell's "handling of tone and the manipulation of paint" three years later. *Vanessa Bell: 1879–1961: An Exhibition to Mark the Centenary of Her Birth* (Sheffield City Art Galleries, 1979), p. 3.

18. Shone, *Bloomsbury Portraits*, pp. 126, 129. Spalding, in *Vanessa Bell*, provides a color reproduction of a portrait of Lytton Strachey done by Vanessa two years earlier. Using the same rapid, loose style, she captures him seated in a patterned

armchair facing front but looking off to one side. The colors are more subdued than in the later painting.

19. Vanessa Bell, "Life at Hyde Park Gate," unpublished typescript; AG.

20. Wendy Steiner, *Exact Resemblance to Exact Resemblance: The Literary Portraiture of Gertrude Stein* (New Haven: Yale University Press, 1978), pp. 14–16.

21. Lewis, in "Combining the Advantages of Fact and Fiction," concludes that, in spite of all her problems and reservations about the biography, Woolf succeeded in presenting a portrait of Roger Fry that captured the essence of his personality" (p. 317), precisely because she allowed him "to speak for himself" (p. 320).

22. Susan Dick thinks the portraits and "Faces and Voices" are connected. That seems more likely than a connection with the similar project begun in 1933 (see note 11 above).

23. This sketch is one of five in the Monks House Papers; USL. Three others were located by Olivier Bell among some Charleston manuscripts. All, as well as "Uncle Vanya," a possible ninth portrait, appear in *The Complete Shorter Fiction of Virginia Woolf* (London: Hogarth, 1985), pp. 236–40, edited by Susan Dick, who kindly shared her work on the portraits with me prior to publication.

24. "The outline, not the detail" is one example of the way phrases and images from Woolf's essays recur in her fiction. So motifs like flowers, and shapes like rectangles and circles, get from Vanessa's decorative work into her paintings. Both women were interested in some of the more applied areas of their media. For Virginia, these included reading and editing manuscripts, typesetting, book design, and binding. Such activities also appear in her fiction: the narrator of "The Mark on the Wall," for instance, recalls "three pale canisters of bookbinding tools" (HH 38).

25. Lyndall Gordon, in "Our Silent Life: Virginia Woolf and T. S. Eliot," in *Virginia Woolf: New Critical Essays*, ed. Patricia Clements and Isobel Grundy (London: Vision, 1983), pp. 82–83, calls Rachel in *The Voyage Out* "faceless" without relating the description to Vanessa's painting. When Kiely calls Jacob "a featureless or blurred composite" of people's views, he has painting in mind in a general way ("*Jacob's Room* and *Roger Fry*," p. 150).

26. Shone, *Bloomsbury Portraits*, p. 126.

27. Judith Collins, *The Omega Workshops* (Chicago: University of Chicago Press, 1984), p. 285, n. 49. As Henry R. Harrington points out in "The Central Line Down the Middle of *To the Lighthouse*," *Contemporary Literature* 21 (1980): 373, Vanessa does present different parts of a painting from different angles, like the tub and the nude in *The Tub*. She does not present multiple, superimposed views of a person, however, as the Cubists do. For some general analogies between Woolf's work and Cubism, see Jack F. Stewart, "Cubist Elements in *Between the Acts*," *Mosaic* 18, no. 2 (Spring 1985): 65–89.

28. Vanessa Bell, "Notes on Bloomsbury," in *The Bloomsbury Group*, ed. S. P. Rosenbaum (Toronto: University of Toronto Press, 1975), p. 74.

29. Susan Gorsky in "'The Central Shadow': Characterisation in *The Waves*," *Modern Fiction Studies* 18 (1972/73): 449–66, indicates how, in this novel, Woolf presents her characters simultaneously on three levels, as individuals, as types, and, finally, as "communal" characters whose identities merge. While such complexity is most evident in *The Waves*, it can be seen in other characters and other novels by Woolf.

30. Vanessa Bell to Marjorie Snowden, June 7, October 21, 1908; KCL. The painting, to my knowledge, has not survived.

31. Frances Spalding, *Vanessa Bell*, p. 125.

32. Quentin Bell, *Virginia Woolf: A Biography*, 2 vols. (London: Hogarth, 1973), 2:160–61; see also Vanessa Bell to Roger Fry, July 20, 1931?; KCL.

33. Reprinted in a watercolor version in George Spater and Ian Parsons, *A Marriage of True Minds: An Intimate Portrait of Leonard and Virginia Woolf* (New York: Harcourt Brace Jovanovich, 1977), p. 145. Alex Reid and Lefevre Gallery, who sold the painting, have no record of the purchaser.

34. The carpet appears to be *Vases* designed by Duncan Grant and woven by Wilton Carpets in 1932. It is reproduced in Isabelle Anscombe, *Omega and After: Bloomsbury and the Decorative Arts* (London: Thames and Hudson, 1982), color plate XII.

35. Friedländer, *Landscape, Portrait, Still Life*, pp. 235–37.

36. Virginia Woolf, "Foreword," *Catalogue of Recent Paintings by Vanessa Bell* (London: Lefevre Galleries, 1934).

37. "Great Men's Houses," *The London Scene: Five Essays by Virginia Woolf* (New York: Frank Hallman, 1975), p. 23. Compare D IV 13.

38. Sandra M. Gilbert, "Costumes of the Mind: Transvestism as Metaphor in Modern Literature," *Critical Inquiry* 7 (Winter 1980): 393–94.

39. See Virginia Blain, "Narrative Voice and the Female Perspective in Virginia Woolf's Early Novels," in Clements and Grundy, eds., *Virginia Woolf: New Critical Essays*, pp. 115–36, for a recent discussion of Woolf's treatment of this problem.

40. Spalding reproduces all three paintings in her biography of Vanessa Bell. She identifies one woman in *Interior with Two Women* as a model and the other as "(presumably the painter)," (p. 250).

41. Virginia Woolf's life of Vanessa Bell is printed as "Reminiscences," in *Moments of Being: Unpublished Autobiographical Writings*, ed. Jeanne Schulkind (New York: Harcourt Brace Jovanovich, 1976). Clive Bell's comment is quoted in Quentin Bell, *Virginia Woolf*, 1:210.

42. Shone, *Bloomsbury Portraits*, p. 140. Madeline Moore also notes the link between Vanessa Bell and Helen Ambrose. See "Some Female Versions of the Pastoral: *The Voyage Out* and Matriarchal Mythologies" in *New Feminist Essays on Virginia Woolf*, ed. Jane Marcus (Lincoln: University of Nebraska Press, 1981), pp. 84–85.

43. Vanessa Bell to Roger Fry, n.d.; KCL. Various critics and biographers, too numerous to list, have noted resemblances between a number of other characters in Woolf's fiction and people she knew: for example, Julia Craye in "Slater's Pins Have No Points" to Clara Pater; St. John Hirst in *The Voyage Out* to Lytton Strachey; Ralph Denham in *Night and Day* to Leonard Woolf; Mrs. Flanders in *Jacob's Room* to Mrs. Ethel Grant; Mrs. Dalloway to Kitty Maxse; Sally Seton to Madge Symonds; Mr. and Mrs. Ramsay in *To the Lighthouse* to Leslie and Julia Stephen; Orlando to Vita Sackville-West; Bernard in *The Waves* to Desmond MacCarthy; Louis to T. S. Eliot; and Percival to Thoby Stephen.

Other critics have emphasized the way different characters, like Septimus Smith in *Mrs. Dalloway*, relate to aspects of Woolf's own personality and thus constitute partial self-portraits. Probably her memoir pieces or her diaries parallel a painter's self-portraits more closely than do the characters she creates. Vanessa Bell's self portraits are also partial in that they vary in the degree of verisimilitude. One, painted in c. 1915, is in the loose style characteristic of that period in her work. Her facial features are merely suggested. In 1952 she painted herself at her easel with most of her face shadowed and thus featureless. Both paintings are reproduced in *Vanessa Bell: 1879–1961: A Retrospective Exhibition*. In 1958 she painted herself in a large hat and in a somewhat more detailed style. The portrait is reproduced in *Vanessa Bell: 1879–1961: A Memorial Exhibition of Paintings* (Arts Council 1964); in Shone, *Bloomsbury Portraits*, Illustration 161; and in Spalding, *Vanessa Bell*.

44. Virginia Woolf, *To the Lighthouse: The Original Holograph Draft*, ed. Susan Dick (Toronto: University of Toronto Press, 1982), p. 8.

45. Duncan Grant to Virginia Woolf, May 1927; USL.

46. Roger Fry to Virginia Woolf, May 17, 1927, USL.

47. A partial exception is Henry R. Harrington, "The Central Line Down the Middle of *To the Lighthouse*." "It was Roger Fry," he says, "who supplied Virginia Woolf with Lily's argument against illusionist painting, and Vanessa Bell's paintings supplied evidence for that argument. But beneath the level of its formal composition is the painting's meaning, and that meaning is Virginia Woolf's alone" (p. 364). Gayatri Spivak, in "Unmaking and Making in *To the Lighthouse*," in *Women and Language in Literature and Society*, ed. Sally McConnell-Ginet, Ruth Borker, and Nelly Furman (New York: Praeger, 1980), briefly links Lily's creative process with both Vanessa's and Virginia's (pp. 320–21).

48. For a fuller discussion of the woman artist's inferiority complex as reflected in fiction, see my article, "Virginia Woolf and the 'Reign of Error,'" *Research Studies* 43, no. 4 (December 1975): 222–34.

49. *To the Lighthouse: The Original Holograph Draft*, p. 273.

50. Vanessa Bell to Roger Fry, November 2, 1912; KCL.

51. Vanessa Bell to Duncan Grant, April 21, 1923.

52. Spalding, *Vanessa Bell*, p. 124.

53. Gillespie, "Vanessa Bell, Virginia Woolf, and Duncan Grant," p. 157. See also Anscombe, *Omega and After*, pp. 161–62.

54. Vanessa Bell to Roger Fry, October 2, 1932; KCL. Also quoted in Spalding, *Vanessa Bell*, p. 259.

55. In a letter written in 1936, Vanessa answered a query about contemporary women painters by claiming not to know of many and by providing a short list. It included Therese Lessore, Patricia Preece, Frances Hodgkins, Sophie Fedorovitch, and, among the younger ones, Elizabeth Watson, MacKenzie Smith, and Janie Bussy. The letter is in the Fawcett Women's History Library, London. Vanessa does not mention Winifred Nicholson or Clare Leighton who, along with herself, were among twenty-four artists from England included in an international exhibition in Venice in 1934. (See the *Manchester Guardian*, March 28, 1934.) I am indebted to J. J. Wilson for calling both of these items to my attention.

Kenneth Clark indicates that the dinner service was unlike what they had expected. "Instead of a gay cascade of decoration like the best Savona, Duncan and Vanessa conscientiously produced forty-eight plates each of which contained the portrait of a famous woman (Bloomsbury asserting its status as a matriarchy). These are in effect forty-eight unique paintings by Duncan and Vanessa, for which they made innumerable studies, and which will give posterity a good idea of their style in the '30s." *Another Part of the Wood: A Self-Portrait* (London: John Murray, 1974), p. 248. A few of the rejected plates are at Charleston. Anscombe, *Omega and After*, illus. 49, provides a photograph of several of the plates and a brief comment on them (p. 137). See also Spalding, *Vanessa Bell*, pp. 258–59.

56. Anne Thackeray Ritchie wrote a book about Angelica Kaufmann entitled *Miss Angel*, vol. 8 of *The Collected Works of Miss Thackeray* (London: Smith, Elder, 1876) and dedicated it to Julia Stephen. Whether or not either sister read the book, still among those Virginia inherited from her father (WSUL), both must have heard of Kaufmann while they lived at 22 Hyde Park Gate.

57. Vanessa Bell to Marjorie Snowden, May 3, 1904; KCL. Marjorie Snowden may in fact be the model for some of Lily Briscoe's external characteristics and circumstances.

58. Quoted in Joseph Hone, *The Life of Henry Tonks* (London: William Heinemann, n.d.), p. 45.

59. Vanessa Bell to Marjorie Snowden, January 11, 1905; KCL.

60. Vanessa Bell to Roger Fry, July 3, 1911; KCL.

61. Vanessa Bell to Marjorie Snowden, January 11, 1905; KCL. Judging from Germaine Greer's account of the inhibiting influence Sickert had on the women artists associated with him, Vanessa Bell perhaps was fortunate in her decision. See *The Obstacle Race*, pp. 46–49.

62. Gillespie, "Vanessa Bell, Virginia Woolf, and Duncan Grant," p. 153.

63. Vanessa Bell to Virginia Woolf, March 12, 1909; NYPL.

64. Vanessa Bell to Roger Fry, June 8, August 9, November 16, 1911; October 17, 1912; KCL.

65. Vanessa Bell to Marjorie Snowden, January 11, 1905; KCL.

66. Vanessa Bell to Roger Fry, June 23, 1911; KCL.

67. Vanessa Bell to Roger Fry, February 5, 1913; KCL.

68. Vanessa Bell to Roger Fry, April 1916. Duncan Grant also expressed a desire for a combination of realism and lack of it in a letter to Roger Fry, May 1916; KCL.

69. Vanessa Bell to Roger Fry, 1911; KCL. In 1923, too, she reported that her view of Delacroix was closer to Fry's than Duncan's was (Vanessa Bell to Roger Fry, January 31, 1928; KCL).

70. Vanessa Bell to Roger Fry, January 22, 1913; KCL.

71. Vanessa Bell to Roger Fry, 1912?; KCL.

72. Vanessa Bell to Roger Fry, 1920?; KCL.

73. Vanessa Bell to Roger Fry, 1921; KCL. In *The Obstacle Race* Germaine Greer describes the relationship between Bell and Grant as ideal, "possibly one of the greatest love stories of our time" (p. 57). While considerably more productive than most, the relationship certainly was not the idyll Greer makes it. Elsewhere in her book she recognizes "the easy assumption that is made about closely related male and female painters that the man led and the woman followed, which accords her the status of an imitator, and assumes that differences in outlook are evidence of inferiority or incompetence" (p. 103).

Both sisters had men in their lives who accepted them as artists, but the dynamics of such relationships, as Vanessa Bell's years with Duncan Grant make clear, are complex. Their partnership, the parallel issue of Leonard Woolf's impact upon Virginia Woolf's mental health and productivity, and the sisters' relationships with each other's husbands and lovers are more the province of psychobiography than of this study.

74. Roger Fry to Vanessa Bell, June 18, 1930; KCL.

75. Vanessa Bell to Roger Fry, March 2, 1922, KCL.

76. Duncan Grant to Vanessa Bell, December 6, 1948; KCL.

77. Vanessa Bell to Marjorie Snowden, May 3, 1904; September 18, 1908; KCL.

78. Vanessa Bell to Virginia Woolf, March 19, 1919; NYPL.

79. Vanessa Bell to Virginia Woolf, April 20, 1908; NYPL.

80. Ethel Smyth to Vanessa Bell, December 15, 1933; KCL.

81. The painting, although damaged, still exists. It was sold at Sothebys in July 1980. Vanessa also painted Thoby in 1904, a portrait Virginia admired. See Spalding, *Vanessa Bell*, pp. 34, 40. On several other occasions the sisters portrayed the same people, each in her own medium. Both, for example, produced portraits of Lady Strachey. Bell's portrait, done a few years before her subject's death, depicts the elderly woman as a stern, formidable figure, massive in black, but softened by the single pink, fully opened bloom she holds loosely in her lap. Virginia Woolf also attempted to sum up Lady Strachey. In an obituary piece in 1928, she characterized her as "the type of the Victorian woman at her finest—many-sided, vigorous, adventurous, advanced." Her "large and powerful frame, her strongly marked features" are combined with a "manner that was so cordial, so humorous, and yet perhaps a little formidable" (BP 208).

82. The early draft of the novel includes more specific details from Julia Stephen's life, like her knowledge of painting derived from the Prinsep family and its painter associates. See *To the Lighthouse: The Original Holograph Draft*, pp. 21–22 of the text and p. 21 of Susan Dick's introduction. Dick also mentions the gradual elimination of certain biographical details from Mr. Ramsay's characterization (p. 22).

83. Vanessa Bell, notes Anscombe in *Omega and After*, felt "stifled by all the connections with Victorian conventions. If a house could be made free, through decoration, for family life and for work, then so much the better, even if the final effect was somewhat improvised. This hatred of Victorian interiors, representing claustrophobic family life, was an important binding factor among Vanessa's friends" (p. 66).

84. Appropriately *Orlando*, this fanciful biography of Vita Sackville-West, has some of the Sackville ancestors among its illustrations. "Orlando as a Boy" is "The Honourable Edward Sackville, second son of the [fourth] Earl of Dorset" painted by Cornelius Nuie. "The Archduchess Harriet" is a painting of "Mary, the fourth Countess of Dorset, by Marc Gheeraerts the younger." See Frank Baldanza, "'Orlando' and the Sackvilles," *PMLA* 70 (1955): 278. "Marmaduke Bonthrop Shelmerdine, Esquire," however, is "an anonymous, brightly colored painting, still hanging at Sissinghurst, of a romantic young man" according to Joanne Trautmann, "Orlando and Vita Sackville-West" in *Virginia Woolf*, ed. Thomas S. W. Lewis (New York: McGraw Hill, 1975), p. 92; reprinted from *The Jessamy Brides: The Friendship of Virginia Woolf and Vita Sackville-West* (University Park, Pa.: Pennsylvania State University Press, 1973). The illustrations also include a photograph, taken by Vanessa Bell, of her daughter,

Angelica, posing as "The Russian Princess as a Child." See Bell and Garnett, eds., *Vanessa Bell's Family Album*, p. 94.

85. This type of painting perhaps was suggested to Virginia Woolf by the three nineteenth-century paintings on wood which the Woolfs bought in 1919 at the auction of the contents of Monks House. One of the paintings, Leonard Woolf concluded, was of "the Glazebrook children of a hundred years ago. Their spirits, I almost felt and feel, walk in the house. . . ." See *Downhill All the Way: An Autobiography of the Years 1919 to 1939* (New York: Harcourt Brace Jovanovich, 1967), p. 15.

86. Gainsborough, Reynolds, and Romney often painted female subjects dressed in white or pale colors, holding or wearing flowers or standing near them. Such paintings of virginal women were also common in the work of Rossetti. Whistler's *The White Girl* (1861–62) is in the tradition, although it is also influenced by Gautier's poem "Symphonie en blanc majeur" (1852). See Dennis Farr, *English Art: 1870–1940* (Oxford: Clarendon, 1978), pp. 7–8. Vanessa (and possibly Virginia) would have seen Whistler's painting when Arthur Studd, the painter, invited the Stephen family to his Cheyne Walk rooms (Spalding, *Vanessa Bell*, p. 17).

87. The posthumous exhibition also traveled to Newcastle, Manchester, and Edinburgh; then the painting was exhibited in Dublin in 1906. I have dated the beginning of Watts's work on *Lilian* and the exhibitions with the help of Richard Jefferies of the Watts Gallery, Guildford, Surrey (letter, July 1984). *Lilian* currently is in that gallery. According to Mr. Jefferies (conversation, August 1983) and to the *Sunday Telegraph* (November 7, 1971), Watts originally painted his ward holding a bay laurel wreath, but Mrs. Watts, who did not like what she considered a funeral emblem, substituted the basket of roses. Woolf, who read M. S. Watts's *George Frederick Watts: The Annals of an Artist's Life*, 3 vols. (New York: George H. Doran, n.d.) in 1919 (D I 237), would also have seen an engraved version of the painting reproduced in volume 3. In addition, she may have remembered Julia Margaret Cameron's striking photograph called *The Rosebud Garden of Girls* (1868), in which four young women with flowing hair and loose white robes hold flowers and leaves. In Anne Thackeray Ritchie's *From an Island* (1877), St. Julian, a painter whose works are like Mrs. Cameron's photos, sets up a picture for Mr. Hexham, an amateur photographer. The scene is a Tennysonian "dream of fair ladies against an ivy wall, flowers and flowing locks, and sweeping garments." See Ann Wilsher and Benjamin Spear, "'A Dream of Fair Ladies': Mrs. Cameron Disguised," *History of Photography* 7, no. 2 (April–June 1983): 118–20. Woolf's copies of Anne Thackeray Ritchie's works, including *From an Island*, are in WSUL.

88. The portrait of the young Mrs. Pargiter smiles down during the 1880 section of the novel. Watts, who was born in 1817, began exhibiting in 1837, and subsequently painted many portraits, fits the time frame. Similarly Kitty Lasswade, who in 1914 looks at the painting done in her youth, could have been painted by an older Watts.

89. For an insightful discussion of the language theme in the novel and of Miss LaTrobe's modernism, see Sallie Sears, "The Theater of War: Virginia Woolf's *Between the Acts*," in *Virginia Woolf: A Feminist Slant*, ed. Jane Marcus (Lincoln: University of Nebraska Press, 1983), pp. 212–35.

90. See Maria Di Battista, "Joyce, Woolf and the Modern Mind," in Clements and Grundy, eds., *Virginia Woolf: New Critical Essays*, p. 112. Di Battista associates

the painting of the ancestor with "Joyce's garrulous virility and its generative improvidences" and the painting of the long lady with "Woolf's 'feminine' reticence and its sustaining economies." Together they represent the "two masterly styles that have come to define the modern temper."

91. Spalding, *Vanessa Bell*, p. 75.

92. Virginia Woolf, *Pointz Hall: The Earlier and Later Typescripts of Between the Acts*, ed. Mitchell A. Leaska (N.Y.: New York University Publications, 1983), p. 98.

93. Virginia Woolf, "Pictures," *The Moment and Other Essays* (London: Hogarth, 1947), p. 143.

94. Woolf probably knew the two winter scenes with skaters by Hendrick Avercamp, purchased by the National Gallery in the 1890s.

95. The Dutch painter Woolf may have had in mind is Van Eyck or Vermeer. In 1909 Virginia wrote to Vanessa from Dresden that she had seen a painting by Vermeer. "I love it," she wrote (L I 410–11). She may also have known Vermeer's *Young Woman Standing at a Virginal* and *Young Woman Seated at a Virginal*, purchased by the National Gallery in 1892 and 1910 respectively. The National Gallery also owns Van Eyck's well-known painting of *The Arnolfini Marriage*. Two years after the publication of *Mrs. Dalloway*, Roger Fry's *Flemish Art: A Critical Survey* (London: Chatto and Windus, 1927) emphasized the Flemish uncritical enjoyment of everyday life. See, for example, pp. 2, 5, 9. A copy of this book, inscribed to Virginia by the author, is in the HRHRC.

96. Maurice Beebe, *Ivory Towers and Sacred Founts: The Artist as Hero from Goethe to Joyce* (New York: New York University Press, 1964), p. v.

97. Spalding mentions several painters who worked at St. Ives when the Stephens spent their summers there. Julius Olsson, "famous for his nocturnal seascapes," and his fellow marine painters were among them. Whistler came one winter with assistants, one of whom was Sickert. *Vanessa Bell*, pp. 11–12.

98. Woolf's reference to "cattle standing absorbing moisture in sunset pools" recalls the seventeenth-century paintings of Aelbert Cuyp of Dordrecht, which she could easily have seen in the National Gallery; but she is more likely to have had Edwin Landseer, R. A., in mind again. His *Monarch of the Glen*, which depicts a stag, antlered head and foreleg raised, was well-known in the Victorian era.

99. Steiner, *Exact Resemblance to Exact Resemblance*, pp. 5–11, mentions several such motivations.

5 — STILL LIFE IN WORDS AND PAINT

1. S. P. Rosenbaum, "The Philosophical Realism of Virginia Woolf," *English Literature and British Philosophy*, ed. S. P. Rosenbaum (Chicago: University of Chicago Press, 1971), p. 321.

2. G. E. Moore, *Principia Ethica* (Cambridge: Cambridge University Press, 1968; first published 1903), pp. 188–89.

3. Rosenbaum, "The Philosophical Realism of Virginia Woolf," pp. 318–19. Mark Hussey's *The Singing of the Real World: The Philosophy of Virginia Woolf's Fiction* (Columbus: Ohio State University Press, 1986) is a more recent study of Woolf's

view of reality. Alex Zwerdling's *Virginia Woolf and the Real World* (Berkeley: University of California Press, 1986) deals with reality in social-historical rather than in philosophical terms.

4. See *Sowing: An Autobiography of the Years 1880–1904* (New York: Harcourt Brace Jovanovich, 1960), pp. 131–49, 156–57, for Leonard Woolf's early contacts with Moore and for Keynes' "wrong" conclusions about Moore's influence. Two articles by Moore are among the books the Woolfs owned, now in WSUL: "The Refutation of Idealism" (1904) has "L. S. Woolf May 1904" inscribed on the title page. "The Nature and Reality of Objects of Perception" (1906) contains a letter from Moore to Leonard Woolf complaining about the difficulty of writing philosophy and anticipating his reader's disappointment in this latest effort.

5. Paul Levy, *Moore: G. E. Moore and the Cambridge Apostles* (New York: Holt, Rinehart and Winston, 1979), p. 275.

6. Or so J. K. Johnstone identifies it in "Bloomsbury Philosophy," *The Bloomsbury Group: A Study of E. M. Forster, Lytton Strachey, Virginia Woolf, and Their Circle* (New York: Noonday, 1963), p. 20.

7. Leonard Woolf, *Beginning Again: An Autobiography of the Years 1911 to 1918* (New York: Harcourt Brace Jovanovich, 1964), p. 25.

8. Spalding, *Vanessa Bell* (London: Weidenfeld and Nicolson, 1983), p. 66.

9. Rosenbaum, "The Philosophical Realism of Virginia Woolf," p. 339.

10. Levy, *Moore*, p. 15, footnote. Contrast Leonard Woolf's account in *Beginning Again*, pp. 24–25: Fry was "'under the surface' a Moorist." Vanessa and Duncan, along with Clive and Virginia "were deeply affected by the astringent influence of Moore." Vanessa Bell, in her "Notes on Bloomsbury" in S. P. Rosenbaum, ed., *The Bloomsbury Group: A Collection of Memoirs, Commentary, and Criticism* (Toronto: University of Toronto Press, 1975), p. 77, says of the young men from Cambridge, "I had never read their prophet G. E. Moore, nor I think had Virginia, but that didn't prevent one from trying to find out what one thought about good or anything else." The men, she adds, wanted the opinions of "young women who might possibly see things from a different angle."

11. Roger Fry's comments are in his introduction to *The Catalogue of the Second Post-Impressionist Exhibition* (London: Ballantyne, 1912), p. 26. Vanessa's copy is in the Woolf Library; WSUL.

12. Spalding, *Vanessa Bell*, p. 125.

13. See Jaakko Hintikka, "Virginia Woolf and our Knowledge of the External World," *Journal of Aesthetics and Art Criticism* 38, no. 1 (Fall 1979): 5–14. See also William Herman's discussion of "Virginia Woolf and the Classics: Every Englishman's Prerogative Transmuted into Fictional Art," in *Virginia Woolf: Centennial Essays*, ed. Elaine K. Ginsberg and Laura Moss Gottlieb (Troy, N.Y.: Whitston, 1983), pp. 257–68.

14. Brenda R. Silver, ed., *Virginia Woolf's Reading Notebooks* (Princeton, N.J.: Princeton University Press, 1983), p. 194.

15. Denys Sutton, ed., *Letters of Roger Fry*, 2 vols. (London: Chatto and Windus, 1972), 2:598. The letter is to Marie Mauron, whose husband, Charles, had just translated into French the "Time Passes" section of *To the Lighthouse*. It appeared in *Commerce* 10 (hiver 1926): 91–133. Fry adds that the passage from Woolf is "better in the translation, because in translation everything is slightly reduced, less accentuated, and in general better."

16. Roger Fry, *Reflections on British Painting* (Freeport, N.Y.: Books for Libraries, 1969; first published 1934), p. 24.

17. Ibid., p. 26.

18. Roger Fry, *Cézanne: A Study of His Development* (London: Hogarth, 1927), p. 41.

19. Fry, *Reflections on British Painting*, p. 26.

20. Frances Spalding, *Vanessa Bell: 1879–1961: An Exhibition to Celebrate the Centenary of the Artist's Birth* (Sheffield City Art Galleries, 1979), p. 4; Richard Shone, *Bloomsbury Portraits: Vanessa Bell, Duncan Grant and Their Circle* (Oxford: Phaidon, 1976), p. 30. The painting is reproduced in color in Frances Spalding, *Vanessa Bell* (London: Weidenfeld and Nicolson, 1983).

21. Spalding, *Vanessa Bell*, pp. 82, 171. Making a private symbolist of Bell, Spalding wonders if the trios in the painting, especially the one poppy separated by color from the other two, reflect Vanessa's jealousy of Virginia, who was flirting with Clive during this period. Virginia also used triads in *To the Lighthouse* (three parts) and *The Waves* (three men, three women), but I would not necessarily attribute them to love triangles in her life.

22. Shone identifies the painting as such (letter, September 9, 1981). *A Tin Pan* was shown at Heal's in London, October 8–26, 1917, at an exhibition called "The New Movement in Art."

23. Vanessa Bell to Roger Fry, April 11, 1920; KCL.

24. Vanessa Bell to Roger Fry, February 18, 1921; KCL.

25. Vanessa Bell to Roger Fry, February 5, 1913; 1915?; 1917?; KCL.

26. As Shone, *Bloomsbury Portraits*, p. 136, and Spalding, *Vanessa Bell*, p. 153, point out. *Still Life with Beer Bottle* is reproduced in Shone's book (Illustration 82) as is *46 Gordon Square* (Illustration 27). For a discussion of both sisters' interests in views from windows, see chapter 6.

27. Clive Bell, *Civilization and Old Friends* (Chicago: University of Chicago Press, 1973; *Civilization* was first published in 1928, *Old Friends* in 1956), p. 113.

28. Vanessa Bell, lecture at Leighton Park School (1925); unpublished typescript; AG. Clive Bell in "The English Group," *Catalogue of the Second Post-Impressionist Exhibition*, p. 22, had already used the coal scuttle to explain the Post-Impressionist painters' attitude towards objects. So Fry in *The Artist and Psychoanalysis* (London: Hogarth, 1924), p. 16, says, "Rembrandt expressed his profoundest feelings just as well when he painted a carcass hanging up in a butcher's shop as when he painted the Crucifixion or his mistress. Cézanne . . . expressed some of his grandest conceptions in pictures of fruit and crockery on a common kitchen table."

29. Jack F. Stewart in "Spatial Form and Color in *The Waves*," *Twentieth-Century Literature* 28 (1982): 99, points out that "the post-impressionist still life" recurs in Woolf's novels.

30. Richard Shone dates the floral painting in this way. My thanks to him and to Peter Miall of the National Trust for getting the information for me (letter, October 22, 1984). Isabelle Anscombe identifies the fireplace as probably Vanessa's and reproduces it in color in *Omega and After: Bloomsbury and the Decorative Arts* (London: Thames and Hudson, 1981), Figure 11. Monks House also contains Omega chairs with flowers needlepointed on the backs, like those in the music room designed by Vanessa Bell and Duncan Grant and exhibited at the Lefevre Gallery, London, in 1932–33. See Anscombe, Figure 40.

31. Vanessa Bell to Roger Fry, August 15, 1930?; KCL.

32. Richard Morphet, "The Art of Vanessa Bell," *Vanessa Bell: Paintings and Drawings* (London: Anthony d'Offay, 1973), pp. 9–10, 12. As Anscombe notes in *Omega and After*, p. 108, these "vases of arching flowers" first appear at Charleston on Duncan's bedroom doors; Vanessa painted them in 1916. They proliferate in the decorative work of both artists in the twenties.

33. Henri Matisse, "Jazz" (1947), in *Matisse on Art*, ed. Jack D. Flam (London: Phaidon, 1973), p. 111. Proust says of the roses painted by Elstir in *Remembrance of Things Past* that they are "a new variety with which this painter, like some clever horticulturist, had enriched the rose family." Quoted in Gaston Bachelard, *The Poetics of Space*, trans. Marie Jolas (N.Y.: Orion, 1964), p. xxix.

34. Vanessa Bell, lecture at Leighton Park School. Roger Fry, in "The French Group," *Catalogue of the Second Post-Impressionist Exhibition*, p. 25, makes a similar point.

35. An early name for Rachel Vinrace in *The Voyage Out* was "Rose"; that name and a later one Woolf chose for her heroine, "Cynthia," the Elizabethans associated with "a kind of stunted sexuality" and self destruction. See Louise DeSalvo, *Virginia Woolf's First Voyage: A Novel in the Making* (Totowa, N.J.: Rowman and Littlefield, 1980), pp. 22–23. Isobel Grundy notes that Rhoda's name in *The Waves* is "Greek for *rose*." See "'Words Without Meaning—Wonderful Words': Virginia Woolf's Choice of Names," in *Virginia Woolf: New Critical Essays*, eds. Patricia Clements and Isobel Grundy (London: Vision, 1983), p. 217. Barbara Seward, in *The Symbolic Rose* (New York: Columbia University Press, 1960), pp. 127–31, considers briefly Woolf's variable use of this flower in her novels. Seward concludes that "Virginia Woolf's earlier roses of personal fulfillment had blossomed only in delicate moments of ecstatic intuition. They were, like their author herself, bound to decline and then cease to endure in a world that crushes the finer perceptions beneath the weight of war" (p. 131).

36. The other was *Between the Acts* (1941).

37. *Sir Leslie Stephen's Mausoleum Book*, ed. Alan Bell (Oxford: Clarendon, 1977), p. 62.

38. Germaine Greer, *The Obstacle Race: The Fortunes of Women Painters and Their Work* (New York: Farrar Straus Giroux, 1979), pp. 248–49.

39. Max J. Friedländer, *Landscape, Portrait, Still-Life: Their Origin and Development* (New York: Schocken, 1965), p. 281; Ann Sutherland Harris and Linda Nochlin, *Women Artists: 1550–1950* (New York: Knopf, 1976), pp. 59–61.

40. Greer, *The Obstacle Race*, pp. 248–49.

41. Leonard Woolf, *Downhill All the Way: An Autobiography of the Years 1919 to 1939* (New York: Harcourt Brace Jovanovich, 1967), pp. 79–80.

42. Virginia Woolf's first two novels were published by Duckworth. Vanessa Bell did designs for all of her sister's books published by the Hogarth Press except for *Orlando* (1928) and *Letter to a Young Poet* (1932). Vanessa Bell may have decorated a set of plates illustrating *Orlando*, possibly for Vita Sackville-West; unfortunately, none now remain (L V 355). She also did what Richard Kennedy calls "a very stylish typographical design for the Uniform Edition" of Woolf's works which the Hogarth Press began publishing in 1929. See *A Boy at the Hogarth Press* (London: Heinemann, 1972), p. 80, as well as L IV 67. All of the dust-jacket designs discussed here are

available in the WSUL, except for *Between the Acts*, *Roger Fry: A Biography*, and *Virginia Woolf and Lytton Strachey: Letters*.

43. Vanessa Bell to Virginia Woolf, June 27, 1929; NYPL. I saw several of Vanessa Bell's sketches for dust-jacket designs at the Anthony d'Offay Gallery in 1978.

44. Quoted in John Lehmann, *Thrown to the Woolfs* (London: Weidenfeld and Nicolson, 1978), p. 27. Lehmann includes the quotation in his discussion of *The Waves*. The letter, NYPL, however, is tentatively dated August 2, 1932. John Lehmann stresses these procedures to counter any notion that Vanessa Bell's jackets are "an integral part of Virginia's books" (p. 27).

45. *Downhill All the Way*, p. 76.

46. As Jean Peters, a collector of Hogarth Press books, notes. See "Publishers' Imprints," in *Collectible Books: Some New Paths*, ed. Jean Peters (New York: R. R. Bowker, 1979), p. 214.

47. *Downhill All the Way*, pp. 76–77.

48. The portrait of Iris Tree (1915) is a good example. It is reproduced in Shone, *Bloomsbury Portraits*, color plate V. Shone also reproduces a sketch for the portrait of Lady Strachey (p. 41). The painting (c. 1925), in which the subject also is dressed in black and holds a full-blown pink rose, is at Charleston. As Linda Nochlin notes in *Women Artists: 1550–1950* (co-authored with Ann Sutherland Harris [New York: Knopf, 1976], p. 284), Matisse's portraits often exhibited a similar simplification and flattening of figures dressed in dark clothing against more brightly colored backgrounds. Nochlin also reproduces the portrait of Iris Tree in black and white (figure 121).

49. See, for example, the painting of Duncan Grant and Henri Doucet in the studio (1912) and *Street Corner Conversation* (1918).

50. Henri Matisse, "Black is a Colour" (1946), in Flam, ed., *Matisse on Art*, p. 106. Critics frequently note the influence of Matisse on Vanessa Bell's early paintings. See, for example, Shone, "Vanessa Bell," in *Vanessa Bell: 1879–1961*, p. 3, and Richard Morphet, "The Art of Vanessa Bell," p. 9.

51. Paul Rand, "Black in the Visual Arts," in *Graphic Forms: The Arts as Related to the Book* (Cambridge: Harvard University Press, 1949), pp. 35–42.

52. A drawing for this dust jacket includes a pair of woman's dancing slippers in addition to the fan and the bouquet. The white shape, in this earlier rendition, has straight rather than curved edges and seven black ovals rather than five within it. See Lehmann, *Virginia Woolf and Her World* (New York: Harcourt Brace Jovanovich, 1975), p. 50.

53. Other dust-jacket designs that have the quality of pen-and-ink drawings are *The Death of the Moth* (1942) and *Between the Acts* (1941). Bell also used the combination of black and pink for her *A Room of One's Own* (1929) design. In addition to the instances discussed, flowers appear on the jackets for *The Waves* (1931), *A Haunted House and Other Stories* (1943), and *The Common Reader*.

6—LANDSCAPES OF THE MIND AND EYE

1. Richard Shone, *Bloomsbury Portraits: Vanessa Bell, Duncan Grant and Their Circle* (London: Phaidon, 1976), p. 75.

2. Ibid., p. 79.

3. Kenneth Clark, *Landscape into Art* (London: John Murray, 1976), p. 168, points out, however, that an artist with "a consistent personal style" does not reveal whether his or her paintings were done "direct from nature." In the case of the Impressionists, the "mode of vision and not the physical fact of being out of doors" created the impact.

4. Vanessa Bell to Roger Fry, August 15, 1930; KCL.

5. Vanessa Bell to Roger Fry, September 16, 1921; KCL.

6. Vanessa Bell to Roger Fry, September 11, 1925; KCL.

7. Vanessa Bell to Roger Fry, September 13, 1928?; KCL.

8. Vanessa Bell to Roger Fry, April 25, 1929; KCL.

9. Ibid.

10. Vanessa Bell to Maynard Keynes, December 6, 1921; December 17, 1921; 1914; 1925?; KCL.

11. See, for example, Vanessa Bell to Roger Fry, April 5, 1922; September 4, 1912; 1915?; KCL.

12. For a discussion of the tradition within which Woolf's thinking on the subject of art imitating nature occurs, see Tzvetan Todorov, "The Romantic Crisis," *Theories of Symbol*, trans. Catherine Porter (Ithaca, N.Y.: Cornell University Press, 1982), pp. 147–221.

13. Jack F. Stewart, "Historical Impressionism in *Orlando*," *Studies in the Novel* 5 (Spring 1973): 71–85, discusses in some detail the treatment of landscape in Woolf's mock biography.

14. "Portraits of Places" was an unsigned article in *The Guardian*, October 3, 1906, p. 1631. S. P. Rosenbaum called my attention to this previously unidentified piece. Since then, it has been reprinted in the *Virginia Woolf Miscellany* 26 (Spring 1986): 3–4, and in *The Essays of Virginia Woolf*, vol. 1 (1904–1912), ed. Andrew McNeillie (London: Hogarth, 1986), pp. 124–27.

15. *Letters of Roger Fry*, 2 vols., ed. Denys Sutton (London: Chatto and Windus, 1972) 2:534. In a letter to Gerald Brenan dated October 27, 1933, however, Fry praises Brenan's landscape descriptions as more like the visual artist's than Virginia Woolf's (*Letters of Roger Fry* 2:684).

16. Vanessa Bell to Virginia Woolf, August 26, 1910; NYPL.

17. Vanessa Bell to Virginia Woolf, September 2, 1909; NYPL.

18. "Lecture given at Leighton Park," 1925, unpublished typescript; AG.

19. Ibid.

20. Roger Fry, "Vanessa Bell and Othon Friesz," *The New Statesman* 19, June 3, 1922, p. 237. For Fry's changing views on the importance of color in painting, see Jacqueline V. Falkenheim, *Roger Fry and the Beginnings of Formalist Art Criticism* (Ann Arbor, Mich.: UMI Research Press, 1980), pp. 96, 100, 103.

21. Fry, "Vanessa Bell and Othon Friesz," p. 238.

22. Paul Roche, *With Duncan Grant in Southern Turkey* (London: Honeyglen, 1982), p. 2.

23. *Vanessa Bell: 1879–1961: An Exhibition to Celebrate the Centenary of the Artist's Birth* (Sheffield City Art Galleries, 1979), p. 7.

24. See Ronald Pickvance, "Introduction," *Vanessa Bell: 1879–1961: A Memorial Exhibition of Paintings* (Arts Council, 1964) pp. 6–7; Neville Wallis, "Vanessa Bell and Bloomsbury," *The Connoisseur* 156 (August 1964): 247–49; and Richard Shone, "Vanessa Bell," *Vanessa Bell: 1879–1961: A Retrospective Exhibition* (New York: Davis and Long, 1980), pp. 3–5.

25. G. E. Moore, "The Refutation of Idealism," *Mind: A Quarterly Review of Psychology and Philosophy* 12, no. 48 (1903): 14. Leonard Woolf's offprint is in WSUL.

26. See S. P. Rosenbaum, "The Philosophical Realism of Virginia Woolf," *English Literature and British Philosophy*, ed. S. P. Rosenbaum (Chicago: University of Chicago Press, 1971), p. 323, and Madeline Moore, "Nature and Community: A Study of Cyclical Reality in *The Waves*," *Virginia Woolf: Revaluation and Continuity*, ed. Ralph Freedman (Berkeley: University of California Press, 1980), p. 225.

27. "Blue and Green" was eliminated from *A Haunted House and Other Stories* (1944). It has been reprinted in the *Virginia Woolf Miscellany* 22 (Spring 1984), 5. See also Rosenbaum, "The Philosophical Realism of Virginia Woolf," p. 323.

28. See Ellen Hawkes, ed., *Friendships Gallery* by Virginia Woolf, *Twentieth Century Literature* 25 (1979): 272.

29. *Virginia Woolf's Reading Notebooks*, ed. Brenda R. Silver (Princeton, N.J.: Princeton University Press, 1983), p. 13.

30. Vanessa Bell to Roger Fry, no date, c. 1925; KCL.

31. Max J. Friedländer, *Landscape, Portrait, Still-Life: Their Origin and Development* (New York: Schocken, 1965), p. 133. James A. W. Heffernan, in "The English Romantic Perception of Color," *Images of Romanticism: Verbal and Visual Affinities*, ed. Karl Kroeber and William Walling (New Haven: Yale University Press, 1978), p. 140, contrasts the Augustan view of color "firmly regulated by the decisiveness and divisiveness of line" to the Romantic refusal to "circumscribe the vitality and spontaneity of colors." Peter and Margaret Harvard-Williams, in "Perceptive Contemplation in the Work of Virginia Woolf," *English Studies* 35 (1954): 97–116, note "the heightened perception of colour" in Woolf's fiction (110). See also Allen McLaurin, *Virginia Woolf: The Echoes Enslaved* (Cambridge: Cambridge University Press, 1973), pp. 70–84, and Jack F. Stewart, "Spatial Form and Color in *The Waves*," *Twentieth-Century Literature* 28 (1982): 90–93. Ezra Pound had a similar experience of the world as color which he described in *Gaudier-Brzeska: A Memior* (London: Marvell, 1960; first published 1916), p. 87. Virginia Woolf read this memoir in 1917 (D I 90).

32. James Naremore uses Bernard's perception as the title and controling idea for his study, *The World Without a Self: Virginia Woolf and the Novel* (New Haven: Yale University Press, 1973). He does not relate the perception to painting.

33. Peter Stowell, in *Literary Impressionism, James and Chekhov* (Athens: University of Georgia Press, 1980), p. 25, points out that one way literary impressionism parallels the "innocence of eye" of the Impressionist painters is by presenting children or young, inexperienced people responding to situations.

34. Peter Coveney, *The Image of Childhood*, rev. ed. (Baltimore: Penguin, 1967), p. 314. Coveney characterizes this response as "sensuous, dreamy, non-intellectual, and unrelated to external realities." One should add to these qualities, which Coveney overstates, freshness and spontaneity.

35. Isabelle Anscombe, *Omega and After: Bloomsbury and the Decorative Arts* (London: Thames and Hudson, 1981), p. 53. Roger Fry was also fascinated with children's perceptions and with their drawings. See Anscombe, p. 75; Falkenheim, *Roger Fry*, pp. 93–94.

36. See chapter 1.

37. Vanessa Bell to Roger Fry, August 18, 1932?; KCL.

38. Vanessa Bell to Roger Fry, August 15, 1930; KCL.

39. Other people have labeled her, however, and used the term in a variety of ways. See, for example, Mario Praz, *Mnemosyne: The Parallel Between Literature and the Visual Arts* (Princeton, N.J.: Princeton University Press, 1974), p. 188; Jack F. Stewart, "Impressionism in the Early Novels of Virginia Woolf," *Journal of Modern Literature* 9, no. 2 (1982): 237–66; and Jean Alexander, *The Venture of Form in the Novels of Virginia Woolf* (Port Washington, N.Y.: Kennikat, 1974), p. 223.

40. A number of art historians note the influence of Whistler on Vanessa Bell. See, for example, Spalding, *Vanessa Bell: 1879–1961*, p. 2; and Shone, *Bloomsbury Portraits*, pp. 20, 22, 23.

41. Owned by Virginia Woolf, this painting was hung first in London and then, when the Woolfs moved their belongings from the city during the World War II air raids, at Monks House. My thanks to Mrs. Trekkie Parsons for this information.

42. Fry, "Vanessa Bell and Othon Friesz," p. 238.

43. Vanessa Bell to Roger Fry, August 30, 1920?; KCL.

44. The painting is reproduced in Shone, *Bloomsbury Portraits*, Illustration 151.

45. A window also appears in Vanessa Bell's design for *Mr. Bennett and Mrs. Brown*.

46. See, for example, James Naremore, "Nature and History in *The Years*," in Ralph Freedman, ed., *Virginia Woolf: Revaluation and Continuity* (Berkeley: University of California Press, 1980), p. 246, and Dorothy Brewster on *Night and Day* in *Virginia Woolf's London* (Westport, Conn.: Greenwood, 1979), p. 33.

47. "For me," Matisse writes in a state of mind similar to Woolf's, "the space is one unity from the horizon right to the interior of my work room, and . . . the boat which is going past exists in the same space as the familiar objects around me; and the wall with the window does not create two different worlds." See *Matisse on Art*, ed. Jack D. Flam (London: Phaidon, 1973), p. 93.

48. For a discussion of the metaphorical nature of the term "stream of consciousness" and some alternative metaphors, see my "May Sinclair and the Stream of Consciousness: Metaphors and Metaphysics," *English Literature in Transition* 21, no. 2 (1978): 134–42.

49. Clive Bell to Vanessa Bell, November 3, 1931; KCL.

50. Praz, *Mnemosyne*, refers specifically to *The Waves*, p. 188. See also Peter and Margaret Harvard-Williams, "Perceptive Contemplation," p. 112.

51. Madeline Moore, "Nature and Community," p. 227, notes the "common structure" of these passages.

52. Henry R. Harrington, "The Central Line Down the Middle of *To the Lighthouse*," *Contemporary Literature* 21 (1980): 373–75, deals with the two points of view in Bell's *The Tub*.

CONCLUSION—DESTRUCTION AND CREATION

1. Quentin Bell, *Virginia Woolf: A Biography*, 2 vols. (London: Hogarth, 1973), 2:218.

2. Frances Spalding, *Vanessa Bell* (London: Weidenfeld & Nicolson, 1983), p. 316.

3. Ibid. Spalding quotes Peter Quennell's description of the wreckage.

4. "Anon," ed. Brenda Silver, *Twentieth Century Literature* 25, nos. 3/4 (Fall/Winter 1979): 403.

5. "Notes for Reading at Random," ed. Brenda Silver, *Twentieth Century Literature* 25, nos. 3/4 (Fall/Winter 1979): 377.

6. Virginia Woolf, "Pictures and Portraits," *The Athenaeum* 1 (January 9, 1920): 46.

Selected Bibliography

Abel, Elizabeth, ed. *Writing and Sexual Difference*. Chicago: University of Chicago Press, 1982.

Alexander, Jean. *The Venture of Form in the Novels of Virginia Woolf*. Port Washington, N.Y.: Kennikat, 1974.

Annan, Noel. *Leslie Stephen: His Thought and Character in Relation to His Time*. London: MacGibbon and Kee, 1951.

Anscombe, Isabelle. *Omega and After: Bloomsbury and the Decorative Arts*. London: Thames and Hudson, 1982.

Arnheim, Rudolf. *Visual Thinking*. Berkeley: University of California Press, 1969.

Bachelard, Gaston. *The Poetics of Space*. Translated by Marie Jolas. New York: Orion, 1964.

Baldanza, Frank. "'Orlando' and the Sackvilles." *PMLA* 70 (1955): 274–79.

Baron, Wendy. *Sickert*. London: Phaidon, 1973.

Bazin, Nancy. *Virginia Woolf and the Androgynous Vision*. New Brunswick, N.J.: Rutgers University Press, 1973.

Beach, Joseph Warren. "Expressionism: Woolf, Frank," in *The Twentieth Century Novel: Studies in Technique*, pp. 485–93. New York: Century, 1932.

Beebe, Maurice. *Ivory Towers and Sacred Founts: The Artist as Hero from Goethe to Joyce*. New York: New York University Press, 1964.

Bell, Clive. *Art*. New York: Capricorn Books, 1958; first published 1913.

———. *Civilization and Old Friends*. Chicago: University of Chicago Press, 1973. *Civilization* first published in 1928, *Old Friends* in 1956.

———. "The English Group." In *Catalogue of the Second Post-Impressionist Exhibition*. London: Ballantyne, 1912.

Bell, Quentin. *Victorian Artists*. Cambridge: Harvard University Press, 1967.

———. *Virginia Woolf: A Biography*. 2 vols. London: Hogarth, 1973.

———. "Virginia Woolf, Her Politics." *Virginia Woolf Miscellany*, 20 (Spring 1983): 2.

Bell, Quentin, and Angelica Garnett, eds. *Vanessa Bell's Family Album*. London: Jill Norman and Hobhouse, 1981.

Bell, Vanessa. *Notes on Virginia's Childhood*. Edited by Richard F. Schaubeck, Jr. New York: F. Hallman, 1974.

———. "Notes on Bloomsbury." In *The Bloomsbury Group: A Collection of Memoirs, Commentary and Criticism*, edited by S. P. Rosenbaum, pp.73–84. Toronto: University of Toronto Press, 1975.

Bernikow, Louise. *Among Women*. New York: Harper, 1981.

Bradbury, Malcolm. "Putting in the Person: Character and Abstraction in Current Writing and Painting." In *The Contemporary English Novel*, edited by Malcolm Bradbury and David Palmer, pp. 181–208. Stratford-Upon-Avon Studies 18. New York: Holmes and Meier, 1979.

Bradbury, Malcolm, and James McFarlane, eds. *Modernism: 1890–1930*. Sussex: Harvester, 1978.

Brewster, Dorothy. "Fiction: Shaping the Globe." In *Virginia Woolf*, pp. 79–161. New York: New York University Press, 1962.

———. *Virginia Woolf's London*. Westport, Conn.: Greenwood, 1979.

Burne-Jones, Georgiana. *Memorials of Edward Burne-Jones*. 2 vols. London: Macmillan, 1904.

Cameron, Julia Margaret. *Victorian Photographs of Famous Men and Fair Women*. London: Hogarth, 1926.

Chesterton, G. K. *G. F. Watts*. London: Duckworth, 1906.

Clark, Kenneth. *Another Part of the Wood: A Self-Portrait*. London: John Murray, 1974.

———. *Landscape into Art*. London: John Murray, 1976.

Clements, Patricia, and Isobel Grundy, eds. *Virginia Woolf: New Critical Essays*. London: Vision Press, 1983.

Clutton-Brock, Alan. "Vanessa Bell and Her Circle." *The Listener*, May 4, 1961, 790.

Collins, Judith. *The Omega Workshops*. Chicago: University of Chicago Press, 1984.

Concise Catalogue of British Paintings. Vol. 2. Manchester: Manchester City Art Gallery, 1978.

Coveney, Peter. *The Image of Childhood*. Rev. ed. Baltimore, Md.: Penguin, 1967.

DeSalvo, Louise A. *Virginia Woolf's First Voyage: A Novel in the Making*. Totowa, N.J.: Roman and Littlefield, 1980.

Dowling, David. *Bloomsbury Aesthetics and the Novels of Forster and Woolf*. New York: St. Martin's, 1985.

Edel, Leon. *Bloomsbury: A House of Lions*. Philadelphia: J. B. Lippincott, 1979.

Falkenheim, Jacqueline. *Roger Fry and the Beginnings of Formalist Art Criticism*. Ann Arbor, Mich.: UMI Research Press, 1980.

Farr, Dennis. *English Art: 1870–1940*. Oxford: Clarendon, 1978.

Fishel, Elizabeth. *Sisters: Love and Rivalry Inside the Family and Beyond*. New York: William Morrow, 1979.

Fishman, Solomon. *The Interpretation of Art: Essays on the Art Criticism of John Ruskin, Walter Pater, Clive Bell, Roger Fry, and Herbert Read*. Berkeley: University of California Press, 1963.

Flam, Jack, ed. *Matisse on Art*. London: Phaidon, 1973.

Fleishman, Avrom. *Virginia Woolf: A Critical Reading*. Baltimore, Md.: Johns Hopkins University Press, 1975.

Frank, Joseph. "Spatial Form in Modern Literature." *Sewanee Review* 53 (1945): 221–40; 433–56; 643–53.

———. "Spatial Form: An Answer to Critics" and "Spatial Form: Some Further Reflections." *Critical Inquiry* 4 (1977–78): 231–52, and 5 (1978–79): 275–90.

Freedman, Ralph, ed. *Virginia Woolf: Revaluation and Continuity*. Berkeley: University of California Press, 1980.

Friedländer, Max J. *Landscape, Portrait, Still-Life: Their Origin and Development*. New York: Schocken, 1965.

Fry, Roger. *The Artist and Psychoanalysis*. London: Hogarth, 1924.

———. *Cézanne: A Study of His Development*. London: Hogarth, 1927.

———. *Flemish Art: A Critical Survey*. London: Chatto and Windus, 1927.

———. "Introduction." In *The Catalogue of the Second Post-Impressionist Exhibition*. London: Ballantyne, 1912.

———. *Reflections on British Painting*. Freeport, N.Y.: Books for Libraries, 1969; first published 1934.

———. *Transformations: Critical and Speculative Essays on Art*. Freeport, N.Y.: Books for Libraries, 1968; first published 1927.

———. "Vanessa Bell and Othon Friesz." *The New Statesman* 19 (June 3, 1922): 237.

Garnett, Angelica. *Deceived with Kindness: A Bloomsbury Childhood*. London: Chatto and Windus, Hogarth, 1984.

Garnett, David. *The Flowers of the Forest*. New York: Harcourt, Brace, 1955.

———. "Virginia Woolf." *The American Scholar* (Summer 1965): 371–86.

Garvey, Eleanor, and Peter Wick. *The Art of the French Book: 1900–1965*. Dallas, Texas: Southern Methodist University Press, 1967.

Gilbert, Sandra M. "The Battle of the Books/The Battle of the Sexes: Virginia Woolf's *Vita Nuova*." *Michigan Quarterly Review* 23, 2 (Spring 1984): 171–95.

———. "Costumes of the Mind: Transvestism as Metaphor in Modern Literature." *Critical Inquiry* 7 (Winter 1980): 391–417.

Gillespie, Diane. "May Sinclair and the Stream of Consciousness: Metaphors and Metaphysics." *English Literature in Transition* 21, 2 (1978): 134–42.

———. "'Oh to be a Painter!': Virginia Woolf as an Art Critic." *Studies in the Humanities* 10, 1 (June 1983): 28–38.

———. "Political Aesthetics: Virginia Woolf and Dorothy Richardson." In *Virginia Woolf: A Feminist Slant*, edited by Jane Marcus, pp. 132–51. Lincoln, Neb.: University of Nebraska Press, 1983.

———. "Vanessa Bell, Virginia Woolf, and Duncan Grant: Conversation with Angelica Garnett." *Modernist Studies* 3, 3 (1979): 151–58.

———. "Virginia Woolf and the 'Reign of Error.'" *Research Studies* 43, 4 (December 1975): 222–34.

———. "Virginia Woolf's Miss LaTrobe: The Artist's Last Struggle Against Masculine Values." *Women and Literature* 5, 1 (Spring 1977): 38–46.

Gillespie, Diane and Elizabeth Steele, eds. *Julia Duckworth Stephen: Stories for Children, Essays for Adults*. Syracuse, N.Y.: Syracuse University Press, 1987.

Ginsberg, Elaine K., and Laura Moss Gottlieb, eds. *Virginia Woolf: Centennial Essays*. Troy, N.Y.: Whitston, 1983.

Gorsky, Susan. "The Central Shadow: Characterization in *The Waves*." *Modern Fiction Studies* 18 (1972/73): 449–66.

Grant, Duncan. "Virginia Woolf." In *The Bloomsbury Group: A Collection of Memoirs, Commentary and Criticism*, edited by S. P. Rosenbaum, pp. 65–68. Toronto: University of Toronto Press, 1975.

Greer, Germaine. *The Obstacle Race: The Fortunes of Women Painters and Their Work*. New York: Farrar Straus Giroux, 1979.

Gregor, Ian. "Spaces: To the Lighthouse." In *The Author in His Work: Essays on a Problem in Criticism*, edited by Louis L. Martz and Aubrey Williams. New Haven: Yale University Press, 1978.

Guiget, Jean. *Virginia Woolf and Her Works*. Translated by Jean Stewart. London: Hogarth, 1965.

Hagstrum, Jean. *The Sister Arts: The Tradition of Literary Pictorialism and English Poetry from Dryden to Gray*. Chicago: University of Chicago Press, 1958.

Harrington, Henry. "The Central Line Down the Middle of *To the Lighthouse*." *Contemporary Literature* 21 (1980): 363–82.

Harris, Ann Sutherland, and Linda Nochlin. *Women Artists: 1550–1950*. New York: Alfred A. Knopf, 1976.

Harrison, Charles. *English Art and Modernism: 1900–1939*. London: Allen Lane, 1981.

Harvard-Williams, Peter and Margaret. "Perceptive Contemplation in the Work of Virginia Woolf." *English Studies* 35 (1954): 97–116.

Heffernan, James A. W. "The English Romantic Perception of Color." In *Images of Romanticism: Verbal and Visual Affinities*, edited by Karl

Kroeber and William Walling, pp. 133–48. New Haven: Yale University Press, 1978.

Heilbrun, Carolyn. *Reinventing Womanhood*. New York: W. W. Norton, 1979.

Heinemann, Jan. "The Revolt Against Language: A Critical Note on Twentieth-Century Irrationalism with Special Reference to the Aesthetico-Philosophical Views of Virginia Woolf and Clive Bell." *Orbis Litterarum* 32 (1977): 212–28.

Hintikka, Jaakko. "Virginia Woolf and Our Knowledge of the External World." *Journal of Aesthetics and Art Criticism* 38, 1 (Fall 1979): 5–14.

Hone, Joseph. *The Life of Henry Tonks*. London: William Heinemann, n.d.

Howe, Irving, ed. *The Idea of the Modern in Literature and the Arts*. New York: Horizon, 1967.

Hussey, Mark. *The Singing of the Real World: The Philosophy of Virginia Woolf's Fiction*. Columbus: Ohio State University Press, 1986.

Hutchison, Sidney. *The History of the Royal Academy: 1768–1968*. New York: Taplinger, 1968.

Johnson, Lee McKay. *The Metaphor of Painting: Essays on Baudelaire, Ruskin, Proust, and Pater*. Ann Arbor, Mich.: UMI Research Press, 1980.

Johnstone, J. K. *The Bloomsbury Group: A Study of E. M. Forster, Lytton Strachey, Virginia Woolf, and Their Circle*. New York: Noonday, 1954.

Kennedy, Richard. *A Boy at the Hogarth Press*. London: Heinemann, 1982.

Kermode, Frank. *Modern Essays*. London: Collins, 1971.

———. *The Sense of an Ending: Studies in the Theory of Fiction*. New York: Oxford University Press, 1967.

Kiely, Robert. "*Jacob's Room* and *Roger Fry*: Two Studies in Still Life." In *Modernism Reconsidered*, edited by Robert Kiely, pp. 147–66. Cambridge: Harvard University Press, 1983.

Kirkpatrick, B. J. *A Bibliography of Virginia Woolf*. London: Rupert Hart-Davis, 1957.

Langer, Suzanne. "Deceptive Analogies: Specious and Real Relationships Among the Arts." In *Problems of Art: Ten Philosophical Lectures*, pp. 75–89. New York: Charles Scribner's, 1957.

Lehmann, John. *Thrown to the Woolfs*. London: Weidenfeld & Nicolson, 1978.

———. *Virginia Woolf and Her World*. New York: Harcourt Brace Jovanovich, 1975.

Levy, Paul. *Moore: G. E. Moore and the Cambridge Apostles*. New York: Holt, Rinehart and Winston, 1979.

Lewis, Thomas, S. W., ed. *Virginia Woolf*. New York: McGraw Hill, 1975.

Lister, Raymond. *Victorian Narrative Paintings*. New York: Clarkson N. Potter, 1966.

Love, Jean. *Virginia Woolf: Sources of Madness and Art*. Berkeley: University of California Press, 1977.

McLaurin, Allen. "A Note on Lily Briscoe's Painting in *To the Lighthouse*" *Notes and Queries* 26 (August 1979): 338–40.

———. *Virginia Woolf: The Echoes Enslaved*. Cambridge: Cambridge University Press, 1973.

McNaron, Toni A. H. "Billy Goat to Dolphin: Letters of Virginia Woolf to Her Sister, Vanessa Bell." In *The Sister Bond: A Feminist View of a Timeless Connection*, edited by Toni A. H. McNaron, pp. 93–103. New York: Pergamon, 1985.

Majumdar, Robin, and Allen McLaurin, eds. *Virginia Woolf: The Critical Heritage*. London: Routledge and Kegan Paul, 1975.

Mann, Charles W. "'Your Loving Auntie and God Mama, Julia Cameron.'" *History of Photography* 7, 1 (January 1983): 73–74.

Marcus, Jane. "Liberty, Sorority, Misogyny." In *The Representation of Women in Fiction: Selected Papers from the English Institute, 1981*, edited by Carolyn Heilbrun and Margaret Higgonet, pp. 60–97. Baltimore, Md.: Johns Hopkins University Press, 1983.

———, ed. *New Feminist Essays on Virginia Woolf*. Lincoln, Neb.: University of Nebraska Press, 1981.

———, ed. *Virginia Woolf: A Feminist Slant*. Lincoln, Neb.: University of Nebraska Press, 1983.

Mares, Cheryl Jean. "'Another Space of Time': The Dominion of Painting in Proust and Woolf." Ph.D. dissertation, Princeton University, 1982.

Mitchell, W. J. T., ed. *The Language of Images*. Chicago: University of Chicago Press, 1980.

Moore, G. E. *Principia Ethica*. Cambridge: Cambridge University Press, 1968; first published 1903.

———. "The Refutation of Idealism." *Mind: A Quarterly Review of Psychology and Philosophy* 12, 48 (1903): 14.

Morphet, Richard. "The Art of Vanessa Bell." In *Vanessa Bell: Paintings and Drawings*. London: Anthony d'Offay, 1973.

Mortimer, Raymond. *Duncan Grant*. London: Penguin, 1948.

Naremore, James. *The World Without a Self: Virginia Woolf and the Novel*. New Haven: Yale University Press, 1973.

Novak, Jane. *The Razor Edge of Balance: A Study of Virginia Woolf*. Coral Gables, Fla.: University of Miami Press, 1975.

Ortega y Gasset, José. *The Dehumanization of Art*. Princeton: Princeton University Press, 1948.

"Our Vortex." *Blast* 1–2 (1914–15): 151–52.

Peters, Jean. "Publishers' Imprints." In *Collectible Books: Some New Paths*, edited by Jean Peters, pp. 198–224. New York: R. R. Bowker, 1979.

Pickvance, Ronald. Introduction to *Vanessa Bell: 1879–1961: A Memorial Exhibition of Paintings*. London: Arts Council, 1964.

Poole, Roger. *The Unknown Virginia Woolf*. Cambridge: Cambridge University Press, 1978.

Pound, Ezra. *Gaudier-Brzeska: A Memoir*. London: Marvell, 1960; first published 1916.

Praz, Mario. *Mnemosyne: The Parallel Between Literature and the Visual Arts*. Princeton, N.J.: Princeton University Press, 1974.

Rand, Paul. "Black in the Visual Arts." In *Graphic Forms: The Arts as Related to the Book*. Cambridge: Harvard University Press, 1949.

Rice-Sayre, Laura, and Henry Sayre. "Autonomy and Affinity: Toward a Theory for Comparing the Arts." *The Arts and their Interrelations, Bucknell Review* 24, 2 (Fall 1978): 86–103.

Richardson, Dorothy. "Continuous Performance: The Film Gone Male." *Close-Up* 9, 1 (March 1932): 36–38.

Roche, Paul. *With Duncan Grant in Southern Turkey*. London: Honeyglen, 1982.

Rosenbaum, S. P. ed. *The Bloomsbury Group: A Collection of Memoirs, Commentary and Criticism*. Toronto: University of Toronto Press, 1975.

———. "The Philosophical Realism of Virginia Woolf." In *English Literature and British Philosophy*, edited by S. P. Rosenbaum, pp. 316–56. Chicago: University of Chicago Press, 1971.

Rosenthal, Michael. "Literary Criticism." In *Virginia Woolf*, pp. 244–60. London: Routledge and Kegan Paul, 1979.

Schlack, Beverly. *Continuing Presences: Virginia Woolf's Use of Literary Allusion*. University Park, Pa.: Pennsylvania State University Press, 1979.

Seward, Barbara. *The Symbolic Rose*. New York: Columbia University Press, 1960.

Shone, Richard. *Bloomsbury Portraits: Vanessa Bell, Duncan Grant, and Their Circle*. Oxford: Phaidon, 1976.

———. "Introduction." In *Duncan Grant and Bloomsbury*. Edinburgh: The Fine Arts Society, 1975.

———. "Vanessa Bell." In *Vanessa Bell: 1879–1961: A Retrospective Exhibition*. New York: Davis and Long, 1980.

Silver, Brenda R. *Virginia Woolf's Reading Notebooks*. Princeton, N.J.: Princeton University Press, 1983.

Sitwell, Sacheverell. *Narrative Pictures: A Survey of English Genre and Its Painters*. London: B. T. Batsford, 1969.

Spalding, Frances. *Vanessa Bell*. London: Weidenfeld and Nicolson, 1983.

———. *Vanessa Bell: 1879–1961: An Exhibition to Mark the Centenary of her Birth*. Sheffield Art Galleries, 1979.

Spater, George, and Ian Parsons. *A Marriage of True Minds: An Intimate*

Portrait of Leonard and Virginia Woolf. New York: Harcourt Brace Jovanovich, 1977.

Spencer, Sharon. *Space, Time and Structure in the Modern Novel*. New York: New York University Press, 1971.

Spender, Stephen. *The Struggle of the Modern*. Berkeley: University of California Press, 1963.

Spivak, Gayatri C. "Unmaking and Making in *To the Lighthouse*." In *Women and Language in Literature and Society*, edited by Sally McConnel-Ginet, Ruth Borker, and Nelly Furman, pp. 310–27. New York: Praeger, 1980.

Steiner, Wendy. *Exact Resemblance to Exact Resemblance: The Literary Portraiture of Gertrude Stein*. New Haven: Yale University Press, 1978.

———. "The Temporal versus the Spatial Arts." In *The Colors of Rhetoric: Problems in the Relation Between Modern Literature and Painting*, pp. 33–50. Chicago: University of Chicago Press, 1982.

Stephen, Leslie. *Mausoleum Book*. Edited by Alan Bell. Oxford: Clarendon Press, 1977.

Stewart, Jack. "Cubist Elements in *Between the Acts*." *Mosaic* 18, 2 (Spring 1985): 65–89.

———. "Historical Impressionism in Orlando." *Studies in the Novel* 5 (Spring 1973): 71–85.

———. "Impressionism in the Early Novels of Virginia Woolf." *Journal of Modern Literature* 9, 2 (1982): 237–66.

———. "Spatial Form and Color in *The Waves*." *Twentieth Century Literature* 28 (1982): 86–107.

Stowell, Peter. *Literary Impressionism, James and Chekhov*. Athens: University of Georgia Press, 1980.

Sutton, Denys, ed. *Letters of Roger Fry*. 2 vols. London: Chatto and Windus, 1972.

———. *Walter Sickert: A Biography*. London: Michael Joseph, 1976.

Szladits, Lola. "The Life, Character and Opinions of Flush the Spaniel." *Bulletin of the New York Public Library* 74 (1970): 211–18.

Thorpe, James. *English Illustration: The Nineties*. New York: Hacker, 1975.

Todorov, Tzvetan. "The Romantic Crisis." In *Theories of Symbol*, translated by Catherine Porter, pp. 147–221. Ithaca, N.Y.: Cornell University Press, 1982.

Torgovnick, Marianna. *The Visual Arts, Pictorialism, and the Novel: James, Lawrence, and Woolf*. Princeton, N.J.: Princeton University Press, 1985.

Trombley, Stephen. *All that Summer She Was Mad: Virginia Woolf: Female Victim of Male Medicine*. New York: Continuum, 1982.

Wallis, Neville. "Vanessa Bell and Bloomsbury." *The Connoisseur* 156 (August 1964): 248.

Ward, Lynd. "The Illustrator and the Book." In *Graphic Forms: The Arts as Related to the Book*, pp. 53–61. Cambridge: Harvard University Press, 1949.

Watts, M. S. *George Frederick Watts: The Annals of an Artist's Life*. 3 vols. New York: George H. Doran, n.d.

Weisstein, Ulrich. "Literature and the Visual Arts." In *Interrelations of Literature*, edited by Jean-Pierre Barricelli and Joseph Gibaldi, pp. 259–61. New York: The Modern Language Association, 1982.

Wendorf, Richard. "Ut Pictura Biographia: Biography and Portrait Painting as Sister Arts." In *Articulate Images: The Sister Arts from Hogarth to Tennyson*, edited by Richard Wendorf, pp. 98–124. Minneapolis: University of Minnesota Press, 1983.

Whistler, James McNeill. "Ten O'Clock Lecture." In *The Gentle Art of Making Enemies*. New York: Dover, 1967.

Williamson, Hugh. "Illustration." In *Methods of Book Design: The Practice of an Industrial Craft*. London: Oxford University Press, 1956.

Wilsher, Ann, and Benjamin Spear. "A Dream of Fair Ladies: Mrs. Cameron Disguised." *History of Photography* 7, 2 (April–June 1983): 118–20.

Wong, Sau-Ling Cynthia. "A Study of Roger Fry and Virginia Woolf from a Chinese Perspective." Ph.D. dissertation, Stanford University, 1978.

Woolf, Leonard. *Beginning Again: An Autobiography of the Years 1911 to 1918*. New York: Harcourt Brace Jovanovich, 1964.

———. *Downhill All the Way: An Autobiography of the Years 1919 to 1939*. New York: Harcourt Brace Jovanovich, 1964.

———. *Sowing: An Autobiography of the Years 1880–1904*. New York: Harcourt Brace Jovanovich, 1960.

———. *The Wise Virgins: A Story of Words, Opinions, and a Few Emotions*. London: Edward Arnold, 1941.

Woolf, Virginia (See also Abbreviations. pp. xi–xii) "Anon." Edited by Brenda Silver. *Twentieth Century Literature* 25, 3/4 (Fall/Winter 1979): 380–441.

———. Foreword to *Catalogue of Recent Paintings by Vanessa Bell*. London: Lefevre Galleries, 1934.

———. "Friendships Gallery." Edited by Ellen Hawkes. *Twentieth Century Literature* 25 (1979): 272.

———. Introduction to *By the Ionion Sea: Notes of a Ramble in Southern Italy*, by George Gissing. London: Jonathan Cape, 1933.

———. "Notes for Reading at Random." Edited by Brenda Silver. *Twentieth Century Literature* 25, 3/4 (Fall/Winter 1979).

———. "Pictures." *The Moment and Other Essays*. London: Hogarth, 1947.

———. *Pointz Hall: The Earlier and Later Typescripts of Between the Acts*. Edited by Mitchell A. Leaska. New York: New York University Publications, 1983.

———. "Portraits of Places." *The Guardian* (October 3, 1906), p. 1631.

———. "The Reader." Edited by Brenda Silver. *Twentieth Century Literature* 25, 3/4 (Fall/Winter 1979): 433.

———. *Recent Paintings by Vanessa Bell*. London: The London Artists' Association, 1930.

———. "Roger Fry." *The Moment and Other Essays*. London: Hogarth, 1947.

———. *To the Lighthouse: The Original Holograph Draft*. Edited by Susan Dick. Toronto: University of Toronto Press, 1982.

Woolmer, J. Howard. *A Checklist of the Hogarth Press*. Andes, N.Y.: Woolmer/Brotherson, 1976.

Zwerdling, Alex. "Julia Stephen, Mrs. Ramsay, and the Sense of Vocation." *Virginia Woolf Miscellany* 22 (Spring 1984): 4.

———. *Virginia Woolf and the Real World*. Berkeley: University of California Press, 1986.

Index

VW = Virginia Woolf; VB = Vanessa Bell
References to illustrations are in *italics*.

THE SISTERS' ARTS
was composed in 10½ on 12½ Janson on a Mergenthaler Linotron 202
by Eastern Graphics;
printed by sheet-fed offset on 50-pound, acid-free Glatfelter Natural,
and Smyth sewn and bound over 88-point binder's boards in Holliston Roxite B,
by Edwards Brothers, Inc.;
with dust jackets printed in 1 color by Edwards Brothers, Inc.;
designed by Mary Peterson Moore;
and published by
SYRACUSE UNIVERSITY PRESS
SYRACUSE, NEW YORK 13244-5160